Joshua Wolf Shenk is an essayist, author and curator based in Los Angeles. He is a contributor to *Atlantic, Slate, Harper's* and other magazines. His first book, *Lincoln's Melancholy,* was a *New York Times* notable book and won prizes from the Lincoln Institute and Mental Health America. Shenk directs the Arts in Mind series on creativity and serves on the general council of The Moth.

Praise for Powers of Two

'We sometimes think of creativity as coming from brilliant loners. In fact, it more often happens when bright people pair up and complement each other. Shenk's fascinating book shows how to spark the power of this phenomenon'
Walter Isaacson, author of *Steve Jobs*

'In this surprising, compelling, deeply felt book, Joshua Wolf Shenk banishes the idea of solitary genius by demonstrating that our richest art and science come from collaboration: we need one another not only for love, but also for thinking and imagining and growing and being' Andrew Solomon

'All future accounts of artistry and innovation will be enriched by the treasures Joshua Wolf Shenk has uncovered in the creativity of pairs'
Lewis Hyde

'Wise, funny, surprising, and completely engrossing' Susan Orlean

'*Powers of Two* is filled with keen insights into the human condition and terrific examples of creativity at work.
This is an inspiring book that also happens to be a great read'
Daniel H. Pink, author of *Drive*

'Fascinating . . . highly readable. We may like to think that we live in a world of creative individualism, but this insightful book should convince even the sceptical that when it comes to creating something new and exciting, it really does take two'
Sunday Business Post

'An interesting thesis' *The Economist*

Books by Joshua Wolf Shenk

Powers of Two: Finding the Essence of Innovation
in Creative Pairs

Lincoln's Melancholy: How Depression Challenged
a President and Fueled His Greatness

POWERS OF TWO

FINDING the ESSENCE of INNOVATION in CREATIVE PAIRS

JOSHUA WOLF SHENK

JOHN MURRAY

First published in Great Britain in 2014 by John Murray (Publishers)
An Hachette UK Company

First published in paperback in 2015

1

A CIP catalogue record for this title is available from the British Library

Paperback ISBN 978-1-84854-592-2
Ebook ISBN 978-1-84854-591-5

Book design by Greta D. Sibley

Illustrations by Josh Ceazan (page 51) and Precision Images (page 100)

Grateful acknowledgment is made for permission to reprint an image from the
following copyrighted work: Figure 1 from "Inclusion of Other in the Self Scale
and the Structure of Interpersonal Closeness" by Arthur Aron, Elaine N. Aron, and
Danny Smollan, originally published in the *Journal of Personality* and *Social Psychology*,
copyright © 1992 by the American Psychological Association.

Printed and bound by Clays Ltd, St Ives plc

John Murray policy is to use papers that are natural, renewable and
recyclable products and made from wood grown in sustainable forests.
The logging and manufacturing processes are expected to conform to the
environmental regulations of the country of origin.

John Murray (Publishers)
338 Euston Road
London NW1 3BH

www.johnmurray.co.uk

For Mom and Sidney

Contents

The world is not comprehensible, but it is embraceable: through the embracing of one of its beings.

— *Martin Buber*

The smallest indivisible human unit is two people, not one; one is a fiction. From such nets of souls societies, the social world, human life springs. And also plays."

— *Tony Kushner*

Note on quotations: When I quote historical figures or non-native English speakers "sic," indicating that the language is accurate as rendered, can be assumed throughout. As a general practice, I did not identify the source of quotations in the text, but exhaustive documentation can be found in the notes.

Prelude

On March 29, 1967, around two p.m., John Lennon came to Paul McCartney's house in London, and they headed up to Paul's workroom, a narrow, rectangular space full of instruments and amps and modern art.

The day before, they'd started a new song, meant for Ringo Starr to sing. Today, they intended to finish it off. Hunter Davies, a columnist with the *Sunday Times,* was on hand, and his account offers a rare window onto how John and Paul worked.

John took up his guitar, and Paul started noodling at the piano. "For a couple of hours," Davies wrote, "they both banged away. Each seemed to be in a trance until the other came up with something good, then he would pluck it out of a mass of noises and try it himself."

"Are you afraid when you turn out the light?" John offered.

Paul repeated the line and nodded. They could begin each of the verses with a question, John suggested, and he gave another one. *"Do you believe in love at first sight?"*

He interrupted himself. "It hasn't got the right number of syllables." He tried breaking the line between *believe* and *in love,* putting in a pause long enough to create the right rhythm. It didn't work.

"How about," Paul said, *"Do you believe in a love at first sight?"* John sang it and instantly added another line. *"Yes, I'm certain it happens all the time."* They switched the order of the lines and sang them over and over again:

Would you believe in a love at first sight?
Yes I'm certain it happens all the time.
Are you afraid when you turn out the light?

It was now five o'clock. John's wife came by with a friend. They talked about the lines to the song so far, and, in the midst of the chatter, John said — almost to himself — in answer to what's seen when the light is out: "I know it's mine." Someone said it sounded smutty.

They chatted some more. Paul started improvising on the piano before breaking into "Can't Buy Me Love." John joined in, shouting and laughing. Then they both began to play "Tequila," a 1958 hit by the Champs.

"Remember in Germany?" John said. "We used to shout out anything." They did the song again, with John throwing in new words at the crescendo of each line: *knickers* and *Duke of Edinburgh* and *tit* and *Hitler.*

"They both stopped all the shouting and larking around as suddenly as they'd begun it," Davies wrote. "They went back, very quietly, to the song they were supposed to be working on." John sang a slight modification of the line they'd agreed on. *"What do you see when you turn out the light?"* Then he answered the question. *"I can't tell you, but I know it's mine."*

Paul said it would do and he wrote the lines on a piece of exercise paper. Then he wandered around the room. Outside the window, the eyes and foreheads of six girls could be seen as they jumped up and down on the sidewalk on Cavendish Avenue, trying to catch a glimpse over the front wall into Paul's property. John began to play a hymn on the piano. After playing with his sitar, Paul went to his guitar, where, Davies wrote, he "started to sing and play a very slow, beautiful song about a foolish man sitting on the hill. John listened to it quietly, staring blankly out of the window." Paul sang the song over and over again. "It was the first time Paul had played it for John," Davies wrote. "There was no discussion."

It was now about seven o'clock. They were due soon around the corner at the EMI Studios on Abbey Road. They lit a joint and passed it between them. They decided to call Ringo and tell him they would do the song that night.

Introduction: 1 + 1 = Infinity

For centuries, the myth of the lone genius has towered over us like a colossus. The idea that new, beautiful, world-changing things come from within great minds is now so common that we don't even consider it an idea. These bronze statues have come to seem like old-growth trees — monuments to modern thinking that we mistake for part of the natural world.

We can be forgiven the mistake because creativity is so inexplicable. How, from all the sounds in the universe, from all the syllables and protean rhythms, does a great song arise? How do we account for the emergence of a good idea — the movement from chaos to clarity?

The dominant idea today is that, because creativity resides within the individual, we best expose it by telling stories of those rare geniuses — the ones who made the Sistine Chapel or *Hamlet,* the light bulb or the iPod. This model basically follows the declaration made by Thomas Carlyle in the 1840s: "The history of the world is but the biography of great men."

The most common alternative to the lone-genius model locates creativity in networks. See, for example, Herbert Spencer's retort to Carlyle that "the genesis of the great man depends" on a "long series of complex influences." "Before he can remake his society," Spencer wrote, "his society must make him." Rather than focus on the solitary hero snatching inspiration from the heavens (or the unconscious), this concept emphasizes the long, meandering course of innovation. Instead of heroic individuals, it prioritizes heroic *cultures* — the courts of sixteenth-century Florence, say, or the coffee shops of Enlightenment London, or the campus of Pixar.

The trouble with the first model of creativity is that it's a fantasy, a myth of achievement predicated on an even more fundamental myth of the enclosed, autonomous self for whom social experience is secondary. The lone-genius idea has become our dominant view of creativity not because of its inherent truth — in fact, it neglects and obscures the social qualities of innovation — but because it makes for a good story.

The network model has the opposite problem. It is basically true, but so complex that it can't easily be made into narrative. Where the lone-genius model is galvanizing but simplistic, the network model is suitably nuanced but hard to apply to day-to-day life. An argument can be made — a rigorous, persuasive argument — that every good new thing results from a teeming complexity. But how do you represent that complexity in a practical way? How do you talk about it, not just at Oxford or the TED Conference, but in kitchens and bars?

Fortunately, there's a way to understand the social nature of creativity that is both true and useful. It's the story of the creative pair.

Five years ago, I became preoccupied with this thing we call "chemistry" or "electricity" between people. My first impulse was personal: I wanted to understand the quality of connection whose presence accounted for the best times of my life and whose absence made for the worst. This led me to think about Eamon Dolan, who edited my first book, *Lincoln's Melancholy*. My relationship with Eamon was an example of the chemistry that intrigued me. As I reflected on this, it occurred to me that the question of chemistry itself — and an inquiry into it based on eminent creative pairs — would get right to the nexus of our interests.

I made a list of creative pairs I wanted to know more about: the Beatles' John Lennon and Paul McCartney; Steve Jobs and Steve Wozniak, who created Apple Computer; Marie and Pierre Curie, who discovered radioactivity; and many other notable duos. I thought that if I could begin to understand these relationships, I could learn something profound about how people buoy each other. I imagined each pair in turn, and thought about the electrified space between them, and planned to write a biography of that space.

The project took on a new direction when I thought about Vincent van Gogh and his brother Theo. What was *that* story? I knew Theo as the recipient of Vincent's correspondence and I had seen him described as Vincent's supporter. But I soon learned there was much more to it. Theo was, in fact, a hidden partner in what I came to see as a true creative pair. I found so many other examples of hidden partners — you'll meet a number of them in this book — that it began to seem more like the rule than the exception: one member of a duo takes the lone-genius spotlight while the other remains in history's shadows.

Then there were cases in which two creative people, each well known individually, turned out to have influenced and affected each other profoundly — Ann Landers and Dear Abby, for example, twin sisters whose rivalry fueled careers in advice-giving, and C. S. Lewis and J.R.R. Tolkien, whose distinct works were inexorably influenced by their creative exchange. Yet, for decades, even scholars of Lewis and Tolkien assiduously downplayed how they affected each other.

On top of my original question about the nature of creative relationships, I found myself asking a second one: Why have so many of these relationships been obscured and neglected?

The depths of the problem came home to me at a dinner hosted by a university where I gave a talk. A business professor asked whether I had considered the relationship between golfers and caddies. I hadn't. All I knew about caddies I'd learned from *Caddyshack*. The professor told me that I ought to look into it; he'd played professionally as a young man, and the dynamics of a PGA match were really interesting in terms of relationships. "You see, the golfer is — by the rules of the pro tour — required to go out alone, and the caddie is the only exception," he explained. "It's not like baseball, where the manager can come to the mound for a talk or where they can meet in the dugout. So the caddies end up not just as helpers but as strategists and psychologists."

Was there any pair in particular he would suggest as an example?

"Of course," he said. "Tiger Woods and Steve Williams."

Indeed, it turns out that Tiger's caddie from 1999 to 2011 did far more than carry his bags. He did more, even, than advise and succor his boss. Williams also taunted Woods — to get his blood up — and deliberately misled him when he thought it would improve his play. At the 2000 PGA Championship, in the fourth round and on the fairway of the seventeenth hole, Woods needed a birdie to catch the leader. Williams had calculated ninety-five yards to the flag — but he told Woods ninety. "Tiger's distance control was a problem," Williams explained to *Golf Magazine*. "So I would adjust yardages and not tell him." At the seventeenth, Woods hit the ball two feet from the pin and went on to win the three-hole playoff. Williams told *Golf* that he'd given Tiger incorrect yardages for the better part of five years.

The hidden nature of partnership extends beyond particular pairs to whole categories of relationships. Most fields have parallels to the unknown caddie, critical roles that are essentially hidden from public view. These workers matter enormously to insiders. But they rarely get general attention. It's not just that Theo van Gogh happens to be unknown to the public. It's that art dealers are largely unknown (and curators and fabricators and assistants and on and on). In the movie business, actors and directors go on *Conan*, not cinematographers and editors. Nor does Conan's longtime partner executive producer Jeff Ross step out from behind the cameras.

In some cases, the silent partner eventually gets attention. After three decades, the artist Christo began to share public credit with his wife and partner, Jeanne-Claude, for what had always been their collective work. Elsewhere, ostensible lone geniuses actively obscure the truth. George Lucas's original *Star Wars* films owed a great deal to his partnership with his first wife, the Academy Award–winning film editor Marcia Lucas, who biographer Dale Pollock said was her then husband's "secret weapon." "She was really the warmth and the heart of those films," said Mark Hamill, who played Luke Skywalker. But after their divorce, authorized histories of the franchise barely mentioned her.

Not that George Lucas has had to do much to obscure his ex-wife's role. In a lone-genius culture, all it takes is a slight advantage for the ball to begin to roll down the hill. With reputation, as with money, the Gospel according to Matthew applies: "To all those who have, more will be given, and they will have an abundance; but from those who have nothing, even what they have will be taken away." The sociologist Robert Merton found that when two scientists collaborated, whoever was better known got the lion's share of the credit. And if two scientists came up with an idea separately at about the same time, the one who was better known received far more recognition for it. Merton called it the Matthew effect.

Lone-genius culture has robbed many women of the recognition they are due, as when Linus Pauling won the Nobel Peace Prize in 1962 for peace activism that his wife, Ava Helen Pauling, led him into. Until relatively recently, creative men have often taken credit for the labor of their wives, whether as research assistants, editors, or even de facto CEOs of the enterprises that bear their husbands' names. This sort of prejudice extends beyond women, of course. Vivien Thomas was a technical wizard who, alongside Dr. Alfred Blalock, pioneered modern heart surgery. Yet Thomas, an African American man, was for several years classified in the hospital payrolls as a janitor, even as he ran labs and trained doctors.

Another reason interdependence so frequently remains hidden is that, even when viewed directly, it can be hard to understand, and not just for outsiders but for the principals themselves. Legendary editor Maxwell Perkins shaped Thomas Wolfe's unwieldy manuscripts into the epic novels *Look Homeward, Angel* and *Of Time and the River,* and Wolfe exuberantly praised his partner in the dedication of the latter book. Then a critic charged in the *Saturday Review* that Wolfe's "incompleteness" as an author could be seen in "the most flagrant evidence" that "one indispensable part of the artist has existed not in Mr. Wolfe but in Maxwell Perkins." Wolfe raged at the idea that he couldn't "perform these functions of an artist for myself." In a tantrum, Wolfe then broke with the man who had helped make him.

F. Scott Fitzgerald, another author nurtured by Maxwell Perkins, once declared that the test of a first-rate intelligence was the ability to hold two opposing ideas in mind without cracking up. Thomas Wolfe could not accept that he was both a complete artist and a dependent partner.

In Wolfe's defense, interdependence can be hard for any of us to grasp in a genius-obsessed culture. "A time is marked," Lawrence Lessig writes, "not so much by ideas that are argued about as by ideas that are taken for granted." We certainly take for granted that the core unit of creative achievement is the individual. From the tests given to schoolchildren to the statistics that rank players in major league baseball to *Fast Company*'s "most creative people in business" list and all the way to the MacArthur Fellowship (the "genius grant"), we return over and over to the notion that creativity originates — imagine me tapping my skull — *in here.* We speak of a Supreme Court justice's opinion as though he or she wrote it entirely alone, the same way the legendary Michelangelo painted the Sistine Chapel. In fact, the justices work just as Michelangelo did, among a scrum of colleagues and acolytes. Many of the biggest creative stars of our time — from Justin Bieber to Mario Batali to Doris Kearns Goodwin — are best understood not as solo actors but as brands representing collectively produced bodies of work.

Where did the myth of the lone genius come from, anyway? The very short answer is that it emerged in the Enlightenment, grew popular in the Romantic era, and took its final shape in the contemporary United States. From the start, the myth was entwined with a view of human nature as a product of the atomized self. So much of what we believe to be true about how we develop, how we operate, and indeed who we are evolved in the shadow of an erroneous idea about human beings as self-contained, cut off, solitary.

For example, for all the diversity of modern psychology — from psychoanalysis to biological psychiatry, from B. F. Skinner's behaviorism to the developmental theories of Jean Piaget — the overwhelming focus has been on the experience of the individual. The popular "hierarchy of needs" formulated by the psychologist Abraham Maslow made one of the field's assumptions explicit: Maslow ranked human needs from the most basic to the most exalted, with physiological needs (for, say, food and excretion) at the bottom, topped by safety needs in the second-lowest position. In the second-highest position are esteem needs (self-esteem, confidence), and self-actualization is at the pinnacle. Stuck ingloriously in the middle: love/belonging needs. In other words, Maslow saw connection with others as more advanced than using the toilet and having a home but just a step along the way to personal growth and fulfillment.

Today, a burgeoning movement in science and creativity studies has laid the foundation for a new understanding. The epochal changes in the seventeenth and eighteenth centuries that led to the myth of the lone genius were products of massive shifts at the intersection of politics, economics, and culture (the emergence of the nation-state, the birth of the market economy, the shifting role of religion in everyday life). Today, amid similarly massive shifts (the birth of the Internet and its far-reaching effects; the global economy; scientific advances that give new insight into everything from child development to complex systems), these core ideas are finally being taken apart. In recent years, an impressive new body of scholarship on human connection—including social psychology, relationship studies, and group creativity—has emerged. Steven Johnson's book *Where Good Ideas Come From* advances what we could call a network theory of human achievement, one that has its best metaphor in ecology, the constant interdependence of many unseen forces that "compulsively connect and remix that most valuable of resources: information."

Yet, while this emphasis on groups and networks is valuable and truthful, it is an insufficient corrective to the lone-genius model. "Genius" is a story made up to account for the broad and ultimately mysterious nature of creativity. It contains and contextualizes something immense. Once the illusion of an autonomous Tiger Woods or Vincent van Gogh or Thomas Wolfe is exposed, it is tempting to try to tell the full story, to study the entirety of the individual's immediate circles, all the influences absorbed from near and far. Soon, this exercise leads us to the idea articulated by Percy Bysshe Shelley: "Every man's mind is . . . modified by all the objects of nature and art; by every word and every suggestion which he ever admitted to act upon his consciousness."

Anyone with some intellectual ambition can appreciate this notion—alongside the critique of the "author" associated with Michel Foucault and Roland Barthes. But the utter complexity of this idea makes it hard to hold in mind, let alone apply to everyday life. The brightest among us could read an exegesis of *The Odyssey* and *The Iliad* as the accumulation of generations of oral tradition and myth, and yet still refer to the author as Homer. It is well known that Homer is an amalgamation, but contests between mind-bending truths and simple fictions are lopsided, to say the least.

The network model also brushes over the subject of intimate relationships. We all know intuitively that life happens in close connection with other people, though it's often tempting to look away from this obvious truth. "On some level, people like to focus on groups because it's more comfortable," said Diana McLain Smith, a family therapist turned adviser to leadership teams and the author of *The Elephant in the Room: How Relationships Make or Break the Success of Leaders and Organizations*. "They don't have to think of people as people. When I show up talking about relationships, people always laugh nervously. They say, 'It's like couples therapy at work.' There's this unease around acknowledging it, because it's outside of the cultural norm of the rational organizational life. But it's what everybody is *really* talking about, around the water cooler, at the bar after work, with their spouse at home. Relationships are really all people think about. Except, they don't think about it very well, which is part of the problem."

The pair is the primary creative unit. In his study of creative circles ranging from the French impressionists to the founders of psychoanalysis, the sociologist Michael Farrell discovered that groups created a sense of community, purpose, and audience but that the truly important work ended up happening in pairs, as with Claude Monet and Pierre Auguste Renoir, and Sigmund Freud and Wilhelm Fliess.

Why is this? For one thing, it's probably true that we're set up to interact with a single person more openly and deeply than with any group, given that our psyches take shape through one-on-one exchanges with caregivers.

The dyad is also the most fluid and flexible of relationships. Two people can basically make their own society on the go. When even one more person is added to the mix, the situation becomes more stable, but this stability may stifle creativity, as roles and power positions harden. Three legs make a table stand in place. Two legs are made for walking or running (or jumping or falling).

Pairs naturally arouse engagement, even intensity. In a larger group, an individual may lie low, phone it in. But nobody can hide in a pair. "The decisive characteristic of the dyad is that each of the two must actually accomplish something," wrote Georg Simmel, "and that in the case of failure only the other remains — not a supra-individual force, as prevails in a group even of three." This gives every pair its color and quality, Simmel said. "Precisely the fact that each of the two knows that he can depend only upon the other and on nobody else, gives the dyad . . . a special consecration."

So this is what I mean when I say that the pair is the primary creative unit. It's not the only significant unit, of course. If you're listening to a jazz trio or studying the U.S. Senate, the entire group is obviously relevant. But even these threes and one hundreds are shaped by dyads among them.

But this is another crucial point, which is that pairs not only enact creativity, but also allow us to model it. In *Where Good Ideas Come From,*

Steven Johnson identifies patterns that characterize innovation in everything from coral reefs to cities to the Internet. "In the language of complexity theory," Johnson writes, "these patterns ... are fractal: they reappear in recognizable form as you zoom in and out, from molecule to neuron to pixel to sidewalk. Whether you're looking at the original innovations of carbon-based life, or the explosion of new software tools on the Web, the same shapes keep turning up."

Such is the case for the shape of the dyad. The goal here is to understand the nature of creative dichotomies as well as the dichotomous nature of the creative process itself. This process is characterized by a push-pull between two entities, whether those entities are two people, two groups of people, or even, as we'll see, a single person and the voice inside her head.

This book follows the progression that pairs themselves follow. By comparing hundreds of creative pairs, I found that they moved through six stages:

I. *Meeting*. Looking at the earliest encounter of individuals who will form a pair, the conditions and characteristics that engender chemistry or electricity — unusual similarities coinciding with unusual differences — become clear.

II. *Confluence*. Over time, two individuals move beyond mere interest and excitement in each other — they truly become a pair by surrendering elements of their singular selves to form what psychologists call a "joint identity."

III. *Dialectics*. In the heart of their creative work, pairs thrive on distinct and enmeshed roles, taking up positions in archetypal combinations that point to the essential place of dichotomy in the creative process.

IV. *Distance*. To thrive for the long term, pairs need more than closeness. They must also find an optimal distance from each other, carving out sufficient space in which to cultivate distinct ideas and experiences in order to give a partnership an ongoing frisson.

V. *The Infinite Game*. At the height of their work, pairs operate at the nexus of competition and cooperation, a dialectic that reveals the stark nature of power and the potential for conflict.

VI. *Interruption.* Looking at how pairs end, we see them driven apart by the same energies that pushed them forward. They lose, not their spark, but their balance, often due to some critical change in the context around them. And yet, considering how they remain bound up in each other practically and psychologically, we can also say that creative pairs never truly end.

Before we start, you may want to know just what I mean by *creativity*. I have borrowed a broad definition from the psychologist Mihaly Csikszent-mihalyi: "to bring into existence something genuinely new that is valued enough to be added to the culture." I've included the arts — writing, music, dance, and so on — as well as science, technology, social activism, and business. I've mostly avoided politics, but virtually every other kind of pair was fair game so long as two people made something together that contributed to the culture beyond what either could have created on his or her own.

A few quick points about process. First, almost every name you'll encounter in this book is well known or involved with a well-known project, though I spent a great deal of time with pairs who are not household names. My first challenge was to understand the essential dynamics of pairs, and for that I had to go wide. The next challenge was to represent the core dynamics with true stories, and for this purpose, I found the narratives and vignettes of easily recognizable pairs to be most evocative.

One of the byproducts of this strategy is that much of the evidence presented in the book is drawn from public material. As much as possible, I relied on direct testimony from the principals themselves and from the people who observed them. I also interviewed some eminent pairs myself, including James Watson (of Watson and Crick), Marina Abramović and Ulay, and David Crosby and Graham Nash. To learn about Matt Stone and Trey Parker, I talked to many members of their inner circle. Probably my most memorable interview was a session with Tenzin Geyche Tethong, who was the Dalai Lama's private secretary (read: chief of staff) for more than forty-five years.

Still, this is primarily a work of synthesis, undergirded by my curiosity about the questions I posed at the outset: What is this thing we call chemistry? What does that teach us about the creative process?

When I started this book, I wanted to see whether looking closely at a wide sample of sublime pairs would yield lessons that applied across recording studios and laboratories and boardrooms and sports fields. That turned out to be the case. There is a common story to creative relationships — an arc they follow, themes that light them up.

Yet my attitude toward this material is not that of the hunter who has bagged his game. Rather, even after five years, I feel like an explorer gazing through binoculars, trying to see a strange and wonderful beast in the tall grass. That's partly because I'm dealing with two subjects, creativity and intimacy, that are inherently mysterious and beset with paradox.

My method has its strengths and limitations, as I try to walk the line between exploring broad truths and exploring the idiosyncrasies and contradictions of real people.

But I also want to confess that my own position is a humble one. I am among the more isolated people I know. I am not quite like Ralph Ellison's invisible man in a dank basement lit up by hot-wired bulbs. But I have spent the vast majority of my adult life alone. Even when in the company of others, I struggle to direct my attention outward, rather than toward the constant murmuring and shouting in my head.

So as I look at the characters in this book, my face is pressed up against the glass. I take comfort from writers who work on subjects where they feel their own deficits keenly — William James, for example, whose sublime discourse on religious experience proceeded from his own struggle for faith. James made his distance an asset, bringing a fervent curiosity and a helpful naïveté — a willingness to name an experience that people who know it intimately might take for granted.

When it comes to connection, I know I'm not alone in wanting more. Even many accomplished people hunger to be part of that equation in which one plus one equals infinity. And many people are enmeshed in partnerships that the world around them doesn't appreciate or that they themselves don't have a vocabulary to describe.

This book is written in the faith, underscored by experience, that more is possible — more intimacy, more creativity, more knowledge about this primary truth: that we make our best work, and live our best lives, by charging into the vast space between ourselves and others.

Whence come you, Hawthorne? By what right do you drink from my flagon of life? And when I put it to my lips — lo, they are yours and not mine. I feel that the Godhead is broken up like the bread at the Supper, and that we are the pieces. Hence this infinite fraternity of feeling . . .

My dear Hawthorne, the atmospheric skepticisms steal into me now, and make me doubtful of my sanity in writing you thus. But, believe me, I am not mad, most noble Festus! But truth is ever incoherent, and when the big hearts strike together, the concussion is a little stunning . . .

I can't stop yet. If the world was entirely made up of Magians, I'll tell you what I should do. I should have a paper-mill established at one end of the house, and so have an endless riband of foolscap rolling in upon my desk; and upon that endless riband I should write a thousand — a million — billion thoughts, all under the form of a letter to you. The divine magnet is on you, and my magnet responds.

— *Herman Melville to Nathaniel Hawthorne, November 1851*

PART I

MEETING

When the quickening comes. When the air between us feels less like a gap than a passage. When we don't know what to say because there is so much to say. Or, conversely, when we know just what to say because somehow, weirdly, all the billions of impulses around thought and language suddenly coalesce and find a direction home.

Sometimes you meet someone who could change your life. Sometimes you feel that possibility. The sense that, in the presence of this celestial body, you fall into a new orbit; that the ground beneath you is more like a trampoline; that you may be able — with this new person — to create things more beautiful and useful, more fantastic and more real, than you ever could before.

How does this happen? What conditions of circumstance and temperament foster creative connection? In other words: Where and how does it begin? And which combinations of people make it most likely?

When we answer these questions, by looking at initial contact in a variety of pairs, we catch sight of our first enduring theme: the heart of creative connection is the felicitous combination of the familiar and the strange. I've come to think of this combination as complementarity—and from what I've seen time and again, it's the essential seed for how two people come to not only support each other, but also startle and vex each other, leading to daring work that neither could achieve alone.

Put another way: The individuals in great dyads will be very different from each other and very much alike. These simultaneous extremes generate the deep rapport and energizing friction that define a creative pair.

1

"You Remind Me of Charlie Munger"

Matchups and Magnet Places

Similarity is a good place for us to start, because common interests and sensibilities usually bring future partners together in the first place. I saw three kinds of meetings: an introduction made by a mutual acquaintance; an encounter at a place of common interest; and a seemingly chance meeting that turned out to be driven by a subterranean similarity.

In 1957, a twenty-seven-year-old investor in Omaha, Nebraska, pitched some family friends named Edwin and Dorothy Davis to join a fund he managed. Dr. Davis hardly seemed to listen. But after he conferred with his wife, they agreed they'd put in $100,000 — most of their net worth, and a huge sum to the investor, Warren Buffett, whose portfolio at the time came to $300,000.

Buffett asked Dr. Davis why he'd take such a big risk. "You remind me of Charlie Munger," Davis replied. Two years later, when Munger, a thirty-five-year-old lawyer in Los Angeles, returned to his hometown of Omaha for a visit, the Davis family arranged for the two men to meet. Thus began the partnership behind what's probably the most successful investment operation in the history of capitalism.

The human mind naturally matches like and like. It satisfies a primal need. It's like those memory games children play. You turn over a card showing a watermelon, and a sudden appetite arises: seeking the other watermelon card feels as natural and urgent as breathing.

In pretty much the same way, people match friends they think have

3

things in common. That's why one day in 1971, a teenager named Bill Fernandez introduced a sixteen-year-old high-school friend named Steve to another Steve, a twenty-year-old college kid who lived on Fernandez's block. "One day," Fernandez remembered, "Steve Jobs bicycled over to hang out with me and do electronics projects in the garage, and out in front was [Steve] Wozniak washing his car. So I thought to myself, Okay, this Steve is an electronics buddy. He's an electronics buddy. They'd probably like to meet each other."

Sometimes introductions spring from practical needs. When Józef Kowalski discovered that his young Polish friend Marie Skłodowska, a physics student in Paris, needed lab space, he thought she might get help from a physicist he knew named Pierre Curie.

In a screenplay about great partners, a conduit like Edwin Davis or Bill Fernandez or Józef Kowalski would be excised, because we cherish the romantic notions of matches made by fate.

But if there is such a thing as fate, it works through human agents. Unlike in the movies, where the girl who will change the hero's life just walks up to him in the doctor's waiting room, most significant real-life connections emerge from other connections. Consider a study by the sociologists Duncan J. Watts and Gueorgi Kossinets on how friendships form on a university campus. Roughly 45 percent of new pairs met through mutual friends, and another 41 percent of new pairs met through mutual friends *and* shared contexts (like classes). The formation of new ties varied with network distance, meaning that individuals who were separated by two intermediaries (that is, they shared neither friends nor classes) were thirty times less likely to become friends than individuals who were separated by just one intermediary.

The fact that sublime, life-changing introductions often emerge from other, more mundane relationships may seem obvious to the socially sophisticated, but it's a crucial lesson for those of us who seek to connect from a place of relative isolation. As John Cacioppo and William Patrick observed in their book *Loneliness: Human Nature and the Need for Social Connection*, people starved for intimacy tend to lose their bearings even in ordinary encounters. Frustrated with the awkwardness they feel, they may retreat further. The way up from the bottom of this social staircase is not to leap straight for the top but to simply take the first step: Say hello to the guy in the elevator. Make eye contact in the conference room. For

God's sake, call your mom. Even the smallest moment of authentic contact can be elevating. Like a pianist warming up with scales before tackling a sonata, we can use social niceties or bland factual exchanges to set ourselves up for the possibility of something more advanced — sharing a risky idea, say.

Just as loneliness can be a downward spiral, so can connection whorl us up into higher spheres. When we get moving, we can move quickly, because, as the science of social networks shows, we're even more broadly interconnected than we realize. A 2011 study of Facebook found that, of its 721 million users at the time, the average number of links from one arbitrarily selected person to another was 4.74 — less, even, than the "six degrees of separation" made famous in John Guare's play of that name.

But making those links isn't necessarily easy. In fact, some clusters of society can be devilishly hard to penetrate. One key to fluid movement is what the psychologist Karen Fingerman calls "consequential strangers." These are people outside your inner circle who have enough interest in you to make connections but enough distance from you to be exposed to interesting people in other spheres. According to a study by the sociologist Mark Granovetter, well over half of a sample of professionals in Newton, Massachusetts, got their jobs through personal connections. And more than 83 percent of the personal connections that led to jobs involved only occasional or rare contact.

This may tempt you into magical thinking — that someone in the outer reaches of your circle will swoop down and deliver you to someplace new. But it's more accurate to view these relationships as magnifiers of your own interest and attention. In all the cases I've mentioned so far, both future members of a pair had given the conduit a reason to introduce them. They hadn't just dreamed their private dreams. They had taken steps, however tentative, to realize a vision. When you speak of what you want, and even one person hears, it may begin a generative loop.

The second major way people meet vital partners — and enact the loop between personal interest and social connection — is by going to what the sociologist Michael Farrell calls a "magnet place," or a locus for people with shared interests or yearnings.

Schools are obvious magnet places. Matt Stone and Trey Parker, the cocreators of *South Park*, met in an undergraduate film class at the University of Colorado. The psychologists Daniel Kahneman and Amos Tversky, who would go on to create behavioral economics, first connected when Kahneman invited Tversky to talk to his class at the Hebrew University in Jerusalem. Larry Page and Sergey Brin, the cofounders of Google, met on a tour Brin led in the spring of 1995 for students (including Page) who had been admitted to Stanford's grad school. James Watson, a twenty-three-year-old American whiz-kid biologist, met Francis Crick, a thirty-five-year-old Brit trained in physics meandering through his PhD thesis, when Watson went to Cambridge University's Cavendish Laboratory to work on x-ray crystallography, a method to study the atomic structure of molecules. Together they would discover the structure of DNA.

Magnet places exude a power even for people who come without any concrete ambition. In 1967, a twenty-year-old poet and artist and dreamer named Patti Smith was drawn as though by a magnet to the Brooklyn neighborhood around an art college called the Pratt Institute, where some of her friends went to school. "I figured if I placed myself in their environment that I could learn from them," she wrote in her memoir *Just Kids*. When she went to her friends' house, it turned out they had moved, but the boy who answered the door pointed her to the back room where his roommate, also a Pratt student, lay sleeping. It was Robert Mapplethorpe, who would become Smith's creative alter ego.

Indeed, a magnet place needn't even be an institution; it could be an event that lasts only a matter of hours, like the Atlanta church service in the fall of 1950 where two young preachers, Ralph David Abernathy and Martin Luther King Jr., met, the first contact of a partnership that led to the American civil rights movement. In 2007, Mark Zuckerberg, the twenty-three-year-old CEO of Facebook, went to a Christmas party at the home of another Silicon Valley entrepreneur and met a Google executive, Sheryl Sandberg, who three months later signed on as Zuckerberg's COO.

Sometimes, the magnetic pull radiates from one member of the eventual pair. Susan B. Anthony, a teacher, abolitionist, and temperance advocate, was a young soldier in reform movements when she came to Seneca Falls, New York, in 1851 for an antislavery conference. Elizabeth Cady Stanton, though only five years older, was that movement's general, having drafted a Declaration of Sentiments that sounded a call for equality of the sexes unlike any the world had yet heard. They met on the street, and

Stanton immediately took a liking to the younger Anthony, who would become her chief aide.

Even as we note the great outcomes of these meetings, we should keep in mind how humbly, and with how much effort, they may begin. One day in 1960, a fourteen-year-old girl in Cincinnati, Ohio, danced her heart out for a visiting ballerina from New York, who was scouting for scholarship students for the School of American Ballet, affiliated with the choreographer George Balanchine's company. Roberta Sue (Suzi) Ficker had danced for years and had often played a game with her friend where they would fall into armchairs and pretend they were collapsing into the arms of Balanchine's leading men. Her technical skills weren't enough to win her a scholarship. But when the scout heard that Ficker's mother planned to move her girls to New York City, she suggested they call the school directly for another try.

On August 16, 1960, her fifteenth birthday, Ficker had her audition. When she got to the rehearsal space, she was surprised to see Balanchine himself. He watched her dance with his head tilted back. She sang to accompany herself, hoping to fill the room's "loud silence." "It just seemed to go on forever," she remembered. Finally Balanchine clapped his hands, said, "Fine. That's enough. Thank you. Goodbye," and left the room.

She got a call the next day. She had been accepted.

Some meetings seem accidental, but we just need to brush up on the context in order to see the influence of a magnet place. On July 31, 1960, Valentino Garavani, a twenty-eight-year-old fashion designer, came to a café on the Via Veneto in Rome with some friends, but they couldn't find a table. Someone in Valentino's group saw a handsome younger man — a twenty-two-year-old architecture student named Giancarlo Giammetti — sitting alone and asked if they could join him. Giancarlo and Valentino took a fancy to each other, began to date, and soon found themselves in business together, with Giancarlo building an infrastructure to prop up Valentino's dream: to dress the world's most beautiful women.

It wasn't chance, though, that caused their paths to cross. Valentino had come from a small town in the north of Italy; he was a dogged, relentless kid who made his way out of the provinces to Paris, where he was an apprentice designer. Then he broke out on his own and returned to

Rome; he felt intuitively that the heat was there. Giancarlo was born in the city—his father had an electronics shop near the Via Veneto. But he was not from the privileged class, and it was no small bit of gumption for him to thrust himself into the scene made iconic by the Fellini film *La Dolce Vita*. Describing them meeting by "chance" at a hot-spot café in early 1960s Rome would be like describing an "accidental" encounter at New York City's Studio 54 in the late 1970s. "Valentino and Giancarlo were at the right place at the right time," Matt Tyrnauer, the director of *Valentino: The Last Emperor*, told me, "but it wasn't an accident. They put themselves in that café, which was itself the epicenter of an historical moment."

Cafés are the epitome of city life, places where people brush up against new bodies and minds—the Enlightenment itself was fueled by the invention of the coffeehouse. And cities are magnet places writ large. Full of jangles and crowded spaces, they draw, and keep, people who endure the hassle because they're seeking something—namely, one another.

Cities beget creative connection, and that's one major reason they are thriving today. In the 1990s, when information technology unleashed workers from their cubicles, some social scientists predicted the demise of urban living, but the past two decades have actually seen sharp increases in urban populations throughout the world, and especially dramatic concentrations of what Richard Florida calls "the creative class."

Physical contact matters a great deal in creative work. A study in the late 1980s by Bell Communications Research looked at a large industrial research and development laboratory with about five hundred employees in the fields of physics, engineering, and computer and behavioral science. Researchers within the same discipline were twice as likely to collaborate with colleagues on the same floor than with ones just an elevator stop away. Researchers in separate departments who sat close together were six times more likely to collaborate with one another than with those in their own departments on separate floors.

This study was published before the widespread use of e-mail, but even in the age of laptops and smartphones, the best work still seems to emerge from person-to-person contact. According to a 2010 study of thirty-five thousand papers in biomedicine that had at least one author from Harvard, the work of physically close collaborators resulted in many more citations (an indication of the importance of the research) than the work of collaborators who were farther from one another. According to the study, citations were negatively affected not only by collaborators' working on different campuses but also by their working in different buildings on the same campus.

Perhaps the most striking endorsement for direct interaction comes from the very companies who profit from virtual exchange. Yahoo insists that employees work in the office (rather than telecommute). When asked how many Google employees telecommute, the company's chief financial officer, Patrick Pichette, replied: "As few as possible."

Bodies matter, in part because of the well-established importance of nonverbal communications; several studies have shown that gestures are more than four times as important as words.

And the advantages of personal contact include experiences we can't consciously register. In a shared space, people plug into what the psychologist Daniel Goleman has called "neural WiFi," "a feedback loop," he writes in *Social Intelligence*, "that crosses the skin-and-skull barrier between bodies." When scientists videotape conversations and slow them down to watch frame by frame, they detect synchronies between nonverbal elements — a shared rhythm very much like the beat that guides an improvisation in jazz. The movements themselves are coordinated to within a fraction of a second — our brains are taking in data on the order of milli- or microseconds. But conscious processing of information happens in the comparatively sluggish scale of seconds. When two people talk to each other, writes Goleman, "our own thoughts can't possibly track the complexity of the dance."

The core value of a magnet place is the juxtaposition of mutual interests. Typically, we see this in places of concentration — like in the places favored by geeks. But it may also happen in places of relative isolation, as when two geeks find each other in a crowd of jocks. When a Danish teenager named Lars Ulrich moved to Newport Beach, in Orange County, California, in 1980, he found himself totally alone in his obsession with the New Wave of British Heavy Metal, which included bands like Saxon, Iron Maiden, and Def Leppard. In his high school, Lars told biographer Mick Wall, "it was literally five hundred kids in pink Lacoste shirts and one guy in a Saxon T-shirt — me . . . I was an outsider — doing my own thing . . . I'd walk around school with a Saxon T-shirt on and people would look at me as if I was from another planet."

Lars felt so isolated that he took out a classified in a paper called the *Recycler:* "Drummer looking for other metal musicians to jam with." James Hetfield answered the ad. He was so shy that he couldn't make eye contact, Ulrich remembered, but he had the same fervent interest in music. Metallica, the band they cofounded, would go on to sell more than one hundred million albums.

Of course, many pairs don't have a first-meeting story that we know about — or even that they know about. Most siblings — Orville and Wilbur Wright, William and Dorothy Wordsworth, Joel and Ethan Coen — won't remember a time they didn't know each other. But even within that milieu, it is striking how many of these pairs create a world unto themselves based on shared interests. Vincent and Theo van Gogh were the first and third of six surviving children but their unusual rapport was noticeable to their sister Elisabeth, who said that even as a boy, Theo considered Vincent "more than just a normal human being." "I adored him more than anything imaginable," Theo said.

The other common feature of early-intimacy pairs like siblings is that, as much as they share a world together from the start, their creative work begins only after a critical separation. After the death of his wife, John Wordsworth sent his son William away to school and his daughter Dorothy to live with relatives. They hardly saw each other for nine years. The Coen brothers went to the same high school and college, but Joel studied film in a graduate program at NYU and Ethan did graduate work in philosophy at Princeton. After Ethan graduated, he joined his brother in New York to write screenplays.

The point is that pairs with deeply entwined early lives must also develop disparate experiences, attitudes, or emotional styles. This is the next layer to unpeel in meeting stories. The catalyst is not similarity alone but the joining of profound similarities with profound differences.

2

Identical Twins from the Ends of the Earth

The Convergence of Homophily and Heterophily

On a warm, humid day in July 1957, Paul McCartney came around to check out a band called the Quarry Men at a fair in the field behind St. Peter's Church in Woolton, a suburb of Liverpool. He met up with his friend Ivan Vaughan, who had suggested he come. After two sets by the Quarry Men — separated by a demonstration of dog-handling by the Liverpool police — the band headed across Church Road to St. Peter's social hall. Ivan and Paul followed them, and Ivan introduced him to the band, and to its leader, John Lennon.

Paul wore black trousers that narrowed down the shin and a white jacket with silver threads. When John first saw him, he thought he looked like Elvis. This was a big deal. A year before the boys met — in May 1956 — Elvis Presley's first breakout single, "Heartbreak Hotel," hit the UK charts. "Nothing really affected me until Elvis," John said. "All we ever wanted to be was Elvis Presley," Paul said.

John and Paul received rock 'n' roll with the force of revelation and they sought to make lives according to the new faith. Shortly after his fourteenth birthday, Paul traded in a trumpet his dad had bought him for a Zenith 17 guitar. Around the same time, John got a Gallotone Champion and put a band together from among his friends. Onstage, John wore a checked shirt and had his hair swept back in a ducktail. He left his glasses off — though he could hardly see people without them, it mattered more how people saw him.

Paul, too, had commanded crowds. His whole school class had gathered around as he stood on his desk and played Little Richard's "Tutti Frutti"; another school performance drew a hundred and fifty boys standing ten deep. Paul and John shared a repertory — the songs that could be heard only via the tenuous signal of Radio Luxembourg or at the listening booth in the local music shop. The Quarry Men played many of those songs at St. Peter's — including "Come Go with Me," by the Del-Vikings, which, according to Beatles scholar Mark Lewisohn, "wasn't merely a song they both knew, it was a song *few* knew; it was hidden gold, a shared secret, a connector of connoisseurs."

The resonance went far deeper than rock 'n' roll. Both boys were the descendants of Irish immigrants to Liverpool, and they shared a rich local argot in which *gear* meant "great," *soft* meant "stupid," and *eh oop* could mean anything from "hello" to "let's go." They had similar body types (Paul would grow to be five foot eleven and John just a half inch shorter) and similar good looks.

John and Paul are a classic illustration of homophily, literally "love of the same." For primates, familiarities signal safety — and in higher-order brains, this comfort forms the foundation for connection. People report feeling more at ease when there is similarity in factors like income, education, physical appearance, ethnicity, and race.

Similarities stand out in our minds especially when, as is often the case with future creative pairs, they are uncanny. In 1975, the performance artist Marina Abramović went to Amsterdam to perform on Dutch television. The host gallery set her up with an artist to guide her around town and help with her performance — a German man named Uwe Laysiepen, known as Ulay. As the two talked, she remarked on the serendipity that the invitation to perform had come on her birthday. "When is your birthday?" Ulay asked. She said November 30. "That can't be your birthday," he said. "That's *my* birthday"— and to prove it he reached for his diary, where he had torn out his birthday's page, as he did every year. Marina then showed him her diary — her November 30s were torn out too.

"There was a recognition," Ulay said, "like you have found a lost brother or a lost sister or something like this." They soon embarked on a career-making collaboration that lasted twelve years.

Yet the comfort of similarity is only one ingredient for creative progress. Think about an outstanding dinner party. As guests arrive to the smell of good food and the sight of drinks laid out, there's instantly a feeling of ease. Some people know one another already — none are farther apart than two degrees. Many have similar interests or backgrounds. The early part of the evening should be weighted toward familiarity, but when the dinner begins, the priority shifts from comfort to stimulation. Disparate experiences are shared; disagreements erupt.

We need similarities to give us ballast, and differences to make us move. One study for the National Bureau of Economic Research looked at the two reasons venture capitalists choose partners: for their ability or for their affinity, such as a shared ethnic background or having worked at the same firm. Similarities of ability enhanced performance, but similarities of affinity "dramatically reduces the probability of investment success," the study found. The problem isn't the similarity itself. That's fine as a foundation. The problem is when members of a group look at situations the same way, and fail to appreciate difficulties coming down the pike, loyalty and devotion can outstrip independent thinking.

In some areas of life, a strong weight toward similarity and against difference may work out fine. But creative work depends on exchanges across an expanse, on the coming together of strangers. "Without Contraries is no progression," William Blake wrote in *The Marriage of Heaven and Hell*. Ira Gershwin's definition of a song — "two arts under emotional pressure coalescing into a third" — could also be applied to creativity generally. Gershwin was speaking of music and lyrics. But these can be understood as symbols for disparate fields or perspectives with the same common problem that, in every case, as Gershwin wrote, "the relation and balance of the two arts . . . has to be resolved anew."

In his book *The Act of Creation*, Arthur Koestler called this relation and balance "bisociation"—"the sudden interlocking of two previously unrelated skills, or matrices, of thought." This is the stuff of creative breakthroughs, which helps explain why, in the history of innovation, the outsider with critical knowledge and a fresh perspective so often plays a crucial role — why mavericks, for example, and not the pedigreed employees of Western Union or IBM, invented the telephone and the personal computer.

Outsiders do more than create novel products. According to Thomas

Kuhn's theory of paradigm shifts, they are often responsible for usher-ing in a whole intellectual atmosphere. The authors of a new paradigm can't be total strangers to the field or they won't have the knowledge to do their work, let alone the influence to effect change. But they can't be vested insiders either, or they'll be constrained by convention. Insiders are especially vulnerable to stasis in the very fields, like academia, that profess to value originality and iconoclasm. People in power naturally re-ward sycophants and line-toers, and the absence of empirical standards can give them free rein.

Yet, just as legacy cultures can grow stodgy, a culture of newbies can innovate itself right into ridiculousness. The dot-com boom of the late 1990s was a classic example.

The best climate for progress is a mix of deference and defiance. Cor-porate teams do well with a clear mission and a deviant who asks un-comfortable questions. Studying the networks out of which Broadway musicals emerged, the sociologists Brian Uzzi and Jarrett Spiro found that the best-selling and most acclaimed work came from environments with an optimal mix of intimates and strangers — people who had worked together closely before, plus people in the field who were new to one another.

At the root level of the dyad, this juxtaposition is essential. "The two people who have the most creative potential," the psychologist and man-agement consultant Diana McLain Smith told me, "are the people who are most different. The question is how do they harness that difference in the service of creativity instead of canceling each other out."

Judging from the number of times Paul McCartney has told the story, one moment stood out for him on that sticky summer day in 1957 when he met his future partner. It came just as McCartney ambled onto the field at St. Peter's — behind the sandstone church with its looming clock tower — and caught the sounds of the Del-Vikings' song "Come Go with Me," a mellifluous doo-wop that opens, on the record, with an infectious melody of *dooby*s and *wah-wah-wah-wah*s before invoking a lovelorn plea that, as in the title, a certain darlin' "come and go with me" and not send the speaker away "beyond the sea."

Paul knew the song well enough to realize that John — wearing a checked shirt, his hair piled atop his head in a style reminiscent of Elvis Presley — was doing something odd and wonderful when he sang the opening verse this way:

Come come come come
And go with me
Down down down down to
The penitentiary

Paul thought it was "ingenious." John had taken a sweet love song and infused it with the outlaw flavor of the blues, and he had reached his arms across the ocean to wrap up Liverpool and the American South. (*Penitentiary* wasn't a common word in the UK.) It was a small moment but it signaled John's impudence and bravado. "I warmed to him immediately hearing that," Paul said.

The Quarry Men were set to play a dance that night at 8 p.m., which is why after the gig some members of the band — including John Lennon — as well as Ivan Vaughan and Paul McCartney, hung around the church social hall.

That's where Paul picked up a guitar, turned it around so he could play it left-handed, and began to show off the songs he knew — the staples of early rock 'n' roll by Eddie Cochran, Carl Perkins, and Little Richard. In just a few songs, Paul demonstrated his mastery of chords and lyrics — including Cochran's "Twenty Flight Rock," a song other kids had a hard time even deciphering. He not only knew the chords but could adjust on the fly to play them in reverse on a right-handed guitar. John, by contrast, didn't even have the guitar tuned right; he was playing it like a banjo. "Right off, I could see John was checking this kid out," Pete Shotton, John's best friend, recalled.

For Paul to register John's daring — and for John to register Paul's proficiency — took only moments, but those moments suggested the extent to which they could complement each other.

Paul came from a warm, close-knit family where the importance of music was epitomized by the upright piano that dominated their tiny living room. Music for Paul was family sing-alongs and brass band concerts with his dad. When he began to write songs, Paul wasn't thinking about rock 'n' roll. He wanted to write for Sinatra.

John, by contrast, spent most of his youth in his aunt Mimi's house, a prim, stuffy place. Quite unlike Paul's cozy childhood, John's life was marked by vectors and divisions. He had been hustled off to Mimi's from the wreckage of his charming, dissolute parents.

For a teenage Paul, Elvis was a major variation on a familiar, and familial, theme. For all his innovation, Elvis also represented a continuity of tradition in big, brash musical performance.

For John, the man from Memphis brought everything he disliked about the world around him into sharper relief. "Rock and roll then was real," he said. "Everything else was unreal."

The irony is that John, who was more fractured and defiant, was by far the more social musician. His charisma came, as charisma usually does, from a bottomless need to be loved. And his ambition came from a sense that if he was going to have a world he liked, he'd have to make it himself. He had his boyhood buddies act out the stories from his favorite books, sent them on raids, orchestrated pranks. He was always running a gang. When rock 'n' roll came into his life, he made his gang into a band. He insisted Pete Shotton join, though Pete protested he could hardly play. John didn't mind. He could hardly play himself.

This rebellious impulse took him to dangerous places. By the time John met Paul, his boyhood hijinks had progressed to shoplifting. Had John not wound up in a truly outstanding band — which is to say, had he not met Paul — he said he would probably have ended up like his dad, a likable ne'er-do-well alternating between odd jobs and petty crime. "Even I sometimes worried that he seemed destined for Skid Row," Pete Shotton remembered.

Paul might have ended up teaching — this was one path he considered — or doing some other job where he could rely on his smarts and still live inside his own mind. He was studied and careful — even his abandon was more or less by the book. It's telling that he had the Elvis look down far better than John did. He could also scream like Little Richard. Paul had the astonishing power of a mime, whereas John could be only himself.

John was twenty months older — a world apart for a teenager. He was the badass older brother Paul never had. For John, Paul presented as a studious and charming sidekick who was as good as him or better and who could do something few others could: keep up with him. Another boy in the hall said that after Paul's performance, the two kids were "circling each other like cats."

Obviously, any two people differ from each other in some ways and resemble each other in others, but in potent pairs, it's taken to an uncanny extreme, as if they were identical twins from opposite ends of the globe. When Graham Nash and David Crosby met in 1966, Nash was a dapper, goateed Englishman from the north of England whose songs reflected a pure pop simplicity, whereas Crosby was a Southern California poet-sailor-mystic whose songs pushed the edges of pop so hard they nearly broke into jazz.

Like most great pairs, they were an archetypal odd couple. And yet in some ways it was as though they were twins separated at birth. Both men had reached the peak of pop success — Nash in the Hollies and Crosby in the Byrds — but were feeling constrained and unappreciated by their bands. Within the exploding rock scene of the 1960s, both reserved their greatest fondness for harmonic singing — and in the canon of harmony, both reserved special devotion for the style of the Everly Brothers, who sang melodic lines mostly based on parallel thirds, so that each line could stand on its own and magnify the other.

Steve Jobs and Steve Wozniak are another case where the similarities approach the level of twin peaks — and the differences feel as gaping as a great canyon. Jobs and Wozniak were both kids of the counterculture who nurtured a genuine political radicalism, pranksters who delighted in clever ways to give the world the middle finger, and gadget geeks who had a soaring idealism about how they could affect people's day-to-day lives. In his memoir *iWoz*, Wozniak remembered an early conversation with Jobs about who was better, Dylan or the Beatles. "We both favored Dylan," he wrote, "because the songs were about life and living and values in life and what was really important . . . To us, Dylan's songs struck a moral chord. They kind of made you think about what was right and wrong in the world, and how you're going to live and be." Each thought he was bound to do magnificent things.

Yet, while they shared a distinct vision, their temperaments and characters diverged sharply. Jobs could bore into people like a laser beam, changing minds with what came to be described, famously, as a "reality distortion field." Wozniak described himself as "shy" and "terribly awkward" and "scared to talk because I thought I'd say the wrong thing." Jobs had a beguiling charm, though he could throw fits like a toddler. Wozniak was patient and dogged.

Perhaps my favorite example of juxtaposed extremes is Bob and Mike Bryan. At first glance, they seem nothing but the same — they are, after all, identical twins who play doubles tennis together and are often seen in public in matching K-Swiss outfits. They've ruled the world of doubles tennis for a decade — and they present as a totally unified force. Even good friends have a hard time telling them apart. Their thinking is so aligned that they don't confer between points. Both Mike and Bob will answer to either Bob or Mike.

Yet tennis insiders are as struck by their differences as anything else. "You don't ever confuse them on the court," said Rajeev Ram, a frequent opponent. Bob is a lefty, an inch taller than his brother, and a better shot. According to Mike, he's the more inventive of the two — he writes the songs for their band and runs their Twitter feed — and the more hot-headed. Mike, who is right-handed, has a stronger return and a more strategic game. He's the more organized of the two — and the more sensitive. "If I rip him on the court," Bob said, "his level of play will drop. With me, it's the opposite." They work together as smoothly, and as separately, as two hands on the same body.

3

"Like Two Young Bear Cubs"

The Varieties of Electric Experience

Electricity—that common image for the experience of mutual potential—is a good metaphor in part because it conveys such disparate emotional experiences. Electricity may feel as natural and easy as plugging into a socket. When the writers—and soon-to-be partners—Kelley Eskridge and Nicola Griffith met, Nicola writes, "Every single cell in my body lined up like iron filings and pointed at her.'" When Marina Abramović and Ulay met, Marina said, "We go straight to his house and stay in bed for ten days."

Pairs may also find first contact uneasy—like they've touched their hands to a live wire. After seeing Pablo Picasso's painting *Les Demoiselles d'Avignon,* Georges Braque told the artist, "It's as if you were trying to make us drink petrol to spit fire," but the energy of the moment propelled the two of them toward the creation of cubism. When Ralph Abernathy first saw Martin Luther King Jr. preach, he sat in the pews "burning with envy at his learning and confidence." Within hours of meeting, Sergey Brin and Larry Page broke into a sharp argument—clashing, one journalist noted, like "two swords sharpening each other." In 2010, thirty-six years after the magician Penn Jillette met his partner, Teller, he said: "We often hate each other, but it's the kind of hatred that's like flint and steel—the sparks that come out make it worth the while."

Many great pairs do not much like each other at first. When C. S. Lewis initially noticed J.R.R. Tolkien, at an Oxford faculty meeting, he came home and wrote: "No harm in him: only needs a smack or so." The two

19

men soon found themselves on opposite sides of a great curricular debate—whether English literature studies should be based on ancient and
medieval texts and languages or include "modern" works. Tolkien took the
former view—he found anything later than Chaucer suspect—Lewis the
latter.

Lewis was wary. "At my first coming into the world," he wrote in *Surprised by Joy,* "I had been (implicitly) warned never to trust a Papist and at
my first coming into the English faculty (explicitly) never to trust a phi-
lologist. Tolkien was both." But Lewis soon learned that his ideological enemy had founded a club called the Kolbíter—"Coalbiters"— after the Old
Norse word for men who sat around swapping stories in the cold, so close
to the fire that, Lewis wrote, "they look as if they were biting the coals."
This was a group of Oxfordians who read Icelandic sagas and myths in the
original language. Lewis was exhilarated to learn of the Kolbíter; he loved
these texts. He and Tolkien discovered a mutual interest in what they
called "northernness," and over time became "great friends," said E. L. Ed-
monds, a student at Oxford in the mid-1930s. "Indeed, they were like two
young bear cubs sometimes, just happily quipping with one another."

Where there is discomfort with promising pairs, it tends to be galvanizing—or perhaps it's that certain pairs move (eventually) toward promising discomfort rather than retreating to the safety of isolation. In 2004,
the filmmaker Lisa Cholodenko found herself at a loss at a coffee shop in
Los Angeles. She was stuck on a script she had been writing and couldn't
get traction. Looking across the room, she spotted another writer she
knew from film circles, Stuart Blumberg. Stuart came to say hello and they
got to talking about Lisa's problem script, which was about two lesbian
moms and their teenage kids who suddenly meet their sperm-donor father. Blumberg listened to the problems and then told Cholodenko: "I've
always thought you should do work that's more commercial." Cholodenko
shot back, "I've always thought you should do work that's more personal."
The next day, they were at work collaborating on the script that became
the film *The Kids Are All Right.*

One trope of first meetings is the endless conversation. "Steve and I
just sat on the sidewalk in front of Bill [Fernandez]'s house for the longest
time, just sharing stories," Wozniak remembered of his first encounter
with Jobs. When Mark Zuckerberg met Sheryl Sandberg at that Christmas party, they talked for about an hour by the door and soon arranged

to continue the conversation in private. According to Carl Jung, when he met Sigmund Freud, they "talked uninterruptedly for thirteen hours."

Both animating conflict and absorbing conversation draw on the same two elements: a shared framework to provide common ground, and sufficient difference to keep things novel and surprising. When Tolkien and Lewis were on opposite sides of the curriculum debate, they shared as much ground as two tennis players facing off on a court.

Promising pairs are the ones who decide to play. Maybe they suffer displeasure for the sake of the work. Good work also *yields* pleasure. "People generally think that teams that work together harmoniously are better and more productive than teams that don't," the psychologist J. Richard Hackman said. But in a study of symphonies, he found that "grumpy orchestras," in Hackman's words, played somewhat better than those whose musicians were happy. "That's because the cause-and-effect is the reverse of what most people believe," Hackman said. "When we're productive and we've done something good together (and are recognized for it), we feel satisfied, not the other way around."

The most telling indicator of success in groups, Hackman found, is not the members' moods before a performance but how they feel afterward. In a 2001 interview with Charlie Rose, Sergey Brin said, with a smile on his face, "You know, Larry's kind of obnoxious." "I'd say Sergey is the obnoxious one," Larry Page retorted, laughing. It helps to take pleasure in a guy's obnoxiousness when you and he have struck gold together. At the time, Google was performing more than seventy million searches a day; three years later, when the company went public, Brin and Page instantly became billionaires.

Not that the pleasure is all in a finished product. Seeing a good idea made better can be its own reward. But it's a peculiar kind of pleasure, one that is often wrapped up in vulnerability, even the risk of humiliation.

The emotional point needs to be made explicit: *Creativity* has become a broad, vague term, a kind of stand-in for universal good, even a synonym for happiness (or, as *innovation,* for profits). But making new, beautiful, useful things is as much about discord as it is about union. The creative impulse is born of a sense of incompleteness and inadequacy. It's often fueled by frustration, by an incessant—though perhaps hard to articulate—sense that things are not as they ought to be, or as they could be. Many of us believe that finding one's partner or soul mate means arriving at a place of consistent satisfaction. But it may be quite the contrary, that a pairing proceeds from an awareness that there is a gulf to cross, and all you have is a dinghy. We may long to be understood by our partners entirely and completely, to be known the way our mothers knew us. But one of the qualities that comes along with strangeness between partners is that they will never fully know each other. As the psychologist Esther Perel explains, drawing on the work of the psychoanalyst Stephen Mitchell, long-term relationships are always beset by a paradox that human beings want both security and novelty. They want ease and familiarity and they also want to be challenged and aroused. They have to negotiate the need for both.

This apparent subversion by close relationships of the self-other distinction is due, specifically, to the other becoming "part of the self"—to the very structure of the self changing, such that the self includes the other in its very make-up.

—*Arthur Aron et al.,* The Self and Social Relationships

He and you join like raindrops on a window.

—*C. S. Lewis,* Surprised by Joy

PART II

CONFLUENCE

One late November afternoon in 1962, John Lennon and Paul McCartney got together to write at Paul's house at 20 Forthlin Road in Liverpool. Their ritual was to come around in the afternoon, just the two of them, when Paul's dad was at work. They would go to the small front room overlooking Jim McCartney's patch of garden and sit opposite each other. "Like mirrors," Paul said.

John sat on a chair pulled in from the dining room. He had his Jumbo Gibson acoustic-electric with a sunburst finish. Paul sat on a little table in front of the telly with his foot on the hearth of the coal fireplace. He played a Spanish-style guitar with nylon strings, strung in reverse for a lefty. In a photograph shot by Paul's brother, Michael, they're both looking down at a notebook on the floor, the page filled with lyrics, a pencil lying on top of it.

McCartney had a song he'd started on the way home from a show in Southport, about forty-five minutes up the coast from Liverpool, and he played the opening for John.

> *She was just seventeen*
> *Never been a beauty queen*

John snorted. "You're joking about that line, aren't you?" he said. Paul agreed it was bad. *Just seventeen* had narrative promise, but *beauty queen* risked cliché. They began to bat around ideas. What rhymed with *seventeen*? *Clean*? *Lean*? Finally, John offered this:

> *She was just seventeen*
> *You know what I mean*

Yep, that would do it. They had joined sin to innocence, taken a promising image and given it a lusty, poetic kick.

Years later, Paul told his brother that he loved his photo of the "I Saw Her Standing There" writing session because it captured how it really was—"the Rodgers and Hammerstein of pop at work." Writing "eyeball to eyeball," as John said, they weren't just frontmen for a rock group; they were composers working in concert. Having already pledged to co-credit all their work, around this time they made it formal, taking equal shares in a company called Northern Songs that would control their publishing. "Historically," writes Mark Lewisohn in *The Beatles: All These Years*, "joint-songwriter agreements enumerated splits of 90:10, 85:15, 80:20, 75:25,

67:33 and every other fiddly fraction down to 50:50. But John and Paul went halves all the way, closeness and ambition shared and matched." Now every lick of music that either one produced (regardless of the other's actual contribution) would be both literally and metaphorically — both legally and emotionally — co-owned.

How does this happen? Blithe accounts of creative connection show two heroes meeting and then tell us, "The rest was history." But there's a big difference in quality, and usually a major gap in time, between the excitement of first contact and the entwinement of mature work. It's not so unusual for two people to come together, excite each other — maybe even knock each other sideways. But exceptional pairs have more than moments of electricity. They come to jointly occupy a house powered by it. Over time, they develop what psychologists call "couple identity," and a coordination of cognitive functions that some scientists even consider a shared mind.

In some ways, this phase can be observed by its tangible indicators, like the rituals that create a shared space or patterns of speech that literally lead to more "we" and less "I." But the big question is less tangible than ethereal: How can the individual submit to the mutual even as the mutual informs the individual? How can we come to feel more vital, more alive — more ourselves — even as we cede independence for interdependence?

And how to describe this progression? I considered gestation, emphasizing the slow and methodical growth of the partnership. I also liked the image of explosion — entities reacting with each other in a contained space until the pressure builds to the point of bursting. In the end, I settled on another image: confluence, when two bodies of water flow into each other, as when the Allegheny joins the Monongahela to create the Ohio River, or when the Mississippi absorbs the Ohio. All these images have something in common — they convey how what happens can't be reversed. After this stage, members of a pair may seek to return to the time before their identities were hitched, to fully restore a sense of the I that preceded the we. But there is no wresting the two rivers apart again. New compounds are formed; maybe even a new organism is born.

4

Presence → Confidence → Trust

The Stages of Confluence

Many ideas about creativity are bound up in the myth of heroic progress, the aha moment, the light bulb incandescing. But while connection, the creative equivalent of love at first sight, may happen in an instant, the movement to true partnership is often slow and meandering.

Take Charlie Munger and Warren Buffett. Though they felt sparks in 1959, they still lived in different cities, worked in different businesses, and had different investing philosophies. In regular phone calls and occasional visits, they began to exchange ideas and advice. Munger learned from Buffett about buying companies with investor capital. Buffett slowly came around to Munger's view that bargain hunting (which he had learned as gospel from his mentor Ben Graham) often made less sense than paying a reasonable price for a good company.

By the mid-1960s, they were investing in some of the same deals. By the late 1960s, they began each day by talking to each other on the phone.

But it wasn't until 1983 that they formalized their partnership, with Munger taking a stake, and the vice chairman position, in Buffett's holding company Berkshire Hathaway.

It's common to find some sizable gap in time between meeting and pairing. J.R.R. Tolkien and C. S. Lewis knew each other for three years before they shared their work. Jerry Seinfeld and Larry David bonded with each other more than a decade before they began to work on what became *Seinfeld*.

When I interviewed Neal Brennan, who co-created the Comedy Central blockbuster *Chappelle's Show* with Dave Chappelle, he emphasized the gradual, rambling way that the partnership developed. Brennan worked the door at a New York City comedy club where Chappelle was a regular. They first clicked when Brennan (an impudent kid — wiry, dark-haired, New England pale, just eighteen years old at the time) suggested a bit for one of Chappelle's jokes. They started hanging around after Chappelle's sets, taking walks, smoking cigarettes, sitting outside the Coffee Shop in Union Square. "We just spent so much time together," Brennan said. "I don't know if I'd say we were working. But we were building an ethos, a sense of what the other one values, a shared history. It's like, you go to a movie, and you both come out of it and you can reference that movie for the rest of your life."

Psychologists call this "tacit knowledge." Widely understood as a key to human interaction — maybe even the DNA of interpersonal exchange — it depends on firsthand observation and interaction: sifting through the slowly accruing sediment of mutual experience. It's the inverse of explicit knowledge — things you can learn about someone from a resumé or Wikipedia.

As I talked to Brennan, I thought of another well-known psychological fact: the study by K. Anders Ericsson that showed a person needs ten thousand hours of "deliberate practice" to become great at something. I mentioned the association, and Brennan seized on it. "It feels like it took ten thousand hours for me and Dave to really get to know each other," he said.

From my observation of pairs, I noticed a progression through three key stages: presence, confidence, and trust.

Presence is the building block for authentic interaction, but it doesn't come easy. "You can enjoy someone a great deal, but still relate to that person on the basis of your own needs," the sociologist Michael Farrell, who studies creative intimacy, told me. "This is 'transference'— meaning, you're not really seeing the other person. You're relating to some heir to your mother or your brother or stuck in the static of your head." In laboratory experiments, Farrell found it sometimes took strangers twenty-five or thirty hours to really be present. "Finally, there is that moment of recognition: 'There really is someone else out there.' Suddenly, there's a real authenticity."

We can feel tenderness for the way people guard themselves, considering the emotional risks. Diane Ackerman, in *A Natural History of Love*, evoked the "utmost vulnerability" of intimate relationships: "We equip someone with freshly sharpened knives; strip naked; then invite him to stand close." There's the possibility of an enlivening exchange, but also the prospect of rejection, even ridicule.

This may sound dour, which is an odd tone, because getting to know a new and dear person is often so much fun. "Laughter," observed the psychologist Daniel Goleman, "may be the shortest distance between two brains." But fun isn't the absence of psychological risk; it's actually a heightened state of risk. As the psychiatrist George Vaillant observed, the negative emotions have built-in insulation. Think of the crouch associated with fear or the head-in-hands posture of sadness; we adopt these positions because they protect us from the outside world. But when we joyously fling our arms up and away, we expose our guts and necks.

Neither intimacy nor creativity is possible without that kind of exposure; at the nexus of creativity and intimacy, we see it twofold. In *The Making of Americans,* Gertrude Stein writes about the shame an author can feel — the sense that "every one must think you are a silly or a crazy one," the expectation that "you will be laughed at or pitied by every one . . . Then someone says yes to it," Stein writes, and the shame lifts like cloud cover on a high peak.

Of course, the "yes" only registers when that "someone" has your confidence. Highly creative people have high standards and distinct sensibilities; they see the world in an unusual way (or they wouldn't be able to make something new out of the materials of that world). Their partners must be a match — and the discovery of a shared sensibility is itself often an impetus to share work. In 1929, J.R.R. Tolkien asked C. S. Lewis if he would look at his epic poem *The Lay of Leithian,* the story of a character named Man Beren who fled from the Battle of Sudden Flame and escaped into the realm of elves, where he fell in love with the elf-maiden Lúthien. Tolkien had been working on the piece for four years but had kept it to himself. No wonder. His academic colleagues at Oxford in the 1920s would hardly have embraced mythical parables soaked with Christian imagery and invented languages. But Lewis said yes to it. "I can quite honestly say," he wrote Tolkien the day after reading it, "that it is ages since I have had an evening of such delight."

The second ingredient of confidence is reciprocity. When you take a step toward another person, does he step toward you in return? After his praise of Tolkien's story, Lewis wrote: "Detailed criticisms (including grumbles at individual lines) will follow." His meticulous notes questioned everything from overarching themes to individual word choices. Lewis suggested specific revisions — and even rewrote sections. Far from dismayed, Tolkien revised the story extensively, responding to most of Lewis's comments. "Tolkien had taken a substantial risk," writes the scholar Diana Pavlac Glyer. "Lewis had offered a generous, detailed response." And then the crucial next step: Lewis took a reciprocal risk. He sent some of his own poems to Tolkien, who offered his own generous and unsparing comments. "He was for long my only audience," Tolkien said of Lewis. "Only from him did I ever get the idea that my 'stuff' could be more than a private hobby. But for his interest and unceasing eagerness for more I should never have brought [The Lord of the Rings] to a conclusion."

Several years later, Tolkien — along with a mutual friend, Hugo Dyson — helped prod Lewis into a transformation that would completely change his life's work: they persuaded him of the essential truth of Christianity. Once a committed atheist, Lewis converted to Christianity, and faith became a central tenet of his writing and his life.

For pairs to jell, it's essential that confidence deepen over time, that each find the other reliable. "He's never late, he never makes mistakes, and he does everything he says he'll do," Penn Jillette said about his partner, adding, "If someone asked what I most liked about Teller, I'd say he was punctual."

Elsewhere in the same interview Penn called Teller one of the "ten best magical minds alive today." But talent matters only when the talent shows up. Creative work often depends on long hours and meticulous attention. Bruce Springsteen and the saxophonist Clarence Clemons had a magical first meeting, with Clemons coming into a bar in Asbury Park, New Jersey, as a howling wind literally blew the door off its hinges. "Bruce and I looked at each other and didn't say anything, we just knew," Clemons said of the moment they first played together. "We knew we were the missing links in each other's lives." And yet, to deliver on the promise, they needed more than windstorms — they needed the consistency of a wind turbine.

The Clemons sax solo that ends "Jungleland" on *Born to Run* took sixteen hours straight to lay down. Bruce and Clarence worked on it all night, literally up to the moment they had to get on the road for a tour.

In ordinary usage, *confidence* and *trust* are synonyms, but there's an important distinction. *Confidence* has a connotation of positive expectations about a system; for example, "I'm confident that this ladder won't collapse." We may be confident in people too, but there is still a flavor of the mechanical. Not long after they met, Steve Jobs and Steve Wozniak built a "blue box" that could hack phone lines and make free long-distance calls. "If it hadn't been for the blue boxes, there wouldn't have been an Apple," Jobs said later. "I'm a hundred percent sure of that. Woz and I learned how to work together and we gained the confidence that we could solve technical problems and actually put something into production. You cannot believe how much confidence that gave us."

If confidence is specific, trust is holistic. If confidence is about what you expect to do with a person, trust is more about how you regard that person. The economist Robert Shiller defines it as "an emotional state that dismisses doubts about others." A common definition in psychology emphasizes the way trust elicits vulnerability. "When you feel trust," the writer George Saunders told me, "you know the other guy is going to cover your back. You can just throw yourself over the cliff, because you know you're going to be caught."

How does trust arise? Some academics propose that it follows from a strain test, when someone takes a risk to benefit another. But what I saw more often in creative pairs was trust developing in concert as pairs took risks together, like when Neal Brennan and Dave Chappelle pitched HBO an idea for a comedy show — and got shot down — or when Warren Buffett and Charlie Munger bought See's Candy and turned a solid profit.

In their early years, Matt Stone and Trey Parker did nothing but take risks together. In 1994, the two went to Hollywood, where they became, almost literally, starving artists: "Down to a meal a day," Stone said. For a while, they both lived in Parker's studio apartment: Parker slept on a futon, Stone on the floor atop a pile of his dirty clothes. "Any money we had was to live or get our own thing going," Stone said. "There is no doubt that adverse conditions increase bonding amongst partners who survive," said Jason McHugh, a producer on several early projects with Parker and Stone. "Making a film production is a little like going to war. And you never forget your buddies."

The big break actually came out of a disappointment. An executive at Fox who had passed on a pilot Trey directed, called *Time Warped*, hired Trey and Matt to make a video Christmas card for him to send to his friends. Trey and Matt went to work shooting stop-motion animation with cardboard cutouts of four foulmouthed kids who watch an epic battle between Jesus Christ and Santa Claus. The video became all the rage in Hollywood — and soon Matt and Trey had a deal to make a pilot for Comedy Central of a show they called *South Park*.

5

The Turn of Faith

The Final Stage

In the final step of bonding, after presence leads to confidence, and confidence settles into trust, trust elevates into faith. To see a pair travel this path, let's return to the student dancer Suzi Ficker and the choreographer George Balanchine — two individuals who, when they first made contact, were separated by a chasm of history and identity and knowledge. Ficker, a fifteen-year-old girl from Mount Healthy, Ohio, had lived in a world of sycamore trees and ice cream parlors and dance classes. Her father drove a meat-delivery truck. When she came to New York, she lived with her mother and sister in a one-room apartment with no stove and a busted toilet. They used the bathroom at the Automat across the street, where they also ate most of their meals.

Balanchine was fifty-six years old, a Russian émigré who had lived under Lenin and Stalin, had danced at the illustrious Ballets Russes under Sergei Diaghilev, and, in America, had essentially created modern ballet. He took his meals at the Russian Tea Room or at home with his wife at the time, the celebrated ballerina Tanaquil Le Clercq. Other long-term collaborators included the composer Igor Stravinsky and the impresario Lincoln Kirstein, with whom he created the New York City Ballet.

A lithe and musical dancer, Ficker was unusually ferocious in both her physicality and her ambition. Balanchine, though he had eighty-some members in his company, on top of the students in his school, noticed her unusual sense of tempo — she had an "inner clock," he said. In her first year, during a photo session for the scholarship students, he looked her in the eye and said: "A few years, maybe less."

Fourteen months after her original audition for Balanchine, Ficker was invited to be a member of the company. When she went to sign her contract, she elongated Suzi to Suzanne and, after thumbing through the New York City phone book, chose the mellifluous Farrell for a last name. She was willing to do more than merely learn or grow. She was ready to remake herself.

After a variety of minor roles, Suzanne Farrell got her big chance in the spring of 1963, when a principal Balanchine lead, Diana Adams, became pregnant and bowed out of a major piece on her doctor's orders. Balanchine was crushed, not just by the loss of his lead two weeks before a premiere but by the pregnancy itself: his obsession with Adams, as with the many ballerinas before her, did not stop at the stage.

When Balanchine shut himself up in his apartment, refusing to answer his phone, the male lead in the piece, Jacques d'Amboise, brought Farrell to Adams's apartment so she could learn the dance. The moves were all in Adams's head, and the music — a complex, atonal score by Stravinsky — was not yet recorded. While Adams lay on the couch making motions with her hands, Farrell threw herself across the parquet floors in the ten-by-twelve-foot room. "There were enough steps to fill a four-act *Swan Lake*," she wrote, "only they seemed to be danced backward and upside down. My head was swimming in a sea of développés, crouches, lunges, and strange musical cues." Still, she learned the movements well enough to dance them before Balanchine. "Mr. B's eyebrows rose and his demeanor changed," Farrell remembered. D'Amboise said the choreographer was "enthralled."

Two days before the premiere, Farrell bungled a rehearsal that was especially high stakes — on hand were not only Stravinsky and Kirstein but also a German film crew, "and the cruel camera eye had witnessed, firsthand, my insufficiencies," Farrell wrote. Afterward, she told Balanchine: "I don't think you should let me do this. I'm just not ready for it."

"Oh, dear," he said, bowing slightly, his hands clasped as though in prayer, "you let me be the judge."

"And I did, forever more," Farrell wrote. "This brief exchange was a turning point in a silent understanding, and our trust was sealed. I would try my hardest to do what he wanted and dance well, and he would be the only judge, relieving me of having to criticize myself."

After this same rehearsal, Stravinsky asked about the new ballerina. "Igor Fyodorovich," Balanchine said, "this is Suzanne Farrell. Just been born."

It was a charged metaphor, suggesting, perhaps, that the girl from Cincinnati had come to exist only now that she existed for him, that her past was but gestation before she sprang into the arms of his imagination. When Diana Adams remarked on the extent of Farrell's accomplishments with Balanchine, he said, "Well, you see, dear, Suzanne never resisted." Farrell herself said as much. "If he thought I could do something, I would believe him, often against my own reasoning," she wrote.

Yet, over time, Balanchine gave himself to his dancer too. He did more than give Farrell parts — starting in 1964, she danced fifteen leading roles in fourteen months. He began to reshape his company around her. Farrell was a poor jumper, so no more jumps. Balanchine ceased to watch the entire performances of his company. When Farrell's parts were complete, he took her directly to supper.

Other ballerinas walked out, but Balanchine didn't care. He now had his eyes firmly fixed on just the one.

In 1964, the New York City Ballet moved to the new Lincoln Center. A much larger stage demanded larger movements. One day, at the regular eleven o'clock class, in a big windowless rehearsal room on the fifth floor of the New York State Theater, Farrell took fourth position in preparation for a pirouette, a move in which the rear foot pushes off the floor to generate a spin and then lifts so that during the spin, it is positioned by the knee of the supporting leg. Typically, in fourth position, a dancer will keep her feet close enough together — say, a foot or a foot and a half — to maintain a steady balance. Balanchine, however, had other ideas. "Why don't you try a big fourth?" he said. Farrell inched her feet a bit farther apart. "Bigger," he urged. She went farther. "Now I was feeling really uncomfortable," she wrote, "with my legs so far apart that the notion of pushing off for a turn was becoming a fantasy."

"More," Balanchine said.

"More," he said again.

Finally, her feet were so far apart that she was about to slip and fall into a split. As the other dancers laughed nervously, and Farrell felt "thoroughly ridiculous," Balanchine smiled in triumph: "*Now* turn," he said. Though expecting to fall on her face, Farrell threw herself into a spin. It was an exhilarating move; not as clean or precise as a more conventional turn, but somehow more free. It was, she wrote in her memoir, a "turn of faith."

In *The Varieties of Religious Experience,* William James describes two common qualities to faith experiences. First, a zest for living — faith is animating; it excites bold ideas or actions. Second, a sense of security, love, and peace — faith is a balm; it stimulates a sense of ease. Both resonate with Farrell's report of her turn of faith, when she felt that *impossible* went out of her vocabulary. "That pirouette," she said, "was really the beginning of our spiritual understanding; indeed, it was not about pirouettes at all, it was about believing in someone even when you might doubt . . . Not to turn, not to believe, to refuse Balanchine's wisdom — that would have been frightening."

A third quality of faith is a fundamental sense of division between it and all other experience. This is one of the roots of the word *sacred* — from the Latin *sanctus,* "set apart." In faith, one feels as though a threshold has been crossed. "Now that I had turned this way once," Farrell wrote, "I could never again turn the old way." Balanchine, for his part, saw she had the willingness, and the skill, to follow him anywhere he might imagine. After the turn, he held his finger in the air "like a magician who has just pulled a rabbit out of a hat," Farrell wrote.

Out of this faith can come a place of true abandon and intense exchange. "He'd give one of his paralyzing combinations; you'd be exhausted even before the music started but Suzanne would zip through it without batting an eye," observed Diana Adams. "Whatever quirky movement or odd rhythm he gave, she'd take it in and feed it back to him. He began to make things harder and harder. She inhaled and kept going."

"And so," writes Joan Acocella in the *New Yorker,* "in collaboration with her, he developed a new style."

Farrell calls it "off-balance" dancing, and its off-balance qualities — the reckless tilts and lunges — were indeed the first thing one noticed about it, but it was also new in its utterly plastic musicality and, above all, in its scale. Farrell's movement came in bolts, in waves, in tearing trajectories. (Balanchine rarely sent her out on-stage without an expert partner, one who could prevent her from hurling herself into the orchestra pit.) Even when her dancing was slow, it was wild: pooling, flooding. And she performed this way not just in Balanchine's new ballets but in his old ones as well. She changed the repertory, and, as other dancers emulated her, she changed the company. In time, she affected every American company.

Her authority was remarkable. Balanchine would ask her, "Is this possible?" She would answer: "Well, it's not possible today but it's not impossible. Let me work on it." "The dynamic of our interaction had changed," she wrote. "Instead of being teacher and student, now, at least on some levels, we were accomplices."

They were a pair. Confluence achieved. In 1965, Balanchine — though he hadn't danced in years — came onstage himself for the debut of his new *Don Quixote*. In the ballet, Farrell washed and dried his feet with her hair, and he walked on his knees across the stage to her. Before the gala crowd, it was a clear announcement: Balanchine was as devoted to his muse as she was to him. Afterward, they clinked glasses at a champagne reception. "For such a big ballet," Farrell said, "and something so visible, so public, we really only existed for each other." They quickly slipped out of the party and went for doughnuts and coffee, just the two of them.

6

"Everybody Just Get the Fuck Out"

The Psychology of "We"

With a grasp of the stages that lead to confluence, let's examine the core qualities of creative pairs who have achieved it. If the approach two people make to each other feels like ascension—each step building on the last—the features of joint identity are more like a mosaic, a series of pieces that connect to one another.

A good place to begin is with ritual, since this is often the foundation of creative practice. Igor Stravinsky came into his studio and, first thing, sat down and played a Bach fugue. When he was writing *The End of the Affair*, Graham Greene produced five hundred words every day, and only five hundred, even if it meant stopping in the middle of a scene. The choreographer Twyla Tharp rises every morning at 5:30, puts on her workout clothes, and catches a taxi to the Pumping Iron gym at Ninety-First Street and First Avenue in Manhattan. "The ritual," she writes in *The Creative Habit*, "is not the stretching and weight training I put my body through each morning at the gym; the ritual is the cab. The moment I tell the driver where to go I have completed the ritual."

Tharp's point is that ritual emerges from the smallest, most concrete action. For pairs, the most basic thing is a regular meeting time. James Watson and Francis Crick had lunch most days at the Eagle pub in Cambridge. Facebook CEO Mark Zuckerberg and COO Sheryl Sandberg begin and end every week with hourlong private meetings. After they began to exchange their work, J.R.R. Tolkien and C. S. Lewis set aside Mondays to meet at a pub and later met with a group, the Inklings, every Thursday night at Lewis's apartment.

Meeting rituals may be tied to moments in time—as when partners like Buffett and Munger begin every day with a call—or to a physical space, as when Lennon and McCartney met at Paul's house to write. Watson and Crick ended up sharing an office at the Cavendish Laboratory in Cambridge because the other scientists in the lab couldn't stand their incessant chatter.

For individuals conducting rituals, the core purpose is to discipline the unruly mind, to make acts that are automatic and definite amid a creative process that involves so many utter unknowns. For pairs, I believe the heart of the matter may be leaving behind an individual life and occupying a space that is shared. Soon after they met, Marina Abramović and Ulay tested their fledgling connection by leaving their homes—hers in Belgrade, his in Amsterdam—to meet in the geographical center: Prague. They began to make some work together—and then to actively conceive of collaborative projects. Soon they made "the radical decision," in Marina's words, to go live in a Citroën HY van that Ulay painted matte black. They slept on a mattress in the back and cooked on a camping stove. "Abramović and Ulay," writes James Westcott, "decided to commit their entire lives, right down to the most basic conditions of daily existence, to the idea of performing together; and since they had no material security, nothing to fall back on, they gave themselves no choice but to succeed."

At the same time that they move toward each other, the two people in a pair leave behind the rest of the world. "Every real friendship is a sort of secession, even a rebellion," C. S. Lewis writes in *The Four Loves*. In the midst of the feverish and entwined six-year collaboration between Braque and Picasso that led to cubism, both artists signed the back of each of their canvases; only they would know who did what. "People always ask Ulay and me the same questions," Marina Abramović told me. "'Whose idea was it?' or 'How was this done?' . . . But we never specify. Everything was interrelated and interdependent."

Similarly, when they began to write together, Neal Brennan and Dave Chappelle agreed never to disclose to others who wrote what. They knew that people would be looking to pick apart the partnership—either exaggerating Brennan's role in handling a tempestuous performer or exaggerating Chappelle's role as a comic genius. (Brennan was once dismissed as

"Dave Chappelle's typist.") When I interviewed him, Brennan flinched at the memory of undue credit at the other extreme, when an agent collared him at a party and called Brennan, within earshot of Chappelle, "the genius behind the guy."

"He was trying to make small talk," Brennan said, "but it's ridiculous, and it's racist. I had people come up to me and whisper, 'Seriously, how much of that script did you write?' Like, you know, 'Between two good white men, explain to me.'"

His reaction to these people, Brennan said, was: "'Yo, man. Everybody just get the fuck out. We've got it. Everyone just stay the fuck away.' In a vacuum, this shit works. The vacuum being mostly me and him, and then Bijan [Shams, the show's editor]. But really, ultimately, me and Dave are the only guys who know how the show works and the only guys who know who did what. We would go in a room together and we would come out with sketches."

This sort of pact is both a sign that a partnership has formed and an impediment to any outsider telling its story. This is one reason many epic partnerships end up as historical footnotes or become entirely effaced: "Things were said with Picasso during those years," Braque said, "that no one will ever say again, things that no one could ever say any more, that no one could ever understand . . . things that would be incomprehensible and which gave us such joy." This was one of the very few lines either man ever spoke about the relationship that helped give birth to modern art.

Alongside the concrete, physical gestures at two-ness comes an unmistakable psychological union that goes down to the bedrock of cognition: language. Many pairs have what we could fairly call a private language. Tom Hanks described the communication between director Ron Howard and producer Brian Grazer as "some gestalt Vulcan." Akio Morita and Masaru Ibuka, the cofounders of Sony, "would sit there talking to each other," Morita's son Hideo said, "and we would listen but we had no idea what they were saying . . . It was gibberish to us, but they were understanding each other, and interrupting them for any reason was forbidden."

Private language emerges organically from constant exchange. Intimate pairs talk fluidly and naturally, having let go of what psychologists call "self-monitoring"—the process of watching impulses and protean thoughts, censoring some, allowing others to pass one's lips. "I don't have to check myself when I'm talking to Crosby," Graham Nash told me. "A lot of people, you check microseconds before you say something how it's going to work out." The psychologist Daniel Kahneman makes the same point. "Like most people, I am somewhat cautious about exposing tentative thoughts to others," he said. But after a while with Amos Tversky, "this caution was completely absent."

"You just get so high-bandwidth," Bill Gates said about talking to Steve Ballmer, his longtime deputy at Microsoft (and eventual successor). "Steve and I would just be going from talking to meeting to talking to meeting, and then I'd stay up late at night, and write him five e-mails. He'd get up early in the morning and maybe not necessarily respond to them, but start thinking about them. And the minute I see him, he's [at the office whiteboard] saying we could move this guy over here and do this thing here." Facebook's CEO Mark Zuckerberg used that same term, *high-bandwidth*, to describe his exchanges with his COO Sheryl Sandberg. "We can talk for 30 seconds and have more meaning be exchanged than in a lot of meetings that I have for an hour," he said.

Over time, evocative phrases emerge. Lea Thau and Catherine Burns, partners for nine years at the helm of *The Moth,* the storytelling series and public radio show, came to refer to "real-life" storytellers, like cops or priests — anyone who was not a professional entertainer — as "dirt farmers." "Lea actually worked with a woman who was the daughter of dirt farmers in Oklahoma," Catherine told me, "and the phrase stuck. We've tried many times to call these stories something else. 'Fantastic tales,' things like that. But nothing else even comes close." I see why. *Dirt farmers* is just three syllables, has an appealing rhythm, and paints a vivid picture. As in E. B. White's definition of poetry, it "compresses much in a small space and adds music, thus heightening its meaning."

I asked Neal Brennan if he and Dave Chappelle had a private language. "Oh yeah," he said. He got out his cell phone and looked at a recent text from Chappelle.

"He just texted me at twelve fifty in the afternoon," Brennan said, "'Ta-ta-tow!' And I texted back, 'Rickety-crickety-clack-clow!'" He laughed. "I have no idea what that means."

Then he changed his mind. "Like I know just what he means."

"What does he mean?" I asked.

"You know what it is? When we wrote *Half-Baked*"— a feature film that preceded *Chappelle's Show*—"we went out and we got a limo. When we turned the draft in and everybody liked it, we rented a limo and did mushrooms and went to the beach, and a buddy of ours also did mushrooms with us, and he kept going, 'Clow!' He just was like freaking out, and he just kept going, 'Clow!' This guy resented us for writing *Half-Baked* together and not including him, and it was me, Dave, and this other guy, and he kept going, 'Fuck everybody on the beach!' And it was me and Dave. We were the only two people there. And, 'Clow!'"

Brennan laughed again.

"So by him writing 'Ta-ta-tow!,' that's him basically saying, 'Show business is insane.' It's almost like a birdcall, of like, 'Ta-ta-tow!' And then I write back, 'Rickety-crickety-clack-clow!' Which is nonsense, and it's also this euphoric, drug-addled way of talking about crazy people, because this guy we used to work with would use the term *rickety-crickety* and he was pretty far out."

I tried to interpret: "So he's basically saying, 'Show business is crazy,' and you're saying, 'Yeah, man,' but in a way no one else could understand?"

Brennan said I'd pretty much got it. But I felt like a translator on deadline. I had arrived at a serviceable interpretation but I knew full well that the essence of the original eluded me.

Over time, the two members of a pair not only develop a private vocabulary but start to match each other in the basic rhythms and syntactical structures of their speech. This is due in part to the astonishing power of mimicry, which psychologists call "social contagion." Just by being near each other, the psychologist Elaine Hatfield has shown, people come to match accents, speech rates, vocal intensity, vocal frequency, pauses, and quickness to respond.

Psychologists used to think that people imitated each other in a deliberate attempt to be liked, but mimicry is far more pervasive than this—and largely nonconscious. Intimate partners share physical postures and breathing patterns too. They use the same muscles so often, the psychologist Robert Zajonc and colleagues found in a study of spouses, that they even come to look alike. Warren Buffett has said that he and Charlie Munger are "Siamese twins, practically." In addition to wearing the same gray suits, the same Clark Kent glasses, and the same combovers, writes Buffett biographer Alice Schroeder, they also share a "lurching, awkward gait" and a flickering intensity in their eyes. Whether or not this is due to what Zajonc calls "repeated empathic mimicry," we can't be sure, but one does wonder.

The larger point about any physical convergence is that it reflects what psychologists call a "shared coordinative structure." Shared mannerisms, like similar walking gaits, often come along with shared emotions and ideas. Just as physical qualities are "highly communicable," write psychologists Molly Ireland and James Pennebaker, so are behaviors, affective states, and beliefs.

Language is an unusually potent mechanism for psychic convergence, because it is so closely tied to thinking. "Linguistic coordination," Ireland and Pennebaker explain, leads to "the cultivation of common ground (i.e., matching cognitive frameworks in which conversants adopt shared assumptions, linguistic referents, and knowledge)."

Using software called Linguistic Inquiry and Word Count, which takes the words of a text and breaks them down into categories, Pennebaker and his colleagues can actually measure how language similarity tracks closeness. With this tool, researchers hit on the surprising significance of a category of words that have no great meaning on their own but take life from the context in which they're used. These are called function words or junk words — prepositions, such as *on* and *for;* pronouns, such as *you* and *I;* and conjunctions, such as *or* and *but.* "Function words are the most forgettable words in our vocabulary," Pennebaker writes in an article with Cindy K. Chung. "Nevertheless, they usually account for over 55% of the words we read, say, and hear."

In scores of studies measuring millions of words of written and verbal exchanges, researchers have found that the closer two people are, the more these function words match in type, frequency, and grammatical structure.

For instance, Pennebaker and Ireland looked at the 337 letters (totaling 174,438 words) exchanged between Sigmund Freud and Carl Jung. When the two men first connected, in 1906, Freud was fifty years old. He had laid out the basics of psychoanalysis, and he saw the thirty-year-old Jung as a promising disciple to help him spread the gospel. As a Christian practicing at a major psychiatric hospital in Switzerland, Jung could help Freud's ideas stretch beyond Jewish intellectuals in Vienna.

In seven fiery years, the relationship passed from intense admiration to deep solidarity and finally to bitter acrimony. The language-matching analysis of their letters tracked the same arc, showing their language mostly in sync from the start, growing through the first four years of their correspondence, and reaching maximum similarity just as their collaboration peaked with a trip together to the United States in 1909. But as the relationship began to decline, their language diverged as well. By 1913, when Jung accused Freud of being arrogant and close-minded, and Freud said that they should "abandon . . . personal relations entirely," their speech had already diverged.

In the peak years, two members of a pair don't just speak similarly; they speak together. One of the most common refrains I've heard about partners — including Lennon and McCartney, Matt Stone and Trey Parker, and Daniel Kahneman and Amos Tversky — is that they finish each other's sentences. When I asked David Crosby and Graham Nash why, despite the intensity and intimacy of their own bond, they still performed with Stephen Stills, their answers came in two voices that, like their harmonies, could easily have been one.

NASH: It's the music.
CROSBY: The guy has created some of the best music we've heard. And we get to sing it if we're singing it with him. We get to do "Love the One You're With." We get to do —
NASH: (*no pause*) "Southern Cross." We get to do "Helplessly Hoping." We get to do all these great songs. You see —
CROSBY: (*no pause*) The guy's good.
NASH: (*no pause*) He's a powerhouse.

The other manifestation of this alignment is in wordless communication that observers commonly describe as "telepathic." Barry Sonnenfeld, who has directed photography on several films for the Coen brothers, remembers Ethan saying, after a take, "Hey, Joel, you know what?" And Joel replying: "Yeah, I know, I'm going to tell him." When the writer David Zax visited *The Daily Show* to profile Steve Bodow, Jon Stewart's head writer at the time, Zax could understand only a small fraction of their exchanges, given the dominance of "workplace argot and quasi-telepathy." "If you work with Jon for any length of time, you learn to interpret the short-hand," Bodow said. For example, Stewart might say: "Cut the thing and bring the thing around and do the thing." "'Cut the thing': You know what thing needs to be cut," Bodow explained. "'Bring the thing around': There's a thing that works, but it needs to move up in order to set up the 'do the thing' thing, which is probably the 'blow,' the big joke at the end. It takes time and repetition and patience and frustration, and suddenly you know how to bring the thing around and do the thing."

I've interviewed many pairs and seen a variety of styles. Some talk over each other wildly, like seals flopping together on a pier, and some behave with an almost severe respect, like two monks side by side. (Watch a video of Merce Cunningham and John Cage for an illustration.) But regardless of a pair's style, I usually came away feeling like I had just met two people who were, while inimitable and distinct, also a single organism.

One way this manifests is in the overwhelming sense that neither I nor any third person can ever be anything but an outsider — that there is no getting inside that shared space. "You see people try to get between them," Scott Rudin said of Matt Stone and Trey Parker. "They shut it down so fast." I heard some version of this over and over again, and it's a critical component of confluence. "Planet Trey and Matt is more important than any planet they reside on," the *New York Times* media reporter David Carr told me. "They're totally sealed off. The ability to form partnerships that have a degree of hermeticism — that's where the great work occurs. When you're doing something that's naughty or against the grain, you need to have someone you can turn to you and say: 'Am I crazy?' And they say, 'Yes and do it anyway.'"

Carr used *crazy* with affection, but it's telling how often the idea of insanity shows up; two creative people making their own reality resembles what psychiatrists call a *folie à deux*, "a madness shared by two." "When I think back on the show," Jerry Seinfeld said in a conversation with his *Seinfeld* co-creator, Larry David, "you would pitch me some premise, some insane, absurd thing. And I would just go, 'Okay.'"

Notice how they finish the thought separately and together.

DAVID: It was something I won't even tell another soul.
SEINFELD: And now we're gonna do it on TV.

Creating something original always runs contrary to the pressure of the common. This is not conformity to be snickered at; it's a biological imperative to be respected. In prehistoric times, if you got thrown out of the pack, you'd die. But I suspect one of the things that happens to creative pairs is that they make their own pack, and they come to know that they're not going to throw each other out, and so they're prepared to take on far greater risks than those of us who haven't made a true society of our own. "Standing next to Clarence [Clemons] . . . you felt like no matter what the day or the night brought, nothing was going to touch you," Bruce Springsteen said. "I had one special reader and that was you," Jean-Paul Sartre told Simone de Beauvoir. "When you said to me, 'I agree; it's all right' then it was all right. I published the book and I didn't give a damn for the critics."

This is essential for creative work. "When you have a body of work that's as complicated and transgressive as what Matt and Trey do," David Carr told me, "the answer to whether something is a good idea or not is very complicated. Many of the things that they've done on the surface seem like manifestly terrible ideas: 'Let's do a musical about Mormons.' 'Let's do a play where the chorus is "Fuck God."' If Trey had asked me about that stuff, I would have said, 'That's a dumb idea.' He asked Matt instead."

Perhaps the strongest lexical indication of union is the most simple — the use of *we*. The closer two people are, the more they will shed singular pronouns in favor of the plural. It's not a conscious choice, James Pennebaker argues. It's simply the way couples begin to think.

Indeed, close couples will actually start to process knowledge in tandem, according to the psychologist Daniel Wegner; he called this "transactive memory." "Nobody remembers everything," Wegner wrote. "Instead, each of us in a couple or group remembers some things personally — and then can remember much more by knowing who else might know what we don't." This age-old process has come to new prominence in recent years because some scientists believe that the hive mind accessed via Google search is actually an extension of it, that the way we draw on gadgets is much the way we've drawn on other people since the Stone Age. One experiment showed that couples of long standing did better retrieving past experiences together than separately. They engaged in "cross-cuing," Clive Thompson explains, "tossing clues back and forth until they triggered each other," as in this couple telling the story of their honeymoon forty years before.

F: And we went to two shows, can you remember what they were called?
M: We did. One was a musical, or were they both? I don't . . . know . . . one . . .
F: John Hanson was in it.
M: *Desert Song*.
F: *Desert Song*, that's it . . .

"They were," writes Thompson, "in a sense, Googling *each other*."

Creative pairs often say that they don't remember who did what. But what's interesting is that intimates may not so much forget distinct contributions as stop coding memories that way in the first place. The discovery of mirror neurons in primates suggests that similar neurological activity is generated whether one is performing a given action or watching it. Though the implications of mirror neurons are hotly debated, the broader field of social cognition — looking at the mental operations involved in processing social stimuli — is rapidly growing in psychology and neuroscience. We don't know precisely how our minds link up with others', but it's becoming increasingly clear that these linkages account for much of what's considered "the mind" in the first place. Call it what you like — maybe *intersubjectivity,* maybe *cognitive interdependence* — but on some level, thinking (and, therefore, being) is social.

Thus the new field of social neuroscience. According to the psychologist John Cacioppo, who coined the term with his colleague Gary Berntson, psychic and physiological boundedness so characterizes human life that the "self" can be understood only as a relational phenomenon. "It sounds like an oxymoron," Cacioppo told me. "But it's not. In fact, the idea that the center of our psychological universe, and even our physiological experience, is 'me' — this just fundamentally misrepresents us as a species." If Cacioppo's theory is borne out, the confluence of creative pairs will come to be seen not as an anomaly but as an unusually clear articulation of the kind of symbiosis that affects all of us all the time.

"Where does it all lead?" Patti Smith wrote in *Just Kids,* her memoir of her relationship with Robert Mapplethorpe. "What will become of us? These were our young questions, and young answers were revealed. It leads to each other. We become ourselves."

Strange. We come to ourselves by giving up the self. The psychologist Arthur Aron and colleagues, including his wife, Elaine Aron, help bring this peculiar truth to life with "self-expansion theory." Aron argues that people are motivated, down to their core, by a wish to become more. One achieves this self-expansion most consistently and dramatically by forming a new attachment with another person, whereby "the resources, perspectives, and identities of a close other are experienced, to some extent, as one's own." Two people do more than get to know each other or come to love each other. They absorb each other. Aron and his colleagues asked a group of subjects the question "Who are you today?" five separate times, once every two and a half weeks, and the ones who had fallen in love since the previous testing gave more varied descriptions of themselves. "The new relationships," Tara Parker-Pope wrote in the *New York Times,* "had literally broadened the way they looked at themselves."

This "inclusion of close others in the self," as Aron refers to it, goes deeper than conscious identity. In one experiment, subjects go over ninety adjectives (like *emotional* and *tactless* and *versatile*) and identify which apply to them and which to their close other. Later, the subjects see those same attribute words flash on a computer screen. The task is to press, as quickly as possible, a key for *yes* if the attribute applies to the subject and a key for *no* if it doesn't.

The essential data, Aron told me, is the time lag between when the adjective appears on the screen and when the subject hits the key. When a person sees attributes that are true of him but false of his close other — or false of him and true of his close other — there is a measurable delay in response. "If I try to think of an aspect of myself — and my partner's not the same — it mixes me up," Aron explained, "because on some level we're the same person."

So the self gets bigger even as it becomes more permeable. And this happens more than the scales indicate. Consider the test of closeness that instructs a subject to circle the picture "that best describes your relationship with your partner."

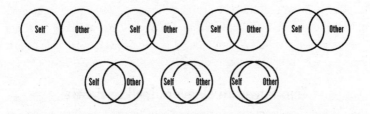

When Aron gave this to the artist Robbi Behr and the writer Matthew Swanson, co-creators of Idiots' Books and Bobbledy Books, they both circled the last choice. "I'd probably choose one where the two circles were even more on top of one another, if there was one," Matthew told me, "with just the faintest sliver of independent self visible outside the middle ground." Robbi said she felt the same, but she objected to the graphic's visual language. Even though the circles on the second row are larger than the first, she told me, "It still suggests on the whole that the closer you become to someone, the less total territory you have. But it's actually the opposite. When we go back and forth, our ideas, our ambitions, our efficiency, our ability — everything gets bigger. The more we overlap, the larger we become, much larger than we were as two individuals."

7

"No Power in Heaven, Hell or Earth"

Creative Marriage

The confluence of pairs has several critical variations.

Asymmetrical. In some pairs, one partner absorbs the other, as when a clear leader works with a deputy or a disciple takes up with a guru. This asymmetry is often signified by the nature of credit. Even though both Balanchine and Suzanne Farrell were changed by their union, Farrell would forever be known as a Balanchine dancer. No one called Balanchine a Farrell choreographer.

Distinct. In a second type of bond, each partner maintains a separate public identity. There may indeed be no public marker of their confluence, no unambiguous sign of union. C. S. Lewis and J.R.R. Tolkien didn't jointly credit any of their published work. Aside from the occasional portraits Robert Mapplethorpe took of Patti Smith, the two never collaborated in the traditional sense, but they relied on each other as muse and adviser. With a distinct pair, people who know both members recognize their essential unity, but their rivers run together underground.

Overt. In the third type of bond, partners join together in rough equality to produce work with which both are publicly associated. This is the traditional idea of collaboration, exemplified by Abramović and Ulay, Watson and Crick, Lennon and McCartney. These pairs typically need to negotiate the question of public credit. Watson and Crick flipped a coin to see whose name would lead on their first paper. Daniel Kahneman and Amos Tversky did the same — and then took turns as lead author afterward. Financial questions are of considerable importance. When Brian Grazer and Ron Howard initiated their partnership, Grazer offered a forty-sixty split in Howard's favor. Howard insisted they split profits fifty-fifty.

When I asked Kevin Morris, Matt Stone and Trey Parker's lawyer, how they organize ownership of their work, he told me: "That's between them. But I'll say it was the easiest thing I've ever done. And that speaks volumes for the guys involved. I would bet that the longevity and success of a partnership correlates to the ease of that moment. And all I'd say is that for Trey and Matt, that moment was extremely easy."

Of course, asymmetrical, distinct, and overt are not precise delineations. Partners may have features of more than one category, and the nature of the partnership may change over time. Initially, Susan B. Anthony fell in line behind Elizabeth Cady Stanton's vision of pursuing women's rights, but they came to be overt partners, and eventually Anthony achieved a higher profile than Stanton.

Categories are useful for classifying broad characteristics, but in the same way we recognize race or ethnicity while avoiding stereotypes, we want to be mindful not just of the categories but of the ways they can be blurred. David Crosby and Graham Nash are another complex case. We could describe them as overt, because they have often written and recorded together and consider themselves partners. Yet they are distinct in the sense that they've maintained their independent identities and performed variously in so many iterations: as solo artists; as a duo; as Crosby, Stills & Nash; and as Crosby, Stills, Nash & Young.

The last critical point about confluence is that it may be either self-determined or imposed from the outside. Every pair resembles a marriage in one way or another. It may be like the romantic ideal, where two people fall in love and declare their allegiance, or it may be like a shotgun wedding, where two people are just fooling around and then discover — whoa, like it or not, they're a couple.

The first arc can be seen with Marie Skłodowska and Pierre Curie. When they met, in the 1890s, each was doggedly independent. At twenty-four, practical, organized, and determined, Marie came to the Sorbonne in Paris to study science, and she found "precious" the freedom of living alone. The last man she'd fallen for had broken her heart. "Stiffened by fine theories and bitter reflections," her daughter Eve Curie wrote, Marie "clung fiercely to her independence."

Pierre, too, had decided to be a bachelor — the only way he reckoned he could be left alone with his scientific imagination. In his diary, he scoffed at how a "mistress . . . wishes to possess her lover, and would find it quite natural to sacrifice the rarest genius in the world for an hour of love." Pierre declared he would "struggle against women" in order to follow an "anti-natural path" of science over marriage. At thirty-five years old, he still lived with his parents.

Let's just say that Marie got him thinking in a new direction. He quickly began to woo her — but she proved elusive, leaving Paris to return to her family and an unknown professional future. He begged her to return — to him, and to science.

A courtship that blurred the romantic and the scientific helps us see a broader point. In many cases, it's hard to separate creative work from other tender longings. While I've not made a study of romance, it does seem that the trajectory of creative and romantic pairs have much in common, including the stages we've seen — the spark at first meeting and the period of gestation leading to union — and those to be discussed: the significance of role-taking, the need for optimal distance, the inevitable conflict that comes from efforts at power equanimity.

The main difference between creative pairings and romantic pairings (or intense friendships), as far as I can see, is not in the internal dynamics so much as in the external product; not in the process so much as in the purpose. What I'm about to say may sound dumb, because it's so simple, but there's no point dressing it up: the thing that distinguishes people who work great together is that they make great work, and that was the only real criterion I considered when I was deciding which pairs to study. I found it helpful, too, because "life" pairs — whose ostensible purpose is happiness — are so often inscrutable. Is it a good relationship? Does any outsider really know? Often, even the people involved don't really know.

With creative pairs, it's clear: if they make great work, that makes the relationship great, so whatever we can learn of them is worthy of appreciation.

Many collaborative pairs are also life partners, and the distinctions often blur. Marina Abramović and Ulay were lovers making art and artists making love. In the years they lived in the van, Ulay said, their sex life was "like that of poor people who don't have a television." Valentino and Giancarlo became collaborators and lovers at the same time, too. Reading Herman Melville's ruminations on Nathaniel Hawthorne, one wonders about where the erotic and the creative intersected, at least for Melville. ("Already," Melville wrote in a pseudonymous review of Hawthorne's work shortly after they met, "I feel that this Hawthorne has dropped germinous seeds into my soul. He expands and deepens down, the more I contemplate him; and further and further.")

"Eroticism is a huge-but-tricky component of these things," the author Kelley Eskridge wrote to me about her life and creative partnership with her fellow writer Nicola Griffith. "I find my own creative process intensely erotic sometimes," Kelley continued, "the act of creating connects me with myself in all the primal ways. And try getting anyone to talk about that! Writing is presented as such a bloodless undertaking, everyone pale and silent and Thinking Great Thoughts in their room. But it's not like that at all. And when other people are involved, they become a part of it, and it can be confusing because it's not necessarily that suddenly we all want to fall down and fuck each other on the floor, you know? It's that creative energy brings all the other energy to the table." In a coauthored essay, Kelley described their lives as "webbed, hyperlinked by shared experience, woven into an ongoing conversation of our selves and the two great bindings between us: our love and our work."

When I asked the psychologist Esther Perel, who has written and lectured widely on eroticism, whether sharp distinctions could be drawn between physical and creative desire, she smiled and said, "Of course not."

If Pierre Curie made distinctions in his mind about his desire for Marie Skłodowska as a woman and his desire for what they could do as fellow scientists, there's no indication in the historical record. One feels a linkage in intensity of his ardor, his plea that she join him in pursuit of "our scientific dream." Though she put him off at first — she had grave concerns about marrying a non-Pole — she slowly moved in his direction. First, she came back to France for another year of study, living on her own, getting to know Pierre, meeting his parents, exploring their common interests. She warmed to him, and he tried to give her both tug and slack — suggesting at one point that they work together in an apartment divided into independent parts, or that he go to Poland and live with her there.

His attitude seemed to be: whatever it takes. Pierre later told Marie that pursuing her was the one thing in his life he had done without hesitation. Over a year after they met, Marie surrendered, too, when she announced to her family that they would marry.

Dramatic pledges, akin to marriage vows, are common for pairs. Jean-Paul Sartre and Simone de Beauvoir declared their partnership superior to marriage: "The comradeship that welded our lives together made a superfluous mockery of any other bond we might have forged for ourselves," Beauvoir wrote in *The Prime of Life*. "No power in heaven, hell or earth can separate us," Elizabeth Cady Stanton wrote to Susan B. Anthony, "for our hearts are eternally wedded together."

Marina Abramović and Ulay took these ideas and made them the center of their art, manifesting what they considered a collective being — a "two-headed body." "I had to find out how to put my ego down," Abramović said, "as did he." Their performance art took shape around this quest. In *Relation in Space,* in 1976 at the Venice Biennale, they started at opposite sides of a gallery, naked, ran toward each other, smacked their bodies together, and then went to opposite sides and began again. In *Breathing In/Breathing Out,* they plugged their noses with cigarette filters, pressed their lips against each other's, and took in each other's exhaled breaths. Fourteen minutes into it, having used up all the available oxygen, they came to the verge of passing out. In *Rest Energy,* Ulay pulled back on an arrow with the weight of his body while Marina held on to the bow with her body weight. The arrow was pointed at her heart. "We had two small microphones near our hearts," Marina said, "so we could hear our heartbeats. As our performance was progressing, heartbeats were becoming more and more intense, and though it lasted just four minutes and ten seconds, I'm telling you, for me it was forever. It was a performance about the complete and total trust."

Yet confluence depends, not just on an internal desire to merge — an effort toward surrender — but also on factors beyond the pair's control. Even after they married, Marie and Pierre Curie worked on distinct projects. He studied the growth of crystals and she the magnetism of tempered steel. When Marie sought a topic for her doctoral dissertation, Pierre still functioned mainly as adviser and sounding board, if a passionately interested one. He reviewed the literature with her, built instruments for her research. But when Marie discovered radioactivity and moved on to the hunt for new elements, Pierre abandoned his own research and devoted himself to hers. After several months of painstaking work, they identified an element they named polonium. Six months later, they found a second element, which they named radium.

From this point onward, their daughter wrote, it was "impossible to distinguish each one's part in the work of the Curies." Their laboratory notebooks contained script in both their hands. Their scientific publications bore both their names. "We found," they would say; "we observed." Explaining polonium, they wrote, "If the existence of this new metal is confirmed we propose to call it polonium, from the name of the original country of one of us." Had the separate research of husband and wife been of equal significance, they might never have taken the next step and gone beyond advising and observing each other to jointly pursuing a single line of inquiry. Now they were fully embedded in a scientific team. "We lived in a preoccupation," Marie wrote, "as complete as that of a dream."

Creativity itself, in a formal sense, is dependent on external conditions. According to the definition I've borrowed from Mihaly Csikszentmihalyi, creativity emerges when something new, beautiful, and useful is validated by the gatekeepers within the relevant field, whether fashion or physics or popular music. The critical distinction is between novelty (doing something different) and creativity (doing something different that is sufficiently surprising and compelling—and good—to be ratified by the culture). Obviously, this raises questions: What about popular work that's actually awful? What about outstanding work that receives no attention? But deconstructing creativity is a job for another day. The stuff we're tending to here has, in one way or another, become part of what we can refer to broadly as "the conversation." And in this sense, creativity is itself dialogical: It depends on a speaker and a hearer; on an artist and an audience; on a generator and a receiver.

Science is an unusual case, because innovations may have empirical foundations, regardless of how the work is received in its time. But in most cases, creative work depends on an audience of sufficient size and power to sustain it. And pairs may be forged by that audience's response.

Take Lennon and McCartney. We can say that their efforts as a pair led to success. But it's also true that it took success to finally make them a pair. For all that pulled them together, there was also considerable entropy — natural forces intrinsic to their characters and situations — tugging them apart. One difference was the nature of their ambition — John's hazy desire for a goal he could never quite name versus Paul's very specific musical vision. Just months after joining the Quarry Men, Paul suggested a new guitarist: a fourteen-year-old boy named George Harrison. For Paul, George's skills made him a slam dunk for the band. John was far more hesitant. "It was too much, too much," John said. "George was just too young . . . George looked even younger than Paul, and Paul looked about ten, with his baby face."

George did join the Quarry Men, but only because he "insinuated himself," Pete Shotton explained, "by doggedly tagging after John." At first, George's presence actually heightened the gulf between John, the art-college bohemian, and the two kids in grammar school. "John would be friendly to us," George remembered, "but at the same time you could tell that he was always a bit on edge because I looked a bit too young, and so did Paul."

This was just the first suggestion of an ongoing theme — John, the whirling dervish of emotion, constantly threatened to spin away from Paul, who remained centered on the band. In July 1958, a year after John and Paul met, John's mom, Julia, was struck and killed by a car. "I thought, 'Fuck it, fuck it, fuck it,'" John remembered. "That's really fucked everything. I've no responsibilities to anyone now." Paul said later that he and John were drawn together by the tragedy because Paul had lost his own mum two years before. "We both understood that something had happened that you couldn't talk about — but we could laugh about it, because each of us had gone through it," Paul said. "It wasn't OK for anyone else."

But in the short term, Julia's death drew John into his own private world. He drank more — and he could be a nasty drunk. "I was in a blind rage for two years," John said. "I was either drunk or fighting. There was something wrong with me."

Meanwhile, even as Paul presented himself as a musical partner, John made a friend in art college who personified another path. Stuart Sutcliffe, a talented painter, was a sweet, moody, handsome boy who read Joyce and Kierkegaard. In the era of Jack Kerouac and Allen Ginsberg, Stuart was a kind of Beat ideal to John — an embodiment of an authentic life. "I looked up to Stu," Lennon said. "I depended on him to tell me the truth. Stu would tell me if something was good and I'd believe him."

John often said later that Stu was his alter ego and a guiding force in his life. When Stu joined the Quarry Men as a bass player — John didn't care that he could hardly play — John had his best friend and his best partner in the same circle. Paul fumed. "He and I used to have a deadly rivalry," Paul said of Stuart. "When I look back on it I think we were probably fighting for John's attention."

Paul was also fighting for the band's future, which often seemed in real doubt. They couldn't get a decent drummer — the good ones were all with higher-status bands. When the Beatles — John and Stu gave the band the new name — went to Hamburg to play the red-light district, they were less like performers, Philip Norman wrote, than "old-fashioned fairground barkers."

After a few months in Germany, they hit bottom. A club owner they had crossed retaliated by having George — only seventeen — deported for violating curfew. Soon after, Paul and Pete Best — the drummer they had snagged for the sojourn — lit a condom on fire and were arrested for attempted arson. Stuart fell for a German girl named Astrid Kirchherr and decided to stay behind. (The next year, after a rash of sudden and severe headaches, he died — at age twenty-one — of a cerebral hemorrhage.) John was left to get home with a guitar in his hand and an amp strapped to his back. "It was quite a shattering experience to be in a foreign country, pretty young, left there all on my own," he remembered.

They were kids. Paul was eighteen, John twenty. For all their zest, they had fragile, easily disrupted identities and wild imaginations in which free-floating desires could fix on any of a number of outlets. Whatever a pair's age or experience, this is a common quality at the outset, because the dawn of a connection presents a daunting mix of potential and uncertainty. Confluence means giving something up, leaping into an unknown.

In the winter of 1960–1961, John and Paul were both ambivalent. When John got home from Hamburg, he remembered, "I was so fed up I didn't bother to contact the others for a few weeks . . . I didn't know what they were doing. I just withdrew to think whether it was worth going on with. I thought, 'Is this what I want to do?' I was always a sort of poet or painter and I thought, 'Is this it? Nightclubs and seedy scenes, being deported, and weird people in clubs?'"

More than the mumblings of a discouraged teenager, these were real questions of an artist as a young man. "I thought hard about whether I should continue," John said. "Now, when George and Paul found out, they were mad at me, because they thought, 'We could have been working now.' But I just withdrew. You see, part of me is a monk and part of me is a performing flea. Knowing when to stop is survival for me."

Paul had his own questions. Underneath his swagger of teenage rebellion, he had respectable yearnings. Just as Stuart Sutcliffe represented for John the path of the true artist, so did Jim McCartney exemplify for Paul the path of the solid, lovable workingman. And just as Paul felt a rivalry with Stuart, so did John compete with Paul's dad. "I was always on at Paul to ignore his dad and just wear what he wanted," John said. "He wouldn't go against his dad and wear drainpipe trousers. And his dad was always trying to get me out of the group behind my back, I found out later. He'd say, 'Why don't you get rid of John, he's just a lot of trouble.'"

"I was always saying, 'Face up to your dad, tell him to 'fuck off,'" John remembered. "'He can't hit you. You can kill him; he's an old man.' He treated Paul like a child, cutting his hair and telling him what to wear at seventeen, eighteen. But Paul would always give in."

For a long time, Paul had stuck with the band over his dad's objections, but now he faced an ultimatum: "Get a job," Jim McCartney said, "or don't come back." So Paul delivered parcels and then went to work at a coil-winding factory for seven pounds a week.

In Paul's story of what happened next, John and George told him about a gig at the Cavern, a club in Liverpool, and he made a dramatic decision. "I've got a steady job here," he remembered telling his mates. "But then — and with my dad's warning still in my mind — I thought, 'Sod it. I can't stick this lot.' I bunked over the wall and was never seen again by Massey and Coggins."

John's memory was that he gave Paul an ultimatum. "His dad told him to get a job; he dropped the group and started working on the lorries, saying, 'I need a steady career.' We couldn't believe it. I told him on the phone, 'Either come or you're out.' So he had to make a decision between me and his dad then, and in the end he chose me."

Both memories miss a larger truth. Paul and John had been circling each other for years. What tossed them headlong into their partnership wasn't a decision they made. It was that the Beatles suddenly became hugely popular. Their residency in Hamburg—and the slavish hours they put in there—had made them a drastically tighter, sharper band. Before Hamburg, Lennon said, the band constantly heard, "You'll do all right, you'll get work someday." But after their first show back in England, "suddenly we were a wow," Lennon said. "We stood there being cheered for the first time."

When the work gets really good, pairs often find midwives to help birth the next phase of their union. When the Beatles became the rage at the Cavern, the manager of a local music store, Brian Epstein, came around to see what the fuss was about, and he soon offered to manage the band. In June 1962, after rejections from most recording labels in London, Parlophone's George Martin took a chance on them, and the Beatles finally congealed as a band, dumping the taciturn Pete Best and adding Ringo Starr.

But as their world got bigger, John and Paul got tighter. For a short spell, the primary nature of the trio with George Harrison had been so prominent that they briefly called their band Japage 3—for John, Paul, and George. As the band exploded, John and Paul seriously considered whether to include George in the songwriting team. "We decided we'd just keep to two of us," Paul said, and the shift was palpable. "An attitude came over John and Paul of 'We're the grooves and you two, just watch it,'" George remembered. John and Paul even had separate legal agreements as songwriters, and they appointed Brian Epstein to manage them, as a pair, as well as the band. Mark Lewisohn wrote, "From October 1, 1962" (the day they signed the contracts with Epstein), "unstoppable twin energies—the Beatles, and Lennon-McCartney—were running strong, together and separate, side by side and neck and neck, parallel missions that intertwined, mutually reinforcing." "To me," said Alistair Taylor, Brian Epstein's assistant, "it looked like John and Paul leading George and Ringo against the rest of the world."

Everything is two things that converge. This range of
convergence is really the great area of speculation.

— *Robert Smithson*

PART III

DIALECTICS

Ordinarily, we think about character in terms of individuals: What's your Myers-Briggs personality type? Are you a depressive? An optimist? But in order to understand creative relationships, we need to grasp the character of two people together, how disparate qualities come into dynamic relation with one another. Clearly etched but intricately entwined roles are the primary way to understand what pairs do and, indeed, who they are.

Obviously, roles can emerge from specialties, from discrete skills or training. Drummers need guitar players. Architects need contractors. Francis Crick was trained as a physicist, James Watson as a biologist, and this allowed them to fill in gaps in the other's knowledge as they attacked the question of DNA. Crick could explain complicated x-ray diffraction techniques to Watson, and Watson could tutor Crick on bacteriophages, viruses whose replication process shed light on the nature of DNA.

But after looking at hundreds of instances of roles, I've become most intrigued by the distinctions that run beneath the surface. I've noticed that three archetypes recur most often — the star and the director; the liquid and the container; the dreamer and the doer — and each speaks to a significant dialectic in the creative life. *Dialectic* is a fancy word, but really it just describes the process by which something singular emerges out of an interaction or duality.

Virtually all the great wisdom traditions return to a concept of connected, overlapping opposites, whether it's the Taoist idea of yin/yang or the Hegelian idea of thesis/antithesis (which combine in synthesis). In recent decades, the science of coordination dynamics has demonstrated empirically that these philosophies actually mirror the way the natural world — as well as the human mind — works. It turns out that, amid infinite potential complexity, things tend to organize repeatedly into pairs. Think of the dual strands of DNA, which are made up of pairs of bases. Like life itself, everything digital springs from pairs too — in this case, 1s and 0s.

Pairs, too, proceed from basic dialectics. They may take shape when each member of a team tends to a particular role, as with a player and a coach. There are also dialectics of turn-taking, as with a spotter and a sniper on a military team, where there are two defined roles but no one person assigned definitively to either. In a final twist, we see how dialectics shape the internal workings of the creative mind itself — how even the thinking of a solitary person is, in a sense, relational.

8

In the Spotlight (in the Shadows)

The Star and the Director

Every spring, Berkshire Hathaway holds its annual shareholder meeting, a three-day affair that's been called the "Woodstock of capitalism." At the main event, Warren Buffett and Charlie Munger take the stage to answer questions. Buffett is the consummate showman—"the Oracle of Omaha"—waxing on about business and public policy. After his pontifications, he turns to Munger for input, and Munger gives his signature line: "I've got nothing to add."

Many partnerships have one member in the spotlight and another offstage. Sometimes, there's a literal stage, as with collaborators in the theater. But even there, the dichotomy applies more often than in the obvious case. A play's director, for example, is on a metaphorical stage—markedly identified with the creative product—in relation to, say, her producers or set designers, who themselves have public roles relative to their deputies. The key word is *relative*. Facebook's CEO Mark Zuckerberg speaks for his company, assumes final credit and blame. He is onstage compared to his COO, Sheryl Sandberg. But Sandberg, a star in her own right, is herself the onstage partner in relation to Nell Scovell, the cowriter of Sandberg's best-selling manifesto *Lean In*. (Scovell's name does not appear on the book cover, though Sandberg credits her in the acknowledgments as her "writing partner.") Most major offstage partners have offstage partners themselves.

The irony is that, while our eyes naturally follow the star, a pair's center of gravity is often with the one we see less. "You know your judgment is better than mine, so what you decide is the one that stands," Laura Ingalls Wilder, the putative author of the Little House on the Prairie books, wrote to her daughter, Rose Wilder Lane. The offstage partner, the daughter, in this case, decisively shaped—and probably directed—the work that made her mother famous. Similarly, though Charlie Munger receives less attention, initiates less action, and has a smaller share of the joint enterprise than Warren Buffett does, a Buffett quip is suggestive: "Charlie does the talking," Buffett said once at a Berkshire Hathaway annual meeting. "I just move my lips."

It will come as no surprise that history often neglects the offstage partner. The poet William Wordsworth drew on his sister Dorothy's journals for imagery, ideas, and language, though she forsook public recognition. "I should detest the idea of setting myself up as an author," she wrote. "Give Wm. the pleasure of it." William's pleasure included taking experiences that he and Dorothy had shared, fashioning them into verse with the aid of her observations, and then presenting them as the products of his high mind alone. "I wandered lonely as a cloud / That floats on high o'er vales and hills" begins his famous poem "Daffodils," which drew on a walk he took with Dorothy and on her journal's account of it.

It may seem unjust when a partner is uncredited, and we shouldn't fail to acknowledge the way that offstage partners are often *used*. "He said frankly that he used me as a butcher uses his steel," Stanislaus Joyce said of his brother James, for whom "Stannie" long served as patron, researcher, gopher, and babysitter.

But often a partnership's mission depends on one member remaining offstage. Though we remember Mohandas Gandhi as a solitary hero, he in fact directed what the scholar Ian Desai calls "one of the 20th century's most innovative social enterprises." One key deputy was Mahadev Desai (no relation to the scholar), who acted as Gandhi's stenographer, confidant, interpreter, ghostwriter, editor, and all-around aide. Before Gandhi rose each morning, Desai laid out the plans for the day. After Gandhi retired, Desai made notes for the movement's official record. According to Desai's son, Gandhi would often examine Desai's texts and make only a single change: at the end, he would cross out the initials *M.D.* (Mahadev Desai) and replace them with *M.K.G.* (Mohandas K. Gandhi).

But for Desai and the rest of Team Gandhi, invisibility was part of the strategy. Their success depended on a global impression of a small, humble man on a cane standing up to the British Empire. "By effacing their own efforts," Ian Desai writes, "Gandhi's associates reinforced his image as a simple and self-reliant crusader."

Decades later, in the southern United States, a civil rights movement arose that also depended — so far as the TV-watching world knew — on a single charismatic leader. As Martin Luther King Jr. was filmed and photographed, Ralph Abernathy worked mostly off camera. In mass meetings at black churches, Abernathy would give the crowd the facts on the ground and rouse them to fight, all while providing low comic relief amid the high tension. Then King would ascend to the pulpit and give a sermon underlaid by moral urgency and a philosophy of nonviolence. "They're a classic Don Quixote/Sancho Panza team — the high road and the low road together," Taylor Branch, author of a trilogy of books on America in the King years, told me. "Abernathy was an extremely gifted preacher. He connected with people and built up their courage. He was street-smart and earthy and funny and really good off the cuff. King was funny in private, but in public he tended to be stilted. He was very conscious of being able to preach in St. Paul's Cathedral as well as tiny rural churches."

One of their contemporaries, the pastor Nelson Trout, thought of Abernathy and King as "Mr. Rough and Mr. Smooth." For a movement appealing to a world's conscience and looking to transcend belittling stereotypes of black Americans, there was no doubt who was the best man to play the starring role. Starting with the Montgomery bus boycott in 1955 and 1956, King became the face of the civil rights movement, its spokesman, its philosopher-king. "America's Gandhi," *Time* magazine declared in a cover story that named King "Man of the Year" for 1963. In the story, King called Abernathy — his sidekick, his warm-up act, his constant companion — "my dearest friend and cellmate."

When a movement makes a star by putting one figure out in front, it's often because that person is better suited for the brand. The Little House on the Prairie books were sold as Laura Ingalls Wilder's story, the tale of her romantic, hardscrabble childhood on the frontier in the 1870s and 1880s. Laura's daughter recognized that publicly identifying with her mother's books would be bad for *her* brand. "This kind of work is called 'ghosting,'" Rose Wilder Lane said of her work on Little House, "and no writer of my reputation ever does it."

Putting aside the question of who stands out in front, why is it so often just one person? This leads to a slightly abstract point, but bear with me, because it suggests something important about the power of the star-director team. One aspect of this archetype's potency is that members of an audience want to identify with a single individual, a person with whom they can have an imagined relationship. It's well known in publishing that coauthored books are generally a tougher sell than works by a single author because readers expect (often unconsciously) to be in direct communion with an author—a creative pair of author and reader, if you will. Curl up with a book by Vladimir Nabokov and you imagine him speaking directly into your ear. You get to feel like his muse, his confidant, his best friend. But if you were forced to consider the role of Vera Nabokov—who served for six decades as her husband's editor, agent, researcher, and secretary—that sense of primary contact would be disrupted. Instead of feeling like you were in a relationship with the author, you'd suddenly feel like an outsider.

It is counterintuitive to consider the offstage partner in many of these relationships as the director when, often, the onstage partner, the star, is highhanded and commanding. Certainly, power dynamics between members of pairs are complex—this is the subject of a later chapter of the book yet to come. The important point here is that the same forces, such as a bottomless hunger for attention, that impel someone to thrust him- or herself before a crowd often come with very specific deficits. Stars do not simply coexist with their offstage partners. They need them like racehorses need their jockeys.

According to the psychoanalyst Michael Maccoby, many of history's stars are straight-up narcissists—from Napoleon to FDR to Bill Clinton; from Henry Ford to Thomas Edison to Steve Jobs. Audacious and persuasive—able to glimpse a future over the horizon and charge toward it, damn the risks—they make for compelling leads. But the narcissist's charisma and gusto, Maccoby observes, coincide with acute challenges.

They often lack self-knowledge and internal restraints. They can be delusional and even paranoid, lost in their own worlds. The metaphor of the spotlight is apt. If you've ever stood in one, you know that the same light source that allows an audience to see *you* makes you blind to *them*.*

If star types bear a resemblance to children, their success frequently depends on their relationships with director types, who often act much like parents, walking the tightrope between patient indulgence and absolute authority. We have to dig to uncover these relationships, or look to the rare cases where they've been artfully exposed, because narcissists so often cultivate the impression of themselves as lone geniuses. For decades, no one except fashion insiders knew about the partnership between Giancarlo Giammetti and Valentino Garavani. *Valentino: The Last Emperor*, the film by Matt Tyrnauer, revealed it, and the movie is among the most affecting portraits of a star-director dynamic I've seen.

When Valentino and Giancarlo met in 1960 at the Café de Paris in Rome, Valentino was already a minor star of the fashion world. He was also going broke. Giancarlo quickly took the job of managing Valentino — the man, the company, and the brand. He forged canny alliances and pioneered the business of fashion licensing. With the world's eyes trained on Valentino's dresses for Jackie Kennedy and Sophia Loren, Giancarlo paid their bills and funded a lavish lifestyle, sometimes by attaching the Valentino name to the most unglamorous products, like bathroom tiles and toilet-seat covers. "It was fun," Giancarlo said. "'Oh, I need two million more dollars this year, what can we do? Let's do bathrooms.'"

On first glance, Giancarlo is clearly the man in the shadows — the operations guy, the one designing shows and stores and financial plans — while

---

* There's a scene I love in a concert film of the singer-songwriter Jeff Tweedy where he remarks on this strange experience. In the film, we hear a man call out from the audience, "Hey, Jeff, I love you, man." Tweedy responds by explaining to the audience that "all I really can see is lights and then blackness, darkness," and he jokes that this actually "resembles quite a bit my interior life in that I'm not quite sure if the voices are real and they're really coming at me from somewhere outside of me. Case in point: 'Jeff, I love you, man.' I don't know if that's real. It could be. It could be me just trying to love myself." It's a funny moment, but there's something poignant and a little haunting about the way that stars can be unsure what exists outside of their minds.

Valentino blows kisses to the crowds. "Living all his life next to me, he accepted a role that was reducing," Valentino said. "But there's a saying, 'When two men ride the same horse, one has to be in the back.'" Indeed, in the film we see Valentino throw a fit because the documentary crew has cameras trained on people other than him. "They can't follow whomever," he shouts to Giancarlo. "They have to follow me! . . . People have to be on their knees in front of me!"

"To be with Valentino as a friend, as a lover, as an employee," Giancarlo said, "is a bit the same. You need a lot of patience."

But Tyrnauer's film also helps us understand the influence Giancarlo enjoys. Whether the two are discussing the design of a dress, reviewing the staging of a show, or even arguing over whether they met at the Café de Paris or at the café across the street, the encounters between Giancarlo and Valentino have the same tone — Giancarlo cool and steady; Valentino hot and erratic — and the same arc: Valentino makes a lot of drama, and Giancarlo makes the decisions.

Once we really look at how creative work is shaped by stars alongside their directors, we have to reconsider — case by case — everything we think we know about how the Great Works of Civilization have been made. Consider the work of Vincent van Gogh. Though his brother Theo never picked up a brush, it's fair to identify him — as Vincent did — as the co-creator of the drawings and paintings that are among the most significant in history. The van Gogh brothers were like aspen trees — entwined at the roots. They had supremely distinct roles, styles, even identities. But from their separate domains, each contributed to a joint project of honest, daring art.

This bears repeating because it's such a surprise: the work of Vincent van Gogh that we treasure emerged from a vision shared fervently and advanced assiduously by two brothers, each playing his role. "Now I feel that my pictures are not yet good enough to compensate for the advantages I have enjoyed through you," Vincent once wrote Theo. "But believe me, if one day they should be good enough, you will have been as much their creator as I, because the two of us are making them together."

Vincent van Gogh was a florid, irascible, driven man who started making art in his late twenties after what seemed, to his family, an endless series of shocks and crises and breakdowns. He did not play the part set for him. The oldest surviving child of a parson's family in the Netherlands, he went to work as a teenager for his uncle Vincent's firm, a leading network of art galleries that prospered amid a flourishing market for prints and reproductions.

Within just a few years, though, Vincent began to curl up at the edges. He did not have the qualities of a salesman; he was dogmatic, not pliant; erratic, not steady; ruthlessly honest, not unctuous. He swallowed books like mugs of coffee and developed an inner encyclopedia of artists he admired. He loved to hold forth. Imagine a hipster clerk in a suburban bookstore scowling at a customer's stack of popular books and chart-topping CDs and enlightening him on the work he *really* ought to buy and you have a sense of just how poorly Vincent fit at Goupil et Cie, which made good money selling images of established works to the middlebrow.

At twenty-three, after stints at Goupil branches in The Hague, London, and Paris, Vincent was fired. The proximate cause — his leaving for holiday without permission — was a pretext. "When the apple is ripe," he wrote Theo, "a soft breeze will make it fall from the tree, and such was the case here."

Vincent's parents once hoped he could take "the crown" of the family and fulfill their exalted expectations. But in the years after Vincent left Goupil, he wandered from the castle onto the barren heath. He worked for spells as a schoolteacher and as a bookseller. He became consumed with religious visions but could not stomach even the first of the seven years of formal study required to join the Protestant clergy. He couldn't even hold the job for which his fiery enthusiasm seemed to suit him, as an evangelist in Belgian coal country. It was there, in a region called the Borinage, that Vincent's madness began to seem less like an occasional lapse and more like an enduring condition. What in his own mind signaled piety, ardor, and devotion to Christ — refusing to wash, wearing rags, sleeping on floors even when beds were offered him — others found bizarre, even frightening. His father wanted to commit him to an insane asylum.

Finally, around 1880, at twenty-seven years old, Vincent made a fateful choice: he would be an artist. He began to work his way — in his own dogged, frenzied, rapturous manner — into that life. But he did not do this alone. Through it all, Vincent would be propped up and influenced (and often led) by his brother Theo.

Four years younger than Vincent, Theo van Gogh shared Vincent's sensitive nature but not his sturdy constitution nor his imperious style. Theo was quieter, more sickly — and where Vincent was oversize in personality and disastrous, like a barge headed into rocks, Theo was swift and steady, like a skiff moving across a lake.

Like his brother, Theo went to work at Goupil when he was still a teenager. Unlike his brother, he did quite well, winning praise for his work in The Hague and Brussels, as well as at a stint at the Exposition Universelle in Paris, where his encounters included a conversation with the president of France. Soon after, he transferred to Paris full-time. He was now a rising employee at a leading gallery in the world capital of art. He began to regularly support his brother. Soon, he was his brother's sole support.

This word, *support,* is important to unpack, because in many popular accounts of Theo, it is given as the summation of his role, but it can be misleading insofar as it makes us think of a banker in Boise — well-off and kind of boring — sending money to his poet brother, the romantic in Greenwich Village. But for Vincent and Theo, the reality was more like a poet living in Boise with a brother who was an editor at Random House in New York City. It took five years before Vincent produced what is now recognized as his first mature piece, *The Potato Eaters,* in the spring of 1885. His truly iconic paintings came years after that. Theo did more than provide financial and emotional support to buoy Vincent up in these years. He was also an arbiter of the work's quality — the one saying, essentially, *Not yet, but keep trying.* He gave his brother something far more valuable than money: encouragement without condescension, taste without haughtiness.

The artist and the dealer is a classic expression of the star-director archetype. In broad terms, the artist is the expressive engine, plumbing her soul for potent, authentic material, often doing the physical labor of making work and attaching her identity to the piece, signing it and declaring: *This is a piece of me.*

The art dealer — again, in broad terms — is charged with finding a context and a market for the artist's work, interfacing with clients, promoting and publicizing, often underwriting the infrastructure necessary for a sale or even supporting the artist directly in return for an ownership stake or commission (which these days typically means a fifty-fifty split).

But a mere recitation of these roles can feel cold and mechanical, like the artist is the red-hot center and the dealer a functionary. When exceptional work gets made and brought to public attention, there is usually a shared core of vision and care.

The van Gogh brothers are a good example. Sons of a devout parson, they came to live in a secular world but never shed an underlying piety, an unapologetic earnestness. "The more people one meets," Theo wrote, "the more one sees that they hide behind conventional forms of conversation, and that what they say when they pretend to be honest, is often so empty and so false." In his brother, Theo saw an inspiring, though often maddening, prophet of authenticity.

For Vincent's part, it's important to remember that he never wanted merely to paint. He came relatively late to art, not because he was a late bloomer but because his real passion was to be an agent of salvation, and though he left the clergy behind, he never stopped preaching. His was a search, as the scholar Debora Silverman puts it, for "sacred art." "In choosing to devote himself to art," Silverman writes, "van Gogh extended the goals of his religious evangelism, service and consolation, to his new calling."

In the same way their relationship led them to art, both brothers saw art as a vehicle for relationships. Vincent told his brother once that, in a pinch, he would "far rather give up painting than see you killing yourself to make money . . . Let's be together whatever happens." In addition to his hopes for the lasting power of the paintings he made and for his and Theo's joint art collection, Vincent dreamed of a movement of painters supporting one another aesthetically and spiritually, living and working alongside one another. This was his true utopian dream.

To fulfill the common objective, both had to do work that, even as it made them more alike, also led them farther apart. Vincent once mused on where they would have stood at a time of revolution. "Both remaining consistent," he wrote, "could with a certain sadness have found ourselves directly opposed to each other as enemies, on just such a barricade, say; you in front of it as a soldier of the government, I behind it as a revolutionary or rebel." Yet these were not so much oppositions as positions in a dialectic — Vincent as Mr. Outside, disheveled, unrespectable, throwing barbs at the establishment even as he sought its approval; Theo as Mr. Inside, clean, put together, in an office, dealing with daily compromises and indignities, all the while yearning for something great and new.

Theo, too, understood implicitly the role of a *relational* opposition. When he began to correspond with the woman he would marry, he took note of a remark of hers, that to be happy, two people who would spend their lives together "should be in complete harmony at the moment they exchanged vows." Theo said he found this "a very beautiful & very young idea, but it is not *true* . . .

"I think it is far more important," he wrote, "knowing that we are what we are, to extend a hand to one another &, in the faith that we are stronger together than alone, to hope and strive, by living together, to reach a point where we see each other's faults & forgive them & try to nurture whatever is good and noble in one another." For Vincent and Theo, forgiveness and faith sometimes eluded them. They lost patience with each other. They made each other furious. But they also spurred and served each other. Inspired by Vincent, Theo made it his mission to not just earn a living but work inside the system to champion the avant-garde. He was among the first dealers to make serious efforts to sell Camille Pissarro, Claude Monet, Paul Gauguin, and others.

This experience came around to strengthen his authority as an adviser to Vincent, whose early works were dark and dreary. Theo urged him to pay attention to impressionism, a movement Vincent knew nothing about until he came, finally, to join his brother in Paris in February 1886. As they walked the avenues, George Howe Colt writes, "the brothers made an unusual pair: Theo striding forward in his pressed suit, polished boots, and carefully trimmed brown beard; Vincent bobbing alongside, gesticulating wildly as he pressed a point, wearing worn boots, patched trousers, a mangy rabbit's fur cap, a scraggly red beard, and a paint-spattered blue smock of the kind favored by Flemish cattle drovers."

Now Vincent was in the swirl of influences of painters in his brother's world. Now Theo was blown along by the windstorm of his brother's energy. It was a hectic, heady time for both men, and when Vincent wrote about his color studies — "seeking oppositions of blue with orange, red and green, yellow and violet seeking *les tons rompus et neutres* to harmonize brutal extremes. Trying to render intense color and not a grey harmony"—he could just as easily have been talking about the oppositions of the two brothers, which made for a fiery whole. Most of Vincent's self-portraits (including several "self-portraits" that may actually be images of Theo) date from this period. He made his first sunflowers. This is where van Gogh really became van Gogh.

9

Jokestein and Structureberg

The Liquid and the Container

On October 18, 1964, Geoff Emerick, an engineer at EMI Studios on Abbey Road in London, noticed a weird buzz coming from the speaker in the control room. "What the bloody hell was that?" he asked Norman Smith, the lead engineer. Smith chuckled and told him to have a look. Emerick approached the glass that looked down over Studio Two and saw John Lennon kneeling before an amplifier with his guitar in hand. Lennon was plucking a note, then turning up the guitar's volume — setting off an escalating shriek, like loons being electrocuted.

"We knew," Emerick wrote, "that if you brought a guitar too close to an amplifier, it would squeal." They also knew that a glass thrown across a room would shatter. The new thing here was Lennon's intentional use of feedback — his deliberate move to throw musical tradition against the wall. In the previous session (for "Eight Days a Week") he had leaned his guitar against an amp, forgetting to turn the volume down. When McCartney plucked a note on his bass, it set off that nasty sound from Lennon's guitar, which John loved. He grew preoccupied with getting it on tape, and we hear it in the five seconds of buzz that open "I Feel Fine." "I defy anybody to find a record — unless it's some old blues record in 1922 — that used feedback in that way," Lennon said in 1980, and he added: "I claim it for the Beatles. Before Hendrix, before the Who, before anybody."

This feedback moment, small in itself, opens a window onto John Lennon's position in his band — and his partnership with Paul McCartney. As the sixties stretched on, as the Beatles began a ride as the most popular and influential musical group in the world, Lennon continued to function as the iconoclast. In early live shows, he would fall into the background and let Paul charm the audience — then he'd twist up his face, make a hunchback pose, and play dissonant chords. At times he played with his guitar slightly out of tune, which, the composer Richard Danielpour told me, "contributes to that raw, raunchy sound." In November 1963, he brooded before the Royal Variety Performance, where the audience would include the Queen Mother and Princess Margaret. "I was fantastically nervous," Lennon said, "but I wanted to say something to rebel a bit." If the audience was unresponsive, he decided, "I'll just tell 'em to rattle their fuckin' jewelry."

At the performance, Lennon's impish suggestion, before "Twist and Shout," that the people in the cheaper seats clap their hands, "and the rest of you, if you'll just rattle your jewelry," went over brilliantly, but John's unruly tendency sometimes made him simply impossible. Consider this exchange with the BBC in 1963:

Q: What's been the greatest influence in your life up to this date, up to this experience with the Beatles?

A: Neil . . . Neil, that's our road manager.

Q: What kind of influence did he have on you?

A: Er, none really.

Q: (*A little desperately*) Is no influence better than some influence?

A: Well, apart from that (*Takes a bite from an apple*), an apple a day keeps the docker away.

Q: It's said, John Lennon, that you have the most *Goon*-type humor of the four Beatles.

A: (*Quickly*) Who said that?

Q: I think I read it in one of the newspapers . . . This is going wrong. I want to get a nice personality bit.

A: I haven't got a nice personality.

Q: What kind of personality would you say you have?

A: (*Cheerfully*) Very nice! (*Laughs*)

McCartney, meanwhile, dutifully answered the same reporter's questions about his education and his lyrics and what he would have done if there had been no Beatles. He functioned as the band's primary diplomat. "Anything you promote, there's a game that you either play or you don't play," he said. "I decided very early on that I was very ambitious and I wanted to play." Among the Beatles, he said, he was the one "who would sit the press down and say, 'Hello, how are you? Do you want a drink?' and make them comfortable . . . You want a good article, don't you? So you don't want to go slagging the guys off . . . Why should I go around slagging people? I really didn't like all that John did."

Geoff Emerick had an unusually close view of John and Paul. As an apprentice engineer at EMI, he watched the Beatles' first-ever Abbey Road session, for "Love Me Do." Later he became the principal engineer on *Revolver, Sgt. Pepper,* and *The Beatles* (aka *The White Album*). "Even from the earliest days," Emerick writes in his memoir *Here, There and Everywhere,* "I always felt that the artist was John Lennon and Paul McCartney, not the Beatles," and he found the distinctions between the two men fascinating.

> Paul was meticulous and organized: he always carried a notebook around with him, in which he methodically wrote down lyrics and chord changes in his neat handwriting. In contrast, John seemed to live in chaos: he was constantly searching for scraps of paper that he'd hurriedly scribbled ideas on. Paul was a natural communicator; John couldn't articulate his ideas well. Paul was the diplomat; John was the agitator. Paul was soft-spoken and almost unfailingly polite; John could be a right loudmouth and quite rude. Paul was willing to put in long hours to get a part right; John was impatient, always ready to move on to the next thing. Paul usually knew exactly what he wanted and would often take offense at criticism; John was much more thick-skinned and was open to hearing what others had to say. In fact, unless he felt especially strongly about something, he was usually amenable to change.

The charmer and the prankster. The sweet, smiling one (who even played mischief carefully), and the one with the impish grin (who guarded the deep truth of his insatiable insecurity). To be around these men was to be struck by endless complementary distinctions. "John needed Paul's attention to detail and persistence," Cynthia Lennon writes. "Paul needed John's anarchic, lateral thinking."

The relationship between order and disorder has been an object of fascination from the time of the ancient Greeks, who extolled the sharp departure from clarity and coherence followed by the pleasing restoration of same. The gods Dionysus and Apollo framed this dialectic. Two sons of Zeus, they embodied the sensual, spontaneous, and emotional aspects of man (the Dionysian) and the rational, ordered, and self-disciplined aspects (the Apollonian).

In *The Birth of Tragedy*, Friedrich Nietzsche claimed this as the core dialectic of creative work generally. Modern creativity research hits on the same key relation of making and breaking, challenging and refining — the "essential tension," noted the psychologist Frank Barron, "between two seemingly opposed dispositional tendencies: the tendency toward structuring and integration and the tendency toward disruption of structure and diffusion of energy and attention." Though I considered *organizer and disrupter* and *maker and breaker*, I settled on *liquid and container* as the primary way to describe this archetypal pair. In its natural state, liquid tends to disperse. Liquid-type creatives are drawn to make lateral associations rather than linear progressions. They're often exciting, excitable characters; boundless. They embody the promise and peril of risk and are simultaneously repelled by and drawn to people who impose constraints, who can offer them shape. Without those constraints, they will spill out onto the sidewalk, evaporate in the sun.

The container sort exudes order and clarity. He is hollow inside; he needs filling up and can take on the character of whatever he becomes a vessel for, whatever he can help deliver. Container types are simultaneously excited by and scared of people who push up against their edges. Electricity depends on the fluid movement of electrons, as with copper wire. Yet wires need casing.

This dialectic is under-recognized in part because of a romantic tradition around the mad artist. "Here's to the crazy ones," said Apple's Think Different TV ad, showing photographs of Alfred Hitchcock, Mohandas Gandhi, Pablo Picasso, and others. "The rebels. The troublemakers . . . the ones who see things differently . . . While some may see them as the crazy ones, we see genius. Because the people who are crazy enough to think they can change the world are the ones who do."

The truth — less amenable to a voice-over by Richard Dreyfuss — is that the "crazy ones" change the world only in partnership with deeply lucid sanity. Alma Reville — known as Lady Hitchcock — effectively served as the CEO of her husband's film career. Gandhi was surrounded by helpers; he was also a deeply pragmatic man with canny political instincts. And for all of Picasso's storied creative power, his anarchic energy worked for him only in the context of constant care and feeding. According to his companion Françoise Gilot — they lived together from 1946 to 1953 — it was a Herculean task just to get him out of bed.

Gilot's account of their morning ritual shows the dramatic — even comical — extent of the structure Picasso required. "He always woke up submerged in pessimism," Gilot wrote in her memoir, "and there was a definite ritual to be followed." First, the chambermaid brought Picasso his café au lait and two pieces of toast as he lay in his large brass bed next to a wood-burning stove. Then the secretary brought the papers and mail. Then, Gilot wrote — this is my favorite line in the sketch — Picasso "would groan and begin his lamentations . . . He would complain of his sicknesses . . . He would declare his misery, and how little anyone understood it. He would complain about a letter from [his ex-wife] Olga. Life was pointless. Why get up. Why paint. His soul itches. His life was unbearable."

Gilot would plead with him: You're not so sick as that. Your friends love you. Your painting is marvelous, everyone thinks so. "Well, maybe you're right," Picasso would say after about an hour of this. "Perhaps it's not so bad as I thought. But are you *sure* of what you say?" She would tell him yes, yes, he would do something extraordinary that day. Finally, he would rise and greet the friends who waited for him in his studio and then work from after lunch until late at night.

"But the next morning," Gilot wrote, "it would begin all over again."

For those of us who have to get ourselves out of bed and make our own breakfasts — impose order on our own lives — the fantasy of the mad artist is alluring. We dream of a release from quotidian cares in the same way we dream of life on a tropical beach. Apple's "crazy ones" marketing (along with just about every SUV commercial ever made) is aimed directly at this fantasy. The myth of the mad artist thrives for the same reason. There's something satisfying about recounting Jackson Pollock's terrifying rages, his stunning departure from the art traditions of his day, his retreat from the wilds of New York City to the barns of Long Island. It's a counternarrative to the burdens of everyday life. But of course, no one is freed of the burdens of everyday life. One may, however, outsource them. Pollock had the aid of his wife, steward, and manager, Lee Krasner — herself an accomplished artist.

Often it may seem like the crazy one is doing all the creative work. Consider the classic double act of comedy — the straight man (also called "the feed" or "deadwood") and the funny man. Carl Reiner and Mel Brooks's *2000 Year Old Man* routine is a model of the form.

REINER: Sir, is it true that you are 2,000 years old?
BROOKS: Oh boy. Yes . . . I'll be — I'm not yet. I'll be 2,000 October 16 . . .

REINER: Sir, could you give us the secret of your longevity?
BROOKS: Well, the major thing, the major thing, is that I never, ever touch fried food. I don't eat it, I wouldn't look at it and I don't touch it. And never run for a bus, there'll always be another.

Yet, while the clown gets the lion's share of attention in these match-ups, typically the straight man is the unheralded leader. "The straight guy is never given enough credit," Mel Brooks said. "For me, the heroes are the straight guys," the ones responsible "for the architecture, for the support, for the drive." In the *2000 Year Old Man,* for example, "the real engine behind it is Carl, not me," Brooks said. "I didn't even start it. I wanted nothing to do with it. I was eating a piece of sponge cake and drinking Manischewitz wine in a corner somewhere at a party, and suddenly Carl comes over with a tape recorder and says, 'I understand, sir, you were at the crucifixion of Jesus Christ.' And I was off." Indeed, if you look closely, Reiner's questions are like a sprung floor on which Brooks turns cartwheels. "The straight guy comes up with the premises," Reiner said. Though Lou Costello got the bigger laughs, he said, it was really Bud Abbott who was the "head guy."

A rule of thumb in Hollywood is that every comic writing pair needs a "Structureberg" and a "Jokestein." This same dialectic resonates in the ancient concept of yin and yang. According to tradition, yin maintains, is immanent and enduring; it contracts and moves inward. It stands for togetherness. Yang is generative; it radiates, expands, moves outward. It stands for apartness.

But we don't necessarily need to study the Tao, because we have the works of Lennon and McCartney. From the earliest days, the material

John initiated tended to be sour and weary. Paul's tended to the buoyant and naïve. The first two songs on their debut album had the primal range of a comic-book universe, where the heroic and the evil juxtapose to suggest the two poles of mankind. The poles here are: (1) love makes us happy ("I Saw Her Standing There," led by Paul), and (2) love makes us unhappy ("Misery," led by John).

Their work grew more complex over the subsequent albums, but lyrically and musically—in substance and form—Paul yearned after pleasing structures. Even a song about "all the lonely people," like "Eleanor Rigby," wondered "where do they all belong?" John's lyrics turned a back to the world. He sometimes gave direct instructions; for example, "Lay down all thoughts, surrender to the void."

But the issue is not just what John did alongside Paul but what he did with Paul's influence, and vice versa. The fallacy of lionizing disorder in art is that, if it's before our eyes as art to begin with, it has been crafted into some form. Paul took the challenging, defiant material John laid before him and found ways, sometimes subtle, sometimes elaborate, to make it work in the vernacular of popular music. A home demo for John's song "Help!," for instance, puts this emotionally raw, aggressively confessional song against a slow, plain piano tune. It sounds like the moan of the blues. This song emerged, John said later, from the sort of depressions "where I would like to jump out the window, you know," and it feels like it.

Paul suggested a countermelody, a line sung behind the principal lyric, and it suddenly made the lonely voice of the demo into a small vocal symphony. The song was also sped up considerably (probably Paul's influence, because John, in one of his crabby moods, later complained about it). The poet Donald Hall described poetry as a meditation on misery, rendered in beauty, and thus a marriage between the two. "Help!" is a desperate song, but it has a manic, buoyant energy—it comes out to shake you, to reach you. It's not incidental that, in the lyrics of the song, John pleaded for "somebody . . . not just anybody" whom he could turn to, open up to, be helped by, after years of a preening independence. John knew himself as someone at risk of floating away. Paul helped put his feet back on the ground.

And John knocked Paul off his, giving complex flavor to songs that otherwise might have been pleasing but anodyne. "Michelle," for example, is almost a send-up of the pretensions of a young man in a beret serenading a girl he likes. Lennon had Nina Simone on his mind when he suggested the bridge: "I love you, I love you, I love you, that's all I want to say." It planted an almost farcical song in the peaty soil of yearning. "You could say that he provided a lightness, an optimism," Lennon said, "while I would always go for the sadness, the discords, a certain bluesy edge."

The distinctions between John and Paul deepened in the wake of *other* influences — the mind-altering kind. In Hamburg, a stimulant called Preludin made the rounds, though Paul felt he had to "exercise caution." "John, particularly, would have four or five during the course of an evening," he told Barry Miles, "and get totally wired. I always felt I could have one and get as wired as they got just on the conversation." After Bob Dylan introduced them to marijuana, in 1964, the drug became a mainstay, though Paul seemed to regret a time they smoked before a writing session. "Better to be straight," he said. "It would just cloud your mind up." Then, in the summer of 1965, on tour in Southern California, Lennon took LSD (with George and Ringo and a host of others, including David Crosby). John and George had first tripped at a dinner party given by their London dentist, who spiked their after-dinner coffee. But this was their first purposeful acid journey — the first for John of what he said must have been "a thousand trips."

McCartney didn't take acid until the fall of 1966, and then only reluctantly, driven by "massive peer pressure," he said. "It was quite spacey," he reported, with "paisley shapes and weird things." He also found it disturbing. "I remember looking at my shirtsleeves," he told Miles, "and seeing they were dirty and not being too pleased with that."

LSD was both a manifestation and a cause of a widening split — one that came out sharply in their process and output. John became more and more preoccupied with evoking mystical states: "Make me sound like the Dalai Lama chanting from a mountaintop," he told George Martin when they were recording his paean to acid, "Tomorrow Never Knows." He suggested that he be suspended from the ceiling, given a push, and recorded while he swung around the mike.

Paul, meanwhile, became more and more interested in formal experimentation, playing Motown on one track ("Got to Get You into My Life") and the Beach Boys on the next ("Here, There and Everywhere"). John and Paul both had Brenell reel-to-reel tape recorders at home. While John used his to record rough demos, Paul, immersed in the experimental work of composers like John Cage and Karlheinz Stockhausen, jiggered the machine to disable the erase head and made tape loops of layered sounds. He brought these to the Beatles' sessions to create the sound for "Tomorrow Never Knows," giving John's homage to the void a place in the material world.

10

Inspiration and Perspiration

The Dreamer and the Doer

One night, Thomas Edison was bantering with colleagues in his office and he made a joke at the expense of his deputy Samuel Insull. "Insull retaliated," wrote Randall Stross in *The Wizard of Menlo Park*, by "telling everyone present how Edison really worked: In the evening, Edison would hand out various assignments to his lab assistants, who were expected to toil through the night. He would then lie down and sleep. In the morning, he would arise, have a good breakfast and exclaim, 'What a wonderful night's work I have done' . . .

"Everyone present," Stross noted, "knew well that it was not far from the truth." Though Edison sold himself as a relentless worker — at his desk eighteen hours a day, his creative fires burning too brightly for him to sleep — he was more a visionary than an executor, more a dreamer than a doer.

I don't mean *dreamer* to be pejorative. Many dreamer-type creators have enormous strength of character. They generate ideas, start new projects, inspire others to join them. They may also start things they can't finish and break promises.

Doer-type creators are the inverse. Productive, efficient, and dependable, they excel at finishing, have a realistic sense of what's possible, and can set priorities and make decisions. Yet doers may struggle to be original, to initiate, to see the long view, and to identify a sense of purpose.

Edison said genius is 1 percent inspiration and 99 percent perspiration. But whose? His real knack was for commanding and beguiling others to execute his ideas. He essentially invented the modern research laboratory: hundreds of workers and a small circle of trusted lieutenants tinkering, testing, revising. Edison's role was as impresario, instigator, chief goader. "Once the groundwork for an invention had been laid," Kathleen McAuliffe writes, "he would leave the details to others."

With creative teams, we often see the union of vision and execution. Pierre Curie tended toward careful thought, delving deep into scientific precepts, while Marie was more active, organized, and results-oriented. Orville Wright was an earthy, funny, shy, mechanical man. Wilbur, his older brother, was more restless, ambitious, and, at times, brooding. Hungry to make his mark on the world, Wilbur initiated the brothers' prodigious mission to build a flying machine. Wilbur also had the insight one day, as he bent a long, thin rectangular box in their bicycle shop, that twisting the wings could offer flexibility and control. But it was Orville who took the lead designing the wind tunnel with which they tested the conditions of flight. Wilbur's interest, Tom D. Crouch wrote in *The Bishop's Boys*, was "in systems, in the big picture. Orville was the one who could make it work."

The maker of a pair is often a hidden partner. You probably know of the pop artist Jeff Koons and his twelve-foot-tall, candy-colored Balloon Dogs. They look like giant metallic versions of balloon animals. (*Balloon Dog (Orange)* sold at Christie's in the fall of 2013 for $58.4 million.) But unless you're a real aficionado, you probably don't know that the piece was actually built by an art fabricator named Peter Carlson, whose firm, Carlson and Company, in San Fernando, California, also made pieces for Isamu Noguchi, Ellsworth Kelly, and the duo Claes Oldenburg and Coosje van Bruggen. (The company closed in 2010, though Carlson has since started another operation.)

The dreamer-doer roles often line up with the star-director roles. But not necessarily. Larry David dreamed up the far-fetched, category-breaking ideas that made *Seinfeld* among the most original and affecting shows ever on television. Jerry Seinfeld smoothed out David's rough edges, talked him down from his constant threats to quit the show, and delivered his material with his winsome, lovable style. David stayed off camera. (His one recurring role on the show was as the voice of George Steinbrenner.) The key to *Seinfeld*, said Rob Reiner, is "you had this curmudgeonly, misanthropic, dyspeptic Larry David being pushed through this very accessible likable Jerry Seinfeld, even though they did share their comic sensibility."

The dreamer and the doer may also—as far as the public is concerned—be joined at the hip. *South Park*'s Trey Parker is the quintessential visionary, a fount of ideas and stories, the sort of creator who inspires a stream of clichés—"true original," "free spirit," "God broke the mold . . ." The aesthetic of *South Park*—often described as "*Peanuts* on acid"—is a cartoon style he developed in high school, and in the show's production, Parker is the "quarterback," says the animator Adrien Beard. Trey is the one who sits alone at his desk late on a Monday night agonizing over five unwritten scenes for an episode that airs Wednesday, lamenting how "the writing part of it is so lonely and sad," taking breaks to eat Chicken McNuggets or, to give his brain a rest, building Star Wars models out of Legos.

Matt Stone is the quintessential doer, in two respects. As a voice in the sound booth, he runs a lot of plays that Trey calls. (Of the regular characters, Trey is the voice of Cartman, Stan, and Mr. Garrison, while Matt does Kyle, Kenny, and Butters.) Matt also protects Trey from distractions, organizes environments conducive to creativity, and runs interference with the networks and studios and lawyers.

To a large extent, their roles proceed from their natural strengths. Trey lives in his own world, friends say, following his fascinations down whatever rabbit holes they lead him. He's long been obsessed with Mormons, and Japanese culture too: he once bought an iron headpiece and body armor in a shop in Tokyo for $270,000. While Trey is morally concerned, he's basically apolitical, and he's more at home playing video games with his girlfriend's son than he is in even the most alluring social situation. When the original cast of *Monty Python* came to the London premiere of *The Book of Mormon*, Trey was so nervous at the prospect of meeting his heroes that he ducked out and went to McDonald's.

Matt Stone, by contrast, "is just the way his name sounds," their old friend and colleague Jason McHugh told me. "Matt is just a very reg-imented person. He gets up at seven a.m. whether he wants to or not. Where Trey is so not grounded. Trey will lose his wallet and his keys once a week." Kevin Morris, Matt and Trey's lawyer, remembered meeting with Matt about a new project in the late 1990s. "Matt came in, his hair a mess. Maybe he was a little hung over. I had this list of ten things that we needed to think about. Matt had already done them all. In Hollywood, producing people tend to make so much noise but they don't do that much. But Matt is always taking hills. He's always gaining ground."

Matt is also an irresistible, if often eviscerating, social presence, deeply engaged with politics and culture. "Matt's favorite thing to do," said the filmmaker Arthur Bradford, a longtime friend who made the documen-tary on *South Park* called *6 Days to Air*, "is hang out with [the blogger and public intellectual] Andrew Sullivan and talk about the European debt cri-sis or WikiLeaks." Matt also had a good old time with the *Python* guys in London and generally acts as the ambassador for the pair when logistical knots need to be untied. With *The Book of Mormon,* Kevin Morris told me, "there were a million deals to be made. Just the key personnel alone — you had sixty people that needed deals. Matt built that whole structure brick by brick. He figured everything out from the assistant choreographer to the cast; it was extraordinary for someone who had never been through it before."

Proving the adage that a little information can be a dangerous thing, many *South Park* fans, after learning something about Matt's role, move to diminish him. "Mocking Stone is a regular pastime among people who discuss *South Park* on message boards," writes Jaime J. Weinman in *Mac-lean's*. "A typical posting reads: 'Trey writes every episode and then does the majority of the voices and most of the music while Matt sits around and laughs at Trey to encourage him.'" In her attempt to clarify, Weinman actually takes this same erroneous thinking a step further. "It's obviously true that Parker is responsible for *South Park* as the crude, foul-mouthed work of art it is," she writes, "and Stone really isn't. But producing a TV series entails more than just the artistry. That's where Stone comes in. While Parker is handling the *creative side of the show,* someone needs to pull together the other elements of production." (Emphasis added.)

But this is a basic mistake about the nature of creativity. Creativity is not the original or the surprising or the aesthetically pleasing. It's when those qualities come into form, take expression, reach an audience. Put another way:

Creativity ≠ Trey
Creativity = Matt + Trey

Creativity is what happens when the dreamer meets the doer.

11

Turn-Taking

Generators and Resonators

But we can't get the whole gestalt of Matt Stone and Trey Parker through the dreamer-doer dialectic. These guys are also comics and they spend a lot of their time developing each other, inspiring each other, egging each other on. Jason McHugh remembers the night that they first seemed to really click; they were working crew on a film by their University of Colorado classmate Amy Brooks. "Trey was DP and Matt was dolly grip," McHugh told me. "We shot from ten p.m. to six a.m. at a restaurant and all night they were just cracking each other up — and the whole crew — with dirty-grandpa jokes. Trey would make one, and Matt would repeat it slightly differently, and they'd just volley back and forth — beating a joke into the ground. That's basically what they've been doing ever since. One will have a spark of an idea that cracks up the other guy and they just follow that forever."

The distinctions between pairs that we've explored through the three primary archetypes are but a means to the larger end of dialectical exchange. Dialectics also take expression through turn-taking. We can name this as another archetype — the generator and the resonator — but one in which each partner may play either side.

I learned the term *resonator* in this context from the scholar Diana Pavlac Glyer's study of C. S. Lewis, J.R.R. Tolkien, and the Inklings. An exchange she described between Tolkien and Lewis helps illustrate how it begins. As we've seen, Tolkien started working on a poem called *The Lay of Leithian* in 1925. (It represented a significant piece of the mythology of Middle-earth that *The Lord of the Rings* continued.) Four years later, he shared it with Lewis, the first time he had ventured to show anyone aside from his high-school English teacher, who had been underwhelmed by it. Lewis's first response was glowing praise — encouragement shouted from the sidelines, the sort of thing most players absolutely depend on.

But Tolkien was just as cheered by the critique that followed. To address Tolkien's text, Lewis created a fictional panel of scholars — he called them Pumpernickel, Peabody, Schick, Bentley, and Schuffer — and wrote the responses in these voices, a technique that carried the implication that Tolkien's work was of great importance. It also made Lewis's criticisms impersonal — even entertaining. (The critique was itself an inventive piece of writing.) If we had to create a curriculum to teach this sort of thing, we might call it "praise-based criticism," and it helps us understand, despite the lavish objections in Lewis's response, why Tolkien later described Lewis as only ever encouraging him.

The generator and the resonator quickly switch places, not only because — as with Lewis and Tolkien — the author sending his manuscript for response will soon be the reader receiving a manuscript. The generator-resonator exchange is even more fine scale, as we see in a glimpse of Lewis's edits.

ORIGINAL TOLKIEN: "his evil legions' marshalled hate"
LEWIS'S SUGGESTION: "the legions of his marching hate"
REVISED TOLKIEN: "the legions of his marshalled hate"

Lewis's suggestion gave Tolkien's original line some depth and movement. As the responder, Lewis became, for a moment, the author. Tolkien adopted the more elegant turn of phrase and line structure, yet retained his own language and intent — simultaneously receiving a critique from an editor and editing a critique from an author friend.

At times, Tolkien simply adopted Lewis's phrasing. Other times he accepted the broad notes but rejected specific fixes. "Almost all the verses which Lewis found wanting," Tolkien's son Christopher wrote, "for one reason or another are marked for revision . . . if not actually rewritten, and in many cases his proposed emendations, or modifications of them, are incorporated into the text."

Perhaps the surest sign of the power in this exchange of ideas is how long Tolkien considered it. As late as the mid-1950s, he was still working on the poem, which was published posthumously. "Some of the revisions to *Lay of Leithian* are at least 30 years later," Christopher Tolkien noted, still in response to Lewis's first edits. Over those thirty years Lewis and Tolkien became two of the most popular authors — ever. Tolkien's *The Hobbit* (1937) and *The Lord of the Rings* (1954–1955) and Lewis's *The Lion, the Witch, and the Wardrobe* (the first of seven Chronicles of Narnia books, published 1949–1954) are among the best-selling books of all time, having sold more than 335 million copies.

Of course, resonators don't just say yes to each other; they improve each other. The Inklings were rough-and-tumble. "We were no mutual admiration society," said Warren Lewis. "Praise for good work was unstinted, but censure for bad work — or even not-so-good work — was often brutally frank."

Handling this balance is enormously delicate. While praise may amplify a work by cheering a creator along, it may also muffle it by keeping the creator from necessary improvements. Criticism can daze and discourage us, or coax or goad us. I love the description that Tim Long, a staff writer on *The Simpsons*, gives of how George Meyer — described by the *Believer* as the show's "Grand Pooh-Bah"— handles this balance. After he reads a draft script, "it's as if you just handed him a baby," Long said, "and it's his responsibility to tell you if your baby's sick."

So much of what two people in a pair do for each other is balance praise and criticism and exploration and curiosity in an ongoing exchange. Emotional management is as important as any discrete creative advance, and balance is key here too, as I saw with my friends the illustrator Robbi Behr and the writer Matthew Swanson, co-creators of two independent presses, Idiots' Books and Bobbledy Books. "As individuals, Robbi and I are capable of tremendous decompensation," Matthew wrote me, "falling into a sudden pit of melodramatic despair, a fog of self-pity, a funk that renders us short-tempered, hostile, and ungracious. But we *never* both succumb to it at the same time. In fact, as soon as one of us starts to go downhill, the other's resolve is strengthened. It's like we're on scales, and when I go 10 percent below neutral, Robbi rises 10 percent above, and vice versa."

Matthew emphasized that this balancing function seemed independent of will. "It's not that we refuse to go south at the same time. It's that we seem unable to. And it's incredibly helpful, because the one who remains on the shore is always able to throw a life preserver to whoever goes under water. I also wonder if, when it comes to maintaining mood/stability/sanity, we're functioning not as individuals, but as two parts of a system with self-regulating equilibrium. As individuals, we occasionally tank, because we can. But as an organism, we're always balanced. So tanking is not a risk."

12

"Everything's the Opposite"

The Psychology of Dialectics

The idea of two people as a single organism in homeostasis may sound exotic, but it's actually a good introduction to how people typically operate. For generations, psychologists looked at the human animal as a collection of fixed traits. Though this legacy still permeates popular culture, the new consensus among social psychologists is that we are something like cubes in an ice tray: We do take regular and reliable shapes, which may persist in certain environments. But these shapes are formed in part by social conditions.

One major turning point came in 1968, when the psychologist Walter Mischel showed that studies had repeatedly failed to find consistency of personality traits across diverse situations. Actually, Mischel said, behavior was highly dependent on situational cues. In 1971, a sensational study brought this home. This was the infamous Stanford prison experiment, which divided twenty-four students — selected for their psychological health and stability — into two groups, prisoners and guards. Over just six days, those in the guard role turned brutish, shooting off fire extinguishers and leaving buckets full of excrement in the cells.

Though this was an extreme illustration, the way circumstances shape how we behave, how we think, and even who we are shows up in all kinds of mundane situations. Think of the contrast between a fifteen-year-old boy speaking politely to his girlfriend's parents and, later the same night, cursing exuberantly at a party with his friends. "Of course we juggle our strategies in response to the people around us," the historian and psychologist Frank Sulloway told me. "It's such a simple idea that you have a hard time thinking it's wrong. Yet a lot of the research in psychology has taken another tack, following an assumption that we are driven by traits that are relatively immutable — or more to the point, that these traits continue to exist regardless of who else is in the room."

It's not that our behavior is entirely determined by others. "Of course you carry around a tool kit of things that may be characteristic of you," Sulloway said. "But you don't use all those tools at any given minute. You pick them in response to what other people are doing."

Sulloway's point applies to the variations in day-to-day life — as we move from talking to our bosses to talking to our children. It also applies, in a broader sense, to the way that character is formed over a lifetime. It turns out that human beings find their niches in very much the same process that Charles Darwin subsumed under his principle of *divergence* — a process that leads to what is now called *adaptive radiation*. In Darwin's famous example, he proposed that fourteen species of Galápagos finches — each with a distinct beak — had evolved from a common ancestor and that the beak variations allowed the birds to minimize competition and maximize resources. Some beaks were best suited to eating insects in trees, others to eating fruits and leaves, and so on.

Human beings also shape themselves to make the best out of their situations. The clearest way to see this is in the patterns of character that show up in relation to birth order. As a rule, firstborns find that they can get attention for anything they do well, so they tend to stake out traditional turf and defend it fiercely. They study hard; play the violin. Younger siblings often find the safe territory spoken for, so they have to go elsewhere. They act the clown; play punk rock. In a study of 121 major historic events — paradigm shifts in science, reform movements, and political revolutions — Frank Sulloway found that later-born children were roughly twice as likely as earlier-borns to take the radical position, while earlier-borns were more likely to defend the status quo. (Charles Darwin and Alfred Russel Wallace, who separately but simultaneously discovered the theory of natural selection, were both later-born children: Darwin was the fifth of six and Wallace the seventh of nine.

The staunchest opponents of evolution, including Louis Agassiz, were oldest children.)*

"Perhaps the most studied aspect of birth order and risk taking," Sulloway writes, "involves participation in dangerous sports. In a meta-analysis of 8,340 participants in 24 different studies of athletic participation, laterborns were found to be 1.5 times more likely than firstborns to engage in dangerous sports such as rugby, football, and soccer, whereas firstborns and only children preferred safer sports such as swimming, tennis, and track." Among the seven hundred brothers who have played major league baseball, younger brothers were 10.6 times more likely to attempt to steal a base, though they were only slightly better base stealers, Sulloway told me. The younger brothers also hit more home runs and—these two go together—struck out more.

The point is that we constantly make (often unconscious) decisions about what to do—and even who to be—depending on what will get us what we want. It's easy to miss this precisely because it is so common. You may know the joke that David Foster Wallace told the graduates of Kenyon College in 2005: Two young fish are floating around when a wise old fish comes swimming by. "Morning, boys," the old fish says. "How's the water?" Then he swims away, and one of the young fish turns to the other and says, "What the hell is water?"

For humans, social influence is the water we swim in—and we often pretend it's not there. In social science, assuming that an individual's behavior is due to internal factors rather than external ones is called the *fundamental attribution error*.

When it comes to appreciating creativity, this error can be toxic, because it leads us to ignore how profoundly people depend on others, not just for help in discrete situations but to shape their very identities. At first glance, John Lennon's rebelliousness might seem intrinsic to his

---

* An important caveat: The birth order Sulloway examines is not always strictly chronological; it is sometimes based on social dynamics. Wilbur and Orville Wright were the third and fourth sons in their family, but the gap between Wilbur and the next-oldest sibling was five years. Practically speaking, Wilbur had the position much like the oldest brother. Also, if a firstborn child dies—or, as with Vincent van Gogh, abandons his role of high achiever or keeper of tradition—a later-born child may take over the part.

character. After all, there was a straight line from the younger kid who stole cigarettes from the store to the older kid who delighted in feedback from an amplifier.

But kids are natural Dionysians, in large part because there's an established order to play against. They can stray with rebellious pleasure and still come home for a hot meal and a bath. When a kid gets punished, he gets to see his entropic desires contained by a force imposing order on them.

As kids grow older, this dynamic becomes harder to maintain. We've all known high-school hell-raisers who grew up to be corporate bureaucrats. Many cultures even condone rebellions, like the Amish *rumspringa,* in which children of this austere tradition go live their own versions of Boys and Girls Gone Wild before returning to the fold — as 90 percent do.

It's a fantasy worthy of a Think Different ad to imagine John Lennon as exempt from this rule — a kid who never grew up because of the force of his own genius. But rebelliousness-as-innate is the exact opposite lesson to take from Lennon — or any rock star or sword swallower or starchitect in a perpetual adolescence. No grownup lives like a kid unless someone around him takes the adult role. John didn't insult reporters *while* Paul charmed them. John *could* insult reporters *because* Paul charmed them. And John reaped a double gain. He benefited from the success and got to rail against it. He got to play the game and be the one who hated the game.

Yet, just as the science of roles helps us understand how character takes shape in relation to other people — the way we come to be reliably *this way* because we know someone else is going to be reliably *that way* — it also helps us see that these roles may be generally consistent but not absolute.

Put another way: While we profit by studying types, we have to resist stereotypes. Roles are not fixed, static things but are themselves creative responses to a complex condition. And while partners thrive with role clarity, they will be stifled by role rigidity.

"I have often thought," William James wrote, "that the best way to define a man's character would be to seek out the particular mental or moral attitude in which, when it came upon him, he felt himself most deeply and intensely active and alive. At such moments there is a voice inside which speaks and says: '*This* is the real me!'" While this experience may feel like it rises up from the inside, it flows from social context. Certain circumstances, James wrote, "are fitted to evoke this attitude, whilst others do not call for it," and noticing these, we can determine "where the man may fail, where succeed, where be happy and where miserable."

Here is where it gets really interesting. "Now as well as I can describe it," James continued, "this characteristic attitude in me always involves an element of active tension, of holding my own, as it were, and trusting outward things to perform their part so as to make it a full harmony, but without any *guaranty* that they will. Make it a guaranty — and the attitude immediately becomes to my consciousness stagnant and stingless."

In other words, conditions beckon our best nature, and we must be able to depend on them. Yet we must not be in conditions that are fixed and unchanging. We need reasonable predictability in our relations. But we also need, if not the constant presence of surprise, at least the potential for it.*

---

* Because it's so essential to our well-being, this business of roles — especially unconscious ones — is a preoccupation for many psychotherapists. "Every relationship is in a sense a division of labor," the psychoanalyst M. Gerard Fromm told me, "and we divide up our positions not just due to our strengths, but also because of our fears. Say you have a man, for example, whose tendency is toward aggression or assertion, and his partner really desires that quality but she's afraid to incorporate it into her own functioning. So they both let the husband 'carry' that for them, enact that for them. On the other hand, maybe the man is very uncomfortable with dependency, feelings of neediness, so both parties may assign that to the women to represent. This division of labor can be quite dysfunctional yet it's not at all uncommon.

"You see, at some level," Fromm continued, "people are essentially saying to each other, 'I'm with you because I want you to help me bring in that part of myself that I need but that I'm afraid of or can't stand.' But it also follows that 'I'm not going to be able to stand you at some point,' because the other person brings these qualities into such sharp relief. And then there is the issue of what people have to repress. Everyone has a range to them, a variety of strengths, and if roles are divided up in this very tidy way and defensively rigid, each person has to submerge an aspect of their strength in favor of keeping the peace. But people get tired of being the one who always has to do one thing or another."

The solution is not a repudiation of roles but a relationship to them that is less rigid. "The question becomes, 'Can one person go to the other person's place?'" Fromm said. "In that marriage I was telling you about, the 'tough guy' can't go to the place that the wife represents of actually needing people and feeling longing, feeling dependent, and conversely she can't go to the place of standing up for herself. Those

Creative people depend on flexibility to an unusual degree, because they have such unusual range. Between 1990 and 1995, Mihaly Csikszent-mihalyi and his students exhaustively studied ninety-one exceptional innovators. "If I had to express in one word what makes their personalities different from others," Csikszentmihalyi noted in *Creativity: Flow and the Psychology of Discovery and Invention*, "it would be *complexity*. By this I mean that they show tendencies of thought and action that in most people are segregated. They contain contradictory extremes — instead of being an 'individual,' each of them is a 'multitude' . . .

"These qualities," Csikszentmihalyi continued, "are present in all of us, but usually we are trained to develop only one pole of the dialectic. We might grow up cultivating the aggressive, competitive side of our nature, and disdain or repress the nurturing, cooperative side. A creative individual is more likely to be both aggressive and cooperative, either at the same time or at different times, depending on the situation. Having a complex personality means being able to express the full range of traits that are

---

are marriages made in hell because they require one person to do one piece of work exclusively. The degree to which a person can go to another person's place is a measure of vitality and range of a relationship — and its creative potential too."

In extreme cases, inflexible roles can even indicate mental illness, as in codependency, when one person rigidly adheres to the position of "the sick one," denying his capabilities, while his friend or relative overly identifies as "the caretaker," denying his own vulnerabilities. At the Austen Riggs Center, a treatment facility for people with severe mental illness, this is a common schism between patients and families, and a key part of recovery is for these roles to be complicated, for the patient to identify his strengths and the caretaker his vulnerability.

Even when it falls short of actual madness, role rigidity can be maddening. Many of us struggle when we visit our families over the holidays, because no matter how competent, distinct, and grown-up we've become, at the family dining table, we revert to old, static patterns. (I'm forty-two years old but still the baby when I'm around my two older brothers.)

Similarly, rigid patterns are a common feature in workplace stagnation, according to the psychologist Diana McLain Smith, whose background in family therapy informs her work advising leadership teams. "When I'm called into a situation," she told me, "it's usually because people are stuck in some pattern. They see each other in fixed, static ways, and the irony is that this keeps people from really performing with consistency, because they are filled with resentment. When you get people to see that they are creating a reality with that other person, this not only enhances relationships, but also individual responsibility."

potentially present in the human repertoire but usually atrophy because we think that one or the other pole is 'good,' whereas the other extreme is 'bad.'" The psychologist Frank Barron found much the same in his creativity research, that creative people "were able to entertain many opposites in psychic life simultaneously — opposites which, for most people, entailed the sacrifice of one to the other." The creativity researcher Alfonso Montuori, a protégé of Barron's, summed up the finding this way: "Creative individuals alternate order and disorder, simplicity and complexity, sanity and craziness in an ongoing process."

According to the Polish psychologist Kazimierz Dabrowski, the term for this ability to set aside a cultivated role, a personality integrated due to instinct and socialization, is *positive disintegration*.

As to how disintegration shapes the way creative pairs work, I will confess this is one of the most challenging subjects I've tried to address, because developing it as a theme seems, on the surface, to contradict the fundamentals of archetypes themselves.

In order to articulate dialectics, we looked first at regular, fixed positions within pairs — John Lennon as the liquid and Paul McCartney as the container; Trey Parker as the dreamer and Matt Stone as the doer. Next, we considered turn-taking, which complicates the picture somewhat but still allows us the clarity of opposition. Lewis and Tolkien may have gone back and forth as generator and resonator, but we can still imagine those distinct roles in relation to each other.

Indeed, dyadic dichotomies, related opposite each other, are one of the basic ways we learn about the world. Mind *versus* body. Nature *versus* nurture. The same is true with creative dialectics. In my experience, the best way to approach a pair at the start is to look for clear divisions and role clarity. Otherwise, the partners remain behind a veil — Matt-and-Trey, for instance, would seem a two-headed beast, impenetrable to observation, without a glimpse of the distinctions between them. But the way to really *deepen* knowledge of pairs is to look at role fluidity.

As an illustration, consider the *taijitu*, where an approach to yin and yang begins with identifying two basic qualities, the black and the white, nestled against each other, each in its own space.

Yet the black and white fields do more than swirl around each other; they contain aspects of each other. Within the white portion lies a black dot, and within the black portion a white dot.

The same is true of creative partners. While it is entirely appropriate to call Matt the doer and Trey the dreamer, we should not take this schism between them too far. Matt can relate to Trey because Matt is a dreamer too. (Like many "doers" in a pair, his operational work is truly visionary.) And Trey can work with Matt because Trey values getting things done.

This doesn't obviate the distinctions we've explored. It's Matt, and not Trey, on the phone multiple times a day with their lawyer. It's Trey, and not Matt, staring at the screen when a script is due. But it suggests how the two stay nimble and how they make something unique.

Consider the scene Arthur Bradford captured in the *South Park* writers' room for the documentary *6 Days to Air*. "You know what's getting a lot of traction in the last six months," Matt says, "is how fucked up the NCAA is and how fucked up it is that players don't get paid."

According to staff writer Vernon Chatman, this is typical Matt — throwing out a premise rooted in politics or current events. "Matt reads a lot, has a lot of strong, rigorous feelings about what he wants to say, and just has this piercing drive to say 'Fuck you' or 'No, no, no'— to call bullshit on something, and a lot of time he's inspired by that," Chatman told me. "Trey is driven a little bit more by character and personal narrative and relationships and stuff like that."

While Matt speaks, Trey slowly paces around the table, looking at the walls. He stops at a refrigerator, takes a soda, cracks it open, and keeps pacing. This is typical Trey, his friends say. Paying keen attention but very much in his own world.

"They're playing on ABC on Sunday in front of like twenty million people," Matt says, "and they can't afford to fly their mom to the game. You look in the crowd and everybody's white . . . [and] all the players are black, or most of them — ninety percent of them are black — and you're like, 'Dude, you're selling their image. You're signing video-game deals!'"

As Matt finishes, Trey is on his second lap around the table. Trey jumps in: "So then, what if Cartman starts a lucrative business of getting crack babies to play basketball?"

Everyone laughs.

"And he videotapes these crack babies and it becomes really big but he doesn't pay the crack babies anything," Trey says. "Because Stan's mom volunteers at the hospital where she holds crack babies, and Cartman sees a really great investment opportunity."

"Yeah," Matt says, and he puts on a face — ready to play a character.

Trey takes up Cartman's voice: "I see. You're going to represent the crack babies against me. How much money they paying you, Kyle?"

Matt (as Kyle): "No, I'm doing it pro bono."

Trey (as Cartman): "What? You're doing it just to get a fucking boner!" Big laughs in the room. "You know I'd be fine if you were doing it for money, I'd understand, but just to get a boner, Kyle. Jesus Christ!"

This was the genesis of "Crack Baby Athletic Association" (season 15, episode 5), a lacerating satire of the NCAA. To study the roles at play, we can begin with the way the original distinction still applies: Trey dreamed up the gestalt of *South Park* in the first place and the show came to life with Matt as his lead producer.

Yet, in this moment, Matt plays the role of dreamer, musing about an injustice he'd like to see addressed, while Trey plays the role of doer, snatching that vision out of the air and attaching it to the reality of a character and narrative.

The conceptual challenge here is to appreciate these reversals, which one can find in every partnership, without forsaking the original distinctions. One helpful image is the way that the Danish physicist Niels Bohr argued that light can be considered both a particle and a wave, depending on how it is observed. With pairs, both role clarity and rule fluidity are important phenomena, and we can choose to focus on either, one depending on our purpose.

It's also helpful to understand that, for every dialectic that exists between two people, there is also a dialectic *within* each partner. Paul wrote optimistic songs to cheer himself up. John was a wise guy because he was so tender. "It is the most violent people who go for love and peace," he said of himself in his peacenik years. "Everything's the opposite." It is oversimplified but perhaps a useful mnemonic to say that every doer has his inner dreamer, every director has her inner star, and so on.

These opposites within each of us often take expression through the people we relate to. When I mentioned this to the psychologist and biographer William Todd Schultz, he said it reminded him of Carl Jung's notion of the compensatory function. "Jung talks about how the psyche is inherently self-correcting," Schultz wrote me, "so if a side of ourselves is not getting expressed — say, we are all 'persona' but no 'shadow'— we unconsciously seek out compensatory opposites, often via relationships. In other words, in part we project our opposite onto another person and get to know it and ourselves via relating with this other person. It's a sort of theoretical glorification of the opposites-attract idea. But Jung said the reason why is balance — we strive to be whole, and so we find others who add to what we've defensively subtracted from ourselves."

With Jung in mind, listen to Taylor Branch account for the bond between Martin Luther King Jr. and Ralph Abernathy: "My theory is that King knew that he had a tendency to get too flowery and too fancy for his own good," Branch told me, "and that Abernathy was a reminder to King of human nature — not to get too full of yourself, your big words and your big applause and your eloquence. King had a very strong part of him that was humble and that made fun of pretense and had an equally strong part of him that loved big words and fancy clothes. I think Abernathy served something in him. He was a reminder of that unattractive side of King."

When we consider the extent of opposites within pairs, as well as between them, we begin to appreciate one of the persistent challenges of studying them. I found over and over again that the moment I hit on a key distinction between partners and put it to one of the partners themselves or to someone who knew them well, I got a refutation in response, some version of: *Well, it's also the opposite.* One example of this pattern showed up in the interview Matt Stone and Trey Parker did with Steve Kroft on *60 Minutes.* Kroft asked them about an observation, made by their longtime producer Anne Garefino, that Matt was the more ruthless satirist of the two of them and that Trey's sense of humor was sweeter. Here's how they responded:

MATT: That Anne's pretty smart.
TREY: Anne's a bitch. (*They both laugh.*)
MATT: See, that was the opposite . . .
TREY: We're just proving the opposite.

MATT: Boy, that Trey is ruthless.

TREY: [*Bleep*] Anne. She's fired.

It's not that Garefino is wrong. Matt *is* the more ruthless of the two. But they don't want to be pigeonholed.

The key thing to remember is that, regardless of what expression it takes, the dialectic remains. With the release of the Apple II in 1977, Steve Wozniak and Steve Jobs defined the personal computer and established Apple as a company that would change the face of technology. Woz, the engineer, said his success with Jobs was due to "my engineering skills and his vision," clearly labeling himself the doer and Jobs the visionary. Wozniak elected to remain the doer, an engineer at the periphery of Apple's organizational chart, free from the responsibilities of managing the business or other people. Meanwhile, over the next thirty-four years, Jobs became arguably the most recognized visionary in the computer industry, leading Apple through innovations like the iPod, iPhone, and iPad.

Yet, we could also paint Woz as the dreamer who conceptualized a powerful new technology, and Jobs as the doer who recognized the potential of the idea and then shaped, refined, and marketed it. As the journalist Gary Wolf observed, Wozniak's Apple II was "essentially the first and last retail computer designed by a single person." As both programmer and electrical engineer, Wozniak imagined the entire design. But the Apple II came into production only by dint of Jobs's ability to push and pull levers of supply chains, and it became popular due to his ability to cultivate and manipulate public opinion. Jobs was a man who made things happen.

Or look at C. S. Lewis and J.R.R. Tolkien. Tolkien was deeper and more dogged; he spent decades creating an entire fictional universe. Lewis was more inclined to skim a subject, coming quickly, adeptly, and boldly to conclusions on everything from the nature of pain and the essence of friendship to the relationship between good and evil.

We could say, then, that one was a miner after ore; the other was the refiner. Had it not been for Lewis, one senses that Tolkien might have spent his entire life in Middle-earth and never surfaced to offer others passage there. Had it not been for Tolkien, one senses that Lewis might never have found the depths out of which he spoke with such facility and ease. By withdrawing from the ordinary world, Tolkien represented disorder. By emphasizing the making and doing and arguing, Lewis represented order.

Yet we could also say that with his fastidious care for the language, customs, and lineage of his Middle-earth, Tolkien was really establishing order, and that in his provocative work, Lewis represented disorder. In both cases, we have the same exciting frisson between the two of them. Which one is Apollo and which Dionysus, who's yin and who's yang — the clear distinctions matter less than that frisson.

"There are always these poles between them," Vernon Chatman said of Matt and Trey. "Everything is great when the power is running between the poles."

13

The "Other" of the Psyche

The Dialogue of Creative Thinking

While this book has been devoted to the intricate, intense interdependencies between people — a necessary and long-neglected subject — the overwhelming influence of others in our lives does not change the fact that Paul McCartney woke up one morning with the tune for "Yesterday" in his head; that Marie Curie first had the idea of radioactivity; and that, from somewhere in his heart or from the ether — but not from his brother Orville, at least not in any direct, traceable way — Wilbur Wright first snatched the ambition of making a flying machine.

But what happens in one's own mental space is not separate from interconnectivity. Rather, it's an extension of it. Much the same dichotomous process that shapes creative exchange between two people also applies when one is thinking alone. Before we explore this further, we need to set aside some romantic misconceptions about solitude. One abiding source of romance is the poet Rainer Maria Rilke. In 1902, Franz Kappus, a nineteen-year-old student at a military school in Vienna, wrote Rilke to ask for some advice and feedback. Rilke answered that he could not be of help. "You ask whether your poems are good," Rilke wrote. "You send them to publishers; you compare them with other poems; you are disturbed when certain publishers reject your attempts. Well now, since you have given me permission to advise you, I suggest that you give all that up. You are looking outward and, above all else, that you must not do now. No one can advise and help you, no one. There is only one way: Go within."

Rilke said it again: "Go within, and scale the depths of your being from which your very life springs forth . . . For the creative artist must be a world of his own and must find everything within himself and in nature, to which he has betrothed himself."

This and nine more letters from Rilke to Kappus over six years came to be published as *Letters to a Young Poet*, one of history's most urgent exhortations on the primacy of self-knowledge.

By this point in our journey, you can probably anticipate the punch line: Rilke, while preaching self-reliance, was himself deep in debt to the opinions, styles, and influence of others. Even as his correspondence with Kappus unfolded, Rilke worked as secretary to the sculptor Auguste Rodin, under whose influence he adopted a whole new style — leaving aside the subjective and sentimental for the compact and unadorned, searching for the literary equivalent of Rodin's clay and bronze.

Rilke had also thrown himself headlong into an affair with the now-legendary muse Lou Andreas-Salomé, who spun like a hurricane through the lives of Nietzsche and Freud and — for nearly thirty years — Rilke. "Though Salomé was a formidable intellectual, novelist and practicing psychoanalyst," wrote Mark M. Anderson, "her most lasting contribution to European culture may well be her role as poetic midwife to the greatest German lyric poet since Hölderlin. It was she who recognized the makings of genius in the bundle of neuroses, preciosity and über-feeling that made up the young 'René Rilke,' helping him through various personal crises to accept the 'Other' in his psyche." Without this, Anderson wrote, Rilke could have never "forged the Modernist style of the *New Poems*, his novel *The Notebooks of Malte Laurids Brigge* or his poetic masterpiece, the *Duino Elegies*."

Among other marks of her influence, Salomé preferred Rainer over his given name, René. He revised his own name to suit her.

Though the gaps between Rilke's advice to Kappus and his actual life were prodigious — Rilke eagerly sought the opinion of others and aggressively pushed his work on publishers — the point here is not that he was a hypocrite. To the contrary, Rilke's story helps us approach what may be the great creative task, as Mark M. Anderson put it, to recognize the "Other" within the psyche, to understand the problem — and approach the solution — of how creative people relate to their own minds.

. . .

The myth that artists need only withdraw into themselves to create has its counterpart in a psychological tradition that pits individuals against the world around them. Sigmund Freud proposed that people had to negotiate between antisocial instincts and the necessity of social realities (and the drive toward sensual pleasures). Men wanted to murder their fathers and claim their mothers sexually, Freud thought. They had to convert those urges — or, at best, sublimate them. For Freud, creativity was a redirection of aggressive wishes into something more palatable. Successors to Freud, including Melanie Klein, began to dig into the way that dyadic exchanges shape the psyche. Klein helped create the idea of "object relations"— how people are shaped by internalized images of their relationships with others. Klein's student Donald Winnicott, an analyst and a pediatrician, advanced this idea to the next crucial stage: a child did not grow up healthy despite his mother, Winnicott observed, but because of exchanges with the mother. Our early experiences are not battles royal; actually, they are the outer experiences that make up the foundation of the inner life — or thought, or consciousness itself, "the basic stuff of the inner world," Winnicott wrote, "that is personal and indeed the self." The self is shaped in dialogue with others.

This dyadic psychology bloomed into many flowers, and I certainly can't paint the full picture here, but one important takeaway has to do with the way that exchange shapes, not only feelings or behavior, but the very stuff of thought.

The psychologist Lev Vygotsky proposed that thinking itself emerges in a social process, through four distinct stages. First, we have external dialogue. As toddlers, we begin to wrap our expanding minds around fragments of language, toss them to adults around us, and receive them back in turn. That volley begins to shape a symbolic representation of matter and thought. Second, we continue this volley out loud, as when toddlers narrate play using dolls or toys.

In the third step, the "speech" goes inside, with internal monologues. A common example is a child narrating an experience to herself, moving her lips, very conscious of the word-by-word parallel with thought. Finally, in the fourth level, we have what psychologists call "condensed inner speech." We can order thoughts and grasp meaning without necessarily being conscious of the actual words.

Thinking, then, is a kind of download of exchanges with other people. And of course the process can happen in reverse, when an internal exchange becomes the template for an interaction. The essential point is that there is an ongoing interaction between the *inter*personal (the self and the other) and the *intra*personal (within the self).

Winnicott's relational model has received many useful refinements over the years. The psychologist Daniel Goleman's work on social intelligence shows that how we think and feel is a function of how we relate to others. The psychiatrist Daniel Siegel has shown that interacting with our own minds is a prerequisite for both mental health and empathy. Meanwhile, it turns out that the relationship one has to oneself is as complex as any society. "We used to think that the hard part of the question 'How can I be happy?' had to do with nailing down the definition of *happy*," writes the psychologist Paul Bloom. "But it may have more to do with the definition of *I*. Many researchers now believe, to varying degrees, that each of us is a community of competing selves, with the happiness of one often causing the misery of another. This theory might explain certain puzzles of everyday life, such as why addictions and compulsions are so hard to shake off, and why we insist on spending so much of our lives in worlds — like TV shows and novels and virtual-reality experiences — that don't actually exist."

To see how this relates to creativity, reflect for a moment on the quality of mind that is the *least* creative — when the mind buzzes like the white noise on a TV screen. This is "monkey mind," a cacophony of voices and sensations. Everything seems possible and nothing gets done.

Contrast that to the clarity of a moment of insight, when suddenly an organic structure emerges from what had been before a mess of scenes or ideas, when the melody line or a sentence comes to mind. We may describe these as "thoughts" that "emerge." But if we pay attention to our own experiences — and to the accounts of exceptionally creative people — what we discover is a kind of dialogue.

Rilke himself offers an excellent example of this inner dialogue. In the winter of 1911–1912, he was in retreat at a medieval castle on the Adriatic coast in northeastern Italy. The estate's owner — a patron of the poet named Marie Taxis — noted that he got off to a hard start: "A great sadness befell him," she wrote, "and he began to suspect that this winter would . . . fail to produce anything."

"Things must first get bad," Rilke told Taxis, "worse, worst, beyond what any language can hold. I creep about all day in the thickets of my life, screaming like a wild man and clapping my hands. You would not believe what hair-raising creatures this flushes up."

The "hair-raising creatures" sound very much like the monkeys of the mind, loose and wild. The fright of encountering them in a feral state is common at the start of a retreat, whether it's a thirty-minute meditation, a three-hour work session, or, as for Rilke, an extended journey of solitude. The static can be acutely uncomfortable. Freed of the social roles of everyday life — those flashlights that guide us through caves — we suddenly encounter the darkness itself, the creatures in its depths.

The heroic work, our teachers enjoin us, is to stay with the discomfort. That's what Rilke did — and something changed. One morning, Taxis noted, the poet received "a tedious business letter. Wishing to deal with it right away, he had to sit down and devote himself to figures and other dry matters. Outside a strong *bora* was blowing . . . Descending from the castle to the bastions overlooking the sea, Rilke walked back and forth deep in thought, preoccupied with his answer to the letter. Then all at once . . . it seemed to him as though in the roar of the wind a voice had called out to him: 'If I cried out, who could hear me up there among the angelic orders?'" Rilke went straight to work and by the end of the day had the first of his *Duino Elegies*.

> *Who, if I cried, would hear me among the angelic orders?*
> *And even if one of them suddenly pressed me against his heart*
> *I should fade in the strength of his stronger existence*

Having a poem descend "as though in the roar of the wind" may seem about as common as being struck by lightning. But what happened to Rilke is a dramatic instance of something rather typical. Over and over again, we hear creative people recounting in their aha moments — the crucial advance, the illumination from the metaphorical light bulb — that an image or a line or an idea *presented itself,* that it came not from the "I" but as though from a distinct source. These visitations seem to produce far superior results than anything one consciously constructs or creates. "The only lyrics that I'm really interested in," Paul Simon said in an interview with the music journalist Paul Zollo, "are the lyrics that I find, not the lyrics that I invent. If it doesn't come to me in that surprising way, I don't tend to believe it or get excited about it."

Zollo asked him to elaborate. "You just have no idea," Simon went on, "that that's a thought that you had. It surprises you. It can make me laugh or make me emotional. When it happens and I'm the audience and I react, I have faith in that because I'm already reacting. I don't have to question it. I've already been the audience."

It's weird. On one level, Simon surely knows the line or lyric is his, yet he feels like an audience to it. "You just have no idea that that's a thought you had." While this may feel familiar, it's worth noticing how hard it is to articulate, let alone explicate. Simon's shifting grammar and points of view emphasize the murkiness of it all.

"With thinking," Henry David Thoreau wrote, "we may be beside ourselves in a sane sense." He went on: "I only know myself as a human entity; the scene, so to speak, of thoughts and affections; and am sensible of a certain doubleness by which I can stand as remote from myself as from another. However intense my experience, I am conscious of the presence and criticism of a part of me, which, as it were, is not a part of me, but spectator, sharing no experience, but taking note of it, and that is no more I than it is you."

One way to clarify the experience is to externalize the origin place of that creative thought — or even personify it, as in the tradition of the muse or daemon or genius itself. The writer Elizabeth Gilbert became strongly associated with a revival of this tradition after she gave a popular TED talk arguing that the modern artist is burdened by the illusion of responsibility for the entirety of creation. People go around thinking that it's all on them to create something wonderful, Gilbert said, and it's just too much to take on.

As an alternative to that idea, Gilbert offered the ancient myths of muses — "basically fairies who follow people around rubbing fairy juice on their projects and stuff." As silly as it might sound, she argued, the idea of the muse actually does a better job describing what it's like to create. We *are* visited, she said, and whether we say by muses or by the unconscious doesn't greatly matter. The point is, we don't create by ourselves, even when we're alone.

Gilbert told the story of the great poet Ruth Stone who had the experience of verse "barreling down at her over the landscape," and Stone having to "run like hell" to get to the house and get a pencil and paper to take down the poem before it went right past her and on to another poet. She also told the story of a Tom Waits breakthrough: He heard a bit of a new song in his head while he was driving on an LA freeway, and he despaired for a moment, afraid he would forget it entirely before he could write it down. So he decided to address the song directly.

"He just looked up at the sky," Gilbert said, "and he said, 'Excuse me, can you not see that I'm driving? Do I look like I can write down a song right now? If you really want to exist, come back at a more opportune moment when I can take care of you. Otherwise, go bother somebody else today. Go bother Leonard Cohen.'"

In these examples, Stone and Waits framed their creative insights as entities — forces or voices that were either metaphorically or literally distinct. Paul Simon's idea of work arising from the unconscious may be quite similar. Listen to this exchange with Paul Zollo:

ZOLLO: Do you ever feel that those thoughts that surprise you come from beyond you?

SIMON: No. Beyond? No. I don't know what that means.

ZOLLO: Many songwriters, including John Lennon, have expressed that they feel like channels, and that songs come through them from a source that is beyond.

SIMON: Well, it's coming from their subconscious. Unless you believe that someone is sending you a signal from another planet or another sphere. But maybe that's an explanation for your subconscious. I don't think that way.

ZOLLO: But doesn't it ever seem to you that the process is rather magical?

SIMON: Yes, and that's why it's more fun to write that way.

ZOLLO: But that magic is something you possess?

SIMON: You don't really possess it. That's the feeling that it comes through, that you're a transmitter. It comes through you. But you don't possess it. You can't control it or dictate to it. You're just waiting. You're just waiting . . . Waiting for the show to begin.

You may have noticed that Simon contradicts himself. Late in this exchange he uses precisely the same image ("you're a transmitter") that he has rejected earlier ("unless you believe that someone is sending you a signal . . . I don't think that way"). The point isn't to catch him in an inconsistency but to see that he is trying to frame an internal dialogue that is essential and elusive.

What we can say for certain is that, whether the exchange is with a part of oneself, or with a muse, or with "basically fairies who follow people around rubbing fairy juice on their projects and stuff"—in all these cases, it *is* an exchange. With this in mind, let's revisit Rilke's advice to young Kappus, wherein he urged him, "There is only one way: Go within"; instructed him, "The creative artist must be a world of his own and must find everything within himself and in nature"; and enjoined him, "Scale the depths of your being." If he sank within himself properly, Rilke said, the young poet would not heed the opinions of others about his poetry, for he would "hear in them your own voice."

But what does it mean, really, to find one's voice? In 2011, a group of high-school poets were invited to the White House for a colloquy, and one of them asked Billy Collins, the former U.S. poet laureate, this very question. What happens, Collins said, is that you read other poets and imitate *their* voices. Early on, he said, "slavish imitation" is actually recommended. Eventually, six or eight influential voices blend together and combine into something singular and original. In other words, you combine your influences in such a distinct and affecting way that no one notices the sources.

"After you've found your voice," Collins continued, "you realize there's only one person to imitate and that's yourself . . . This allows you to be authentic. That's one of the paradoxes of the writing life, that the way to originality is through imitation."

This is where the developmental theories about the origin of thinking and consciousness — and the semimystical questions about the dialogue that creative people experience — become practical: Much like the thinking of a toddler, the stuff of one's creative life begins with an exchange between the individual and other people. From there, it can become an exchange within.

One benefit of this context is that it can help us transcend a kind of catfight between those contemporary figures who describe creativity as a social process and those who emphasize the necessity of solitude. The psychologist Keith Sawyer, the author of *Group Genius: The Creative Power of Collaboration,* looks at the cultural landscape and finds a dangerous underemphasis on collaboration. Susan Cain, the author of the best-selling book *Quiet,* sees a world of introverts oppressed by what she calls "the New Groupthink." Introverts, she points out, make up anywhere from one-third to one-half of the population — and many outstanding creative thinkers are introverts. But these people are beaten down, she argues, when companies and schools eliminate private space and force people into teams and groups. In one fourth-grade classroom, Cain noticed a sign that read RULES FOR GROUP WORK and included YOU CAN'T ASK A TEACHER FOR HELP UNLESS EVERYONE IN YOUR GROUP HAS THE SAME QUESTION.

The problems Cain notices are real enough. It's painful to see the knowledge that human beings are social creatures applied in such an antisocial way. To say, "Oh, creativity is social, so let's just throw everyone in groups," is like saying, "Flowers need water to grow, so let's put them in a lake." Of course, they need just the right amount of water — and sunlight and air.

The conditions required for human beings to thrive in one another's company are also a function of balance.

"Collaboration is good!" versus "Creators need time alone!" is about as helpful as an argument about breathing where one side insists that we absolutely must inhale, all the science says so, and the other side insists, no, no, that view fails to account for the massive body of evidence on the critical need to exhale. The creative body depends on appropriate social support and solitude. We need to be able to get wired up without overheating, and disconnect without going cold.

No one can prescribe these conditions from afar, in part because people vary in their needs. John Lennon, for instance, was so devoid of an internal relation that he had a hard time being by himself. "His reclusive lifestyle notwithstanding," his friend Pete Shotton said, "John could never bear to be left completely alone — even when he was composing his songs. Much of my time at Kenwood was spent idly reading or watching TV while John, a few feet away, doodled at the piano or scribbled verses on a scrap of paper." "If I am on my own for three days, doing nothing," he told Hunter Davies in 1967, "I'm just not here . . . I have to see the others to see myself. It's frightening, really, when it gets too bad. I have to see them [i.e., the others in the band] to establish contact with myself again and come down."

Thoreau, who, like Rilke, became a famous proponent of solitude — and even isolation — represented an opposite extreme. "I find it wholesome to be alone the greater part of the time," Thoreau writes. "I never found the companion that was so companionable as solitude." Yet Thoreau and Lennon both represent the way that the best experiences of connection and solitude come together in work by an individual, just as a complex interdependence — one with real room for idiosyncratic individuality *and* enmeshed identities — is characteristic of the best collaborations.

These extremes may be joined felicitously, and the best example I've seen is Tenzin Gyatso, the fourteenth Dalai Lama. While writing this book, I found myself in Dharamsala, the Tibetan capital in exile, in India, and I interviewed Tenzin Geyche Tethong, private secretary to His Holiness for about forty-five years, a man who had been described to me by a variety of authorities in Dharamsala as the Dalai Lama's most intimate partner. I asked him to tell me about the most significant relationships in the Dalai Lama's life, and we spent some time going over an impressive list, from his root guru, or primary teacher, to the oracles he consults on decisions, to Tenzin Geyche himself. Though the Dalai Lama is credited as the primary author of many books, Tenzin Geyche told me that he didn't believe he had ever sat alone with a keyboard, that the texts of his books emerged in conversations and in public talks.

But what interested me most was the way that the Dalai Lama's day is organized. He wakes up at three thirty every morning, Tenzin Geyche told me (regardless of where in the world he is) and does his meditations and prostrations. As the sun comes up, he begins to circulate among his staff and to receive visitors — and he spends the rest of the day absorbed in company. Here, then, is the exact opposite of the sort of problematic individual psychologists worry over — the person who is not comfortable being alone but can never truly connect. The Dalai Lama is brilliant at being alone and at connecting.

Thoreau, too, had the best of both worlds — enjoying his solitude while enmeshed in a creative culture. He often left his retreat at Walden Pond to go into Concord, Massachusetts, where one of the great intellectual and literary communities in history awaited him, including his indispensable mentor Ralph Waldo Emerson. Indeed, Thoreau's hut at Walden was on land owned by Emerson. In a very real way, Thoreau was held throughout his retreat in the space of a wise elder. From his engagement with others — as a reader, as a writer, as a listener, as a talker — Thoreau took in the material with which to construct a rich interior life. Enough connection allowed Thoreau his solitude. From solitude he returned to connection — when he brought his journal back from Walden Pond.

It is not for everyone in every moment to emphasize both sides of this dialectic. The overstimulated may be appreciated in her simple cry to be left alone. Likewise, the lonely may be loved in his plea for company. *Letters to a Young Poet* reaches so many creative people because they need the message. Rilke himself delivered the message out of his own need.

Around the time he first wrote to Kappus, Rilke confided to a friend that, when he dreamed of his ideal life of poetry, he would hear the voice of his father, sounding over and over again in his head, saying the word *imprudent*. Rilke was also oppressed — that is not too strong a word — by his inner sense of his mother. He spoke of a "fear deep within me lest after years and years of running and walking I am still not far enough from her, that somewhere inwardly I still make movements that are the other half of her embittered gestures." The struggle with these and other influences left Rilke feeling "as if someone had closed the window towards the garden in which my songs live."

Now we understand. Rilke exalted solitude because his (inner and outer) world was too full of the wrong kind of company. The writer and scholar Lewis Hyde reminded us that these *Letters to a Young Poet* were begun when Rilke was only in his late twenties. The book really could, Hyde observed incisively, be called "*Letters* from *a Young Poet*."

But perhaps the title is actually quite right. Perhaps Rilke really needed this young man Franz Kappus as his partner so that he could say what most mattered to him. Perhaps this paean to individuation was actually a case study in a beneficial mutuality, with Kappus acting as a kind of muse who inspired Rilke to voice the thoughts that he himself really needed to hear. Perhaps the author and the primary audience for *Letters to a Young Poet* were the same man.

We learn about friendliness that it does not abolish
the distance between human beings but brings that
distance to life.

— *Walter Benjamin*

Don't you know that "No" is the wildest word we con-
sign to Language?

— *Emily Dickinson*

PART IV

DISTANCE

Like many people, I'm used to thinking about relationships according to the common question "Are you close?" But I've come to see that the better question is about how two people best animate the space between them — how they maintain the élan of curiosity and surprise alongside familiarity and faith.

I didn't go looking for distance in pairs; among the recurring qualities I found, it surprised me the most. But it struck me over and over again that without separation, there can be no relation. Once we've seen creative pairs connect, achieve confluence, and take positions in an ongoing dialectic, the question is how they remain absorbed in a shared endeavor not despite but because of ample room to move.

As an emblem of ideal distance — a distilled and pure illustration — consider this picture: Simone de Beauvoir and Jean-Paul Sartre working in the same café at separate tables. This was just one sign of a relationship built on unanimity of purpose and fueled by individual liberty. Sartre called the model of relationship "federative," suggesting a shared philosophy as a central government with autonomy for the provinces over their internal affairs. Both he and Beauvoir accumulated disparate experiences, wrote separate stories and lectures, nurtured individual interests. Both had other lovers, full-blown affairs, even live-in partners. At one point, Sartre was sleeping with Evelyne Rey, the sister of the editor Claude Lanzmann, who was living with (and sleeping with) Beauvoir. Yet Lanzmann said there was never "the slightest question of rivalry with Sartre." After mornings on her own—Sartre, too, gave his mornings to writing—Beauvoir went to him in the afternoon. As they viewed it, their style of connection enacted a feedback loop where distance served the mutual project, which project magnified their autonomy. It fit with their existentialist belief that, as the philosopher David Banach writes, human beings "are all ultimately alone, isolated islands of subjectivity in an objective world." Yet the vision was not grim-faced and dour but breathless and excited.

Independence seeds interdependence—and vice versa. This was their creed, and Beauvoir wrote a kind of manifesto: "One single aim fired us, the urge to embrace all experience, and to bear witness concerning it. At times this meant that we had to follow diverse paths—though without concealing even the least of our discoveries from one another. When we were together we bent our wills so firmly to the requirements of this common task that even at the moment of parting we still thought as one. That which bound us freed us; and in this freedom we found ourselves bound as closely as possible."

14

Creative Monks and Siamese Twins

The Extremes of Distance

For some pairs, optimal distance seems to come naturally. James Watson and Francis Crick talked about DNA for hours in their shared office at the Cavendish Laboratory, but they also spent long stretches working on separate projects. Crick had his doctoral research; Watson had other duties at the lab. What might have been a liability, both recognized as an asset. "Neither Jim nor I felt any external pressure to get on with the problem," Crick said. "This meant that we could approach it intensively for a period and then leave it alone for a bit."

For others, maintaining distance is a conscious move. David Crosby and Graham Nash — along with Stephen Stills and, later, Neil Young — were intent on performing under a confederation of last names. "It was a deliberate choice," Crosby told me, "because we had seen what happens when you were part of the Byrds or the Hollies. Then you're stuck. That's your identity. With us, we were always individuals, and we could work together as we liked — or not, as we liked."

More striking than the range of intention is the range of practice. At one end of the spectrum, pairs may almost never be in physical proximity, as with the composer Richard Strauss and the librettist Hugo von Hofmannsthal, who collaborated on their celebrated operas through the mail. Strauss often tried to persuade his partner to visit, but, a biographer notes, "the poet remained curiously evasive." Hofmannsthal did pledge his "lasting goodwill in all our future joint concerns." But for him to work well with someone, he needed to be left largely alone — not just physically, he insisted, but intellectually too. He enjoined Strauss not even to mention certain ideas or remind him of agreements but simply to "take me as I am, and take me kindly."

We might be tempted to call Hofmannsthal isolated, but that's not the right word. It's true that he needed considerable physical and psychological space. But creative individuals have often been mistaken for hermits, when the clearer picture would show skillful and productive relationships engaged from a deliberate solitude.

Emily Dickinson is an epic example of such deliberation, as several of her core relationships reflect. Though conventionally sociable as a child, she began, in her late teens and twenties, to withdraw from the usual social activities of women of her station. Her father was a leading figure in Amherst, so she was, ex officio, a town belle, yet she did not call on ladies or submit to being called upon. By her late thirties, she declared, "I do not cross my Father's ground to any House or town." Some of her choices fueled local gossip. For example, when her father's funeral service was held in the family home, she stayed upstairs and listened from her bedroom, with the door ajar.

What she did in that bedroom excited even more interest: she dressed in a costume of virginal white and wrote poetry. Dickinson has been called insane, but this is like calling Mr. Rogers cruel or Bill Clinton prudish. It's not just wrong but the opposite of the truth. That the fantasy of her madness persists is due in no small part to our hobbled understanding of creative distance.

Here's the basic thing: some people engage best face to face, others side by side. Emily Dickinson connected with others through words on a page. About a thousand of her letters survive, and scholars believe this may be only a tenth of what she wrote. "Her letters are beyond brilliant," Christopher Benfey, a Dickinson authority who teaches at Mount Holyoke College, told me, "and you really can't understand her as a poet and a writer without seeing that she approached this form, alongside her poetry, with equal energy and commitment."

Dickinson often aimed her poems at particular readers. Over her lifetime, she sent three dozen letters and nearly fifty poems to the editor Samuel Bowles, with whom she had a special sympathy. "When the Best is gone — I know that other things are not of consequence," she wrote his wife when he left for a sabbatical in Europe. Then there was the writer and activist Thomas Wentworth Higginson, whom she asked to be her "Preceptor," an instructor or teacher. Over twenty-four years, she sent him almost a hundred poems ("many of her best," writes the scholar Brenda Wineapple in *White Heat,* a study of the relationship). She often said he saved her life.

Perhaps Dickinson's most activating muse was her sister-in-law Susan Huntington Dickinson, whom she called "Imagination" itself and a source of knowledge second only to Shakespeare. To Susan, Emily sent more than two hundred letters and two hundred and fifty poems, even though they lived next door to each other.

Dickinson often touched on the paradox of intimacy. "I must wait a few Days before seeing you —" she wrote her sister-in-law. "You are too momentous. But remember it is idolatry, not indifference."

Another of Emily's intriguing paeans described Susan as "a Stranger yet." Those who "cite" Susan the most, the poem said,

> *Have never scaled*
> *her Haunted House*
> *Nor Compromised*
> *her Ghost —*

Then she made the paradox explicit:

> *To pity those who*
> *know her not*
> *Is helped by the*
> *regret*
> *That those who*
> *know her know*
> *her less*
> *The nearer her*
> *they get —*

Belying the common portrayals of Dickinson as a fragile, secluded creature, her writings to and about her sister-in-law show her, as Ellen Louise Hart and Martha Nell Smith write, as "engaged in philosophical and spiritual issues as well as all the complexities of family life and human relationships. She knew love, rejection, forgiveness, jealousy, despair, and electric passion," and she seemed particularly in tune with the paradox of distance — that the fiercest heat of a flame may be best experienced by a hand hovering over it.

Whatever pain she may have felt — and loneliness, too, perhaps — Dickinson brought great intelligence and will to bear in constructing a decidedly social literary life. Many of the engagements she avoided were just the sort of superficial exchanges that most of us would duck if we had the courage. This opened up time for her to read copiously — her favorites included Shakespeare, George Eliot, and Elizabeth Barrett Browning. She also kept current with fifteen magazines and newspapers that came to her family's house, including the *Springfield Republican* and *Harper's Magazine*. In April 1862, when Higginson wrote his "Letter to a Young Contributor" — addressing the many "new or obscure contributors" who might send work to the *Atlantic Monthly* — she was coiled and ready to spring. She wrote on the fifteenth of the same month.

> Mr. Higginson,
> Are you too deeply occupied to say if my verse is alive?
> The mind is so near itself it cannot see distinctly and I have none to ask.

Brenda Wineapple notes that this letter was actually a savvy, even coy, opening move, and fitting for an ambitious woman determined to have contact only with those whom she deemed "the Best." ("The Soul selects her own Society—" she wrote. "Then—shuts the Door—") She wasn't begging for help from Higginson. She was enticing a correspondent—a man she would later ask to be her mentor. And Higginson was certainly enticed. He found Dickinson impressive and intriguing and startling.

Yet he came to appreciate the distance between them as well. After traveling to Amherst to meet her face to face, he wrote: "I never was with any one who drained my nerve power so much. Without touching her, she drew from me. I am glad not to live near her."

· · ·

Today, psychologists might call Dickinson a "highly sensitive person." This is a term coined by the psychologist Elaine Aron, whose research identifies an innate trait of "sensory-processing sensitivity" (meaning a high degree of responsiveness to one's environment) in about 15 to 20 percent of the population. Highly sensitive people have "a rich, complex inner life," are unusually aware of subtleties in their environment, "notice and enjoy delicate or fine scents, tastes, sounds, works of art," and are "deeply moved" by the same. But they also need to withdraw into spaces that afford "privacy and relief from stimulation." They spend a great deal of time alone and often arrange their lives to avoid "upsetting or overwhelming situations."

These people are not chilly but rather have the kind of heat that needs ample room to dissipate. They are highly empathic, highly reactive emotionally, and extremely sensitive to stimuli. Naturally, they become over-aroused easily.

It follows that many creative people who appear deeply isolated might actually be taking what seems, to ordinary folks, an unusual amount of space to recharge. They may be like the monks of creative work — taking what solitude they need for their practice in much the same way that lamas retreat for extended bouts of meditation.

For such people, *introversion* may be a misleading description. It suggests an orientation away from others, when it may be that they are so porous, they need buffers. The psychologist Hans Eysenck (in collaboration with his wife, Sybil Eysenck) proposed that introverts have higher levels of cortical arousal than extraverts, so while introverts often need to minimize stimulation, extraverts often need to maximize it. According to the Yerkes-Dodson law (after the psychologists Robert M. Yerkes and John Dillingham Dodson), performance increases with physiological or mental arousal — but only up to a point, after which stimulation has a negative effect. Perhaps all of us need some version of the balance that highly sensitive people starkly illustrate.

If Dickinson and Hofmannsthal illustrate the path of the creative monk, the artists Gilbert and George exemplify the mode of hyperclose pairs, usually appearing in public together and in matching suits. "Two people make one artist," Gilbert said. "We think that we are an artist," George said. The DJ/performance artists known as AndrewAndrew take this even further; they are artists as Siamese twins, collapsing the distance between them to the greatest possible degree. Shortly after they met, they began living together and working together and threw away everything that didn't match, down to the underwear. Everything they own, from khaki slacks to rattan belts to white-framed eyeglasses, comes in duplicate.

Their effort at twinning goes to the depths of identity. They betray no details that distinguish one from the other. Before I interviewed them, in the lobby of the Ace Hotel in New York City before a DJ set, I signed a required pledge not to reveal either one's last name or birthplace or any details of their lives before they met.

The Andrews did yield a hint of the roles they play. One Andrew — they did not say which — is the chief communications officer of the team, fashioning their website, for example. The other is the chief engineer, tending to the many gadgets they use when they perform. But their efforts to achieve similarity far overshadow any distinction. They read the same books. They celebrate the same birthday — September 9, the day they made their first appearance as AndrewAndrew. They ate identical food for seven years, the amount of time a biologist had told them it would take for every cell in their bodies to regenerate.

But just as it would be a mistake to see Emily Dickinson as an isolate, we shouldn't mistake AndrewAndrew for a merged entity. It may be that, more than most, they're animated or even actualized by their distance.

Let's look at them a bit closer. When Michael Schulman profiled the team for the *New York Times* in 2011, he was impressed by "the discipline it requires" for them to maintain the "depth of their sameness." "When one of them loses a button on a blazer," Schulman wrote, "the other will lose the same one . . . One time at an art gallery, Andrew spilled red wine on his jacket. Instinctively, the other Andrew grabbed a glass and spilled it on himself, too."

What Schulman calls *discipline* could also be described as "constant, unyielding attention." Before the DJ set, as we were talking in a booth in the corner of the Ace lobby, I noticed that one Andrew's hair was dryer than the other Andrew's; his had been gelled to clear, wet-looking peaks. An hour later, on the DJ stand, the first Andrew had put on more product.

They were identical again. But only for the moment. One of the striking things about AndrewAndrew is that their very action against distinctions heightens their awareness of them. Spilling wine, tearing off blazer buttons, applying hair gel — we may think that these erase the differences between the two. But it's actually a case of differences constantly noticed and constantly adjusted.

15

"Somehow We Also Kept Surprising Each Other"

The Varieties of Distance

High-functioning couples commonly say that one key to a good relationship is giving each other plenty of space. But a big reason there are so many dysfunctional couples, romantic and creative, is that it's hard for a lot of us to know what that really means or what it would look like in our lives. The extreme cases we've considered suggest the range. But most people want something between total physical separation and as-near-as-possible fusing.

There's no formula. Optimal distance depends on the temperaments and pursuits of each member of the couple, and how they play together. Obligations vary according to the mechanics of the field — and the phases of work within it. A writer works for years before bringing a manuscript to an editor, then talks to her every day while the book moves toward production. Cofounders of a startup spend sixteen hours a day together doing grunt work, then one recedes to a board role while the other stays at the reins as CEO.

Another complicating factor is that distance can take so many different forms. It may be geographic (whether a partner is across town or across an ocean). It may be temporal (whether the passage of time between contact is an hour or a year). These concrete, measurable qualities intersect variously with the psychological experience of being together or apart. The poets Jane Kenyon and Donald Hall lived in the same house but inhabited a "double solitude," Hall said, writing separately, meeting for coffee in the kitchen without speaking. "In our silence," he wrote, "we were utterly aware of each other's presence." Oprah Winfrey and Gayle King, by contrast, haven't lived in the same city since they worked together in Baltimore more than three decades ago, but a day rarely passes without them talking on the phone, often at length; *O Magazine* reported in 2006 that they talk three to four times a day.

The same basic experience of space — the same rough feeling — can be achieved on a variety of scales. When Bernie Taupin and Elton John were starting out, they worked in different rooms in an apartment they shared in London, Taupin emerging from the bedroom to bring John finished lyrics in the living room, where the pianist put them to music. Now Taupin sends the lyrics by e-mail from his horse ranch in Southern California, and John takes them directly to the studio, where he looks at them for the first time.

Over the course of a long career, transitions in distance are common — for some pairs, the changes can be dramatic. "At this point, it's kinda like a marriage," Matt Stone said in 2011. "It's funny," Trey Parker added, "'cause we're just at that level now where it just doesn't happen anymore that one of us can say to the other, 'You know, one time, I was doing this.' Because, 'Yeah, I know. I was there.'" Yet it was around the time of this interview that the partners were really diverging. Bachelor days — in which they lived, worked, and partied together — were giving way to marriage and family. According to their friend Arthur Bradford, Matt and Trey don't tend to see each other outside of work these days. While both have homes on both coasts, Matt makes New York City his home base and Trey's HQ is in LA. They're still often together in studios, in the writers' room, in retreats, but it's not like the old days.

Penn and Teller made the same transition but with a very different attitude. In their early days, they drove around to festivals and fairs in a Datsun 210 station wagon. They set up together, performed together, did press together, and shared rooms at Motel 6s. "If one of us wanted to have sex, the other one had to walk around the parking lot," Penn said. Today, with a stage act in Vegas and international renown, they live very separate lives. What's striking, though, is that Penn attributes their staying power not to any adjustment in physical distance but to a consistent emotional distance throughout.

"I believe that the volatile groups — Lennon and McCartney, Martin and Lewis . . . were love affairs," Penn said. "Those were two people who fell in love . . . Teller and I started without any natural affection at all. I didn't have that — you know, that feeling you have you want to hug somebody or want to be around them or really feel affectionate toward them, which I feel toward a lot of people, I never felt toward Teller. Our relationship was essentially an e-mail relationship before e-mail. It was very, very sterile, very cold." Even their disagreements, Penn said, were "intellectual." "It was built on respect," Penn continued, "and respect is more important than love . . . I've always believed that what I did with Teller was better than what I do alone. And we're like two guys who run a dry cleaning shop or something and [if] we don't get along, it's not bad at all. We kind of assume that we're not going to get along. We're business partners. So the guy who cleans the Slurpee machine pisses you off. So what? He cleans the Slurpee machine. You deal with it."

Another complexity to distance is that it may emerge over a myriad of exchanges that resist broad characterization but that feel — the word that comes to mind is *microscopic*. What I mean is, the experience of separation from and connection with another person plays out in subtle ways day to day.

Among the most intriguing glimpses of this for me was with Phyllis Rose and Laurent de Brunhoff, who create the iconic books about Babar the elephant. Though most readers probably don't notice, Phyllis, rather than Laurent, has been the acknowledged writer of the text of the Babar books for some time; the credit is on the publication-data page, where the text copyright is assigned to her.

Phyllis's son, Ted, is my best friend, so I've seen Phyllis and Laurent often over the years. I wrote the last chapter of *Lincoln's Melancholy* in their guest cottage in Key West. On the face of it, they live very separate working lives: Phyllis is an essayist and biographer (and the author of a seminal work on creative intimacy, *Parallel Lives: Five Victorian Marriages*). She is the doyenne of her house — a party-thrower, an intellectual provocateur. Laurent is far quieter. I think of him wearing a sweater vest, at his drafting table, drawing elephants.

Also, while Babar accounts for Laurent's work life and identity, it is but a minor piece of Phyllis's world. Yet, when I asked Phyllis and Laurent directly about their exchanges, it became clear to me how freewheeling each book's creation is, and how much depended on what Phyllis described as

Laurent's "twenty-four-hour access" to her ideas and opinions. This is fitting, because the first Babar book, authored and illustrated by Laurent's father, Jean de Brunhoff, began with a bedtime story dreamed up by Laurent's mother, Cécile. When her boys repeated it to their father, Jean developed it into a written and illustrated story.

Seventy-nine years after that first book was published, I met with Phyllis and Laurent as they were developing the sixty-first Babar, and the fifty-fourth of Laurent's tenure as its author and illustrator. Called *Babar's Celesteville Games*, the story joined two fancies shared by Phyllis and Laurent: the Olympics — which they'd been watching the summer before, and during which Laurent sketched elephants diving and playing volleyball — and to do a book on weddings, inspired by a dramatic ceremony they'd attended in India. When I met with them, Laurent was nearly done with the sketches for the book, in which the Olympics comes to Celesteville, and Babar's daughter falls in love with one of the athletes, leading to a wedding. Phyllis had written a draft of the story. Laurent had been peppering her with questions on everything from how many birds it would take to lift up a pair of elephants in a chariot to what expression on a girl's face would communicate *amazed*. "I wasn't joking about twenty-four-hour access," Phyllis told me. "I think one thing that happens as you move through life is that you kind of want things more irregularly, and then the formality of going to an editor — it's not realistic. You just need someone around that you can talk to all the time."

The psychologists Daniel Kahneman and Amos Tversky also enjoyed open access to each other. They spent so much time together that Tversky's fifteen-month-old son described his father's profession by saying: "Aba [Hebrew for "Daddy"] talk Danny." They were "twinned," Kahneman said. Yet the twin-ship thrived with ample time together and apart. "Amos was a night person," Kahneman said, "and I was a morning person. This made it natural for us to meet for lunch and a long afternoon together, and still have time to do our separate things. We spent hours each day, just talking." And they spent hours each day not talking. Each knew the other's mind as well as his own, Kahneman said, yet "somehow we also kept surprising each other."

Starting in 1971, Kahneman and Tversky published a series of papers that challenged long-held views of how people formed opinions and made choices, demonstrating that human judgment often runs against what a rational model would predict. They essentially founded a new field of study, behavioral economics, and their careers exploded.

But a relationship originally buoyed by distance was eventually sunk by the same factor. In 1978, Kahneman took a job at the University of British Columbia in Vancouver, and Tversky went to Stanford, in Palo Alto, California. Though they spent every second weekend together and talked on the phone multiple times every day — sometimes for hours — the collaboration eventually languished. "We had completely failed to appreciate," Kahneman said, "how critically our successful interaction had depended on our being together at the birth of every significant idea, on our rejection of any formal division of labor, and on the infinite patience that became a luxury when we could meet only periodically."

That Lennon and McCartney maintained an ability to surprise each other was facilitated by distance as well. In the days of frenetic touring, the Beatles practically lived together, and the closeness suited them. They cooked up all kinds of schemes for Beatles retreats — a Greek island they'd buy together, or an entire English village with a common green and houses on four sides. "We were going to have a side each," Ringo said.

But in the mid-1960s, they also found a critical separation. John moved to an estate in a wealthy London suburb called Weybridge. Paul made his home in the St. John's Wood section of London, about an hour's drive away. Though they still met for regular writing sessions, their lives in the off-hours had distinctly different flavors, with Paul spending more time at the studio, catching John Cage performances, hanging out at the avant-garde Indica Gallery that he helped fund, and screening his little abstract films for Michelangelo Antonioni, which Paul pronounced, "Dead cool, really."

John spent an increasing amount of time at home, in the sitting room off his kitchen, taking acid, watching TV.

The struggle for space is sometimes like a ground war where every inch must be defended. My friend Adam Goodheart, while writing *1861*, his celebrated study of the origins of the Civil War, had the good fortune to live near the legendary nonfiction writer Richard Ben Cramer. Adam told me that, more than once, Richard gave him this advice: "Don't be afraid to be a son of a bitch." Meaning: Say no, ignore phone calls, hole up and do what you need to do.

Other creators will find that the trick is not so much in saying no as it is in gauging the precise balance of social sustenance and solitary pursuit. As we've seen, being in the same room with another person brings a massive quantity of data that goes way beyond language, way beyond even conscious awareness. The question often becomes, How much should you take in? We live in an especially interesting time for that question, as varieties of technology make both physical and virtual presence easier than ever before. The issue for pairs is how to use the tools. One pair of architects I interviewed work 5,400 miles away from each other. Abigail Turin is in San Francisco; her partner, Stephania Kallos, in London. They talk every day on Skype, Turin told me. But they don't turn on the video. Without daily Skype talks, they might be too far. But video — it's too close.

Optimal distance may seem to contradict the necessity for confluence, but both are basic qualities of pairs that proceed from the simultaneous human need for intimacy and autonomy. This basic tension is with us all from the start. "Our physical and emotional dependence on our parents surpasses that of any other living species, in both magnitude and duration," wrote the psychologist Esther Perel. "It is so complete — and our need to feel safe is so profound — that we will do anything not to lose them." Yet as we develop, we need to crawl with our own legs, stand on our own feet, and dart off in our own directions. The art of living, as Perel wrote, is to "balance our fundamental urge for connection with the urge to experience our own agency."*

It's clear, then, that autonomy and intimacy both serve human health. How do they serve creativity? The overarching answer is that alone time and social connection are each conducive to certain ways of thinking; while each mode has its distinct advantages, the real magic happens when they can be applied in alternating fashion.

In general, when alone, we have greater access to the unconscious, to

---

* Evolutionary history helps explain these dual needs. Human beings have always survived by situating themselves in groups and have thrived by taking positions of maximum specificity within the group. According to psychologist Marilynn Brewer, we follow this same pattern today by seeking identities that are "optimally distinctive," neither so weird that we'll be shunned by a core group, nor so assimilated that we'll lose our pizzazz. These two moves counteract each other like weights balancing on a scale. We're constantly adjusting to keep in equilibrium.

unfettered, wandering, ruminative thinking. An extreme example of this mind state is in sleep, which has long been understood as a fertile time for creativity. "It is a common experience that a problem difficult at night is resolved in the morning after the committee of sleep has worked on it," John Steinbeck wrote in *Sweet Thursday*. Recent research has borne him out.*

Many famous insights — ranging from Dmitri Mendeleev's vision of the periodic table to Keith Richards's riff for "(I Can't Get No) Satisfaction"— have come directly from sleeping states. Even more commonly, breakthroughs emerge from states of relaxation. "When ordinary people are signaled with an electronic pager at random times of the day and asked to rate how creative they feel," writes the psychologist Mihaly Csikszentmihalyi, "they tend to report the highest levels of creativity when walking, driving, or swimming; in other words, when involved in a semiautomatic activity that takes up a certain amount of attention, while leaving some of it free to make connections among ideas below the threshold of conscious intentionality."

But the novel ideas that come to us while sleeping or walking need to be tested and ratified by another way of thinking. "Later on, as we try to fit it into 'reality,' that original thought may turn out to have been trivial and naïve," Csikszentmihalyi wrote. "Much hard work of evaluation and elaboration is necessary before brilliant flashes of insight can be accepted and applied." Or rejected and discarded. A creative person may need to entertain a thousand solutions in order to find the one that works. Unfettered

---

* The writer Sam McNerney calls it the "science of sleeping on it." In one experiment, the neuroscientists Ullrich Wagner and Jan Born asked subjects to transform a long list of number strings; to solve the problem formally would require "a set of algorithms that would scare off most save a handful of math geeks," McNerney writes. "However, the researchers integrated an elegant shortcut that made the task easier. How many people, Wagner and Born asked, would catch it?" Only 20 percent total, even though most worked at the problem for several hours. But of the subjects who took a nap between trials, 59 percent found the shortcut. Sleeping and dreaming, Wagner and Born concluded, "facilitates extraction of explicit knowledge and insightful behavior." Another study, by Deirdre Barrett, a professor at Harvard Medical School, asked seventy-six college students to pick a problem from their lives and focus on it each night before bed. "After one week," McNerney wrote, "Barrett found that about half of the students dreamt about their problem and about a quarter dreamt a solution."

thinking generates the thousand. Analytical thinking helps us see the one that works.

"A key element to creativity," said the psychologist Greg Feist, "is to separate idea generation from evaluation and elaboration. For many creative people, the generation phase is best done in solitude, and they tend to be relatively uninhibited." The presence of other people draws you toward that testing state of mind. You share an idea and see a nodding head or a furrowed brow. Perhaps your partner takes up the idea like a baton in a relay race. Perhaps she puts it away like a broken toy. Even if she doesn't react, you can't help but devote *some* mental energy to imagining what she's thinking.

With ample distance, pairs can move between these two modes of being and thinking. The same rhythms come to affect work sessions, where two partners may move between generating and testing ideas, between focusing on a task and goofing off, between rumination and association. A good illustration is when John and Paul wrote "With a Little Help from My Friends"— the story that opened this book. They played with the lyrics, then broke into old songs and stories, then came back to the song, then broke for cake, then returned again. Their sessions always had this expansive quality. There was no rush and lots of room.

And in the larger scheme of things, they also came to feel that they could choose to be apart or together, as they liked. "We'll work together only if we miss each other. Then it'll be hobby work," McCartney said after they stopped touring. "It's good for us to go it alone." He wrote the score for a film called *The Family Way*. Lennon went to Spain to play the role of Private Gripweed in a movie called *How I Won the War*. "I had a few good laughs and games of Monopoly on my film," Lennon said, "but it didn't work. I didn't meet anyone else I liked." After the band reconvened in November 1966 to begin a new album, John said, "I was never so glad to see the others. Seeing them made me feel normal again."

16

"Desire for That Which Is Missing"

The Erotics of Distance

The phrase *optimal distance* has an unfortunate connotation of something fixed, static. But for many pairs, the right blend of intimacy and distance is a fluid, ongoing process. It emerges not from clarity about space but from ambiguity and uncertainty. Contrary to our simplified model, the moon is not circling the earth. Actually, the moon is in constant free fall toward the earth. The illusion of orbit is created only because the earth itself is constantly moving.

Rather than a set position, optimal distance is more like a dance. It is fitting, then, that the best illustration I've found is that of George Balanchine and Suzanne Farrell.

When we last left them, they were the very picture of confluence. Indeed, when Balanchine walked on his knees across the stage of the New York State Theater in the costume of Don Quixote; when he laid his head in Farrell's lap; when she washed his feet with her hair, the extent of their devotion was clear. "It was obvious that he was dancing not only *with* Farrell but *for* her," wrote Robert Gottlieb. Farrell herself called the gala benefit performance a "spiritual consummation." When they slipped away for coffee and doughnuts, leaving the tony crowd behind at the reception, they entered a world all their own.

In the early days, the main question of space between them was how zestfully they could charge into it. According to the psychologists Arthur and Elaine Aron's self-expansion model (which we explored in chapter 6), the joy of early connection follows a buoyant sense of one's world getting so much bigger. It's like that dream that, within your house, there are rooms you didn't know before. With George Balanchine "choreographing my life," as she put it, Suzanne Farrell could be part of a history that included imperial Russia and the Ballets Russes. With the spry, dutiful, and bold energy of his nineteen-year-old phenom, Balanchine could rediscover his own dances onstage and, afterward, the haunts of his life, like Le Cirque and the Russian Tea Room — and Dunkin' Donuts and the Tip Toe Inn. Their shared world was as big as both of them, and bigger, and they relished it. They had dinner together most nights, and when they traveled with the company to Paris, they took long silent walks along the Seine.

Soon, though, they began to find the boundaries between them. First, the relationship began to blur the professional and the personal, and while that may have been a source of inspiration and expansion, Farrell quickly saw the potential trouble. She had "amorous" feelings for Balanchine. "I was beginning to love the man," she wrote. But where would this lead? She was Catholic, and serious about it, and he was married, to his fourth wife, the dancer Tanaquil Le Clercq, who had become paralyzed from the waist down by polio.

Farrell took comfort in the faith that their love, when it came down to it, was centered on work. But Balanchine advanced on Farrell, asking for more and more of her time, moving not just to engage with her but to control her. He went with her to her apartment door in the evening to "deposit" her, and he smiled at the double-entendre. When he was not with her, he sent a friend to act as escort and bodyguard. When she dared to wear a ring given to her by a young man she liked, Balanchine threw such a fit that she broke off contact with her suitor.

Balanchine had a history. Four times he had married his lead ballerina, binding up in matrimony women who had charmed him as muses. (Some reports said the number was five, counting Alexandra Danilova, though the two never legally married.) It's not clear that his motivation was solely romantic: "If you marry a dancer," he said, "you always know where she is — in the studio working."

The tension between desire and control speaks to a familiar problem. Desire beckons us to try to eliminate gaps. But longing itself — and the thing we long for — depends on the gaps. "To sustain an élan toward the other," writes the psychologist Esther Perel, "there must be a synapse to cross." Simone Weil put it this way: "All our desires are contradictory . . . I want the person I love to love me. If, however, he is totally devoted to me, he does not exist any longer."

There's a word that describes this problem, the poet and scholar Anne Carson notes. The word is *eroticism*.

Eroticism is often considered an adjunct to sex; the dictionary definition is "relating to or arousing sexual desire or excitement." But sex is the act of physically joining with another person — entering, being entered. Sex is copulation, from the Latin *copula*, for "link" or "tie." Eroticism is not the fulfillment of yearning but the heightening of that yearning.

"The Greek word *eros* denotes 'want,' 'lack,' 'desire for that which is missing,'" writes Carson in *Eros the Bittersweet*. "The lover wants what he does not have. It is by definition impossible for him to have what he wants if, as soon as it is had, it is no longer wanting. This is more than wordplay. There is a dilemma within eros that has been thought crucial by thinkers from Sappho to the present day. Plato turns and returns to it. Four of his dialogues explore what it means to say that desire can only be for what is lacking, not at hand, not present, not in one's possession nor in one's being."

It is also a recurring theme in Greek iconography, Carson explains, where poets and painters tended to focus not on the moment a lover opens her arms wide but "when the beloved turns and runs. The verbs *pheugein* ('to flee') and *diōkein* ('to pursue') are a fixed item in the technical erotic vocabulary of the poets."

George Balanchine's art was replete with pursuit and flight. It wasn't just a favorite theme; it was a central preoccupation. "Many of his works," said his longtime lead dancer Jacques d'Amboise, "have to do with a muse, a woman, an ideal that a man attempts to own, touches and passes with for a moment in his life, and is doomed to lose it — and it's necessary to lose it, otherwise there's no striving for anything better anymore if you achieve what you have dreamed of. You must not achieve it. You must not possess it."

D'Amboise was talking about the core function of a muse — to be an object of inspiration and desire who reaches into our souls and psyches, who beckons, tempts, and coaxes that peculiar mix of tenderness and ardor. The Greek Muses were goddesses, so they could always elude a mortal's grasp and thus retain their power. Other muses, like Dante's Beatrice and Petrarch's Laura, attained similarly mythical states in their artists' eyes by dying young.

But for many people, mostly women, who were cast in history as muses to artists, an exquisite problem presents itself — how to be flesh and spirit at once. "How brave and resourceful the muse must be," Francine Prose writes in *The Lives of the Muses,* "to balance, year after year, on the vertiginous high wire that her calling requires — to navigate the tightrope between imminence and absence, to be at once accessible and unobtainable, perpetually present in the mind of the artist and at the same time distant enough to create a chasm into which the muse's devoted subject is moved to fling propitiatory, ritual objects: that is, works of art."

In psychology, the word for art-making as an expression of desire is *sublimation;* it applies anytime an emotion finds an indirect outlet. In Jane Campion's movie *Bright Star,* about John Keats and Fanny Brawne, one scene shows them on opposite sides of a wall. She stands with her cheek against it, and he holds his hand to it on the other side. Because they were unmarried, this was as close to physical intimacy as they were allowed to get. His poetry was a love song that bypassed the walls of that restraint.

Farrell and Balanchine illustrated a similar dynamic. The relationship was intensely physical, and erotic — but not sexual. Their language was a physical language. He placed her in the positions he desired. She answered his questions with her body. Before Farrell, Joan Acocella writes, Balanchine's work had been known for its classicism. With her, it took on a "jazz-baby sexiness," girded with a spiritual yearning — stages filled with "angels and gypsies, visions and confessions." A photograph from these years shows Balanchine demonstrating a male part to be danced by Arthur Mitchell. Balanchine and Farrell face each other, and his left leg is extended between her knees. In all the ways they are far, and in all the ways they are near, it is the embodiment of heat.

They did not have sex, Farrell said.

And yet, their work, she said in the film *Elusive Muse,* "was extremely physical and extremely gratifying ... It certainly was not the orthodox way of having a relationship," she said with a smile. "But it was more passionate and more loving and more *more* than most relationships. We had"—she laughed—"it was terrific. We had a great time." For six years, Farrell and Balanchine worked magnificently across the space between them. In the 1967 ballet *Jewels,* Farrell danced the lead part in the section called "Diamonds," and she found in the ballet's final pas de deux a "glorious blend of victory and surrender between Jacques and me, of leading and following, initiating and receiving."

But if his work knew that the hero must lose his ideal, Balanchine himself was not as wise. Art often knows more than the artist. Perhaps, too, there is something of a child in a creator, wanting to defy all limits but drawn to just those places where limits will be most sharply defined. "Infants," Anne Carson writes, "begin to see by noticing the edges of things. How do they know an edge is an edge? By passionately wanting it not to be."

Balanchine's pattern had long been clear. While he put women in power onstage, in his life he fixated on young ballerinas and made work *on* them. (Such is the language of the ballet, with its provocative syntax.) He often married them—and then moved on.

It was remarkable, then, when Farrell—only twenty-one years old at the time of *Jewels*—refused the master of dance, not because she wanted to push him away, but because she wanted to keep him. She didn't chafe at the contact so much as she sought the sort of contact that requires space. She had bristled at an article in *Newsweek* that called her "not only the alpha but the omega" of Balanchine's young ballerinas. "The exquisite Farrell," the piece read, "is the latest in a forty-year series of Galateas that include Danilova, Geva, Zorina, Tallchief and Tanaquil Le Clercq."

"I hated being on a list," Farrell wrote, "anyone's list."

Farrell's confidence was striking given how sheltered she was. She had no real friends, no hobbies. She lived with her mother and sister and had no life at all outside of Balanchine's company. Yet she did not cower. Wanting more of Balanchine, Farrell insisted on less. This set up a seesaw, because Balanchine reacted by moving toward her more strongly. In the fall of 1967, the *Chicago Sun-Times* reported—perhaps on Balanchine's authority—that the two would wed "shortly." Not long after this, Farrell wrote, she "decided again to try to put a little distance between George and myself." This wasn't easy. When she told him they ought not have dinner together every night, he soon lost so much weight that a company staff member urged her to return to his side and do whatever it took to make him happy. "Why don't you just sleep with him?" one of the male dancers said to her. "Is it such a big deal?"

She did consider marrying him. "It would have given George what he thought he wanted," she wrote. But she also thought that "our unique relationship . . . might not have withstood consummation. The physical side of love is of paramount importance to many people, but to us it wasn't. Our interaction was physical, but its expression was dance." And she danced, she wrote in her memoir, as if her life depended on it. "Dancing was the bottom line — the line that would support or hang me."

Farrell's impulses throughout were to create the best conditions for work. Unlike the traditional muse, whose role is to inspire the master and remain a sort of ghost, she wanted to be fully embodied, to actually coauthor a story from a place of respectful deference but with mutual authority. An effort at cultivating personal power of this sort did not need to be an affront to the union.

But it's not easy to push someone away to keep him close. From this confused place, Farrell struck up a friendship with a dancer two years younger than she — a "nice, quiet boy," she said in her memoir, named Paul Mejia. When he confessed that he loved her, she found herself in a crisis. Spurning him would mean a surrender to Balanchine she was loath to make, but engaging with him meant risking the master's wrath.* She felt so desperate that she contemplated suicide. As she spent more time with Mejia, Balanchine began to treat her coldly — her own mother told her she should give the great man what he wanted, and when her daughter didn't come to heel, she stopped talking to her. Farrell moved into her own apartment and, scared and lonely, found that Mejia was now her only real friend. She soon agreed to marry him. Balanchine, who had obtained his own divorce just two weeks before, was in Hamburg, Germany; a delegation from the company flew there to tend to him.

---

* It's fair to ask just what Farrell felt about Mejia. Did she want to be with him? Her memoir isn't clear, though she does consistently emphasize her preoccupation with Balanchine. "I don't know when I realized that I *was* in love with Paul," she wrote in *Holding On to the Air*. "I was so haunted by possible confrontations that my emotions were reined in. I felt guilty about every moment or thought or feeling I shared with Paul — or anyone else. Nevertheless, I decided to tell Paul that I loved him." Later she wrote: "My relationship with Paul did not diminish what remained, always, the most important thing in my life: my work."

Even after her marriage, Farrell hoped for a relationship with Balanchine that would preserve their work together — one where she had her life, and Balanchine his, and they met on common ground. But Balanchine acted like a spurned lover, or a petulant child. Or perhaps he was a canny operator, hoping to wield the power that remained to him to force the outcome he wanted. He had never appointed an understudy for Farrell before; if she could not perform, the dance would not go on. But now he asked that she teach her role in "Diamonds" to a second. As she and the master grew more distant — he turned away from her when they crossed in the hallway — she offered to leave the company. "No, that's not necessary, dear," Balanchine replied. "But perhaps Paul should leave."

Balanchine's control over Farrell's husband's career turned out to be the last bit of weight under which the Farrell and Balanchine partnership collapsed. On May 8, 1969, two and a half months after Farrell and Mejia's marriage, the New York City Ballet was to present *Symphony in C*, and a male dancer withdrew at the last moment from a role that Mejia had often performed. When Balanchine cast someone who was much less familiar with the role, Farrell sent him a message warning him that if Mejia did not dance that night, they would both resign from the company. She went to her dressing room early and began to apply her makeup. Soon there came a knock on the door. The director of wardrobe, Sophie Pourmel, walked in and collected her costume. "Suzanne," she said, crying, "you're not dancing tonight."

And just like that, she was in exile.

Distance may feel like a rebuke. It may feel like a breakup. It may *be* a breakup. The luxury of observing these pairs in retrospect is that we can often see the span of their whole careers. But when you see your life through your own eyes and in the present tense, you don't know how the story is going to end.

In 1989, after seventeen years playing with the E Street Band, Bruce Springsteen decided that "we got into a rut," that the relationships were "muddy, through codependence, or whatever." He sat down one day and called the band members one by one. Clarence Clemons was in Japan on tour with Ringo Starr's All-Starr Band. As Clemons remembered the conversation, they greeted in the usual way — "Hey, Big Man!"; "Hey, Boss!" Then Springsteen said: "Well, it's all over."

Clemons thought he meant the Ringo tour—that he needed to come back and get to work. He said he'd get home and check in ASAP.

"Naw, naw, naw," Bruce said. "I'm breaking up the band." According to Springsteen's biographer Peter Ames Carlin, as Bruce talked, "Clemons was juggling his surprise and grief with a sudden urge to reduce his hotel room to ruins. So many years on the road, so much sacrifice, the thousands of hours spent waiting for Bruce to hear just the right sound from the recording studio speakers. 'And I'm thinking, "It's all for this? My whole life dedicated to this band, this situation, this man, and what he believes in, then I'm out of town and I get a fucking phone call?"'"

Like Clemons, Suzanne Farrell was dazed to find herself on her own. The problem was more than emotional and artistic. She didn't know if she could support herself. She had dim prospects as a dancer; any American company that hired her would risk alienating Balanchine. And her training had been so firmly in Balanchine's particular style that it was unclear whether she could even fit in anywhere else. She was twenty-three years old.

She and Mejia rented cheap space to practice in. At a local high school, they danced a piece Mejia choreographed. Eventually they went to live in upstate New York. Then Maurice Béjart, the director of a dance company in Belgium, called and offered to hire them both. "Béjart's work was not so much ballet as a sort of extravagant multimedia theater," wrote Joan Acocella. "Many of Balanchine's fans felt as if Farrell had run off with a biker."

As exiles go, this was a felicitous one. Farrell felt like the utter strangeness of the environment allowed her to adapt to it without forsaking her core identity. "Although I transferred my present allegiance," she wrote, "I did not forget who was who or what was what artistically." She never stopped thinking of herself as a Balanchine dancer, and even though Béjart was dumbfounded at his luck—no one, he said, made him as good as she did; she was like a violin, "the music comes out from her body"—he never felt he had a claim on her. She was Balanchine's "spiritual daughter," he said.

In her Belgian years, in many ways, the daughter grew up. She had a new boss she could approach from a place of preexisting authority. She had a new space to play in. And she had a husband she could be with freely. Farrell said that she especially liked checking in to hotel rooms and asking for a double bed.

For his part, after Farrell left, Balanchine was devastated. It took him nearly a year to produce his next work—a ballet called *Who Cares?* Then in 1972 he staged a festival in homage to another of his essential collaborators, the composer Igor Stravinsky, who had died the year before. The pieces burnished Balanchine's sterling reputation and he carried on.

Farrell made several overtures to Balanchine over the years, but he didn't respond. In 1974, five years after their break, she went to see the New York City Ballet in its summer home at Saratoga Springs, New York. Afterward, she sent Balanchine the shortest letter she had ever written.

Dear George,

As wonderful as it is to see your ballets, it is even more wonderful to dance them. Is this impossible?

Love,
Suzi

Balanchine's assistant arranged for the two to meet as she passed through New York City on her way to Brussels. They hugged, opened a bottle of wine, and it was "just sort of like: 'Well, when do we get to work?'" Farrell remembered.

Balanchine cast her in *Symphony in C*—the piece she was to dance the night she'd left the company. In Farrell's dressing room, Sophie Pourmel hooked her into the same white tutu she had taken away six years before.

But things had changed. A new, more durable, more reliable tension existed between them that allowed for a new kind of closeness. She was no longer his "alabaster princess" (Balanchine's words) or "this virginal girl in white" (Farrell's). In the first new Balanchine piece made on her, *Tzigane,* Farrell was a gypsy—"a grownup, sexy, alluring woman," says the writer Toni Bentley, who cowrote Farrell's memoir, "a powerful, solitary woman—not a child anymore." Instead of having her wear the traditional white, he dressed her in a skirt made of shredded red, gold, and black ribbons. Even the old dances took on new life. "There's much more substance to *Diamonds* than there was in the days when Farrell first danced it," Arlene Croce wrote in the *New Yorker* in 1975. "Then it seemed the iciest and emptiest of abstractions with, in the woman's part, an edge of brazen contempt. Farrell, a changed and immeasurably enriched dancer, in stepping back into the ballet has discovered it. She is every bit as powerful as she was before, but now she takes responsibility for the discharge of power; she doesn't just fire away. And whereas she used to look to me like an omnicompetent blank, she's now dynamic, colorful, tender."

When the two resumed their work together, George Balanchine apologized to Farrell for coming on too strong—she said she thought it was a "confession." She remembers him saying, "It was not right. I was an old man. I never should have thought about you that way. You should have had your freedom; you should have had your marriage."

She refused to accept the apology, but the power of their new terms could be seen onstage. Balanchine had always idealized women and given them some authority, but he undermined them too. Now, he had a genuinely powerful woman dancing for him. "Of course," Croce wrote, "the autonomy of the ballerina is an illusion, but Farrell's is the extremest form of this illusion we have yet seen, and it makes *Diamonds* a riveting spectacle about the freest woman alive."

The reconciliation is satisfying, as it was to watch Springsteen return to the stage with the E Street Band and Clarence Clemons in 1999. Yet there is a tinge of melancholy in the recognition that, in art and in life, there is an uncrossable expanse, that for Farrell and Balanchine, or Bruce and the Big Man—for any two people, creative potential depends on separation. One common stage in a pair's lifespan is to come to submit to this fact. In Marina Abramović and Ulay's early collaborations, they shouted at each other, smacked into each other, clamped their mouths together and breathed in and out to the point of near suffocation. But the signature piece of their later years was *Nightsea Crossing*, in which they sat across from each other at a table, silent, motionless, for an entire gallery day—fasting for twenty-four hours, to boot. They performed the piece for ninety nonconsecutive days; they once did it sixteen days straight.

Vincent van Gogh bucked and fought the distance between himself and his brother, but he, too, submitted in the end. In his teens and twenties, Vincent pined for Theo constantly; he regarded boundaries between them as birds regard fences. He shifted so fluidly between "I" and "we" that he seems to have been genuinely confused about the difference. At times he waxed romantic, calling himself and Theo *compagnons de voyage*. At times he turned bitter, telling Theo that if he were to withhold funds, he might as well "cut off my head."

After two years in Paris—during which Vincent often bucked his brother like a bull—he decided he must go south, and he asked the painter Emile Bernard to help him arrange his old studio in Theo's apartment, "so that my brother will feel that I am still here." Once he arrived in Arles, he immediately began to pine again. "During the journey," he wrote Theo in February 1888, "I thought at least as much about you as about the new country I was seeing. But I tell myself that you'll perhaps come here often yourself later on."

"It would be the paradox of Vincent's life," writes George Howe Colt, "that he longed for family, for friendship, for community, but was temperamentally unable to get along with people." At Arles, he dreamed of a community of painters, with himself and Theo as first residents, then he began to fixate on the painter Paul Gauguin as the "father superior" of their art monastery. Persuaded that disciples would follow, Vincent bought twelve chairs to go in the three-room house, which Gauguin, in an answer to Vincent's prayers—and as a grudging submission to his own need for Theo's money—came to share.

Vincent dreamed of connections like handshakes, but his relationships often led to raised fists. Seven weeks into the experiment, Gauguin told Theo it was "absolutely necessary" that he leave. This loss for Vincent came around the same time as the news of Theo's great romance. By December 21, 1888, he was engaged to be married. He wrote his mother and sister immediately, and Vincent, too, may have received word by December 23, 1888. That night, he quarreled with Gauguin, then cut off a portion of his left ear and left it in a box for a girl at a brothel.

Afterward, Vincent asked to go to an asylum, and he seems to have had a revelation around this time, not just that he was subject to fits of madness, but that he was essentially separate, his own vessel on vast and stormy seas. Into his letters crept a recognition of Theo as his own man. Vincent even seemed to speak of their relationship as something past: "The kindness you have had for me isn't lost," he wrote Theo, "since you have had it and you still have it . . . Only transfer this affection onto your wife as much as possible."

Just as Vincent's ear-cutting frenzy coincided with Theo's engagement, so did he fall apart around the time of Theo's wedding and at the birth of Theo's child. Yet between the fuzzy madnesses of his breakdowns, his work took on a crystalline sanity, and perhaps both his mental nadirs and creative pinnacles proceeded from a sense of the only actual way he could reach others: through his work. From behind the window of the asylum at Saint-Rémy-de-Provence, he found elements of the scene that would become *De Sterrennacht* (*The Starry Night*), where a towering cypress is itself towered over by a swirling sky and stars.

Vincent had once longed for a communion with others that I've described as "utopian," It's the perfect last word for our inquiry into distance. Derived in English from the Greek prefix εὖ ("good" or "well"), it alludes of course to a desirable or even perfect place. But, in fact, the first use of "utopian," in a 1516 book by Sir Thomas More, meant the opposite: More coined the word with a prefix οὐ ("not") that had the same "eu" sound, but quite a different meaning—the word originally meant "no place." It alluded to an idea of perfection that can never exist.

Likewise, creative intimacy is a sacred ideal that we reach for and touch but never finally grasp. Emily Dickinson's cool, decisive move to maintain her separateness and relate across an expanse is in perfect contrast to van Gogh's erratic, sloppy trajectory. She was all cat, slinking away, arching her back. He was all dog, bounding into areas forbidden him, whimpering when put into his cage.

Yet both lived out an extreme of the essential human paradox, where intimacy coincides with separateness, and the essential creative paradox, where expression comes, at least in some measure, from frustration. When he made *The Starry Night*, Vincent van Gogh was thirty-six years old and unspeakably lonely, and what he did from this loneliness was paint and write and send his paintings and letters north to his brother—letters that, Adam Gopnik has written, constitute "the longest, warmest, most attentive account of an artist's life seen from the inside that has ever been written."

After reading the letters (and responding to many), Theo tucked them in his bureau; the canvases he stowed under the bed, under the sofa, under the cupboards. He arranged and rearranged them on his walls. "In the bedroom, the 'Orchards in Bloom,'" Johanna van Gogh-Bonger, Theo's wife, wrote. "In the dining room over the mantelpiece, the 'Potato Eaters'; in the sitting room . . . the great 'Landscape from Arles' and the 'Night View on the Rhône.'" His brother was, physically and psychologically, so very far away. But it was also as though Theo lived inside his brother's mind.

If there were only two men in the world, how would they get on? They would help one another, harm one another, flatter one another, slander one another, fight one another, make it up; they could neither live together nor do without one another.

— Voltaire

In Italy, for thirty years under the Borgias, they had warfare, terror, murder, and bloodshed, but they produced Michelangelo, Leonardo da Vinci, and the Renaissance. In Switzerland, they had brotherly love. They had five hundred years of democracy and peace, and what did that produce? The cuckoo clock.

— Orson Welles as Harry Lime in The Third Man

✳

PART V

THE INFINITE GAME

In 1967, ten years after he met Paul McCartney at St. Peter's Church in suburban Liverpool, John Lennon told the story of the meeting to a journalist named Hunter Davies. He remembered Paul playing guitar and how good he was and how much he "dug him." And he remembered worrying what would happen if Paul joined the band. "I'd been kingpin up to then," Lennon said. "Now, I thought, if I take him on, what will happen? It went through my head that I'd have to keep him in line if I let him join."

In 1970, talking with Jann Wenner of *Rolling Stone,* Lennon returned to the same dilemma: "I had a group. I was the singer and the leader; I met Paul and I made a decision whether to — and he made a decision too — have him in the group: Was it better to have a guy who was better than the people I had in, obviously, or not? To make the group stronger, or to let me be stronger?"

Knowing what we know about partnerships, it's tempting to call out an error in Lennon's thinking, to correct his binary view of things. After all, Paul made the group stronger, and he made John stronger. Their confluence gave each man part ownership of an enterprise with infinite value. As they took up distinct and congruent roles, John could, with Paul's help, be even more himself. With sufficient distance, he had ample space to pursue that self — aesthetically and intellectually, as an artist and a druggie, an optimist and a malcontent, a lover and a loner.

Yet alongside the supreme support of their partnership ran audacious challenge. Yearning for interdependence entwined with desire to triumph. And so Lennon's thinking was not in error. Rather, it reflected an inherently complex position: to take someone on in the sense of "hiring, engaging, joining with" coexisted with the other meaning of that phrase, "to oppose in competition."

This tension applies to all great creative pairs, though it manifests in a variety of ways. Sometimes, competition is so subtle that it takes care to even see. Elsewhere it is so conspicuous that it seems strange to call the competitors a "pair." But, in fact, rivals are often dependent on each other, improve each other, and even jointly effect a singular creative outcome. Looking at them in the light of creative partnership, we see in stark relief what applies to all pairs: the potential of negation combined with affirmation, opposition with coordination, competition with cooperation. These sets of qualities charge creative work like the positive and negative poles of a battery. What keeps the current flowing? And what causes a short circuit?

17

My Most Intimate Enemy

Creative Foils

In the mid-1970s, at Everett High School in Lansing, Michigan, nobody could touch Earvin Johnson Jr. on the basketball court. He was only fifteen years old but a local sportswriter had already dubbed him "Magic." "You're special, Earvin," his coach told him. "But you can't stop working hard. Just remember — there's someone out there who is just as talented as you, and he's working just as hard. Maybe even harder." Magic nodded politely but he was thinking, *I'd like to meet this guy, because I haven't seen him.*

"Truthfully," he reflected later, "I wasn't sure anybody like that existed."

He did exist. His name was Larry Bird. He grew up in French Lick, Indiana, with two older brothers. "Mark and Mike were older than me," Bird said, "and that meant they were bigger, stronger, and better — in basketball, baseball, everything. They pushed me. They drove me. I wanted to beat them more than anything, more than anyone. But I hadn't met Magic yet. Once I did, he was the one I *had* to beat."

His freshman year of college, Magic saw Bird on the cover of *Sports Illustrated* and was "blown away by his stats" (32.8 points per game on average and 13.3 rebounds). When the two played in a tournament, he saw that it wasn't just numbers. "I couldn't wait," Magic said, "to call home and tell my boys, 'Man, this dude named Larry Bird is for real.'" Bird was just as impressed: "I've just seen the best player in college basketball," he told his brother Mark. "It's Magic Johnson."

On March 26, 1979, they faced off in the NCAA finals. A sophomore at Michigan State, Magic was now a *Sports Illustrated* cover boy too. A senior, Bird had led Indiana State through an undefeated season. Thirty-five million people — still the largest audience ever for a college championship — watched the game, and they saw Indiana take a drubbing. Double-teamed, Bird missed fourteen of twenty-one shots. When the buzzer sounded, the dueling stars were the very picture of victory and defeat. As Magic, still panting from the game, wrapped one arm around his coach and the other around Bryant Gumbel for a postgame interview, Bird made his way to the Indiana bench, draped a towel over his head, and put his face in his hands. On national TV, Magic stuck out his tongue in delight, praised his coach, dodged the big question about when he'd leap to the NBA. Then the camera cut to Bird, now with his face buried in the towel.

Sports nicely illustrate the fundamentals of competition because they're built on what the philosopher James Carse calls "finite games" — clear contests, bounded in time, with rules designed to produce a winner and a loser (or rankings from the most to the least successful). Any impurities that leach in — a controversial call by the referee, say — are overwhelmed by the final score, the official record, the glum faces of postgame agony, and the raised arms of postgame thrill.

Though competition rouses us with specific promises of victory — a towering trophy, an impressive title — the most primal desire may be for triumph itself. Certainly, direct face-offs improve performance in all manner of conditions, an effect that has been validated empirically: One study found weightlifters able to bench-press an average of two kilograms (about four and a half pounds) more when competing with another person than when facing a crowd alone. Another found that people could squeeze a handgrip twenty-one seconds longer. Competition, compared to solo performance, has also been linked to increased heart rate and blood pressure, even when the challenge requires little physical exertion (as when study participants race toy cars).

What these studies suggest and measure, epic stories help us really see and feel — whether in business (Steve Jobs versus Bill Gates), politics (Abraham Lincoln versus Stephen Douglas), art (Pablo Picasso versus Henri Matisse), or advice-giving (Ann Landers versus Dear Abby). In sports alone, the sheer volume of epic pairings—Jack Nicklaus versus Arnold Palmer in golf, Muhammad Ali versus Joe Frazier in boxing, Chris Evert versus Martina Navratilova in tennis (and we could go on and on)—makes it seem like the rule, not the exception, that great work emerges from rivalry.

The irony is that, while an animating motivation comes from a desire to best someone—which is, at bottom, a desire for separation, for distinction—top players end up developing a strange attachment to one another, even a need for the other. Playing with the best brings out your best, and if the other guy is gunning to beat you, that may be bad for your stress level but it's ideal for your performance.

What makes the attachment between rivals all the more poignant is that defeats, setbacks, and even humiliations may in retrospect seem like a shove down a better path. By 1998, the contest between Steve Jobs (who'd been exiled from Apple and had just returned to save a near-bankrupt company) and Bill Gates was so lopsided that Gates told a journalist: "What I can't figure out is why he is even trying. He knows he can't win." But Jobs, by applying lessons learned in his exile (and by working effectively with others), would make Apple the most valuable company in the world. In his mid-forties, Abraham Lincoln (a one-term congressman and a prairie lawyer) found himself so outpaced by Stephen Douglas (an eminent U.S. senator) that he wrote in a note to himself: "With *me*, the race of ambition has been a failure—a flat failure; with *him* it has been one of splendid success." Yet Lincoln framed an antislavery platform in contrast to Douglas and rode that local rivalry to national renown. In the presidential inauguration of 1861, it was Douglas who held Lincoln's hat.

For stories of winning responses to stinging defeats, nothing beats the saga of Larry Bird and Magic Johnson. In the fall of 1979, Bird started as forward for the Boston Celtics and took his team to a 61–21 record. (The year before, they'd gone 29–53.) But the Celtics didn't make it to the finals; Bird watched the games at a Boston restaurant. In the sixth game, Magic Johnson led his Los Angeles Lakers to the title over the Philadelphia 76ers.

Not only that, but Magic was series MVP.

"I was pissed," Bird said. He was burning still from the NCAA finals, which even decades later he called the "biggest game of my life" and the "toughest loss I ever took." Now Bird considered himself down by *two*.

Bird didn't know it, but he had fueled Magic's performance. The day before game six, Magic had learned that Bird had won Rookie of the Year — he'd gotten sixty-three votes, compared to only three for Magic. "I was jealous and I was mad," Magic said. "I thought I had a great year. When I heard I only got three votes, I took it out on the Sixers. I wanted people to recognize my play the way they had recognized Larry's.

"It wasn't anything personal against Larry," Magic added. "Well, actually, it was."

Watching, anticipating, and responding to each other quickly came to feel like a necessity. Bird called the competition "a crutch" — "I had to have him there," he said. First thing every morning, he would look up Magic's stats in the newspaper. "I didn't care about anything else," Bird said. Magic felt the same. "When the new schedule would come out each year," he said, "I'd grab it and circle the Boston games. To me, it was the two and the other eighty."

In their second NBA season, in 1981, Bird's Celtics took the NBA championship. The next year, Magic's Lakers reclaimed it. At last, in 1984, the two met in the finals — which Bird relished as a long-awaited rematch of their college duel. The Celtics won in seven games. "I finally got him," Bird told his teammate Quinn Buckner late into the celebratory night. "I finally got Magic."

Magic was crushed. "It's probably the first time ever in my life I was depressed," he said. "It took me years to get over it," he wrote in 2009. "Actually, I'm not sure I'm over it yet." Bird savored his rival's pain. "I hope he was hurt," he said around the same time. "I hope it killed him . . . to not only win the game makes you feel good but just knowing that the other guy was suffering, and you know he was."

Yet even this suffering was stimulating. "That championship series redefined his whole career," said Magic's teammate Michael Cooper, "because he never stopped working after that." In 1985, the teams faced off again for the championship. This time, the Lakers took it in six games.

Even their off-court encounters were dramatic. Though Johnson often made friendly overtures, Bird always rebuffed him. In 1986, Converse introduced a Bird shoe and a Magic shoe, and the company persuaded them to shoot a commercial playing off their rivalry. Bird surprised Magic by making small talk between shots and even inviting him for lunch. When they met the next season, Magic found himself saying, "Hey, let's go have a beer." Bird said no way. "If me and him got to be really good friends . . . he could still play the same game," Bird said. "I couldn't. That's just the way it is."

Magic and Bird were foils for each other. *Foil* is the perfect word, because it has two complementary meanings. As a verb, from the French *fouler* (to trample), *foil* means "to prevent something undesirable; to impede, hinder, or scuttle." As a noun meaning "a thing that by contrast emphasizes the qualities of another," it derives from the practice of putting metal foil (from the Latin *folium*) underneath a gem to enhance its shine.

Foils who seek to stymie each other can also bring out each other's best qualities. "If I'd beaten Pete [Sampras] more often," Andre Agassi writes in his memoir, "or if he'd come along in a different generation, I'd have a better record, and I might go down as a better player, but I'd be less." Until recently, research psychology had no vocabulary for these relationships, because it studied competition only through staged encounters. The subjects were always strangers and they performed in contests with a zero-sum game — one guy wins, the other loses, and that's that. But over time, mere competition can evolve into rivalry, which the scholar Gavin Kilduff and colleagues define as a "subjective competitive relationship," where the stakes feel higher "independent of the objective characteristics of the situation."

Put another way: Competition is when you *need* to kick the guy's ass to get what you want. Rivalry is when you *want* to kick the guy's ass. But such animosity — such oppositional passion — can actually lead both parties to each get more of what they want. In a study of runners, Kilduff found that the presence of a true rival in a race (as opposed to mere competitors) led to faster times — an average of twenty-five seconds in a 5K.

Animating passions are hardly restricted to sports. In 1958, *Life* magazine ran a feature on twin sisters, daughters of Jewish immigrants, who "in two short years of rivalry have made themselves the most widely read and most quoted women in the world." Their names were Esther Pauline Friedman and Pauline Esther Friedman but they had come to be known as Ann Landers and Dear Abby, respectively. As young women, they were so bonded that they married in a double wedding. Their husbands ended up in the same army unit in World War II and worked together after the war—but Pauline's husband had the edge over Esther's in business. Esther moved to Chicago, where she won a competition to become Ann Landers. In San Francisco, Pauline got herself hired for a new column written under the name Abigail Van Buren.

Two years later, the sisters' columns were in hundreds of papers, and each woman received thousands of letters a week. They answered every one that came with a return address. Both women were five two, had jet-black hair, and weighed 108 pounds, and when the reporter from *Life* called, he found that they ran their days the same way: each one sent her family off in the morning and then sat down in front of the typewriter with yellow paper and endless cups of coffee.

Though Ann had her column first, Abby's was the first one run in New York City. "I understand why she's disturbed," Abby said. "She wanted to be the first violin in the school orchestra, but I was. She swore she'd marry a millionaire but I did. I'm not trying to be the champion. It's just like playing poker. If you don't *have* to win you get the cards, and she's always just had to win."

"That's her fantasy," Ann answered. "She's just like a kid who beats a dog until somebody looks, and then starts petting it."

The real field of competition was in the number and size of the newspapers carrying their columns. "Their fight for newspapers is a curious battle," *Life* reported, "for neither can help selling the other's column. As soon as a newspaper buys one, its rival in town is virtually forced to buy the other to match reader interest. As a result the two women constantly roar along, neck and neck, whipping like mad, yelling complaints, and kicking dust."

With their styles remarkably similar, each accused the other of imitation. *Life* reported that Ann had sworn off seeing or talking to her sister. "When is she going to quit behaving like this?" Abby asked. Ann asked: "How long am I going to have her hanging over me?" The *Life* piece ended with them answering their own questions.

DEAR ABBY: Never.
ANN LANDERS: Forever.

The conditions for outstanding rivalries bear the same essential features as all great creative pairings. To start, rivals tend to have vast differences in temperament or style alongside extreme similarities in ambition and vision. Bird, who called himself the "hick from French Lick," blended in well in Boston, a city proud of its stolid working class. He was an aggressive player and didn't mind trash-talking and mixing it up with the toughest guys in the league. In scuffles on and off the court, Bird gave as good as he got. He was also taciturn and reclusive. He was rarely seen off the court, except for warm-weather Saturdays, when he mowed his front lawn. Magic, by contrast, luxuriated in the sunny scene of Los Angeles. He celebrated ordinary wins as if they were championship games and enjoyed himself at the Playboy Mansion. "It's just all one big party," Magic said, "one big show, big, big fun."

Yet Bird and Magic played so much alike that the Boston sportswriter Charles Pierce called them "two halves of the same brain." Both had the talent to hot-dog but focused on setting up other players and fueling their teams. *Selfless* was a description commonly applied to both. "That's why we hated each other," Magic said, "because we were mirrors of each other."

Kilduff has found that rivalries are often spurred by similarity. We tend to oppose people whom we can identify with, and rivalries thrive when people are closely matched. That's because contests decided by small margins are likely to elicit counterfactual thoughts, like *If things had gone slightly differently* . . . This memory acts as a spur. "I used to have this thing in my head in the summer," Bird said in a 2012 joint interview with Magic. "I'd go shoot seven hundred jump shots that day and I'd get ready to leave and I'd go, 'God, I know he's shooting eight hundred.' And it would drive me back out there." "I was a thorn in his side," Magic said, and vice versa: "Larry made me have sleepless nights, because I was scared to death that I knew he could beat me. That's what a great player does to you."

Though Magic and Bird are supersize figures, all of us are motivated by opposition—whether tangible or imagined—because human beings have evolved to handle threats. One theory suggests that the rapid increase in brain size that made us human in the first place can be linked to the ability to identify and respond to same-species enemies. "We have been mentally contracted," writes the psychologist David Barash, "to test ourselves when surrounded not only by those who wish us well but also by those who wish us ill."

Another lens on the value of enemies comes from narrative psychology — the study of how we think, act, and frame our identities according to stories we tell ourselves. "We find that when it comes to the big choices people make — Should I marry this person? Should I take this job? Should I move across the country? — they draw on these stories implicitly, whether they know they are working from them or not," the psychologist Dan McAdams said. These life stories, McAdams found, have the same essential features of a movie we'd see at the multiplex or a fairy tale we'd read to a six-year-old. That is, they all have settings, scenes, characters, plots, themes.

And antagonists. Where would Sherlock Holmes be without Professor Moriarty — or Harry Potter without Lord Voldemort? True stories are no exception: whether it's Brave Orchid in Maxine Hong Kingston's *The Woman Warrior* or General Motors' CEO Roger Smith in Michael Moore's *Roger & Me,* the bad guy is a staple, and he's a foil in both meanings of the word. In everyday life, foils may even contribute to our psychological health. McAdams's research has found that "generative" adults — those who have a "concern for and commitment to promoting the development and well-being of future generations"— tend to tell life stories of redemption. In other words, in their minds, they've been on the field with enemies that they've met and obstacles that they've overcome. Another study found that people who benefit most from psychotherapy tend to characterize their problems as outside antagonists. They name their foes — the way Winston Churchill called his depression "the black dog"— and fashion narratives about conquering them. "The story," the psychologist Jonathan Adler said, "is one of victorious battle."

Yet, while it's our nature to seek victory over rivals, if we are to create and achieve, we also need ongoing challenges. From my research, I've come to see three key benefits rivals offer.

First, they push us to work harder. This is *motivation,* as basic a drive in performance as hunger is in physiology. Rivals quicken the blood, animate the spirit.

Second, they model what we need to do. This is *inspiration,* and whether it comes from an example we want to follow, one we want to reject, or one we want to improve on, the impact is much the same.

Third, they keep us in the game. This is *dedication* — perseverance, persistence, tenacity, the power to not just approach a task with zeal but stick with it even when we want to quit.

Just as traditional collaborators need time to achieve confluence, rivals tend to grow entwined over time. Gavin Kilduff has found that the degree of past competition — in quantity and quality — increases present rivalry. The oppositional energy increases, but so does the association of the partner with improved performance. Eventually, rivals at the top of their game may find that no one else really understands them but their opponents; no one else is flying so high, where the air is so thin. William James described his former student Dickinson Miller as "my most penetrating critic and intimate enemy."

In 1989, Larry Bird published his memoir, and Magic Johnson wrote the introduction: "It's like a marriage," Magic said of their bond, "and we can't ever divorce each other."

In the late 1980s, for Bird, the competition with Magic was the only thing keeping him in the game. In 1985, he grievously injured his back while laying a driveway for his mother in French Lick. The pain became so severe that his doctor compared it to getting a finger stuck in a car door—"and somebody is still pushing on the door," the doctor said. Bird thought he might end up in a wheelchair. "I probably should have retired in '88, '89," he said. "But it's that competition. Maybe one more chance for me and Magic to get together in the finals."

No one suspected how it would end. In the fall of 1991, a few weeks into his thirteenth season, Magic Johnson went before cameras at the Los Angeles Forum and told the world that he had contracted HIV and that he would retire from basketball, effective immediately. Given the state of treatment at the time, this diagnosis seemed like a death sentence. Bird told reporters he was "depressed." He played that night but he said later: "I didn't want to be there that night. First time ever . . . had no feel for the game, you know. Just wasn't a good time to be out there. Never had that before." With Johnson gone, Bird said, "I didn't check the papers anymore. It didn't matter. I still wanted to compete but it wasn't the same, it really wasn't."

After the season ended, Bird announced his own retirement. His ongoing back problems had caused him to miss thirty-seven games, but still, it was the absence of his rival he pointed to: "Knowing that he's not there," he said, "it wouldn't feel right."

18

Luke Skywalker and Han Solo

Creative Pairs and Coopetition

For nearly fifty years, Henri Matisse and Pablo Picasso pushed each other, goaded each other, drew from each other, and tried to best each other. It may not be too much to say that, over the course of their careers, they made each other — and shaped the standards for modern art in the twentieth century. In the midst of the landmark international exhibition *Matisse Picasso* in 2003, many observers set the artists against each other, casting their rivalry as a "chess game" (*Smithsonian*) or a "duel" (*New York Times*). "Each time I visited the show at the Tate," wrote the art historian John Richardson in *Vanity Fair*, "acquaintances would come up and ask me whether I thought Matisse or Picasso was the winner. 'You idiot — you are missing the point,' I told one of them. 'The show is not a boxing match.'"

But what, then, to call it? "According to most of the contributors to the catalogue," Richardson wrote, "it is more of a dialogue, although, considering the number of sparks these two artists strike off of each other — sparks that illuminate so much in the work of both — the word 'dialogue' seems too tame." He finally suggested calling them "secret sharers," after the short story by Joseph Conrad.

The trouble here isn't merely semantic. It actually represents a real conceptual challenge. To understand competition as a creative force, we've looked first to understand its potential to spur us on and lead us to attachments with those we oppose. For this task, contests like chess or boxing or basketball serve as useful metaphors and reliable illustrations. *Finite* games — discrete, measurable encounters, as in sports or elections or fights for market share — articulate something essential about how people go toe to toe.

Yet, just as students must master algebra to take on calculus, we must grasp competition to look beyond it. Most creative work does not post to a scoreboard. Encounters that end with a winner and a loser are rarely the most interesting — even in sports. Any fan who has ever muttered, with a broken heart, "We'll get them next year," knows that any one matchup — no matter how much it matters — is embedded in an ongoing narrative.

The critical distinction, as developed by the philosopher James Carse, is between the finite game and the *infinite game.* "A finite game is played for the purpose of winning," Carse wrote, "an infinite game for the purpose of continuing the play." Where finite games follow predetermined rules, intended to eliminate players until one stands on top alone, infinite games are constantly adjusted so that both players can remain standing. Where finite games are impersonal and hew to established forms, infinite games are peculiar to their players and grow increasingly distinct. Finite games are like formal debate, where artificial constraints impose order. Infinite games are like the grammar of a living language, where organic growth magnifies complexity. Where finite games hinge on competition, infinite games operate at the intersection of competition and cooperation.

Motivated as we are to spot enemies and define ourselves against them, these intersecting qualities can be hard to see. Consider the moment in 1997 when Steve Jobs returned to Apple and announced at Macworld Expo that he had negotiated a $150 million investment from Microsoft, settled lawsuits between the two tech giants, and pledged to make Microsoft's Internet Explorer the default web browser on Macintosh computers. Along with scant applause, boos and hisses rolled through the crowd; in one video, we see a man cover his face with his hands in amazed dismay. Microsoft had become, in the eyes of many Mac loyalists, the Evil Empire. To Apple's faithful, Jobs's announcement felt like Luke Skywalker kneeling before Darth Vader.

But Microsoft and Apple had long been more like Luke Skywalker and Han Solo — compatriots in an uneasy alliance. They were actually allies first. In 1978 the Apple II shipped with a version of BASIC software developed by Microsoft, tweaked by Apple, and given the mash-up name Applesoft BASIC. In 1983, Gates played along with a mock version of *The Dating Game* that Jobs hosted to celebrate the Macintosh, and Gates noted on-stage that the next year he expected half of Microsoft's revenue to come from Macintosh applications.

Only later did their central competition emerge, over the market share for their distinct operating systems. Then, just as Microsoft seemed poised for a triumph, it stepped in to aid Apple, eschewing victory in one arena for broader benefits that included ongoing profits from its Mac software and a critical boost Apple could give it in its war against Netscape. (The browser wars appear quaint now but seemed critical at the time.)

Coopetition in business — which the *Financial Times* defines as "combining the advantages of" cooperation and competition to create "a bigger market in complementary areas"— is common. Think of multiple gas stations at the same intersection — the customers each station loses are more than offset by increased awareness of the product — or rival movie studios jointly financing a picture. Toyota and PSA Peugeot Citroën made a minicar together and marketed it under different names. Philips and Sony ran the R&D together to create the compact disc.

But the coexistence of cooperation and competition is more than institutional. It's basic to human relations and the human psyche. Everyone, the psychologist Elaine Aron explains, has two primary relational impulses: to link, or find common ground, and to rank, or establish hierarchical positions.

Even this language may understate the universality of the phenomenon, because it suggests extremes of connection or opposition. But each quality may manifest in far more subtle ways. At bottom, cooperation is a tendency, wrote the author V. Frank Asaro, to "unite, bind, attract, or be orderly or collective." Cooperation is often implicit, as when two people agree to play by the rules of a game or when people obey laws or customs. Competition, meanwhile, is any action contrary to others — any move to "separate, break apart, disunite, be chaotic, or become individualistic." Considered in this broad way, competition doesn't need to be a knockout punch or a lacerating attack. It could be a mischievous shove or a pointed criticism.

Most members of pairs are in coopetition most of the time — though they may not know it. When I asked the novelist Sheila Heti if she felt competition with her creative partner, the painter and filmmaker Margaux Williamson, she wrote me: "I don't think so. Because we have different mediums. How does a writer compete with a painter?"

She went on: "But I can be urged on to doing better work when I see that she's moving quickly in her work, or if her paintings are really great that week, then I can feel like I'm falling behind or slacking off, and I want to do better in my work. I guess they call that 'healthy competition.' I don't want to 'beat' her but I don't want to fall behind."

Two things struck me in this response. First, *comparison* is a species of competition, insofar as it emerges from a sense of distinction and difference — the feeling of being stirred, provoked, swept along by a recognition of the other's separateness. William James calls this — I love the phrase — "the emulous passion," and in an 1892 lecture to teachers, he enjoined them to take it seriously. "The feeling of rivalry," he said, "lies at the very basis of our being, all social improvement being largely due to it . . . The deepest spring of action in us is the sight of action in another. The spectacle of effort is what awakens and sustains our own effort." Of course, he recognized that just as "imitation slides into emulation, so emulation slides into *Ambition;* and ambition connects itself closely with *Pugnacity* and *Pride*." These five instinctive tendencies ("the ambitious impulses") can be hard to separate, he said, and he understood how pride and pugnacity ought be tempered. But even still, the potency of the feelings couldn't be ignored. "Pugnacity need not be thought of merely in the form of physical combativeness," James said.

It can be taken in the sense of a general unwillingness to be beaten by any kind of difficulty. It is what makes us feel "stumped" and challenged by arduous achievements, and is essential to a spirited and enterprising character. We have of late been hearing much of the philosophy of tenderness in education; "interest" must be assiduously awakened in everything, difficulties must be smoothed away. *Soft* pedagogics have taken the place of the old steep and rocky path to learning. But from this lukewarm air the bracing oxygen of effort is left out. It is nonsense to suppose that every step in education *can* be interesting. The fighting impulse must often be appealed to. Make the pupil feel ashamed of being scared at fractions, of being "downed" by the law of falling bodies; rouse his pugnacity and pride, and he will rush at the difficult places with a sort of inner wrath at himself that is one of his best moral faculties. A victory scored under such conditions becomes a turning-point and crisis of his character. It represents the high-water mark of his powers, and serves thereafter as an ideal pattern for his self-imitation. The teacher who never rouses this sort of pugnacious excitement in his pupils falls short of one of his best forms of usefulness.

Sheila Heti's description of "healthy competition" resonates with what James described here as a salutary pugnacity: "I'm not going to be left behind." But the critical point is that this sense of being roused and stimulated, this incitement of the "fighting impulse" that surely belongs in the category of ranking ("I must not be left on the bottom") is also intricately entwined with the tendency of linking. My impression is that Heti's desire is not to get on top and stay there but to join her partner on a higher plane — or perhaps to go even higher, which would only spur on Margaux's emulous passions. This is the key play in the infinite game.

In the fall of 1966, during a stretch of nine weeks away from the Beatles, John Lennon wrote a song on acoustic guitar. He was in rural Spain on the set of a movie called *How I Won the War*. He recorded his first demo there and a second in his home studio several weeks later. On November 24, he played it for the band and its engineers at the EMI Studios on Abbey Road in London. Four weeks later, after scores of hours of studio time, they had a final cut of "Strawberry Fields Forever," and that's when Paul McCartney brought in the song that would become "Penny Lane."

It was a practice, Paul said, of he and John "answering each other's songs." "He'd write 'Strawberry Fields,'" Paul said, "I'd go away and write 'Penny Lane' . . . to compete with each other. But it was very friendly competition because we were both going to share in the rewards anyway . . . But it was this"— Paul stretched his hands out so the fingers faced each other and put one above the other until both were over his head. "We'd get better and better all the time."

The metaphor "answering each other" is apt, because John and Paul worked together — and opposed each other — like a great piece of dialogue. John's song was set in one of the most memorable spots of his childhood, the Strawberry Field orphanage, whose sprawling grounds he'd often visited with his aunt Mimi or other kids in his gang. The song placed a narrator in situ, not just singing about a place but *taking* us there, singing from there, asking questions that had preoccupied him since he was five years old: whether life is real or a dream; whether he was alone in the world in his own "tree"; whether he was "high or low"—above others or below them.*

"Penny Lane" reflects the same structure as though through a funhouse mirror. For his Liverpool mother lode, Paul chose the junction where the 46 and 99 buses terminated. "John and I would often meet at Penny Lane," Paul said. The song itself is an effort at meeting. Like John, Paul not only puts his narrator in the scene but has him self-consciously enter it.

McCartney's song, too, used a landmark to explore something psychological. It was typical that Lennon made his own questions pretty clear in the song—and then, when reflecting on it later, put his finger directly on them, or tried to anyway. ("Am I crazy or am I a genius?" he said was the question of "Strawberry Fields Forever.") It was typical that Paul's meaning was harder to penetrate, and he never really explicated the song. On top of picture-book images in "Penny Lane" of a barber and a fireman going about their orderly way, he overlaid this reflection: "Very strange." It is strange. The skies are alternately blue and bursting with rain. And the song is set simultaneously "in summer" and (with a nurse selling poppies, as was done for Remembrance Day) in November.

Rooted in a common exploration, the songs sharply expose the distinctions between John and Paul. Where "Strawberry Fields Forever" is, musically, "lazily horizontal," wrote Ian MacDonald, "Penny Lane" is "breezily vertical in tune and harmony." Where John seemed to want to use art to explore life, Paul's conception of art and life were deeply blurred. Where Lennon looked on the world and asked if it was real or a dream, McCartney looked on reality as a playwright would his characters.

---

* According to a tour guide at John's boyhood home, Mendips, when Mimi warned him that he'd get caught sneaking into Strawberry Field, he would say, "They're not going to hang me for it, Mimi," which gives new meaning to the song's key line: "Nothing to get hung about."

One finite game between John and Paul had to do with singles. "There was a little competition between Paul and I," John said, "as to who got the A-side"—the cut intended for DJs to play and critics to review, the contender for the charts. Over and over again, John and Paul each threw in his most powerful hand; both wanted to trump the other; both knew that they would pretty much share the pot—at least when it came to public appreciation and financial gain.

With "Strawberry Fields Forever" and "Penny Lane," the consensus emerged that they were both so promising that the label should present them as a "double A side." This is a precise illustration of James Carse's point that in infinite games, the rules change as needed so the players can keep playing.

"Imagine two people pulling on a rope," said George Martin, "smiling at each other and pulling all the time with all their might. The tension between the two of them made for the bond."

The coexistence of ranking and linking goes beyond human relationships. It's a basic part of nature, as in the uniting and dividing of atoms or the alliances and enmities that make up the food chain. From afar, we see an optimal point of tension between cooperation and competition—and we can easily see where one impulse gets out of hand, as when a parasite kills its host.

With humans, too, power alone is rarely satisfying and can actually be dispiriting if it isolates one from others. The magic mix is to have both power (command over resources) and authority or status (the respect that leads to affection, loyalty, and solidarity). Certainly, the most effective leaders have both: a strong CEO will have the power to hire and fire and the authority to inspire and direct.

Whether they see it or not, all competitors depend on the ecosystem around them—and pushing too hard against it will bring them down. Lance Armstrong took performance-enhancing drugs to ride better, rank higher, break away from the pack. But he ended up breaking the compact that made him legitimate—and lost everything.

It's also possible to be too cooperative. A 2012 study found that men seen as "agreeable"—trustworthy, straightforward, altruistic, compliant, modest, and tender-minded—made about 18 percent less than men who were seen as less agreeable. A smaller but still significant gap existed for women—"agreeable" females made about 5½ percent less than those who were not as agreeable. Another study suggests that excessive generosity is regarded as poorly as excessive selfishness.

Optimal *tension* between competition and cooperation is not the same as *balance*. "Balance," writes V. Frank Asaro, "equals motionlessness, equilibrium, steadiness; that is, lack of change." Similarly, the creativity researcher Alfonso Montuori writes, "Any system that focuses on order at the exclusion of disorder soon becomes a rigid, homogeneous equilibrium system where no change is likely or even possible."

For creative advancement, change is essential. And while all creative exchange will have a cooperative element, competition on the whole takes a slight edge. This may seem counterintuitive, since we generally yearn for order, unity, and connection. But progress depends on disorder and fluidity. Sometimes the best aids to our work are people who knock us most off balance.

For Pablo Picasso, some of the biggest jolts of his life came from Henri Matisse. When the two men first encountered each other, in early-twentieth-century Paris, Matisse was leading a movement of artists dubbed Les Fauves—"the Wild Beasts"—but he didn't look the part of a radical. A Frenchman from the north, he wore three-piece suits and had a trimmed reddish beard. His friends called him "the professor." "Tell the American people that I am a normal man," he told the *New York Times* in 1912, "that I am a devoted husband and father, that I have three fine children, that I go to the theater, ride horseback, have a comfortable home, a fine garden that I love, flowers, etc., just like any man."

Twelve years younger than Matisse, the Spaniard Picasso had another style entirely—mercurial rather than steady, impetuous rather than mannered. They presented a perfect contrast in many respects: While Matisse worked during the day, needing natural light and still lifes or models, Picasso worked at night, often from his imagination. While Matisse slowly and methodically developed an aesthetic, Picasso was quick and virtuosic and ravenous for new influences. Matisse was more socially adept, a natural charismatic in galleries and salons; Picasso assumed the air of a disaffected bohemian—and, with his awkward French, he genuinely struggled in high society. But he had a star's instinct for attention, starting with an unerring sense of what—and whom—he should take on.

From 1905 to 1907, Matisse painted and exhibited a series of pieces that quickly became the talk of the town — *La Femme au Chapeau* (*Woman with a Hat*), *Le Bonheur de Vivre* (*The Joy of Life*), and then *Nu Bleu* (*Blue Nude*). With his bright, jarring colors and strange human forms, Matisse introduced a startling roughness, even savagery, into the art scene, picking up where van Gogh and Gauguin and Cézanne had left off — and drawing fierce objections: when *Blue Nude* traveled to America, students at the Art Institute of Chicago held a mock trial charging Matisse with "artistic murder," "total degeneracy of color," and "general aesthetic aberration," and then burned the painting in effigy.

"Before *Blue Nude*," writes the art critic Tyler Green, "Picasso was aware of Matisse and his work, but he wasn't driven to respond to it (nor was Matisse paying that much attention to Picasso). *Blue Nude* changed all that . . . Picasso retired to his studio, wasn't seen for weeks, and only emerged when he'd finished a painting of five whores ready for the male gaze." The large canvas (eight feet high and seven feet eight inches wide) came after hundreds of sketches and studies. It was called *Les Demoiselles d'Avignon* (*The Young Ladies of Avignon*). Five naked prostitutes loom in the foreground looking at us even as we look at them — two with faces like African masks.

The painting was explosive even to the avant-garde. Picasso's dealer called it the "work of a madman." But it came to be seen widely as the single most significant work of twentieth-century art — the initiation of a style known as cubism and the first step toward disrupting the basic expectations of what art could do. Scholars consider Picasso's engagement with Matisse to be unmistakable. "By Picasso's desire to best the roughness and savagery of the *Blue Nude*," said the scholar Kirk Varnedoe, a curator of the international Matisse-Picasso exhibition in 2003, "he reached further than he might otherwise have reached for something even doubly savage and more aggressive and more transgressive than what Matisse had done."

However he had contributed to Picasso's *Demoiselles*, when Matisse saw it he was stunned. "What it did," Varnedoe said, "was push him back deeper into the western tradition, back to Giotto — back to the so-called Italian primitives . . . So that in a sense Matisse pushed Picasso in that direction and Picasso pushed Matisse in this direction, and they became more themselves by virtue of the challenge with the other."

Of course, as we zoom in on Picasso and Matisse, we shouldn't forget the big picture around them. Both were responding to many influences, chief among them Paul Cézanne's. And both had circles surrounding them. The *Demoiselles,* in fact, initiated an epic collaboration between Picasso and the painter Georges Braque, who was initially horrified by the image but soon began working side by side with Picasso (often literally), developing cubism. They became so bound up that Braque said they were "like mountain climbers roped together." Both Matisse and Picasso depended on collectors like Gertrude and Leo Stein, who arranged their first face-to-face meeting and invited both to their Saturday-evening salons.

The worlds of Picasso and Matisse grew bigger and bigger, but the unique place each man had for the other did not diminish; rather, it became magnified. "All things considered," Picasso said, "there is only Matisse." Matisse said, "Only one person has the right to criticize me, that is Picasso."

The story here is not of enemies turned friends but of enmity and comity intertwined, as in a double helix. When we see the mutual respect, and need, and opposition, we understand John Richardson's sneering response to the question of who "won" the Matisse-Picasso exhibition. In this kind of relationship, the last thing in the world you want is the other guy on the floor, unable to get up. The last thing you want is for the game to end.

19

"We All Want the Hand"

Power Clarity and Power Fluidity

Having grasped competition as an animating force and having seen how it becomes entwined with cooperation in an infinite game, we can see how both play out day to day, year to year. Traditional pairs, not just obvious rivals, rank and link, compare and cohere, *take each other on.* To properly view the dynamics of creative pairs, we must look at more than simple opposition and cooperation. We must look at differentials in power.

Power is a real and pervasive force in all relationships. It may be as apparent as medals on a uniform or as subtle as a downward glance. It may also be multifaceted and multilayered. But when you get down to it, one person is usually running the show. Or one person needs the other more. Or one person would find it easier to leave.

"Once in my life I would like the upper hand," George Costanza says in *Seinfeld.* "I have no hand, no hand at all. . . . How do I get the hand?"

"We all want the hand," Jerry answers. "Hand is tough to get. You gotta get the hand right from the opening."

So true. Let's look at the psychology of power. On the savanna, alpha males and females get the greatest prizes, and subordinates make obvious gestures of deference. The same is true in coffee shops and office parks, where people follow patterns flowing from their dominant or subordinate positions. "No two people can be half an hour together," Samuel Johnson said, "but one shall acquire an evident superiority over the other."

"It doesn't take a half hour," Richard Conniff points out in *The Ape in the Corner Office*. In a Stanford study, groups of male college freshmen given a problem to solve sorted themselves into hierarchies in less than fifteen minutes. Even five-year-olds quickly establish social ranks, which prove remarkably stable over time.

Deference hardly needs to be conscious, or even noticeable. "Researchers at Kent State University," Conniff writes, "study very low conversational frequencies. What they're listening to is a deep hum, below 500 hertz, vocal but not verbal, which runs like a foundation beneath speakers' words. In every conversation they have studied, the low-frequency tones of the two speakers quickly converge . . . They don't converge on some comfortable middle ground. Instead, they converge at the vocal level of the more dominant. That is, at some point in the conversation, one person submits and switches to the 'power signal' of the other." And whether they know it or not, observers of an exchange sense who is running the show — which itself can strengthen a hold on power. When researchers studied U.S. presidential debates, they found that in every election between 1960 and 2000, the candidate that adjusted to the other's timbre lost the popular vote.

Power relations affect far more than our vocal hum. People naturally come to differences over ideas and feelings, over grand schemes and minute logistics. In general, the person with power is the person whose position the other one adjusts toward. "One partner," the psychologist Daniel Goleman writes in *Social Intelligence,* "will make a larger emotional shift to converge with the other." Couples tacitly negotiate which partner will have more power in any given situation. Roles, in other words, may give each partner a power domain. (More on this soon.) Yet one member of a partnership will generally carry the day in one crucial respect — the power to affect how the other feels about him- or herself. "The less powerful partner," Goleman writes, "all in all makes the greater internal adjustments in their emotional convergence."

Power is to relationships what gravity is to matter. But unlike a concrete physical phenomenon, power's origins may be obscure or, to start, arbitrary. Being the boss can proceed simply from believing you're the boss — or just projecting the attitude. Attitude induces behavior; behavior leads to expectations; expectations harden into habit. All the while, the idea of power can lead to the actual fact of it, as one party garners the experience of leading or other concrete advantages that come with the top spot.

Though it may upset egalitarian fantasies, power asymmetry in itself is not problematic in relationships. To the contrary, lateral relationships may be less intimate than asymmetrical ones. Consider two busy colleagues who want to connect. The first one reaches out, but the second is busy and lets the call go to voice mail. The second returns the call at his convenience, but now the first one is otherwise occupied. Each one has agency — and they never talk on the phone.

But in an asymmetrical situation, the dominant partner determines the time for the call, the subordinate makes himself available, and the meeting proceeds, and the next meeting, and the one after that. Intimacy accrues by shared experiences, which in this case power disparity has facilitated.

In creative pairs, the power disparity may be clear and recognized, as when a chief like Steve Jobs works with a deputy like Jonathan Ive, or a choreographer like George Balanchine (effectively the CEO of his company) works with a dancer like Suzanne Farrell (effectively an employee). With other pairs, the leader may be apparent only to insiders, as with Trey Parker and Matt Stone (at *South Park,* remember, Trey is the quarterback) or James Watson and Francis Crick. When I interviewed Watson in 2013, nine years after Crick's death, he told me: "Recently, again, I've decided I'm bright, but it was really only because of the death of Crick. As long as Francis was alive, I knew my place." "Francis was the one whose regard moved Jim," a fellow scientist told writer Horace Freeland Judson.

The chief advantage of power clarity is absence of strife. "Although positions within a hierarchy are born from contest," wrote the primatologist Frans de Waal, "the hierarchical structure itself, once established, eliminates the need for further conflict. Obviously, those lower on the scale would have preferred to be higher, but they settle for the next best thing, which is to be left in peace. The frequent exchange of status signals reassures bosses that there is no need for them to underline their position by force."

One reason it makes sense for power disparities to show up in creative partnerships is that a powerful person, in any given situation, has greater access to certain modes of thinking. A number of experiments link a subject's feelings of power to his assumption that others should, and will, see the world as he does. For example, the psychologist Adam Galinsky primed volunteers to feel either powerful or powerless and then asked them to draw the letter *E* on their foreheads. The powerful ones were three times more likely to draw the *E* so that it was correct from their perspective when they were looking in a mirror but reversed to someone facing them.

Powerful people believe that their ideas matter. They get the draft done, build the prototype, ask for the meeting, and make the big pitch. The psychologist Amy Cuddy has found that even the physical posture of power improves performance. "Normally, what people do before they give a speech or go into a sales meeting is sit in a chair, hunching over their notes or their iPhone," Cuddy said. "That's the opposite of what you should be doing. You're making yourself tiny. Instead, you should be walking around the hallway, putting your arms up. Sit at your desk and put your feet up on it. Stand on your tiptoes with your hands in the air."

Yet every single advantage of power can become a disadvantage. People who are more focused on the view out of their own eyes may find their worlds blinkered and narrow. This is the flip side of Adam Galinsky's *E* study. The very move that reflects confidence also reflects inattention to the perspective of others.

This is a pervasive challenge for alphas — and for the cultures around them. According to the approach/inhibition theory, powerful people tend to talk more, interrupt others more, flirt more, and engage in conflict more readily than less powerful people. Left unchecked, they lose their inhibitions entirely. Think of Lyndon Johnson taking meetings while on the toilet or ex–Tyco CEO Dennis Kozlowski throwing a two-million-dollar party for his wife funded in part with company money. These are not stories of mere eccentricity or greed. Power itself does not corrupt, but *pure* power inevitably does. "The skills most important to obtaining power and leading effectively," observes the psychologist Dacher Keltner, "are the very skills that deteriorate once we have power."

"Make no mistake," write the executive coaches Kate Ludeman and Eddie Erlandson, authors of *The Alpha Male Syndrome*, "the world *needs* alpha males. When used appropriately, their courage, confidence, tireless energy, and fighting spirit make them natural leaders in competitive situations. The trouble comes when they use their exceptional strengths inappropriately or carry them to such extremes that they turn into tragic flaws: their confidence becomes arrogance, their toughness becomes belligerence, and their competitiveness becomes a fight to the death in which even teammates are seen as rivals that have to be vanquished." But these strengths and flaws tend to run together. In a survey of 1,507 subjects, Ludeman and Erlandson found that "in general the greater the strengths, the greater the risks." The risks are not just that other people in the organization might be unhappy. In experiments, people primed to feel powerful are more likely to assess others by drawing on stereotypes. One survey found that high-powered professors made less accurate judgments about the attitudes of their lower-power colleagues than those colleagues made about them. For good or for ill, the powerful person tends to see the world from his own point of view. Unchecked, this obviously becomes an enormous problem. And that's why, when we look at consistent, effective, long-term uses of power, we see powerful people turning to their less powerful colleagues for help. The more we look into this, the more it complicates our understanding of power in the first place.

While it's usually clear who has the upper hand in creative pairs, the leader-follower schism can't be absolute. This is the paradox of power dynamics, and it's not easy to summarize. Put one way, it sounds like a contradiction: *High-level creative exchange depends on both hierarchical and fluid power relationships.* Put another way, it sounds like a truism: *To be a strong pair, both members must be able to lead and follow.* As we'll see, research psychology helps anchor the paradox — and stories help bring it to life.

One way to glimpse its essence is to consider the dance of tango. The song "Takes Two to Tango" could be a theme song for this book. It was written by a team of singer-songwriters — Al Hoffman and Dick Manning — and covered in two famous duets by Ray Charles, first with Betty Carter and then with Aretha Franklin. Over the years, it's become a popular idiom for how two people are joined, unbreakable, essential to whatever situation is at play.

I had the song running in my head for some time before the question occurred to me: Why tango? I supposed it had to do with the catchy rhythm and alliteration of the title. But one day I had lunch with the novelist, memoirist — and tango dancer — Jillian Lauren, who told me that tango is actually the most social of dance forms. "Unlike the foxtrot or a waltz or something," she said, "tango doesn't have steps. It has a lot of technique, and it's a lot of work, but it doesn't have set moves that you learn and put into practice. It's really developed live in the exchange."

Then Jillian got to telling me about her experience starting out in tango and how hard she found it, as a woman, to be relegated to the position of follower. "For a strident feminist, it's really an emotional experience," she said, "because you're stepping into this whole other culture. To embrace the power of listening — it's just a really different thing."

According to Jamie Rose, the author of *Shut Up and Dance!*, a guide to relationships based on the principles of tango, among all the partner dances, it is "the most strictly lead/follow." "You can think of it as being like driving a car," Rose writes, "only one person at a time can take the wheel and steer." Yet Rose found that accepting this line of authority was immensely empowering for the follower.

Jillian had the same experience. "At the highest levels," she told me, "the leader is leading, absolutely, but part of leading is paying immensely close attention to the follower and her responses. And the follower is responding, but the nature of her response can, in an instant, change everything. The follower teaches the leader how to lead."

We can make this more concrete by looking again at the value of a subordinate person's perspective. Let's consider that university study that asked high-powered and low-powered professors to assess their colleagues. It turned out that people looking up the totem pole were far clearer about what was going on above them. And this is a common finding. Among siblings, several studies have found, younger brothers and sisters do better than their elders on tests assessing "theory of mind" — that is, the ability to grasp what others intend and believe. The Stanford psychologist Deborah Gruenfeld even found that U.S. Supreme Court decisions tended to be more nuanced when justices wrote from the minority.

Indeed, the low-powered perspective tends to bring with it greater awareness. "While powerful people are paying attention to the potential rewards," Richard Conniff writes, "disempowered people are paying attention to the likely costs. They have to stay alert to what's going on around them because they are more vulnerable to threats of all kinds, from layoffs to nasty assignments nobody else wants to handle."

And effective betas do not submit entirely — that would make them drones, not partners. Many creative relationships have a clear power disparity but a strong sense of mutual authority, so that the pair can benefit from all the clarity of knowing who is dominant and all the creativity of bringing low- and high-powered perspectives on their work. At *Chappelle's Show,* Dave Chappelle had the final call on material. "If it tanks, it's my ass on that stage, not yours," he would tell his co-creator, Neal Brennan. But Chappelle rarely resorted to this kind of decree, usually working out disagreements with Brennan until they were both pleased. Suzanne Farrell submitted to Balanchine but he ceded enormous authority to her as well, including, writes Jacques d'Amboise, "the power to choose which ballets would be on the program and who would dance them." Even the most dramatically asymmetrical relationships — between a boss and an assistant, say — requires some degree of parity to have any value. According to the businesswoman and TV personality Barbara Corcoran, for an entrepreneur, "the most important decision you can make is to let go of the detail into the hands of someone who is just as able as you are." She was talking about her executive assistant Gail Abrahamsen, who wades through hundreds of e-mails a day and decides what gets Corcoran's attention.

The most flagrant risk of this fluidity — a risk for the more powerful one — is that there will be a reversal. The Detours were Roger Daltrey's band. He invited the bassist John Entwistle to join, then the guitarist Pete Townshend. Two years later, the drummer Keith Moon came on too. Daltrey booked the gigs, made the set lists, and drove the van. If you argued with him, Townshend said, "you usually got a bunch of fives." (Meaning that you got punched.) But when the band needed original material, Pete was the one with the knack for it. "I Can't Explain" got the band (now called the Who) their record deal, and it wasn't long before Townshend had taken over. Offering his view of Daltrey at the time, Pete was not subtle: "Keith was a genius," he said. "John was a genius. I was certainly in on the edge of it. You know, Roger was a singer. That was it."

But while Daltrey took his subordinate place, he didn't fold. "I struggled more than anything to find a voice, a *real* voice for this band," Daltrey said. In the late 1960s, Townshend wrote his first full-length rock opera, *Tommy,* which followed the arc of a deaf, dumb, and blind boy. Many of the songs were in the first person, and as Daltrey practiced the material — singing it in the first person — his obsession with being more than a mere ordinary singer grew. Finally, he said to Townshend: "Can I *be* Tommy?"

"And I remember thinking, 'Yeah,'" Townshend said. "Roger *became* Tommy, became this figure, then it equalized, and then we were unbelievably potent, because we were balanced. It was a marriage, but it was a good marriage. Those were glorious years."

Glorious for the creative work, but not for the living of it. "The Who was built on competition," Daltrey said. "The competition was horrendous, on and off the stage." And it often boiled over. At one point, Townshend smacked Daltrey over the shoulder with his electric guitar. Daltrey then hauled off and knocked Townshend unconscious. These squabbles may seem petty, but it's hard to separate them from the essential and generative tension of their arrangement, where a lead singer is not actually the lead figure, where a chief songwriter and visionary also understands that absolute rule is an absolute bore.

20

"I Love to Scrap with Orv"

Conflict

So this is the tension: power clarity can negate conflict but stifle creativity. Along with sufficient clarity, pairs need some fluidity. Thus conflict is an organic part of the process. That's the bad news.

The good news is that conflict is not necessarily bad.

Rather than indicating a problem that needs solving, conflict may emerge out of right behavior — people acting their parts, expressing their opinions, bringing their perspectives to bear. Being a pain in the ass. Being a stickler. Being the one who daydreams and comes late, or being the one who can't stand it when the other guy is late. Insisting the thing needs more work. Insisting the thing needs to be put into production.

Conflict may emerge over substance or process and it may blur the professional and personal. Some guidebooks advise keeping these realms strictly separate. But according to the management scholar Amy Edmondson and the psychologist Diana McLain Smith, both of whom have studied hot topics in the workplace, this is rarely possible. Conflict, by its nature, heats us up emotionally, and when we're emotional, rational boundaries naturally dissolve. Hot topics raise uncertainties that "cannot be reduced by a review of the available facts," Edmondson and Smith write. And they bring into view "differing (usually taken-for-granted) values, belief systems, or interests."

The TV writers Mark V. Olsen and Will Scheffer, a married couple who created and produced HBO's *Big Love,* say they talk to each other with a venom that they'd never allow among their staff. And it's not that they're just disagreeing over a plot point. "There's going to be conflict when all the old baggage comes out," Olsen said. "There are sections of the 210 [freeway in Los Angeles] where we regularly scream our guts out at each other." One of the most memorable moments in my five years of research came when a man described his writing partner to me as a "genius" and the "best thing that ever happened to me" and then told me: "But he drives me way beyond crazy. Sometimes I want to stab him in the eye with a knife." It struck me especially because this was the *second* time someone had used that image (the first time, the sharp implement was a pair of scissors).

Epic conflict is legion in pairs. The filmmaker Werner Herzog's documentary about the actor Klaus Kinski — with whom he made *Aguirre, the Wrath of God* and *Fitzcarraldo,* among other movies — is called *My Best Fiend.* Herzog's "fiend" pun was quite tame compared to Kinski's words for Herzog. In his memoir, he called him "a miserable, spiteful, envious, stingy, stinking, money-hungry, malicious, sadistic, insidious, backstabbing, blackmailing, cowardly person, and a liar through and through."

But going head-to-head may be essential for creative work. Francis Crick said that if he had a flawed idea, "Watson would tell me in no uncertain terms this was nonsense, and vice-versa. If he would have some idea I didn't like, and I would say so, this would shake his thinking." Crick believed it essential to be "perfectly candid, one might almost say rude, to the person you're working with." The death knell to real collaboration, he said, is "politeness."

What's striking about Watson and Crick is that being unsparing with each other served their work, while a second pair of scientists, who were by all accounts in a better position than Watson and Crick to crack the problem of DNA, were stymied by a power dynamic that kept them from engaging at all. In January 1951, the physicist Maurice Wilkins returned from vacation to King's College in London, one of the centers for budding DNA research, and found a young scientist named Rosalind Franklin working in the x-ray lab. Assuming she was his new assistant, he asked her how her research was progressing. "And she just said, 'Go back to your microscopes,' which bewildered me," Wilkins remembered. Unbeknownst to Wilkins, Franklin had been given space in the lab he had been using (and given his PhD student as an assistant) so she could do her own DNA research, not a subset of his. The lab's director, J. T. Randall, hadn't even mentioned Wilkins to Franklin when he hired her. She was a star researcher — she made the crucial discovery that there was not just one but two forms of DNA. But she and Wilkins were in a cold war.

Sixty miles north, in Cambridge, Watson and Crick were heating each other up. "We had evolved unstated but fruitful methods of collaboration," Crick wrote, "something that was quite missing in the London group. If either of us suggested a new idea the other, while taking it seriously, would attempt to demolish it in a candid but nonhostile manner. This turned out to be quite crucial."

In January 1953, Watson visited Wilkins's London office, and Wilkins showed him a critical photograph of Franklin's. "The instant I saw the picture my mouth fell open," Watson said. Known as Photo 51, it was an x-ray image of the "B" form of DNA. Watson and Crick had surmised that the DNA structure might form a helix but had no data to confirm it. Photo 51 not only showed a helical pattern but showed it clearly enough to reveal the distance between each helical twist.

The question remained: How did the four bases, those molecular building blocks of DNA — adenine, thymine, guanine, and cytosine (or A, T, G, and C) — align within the helix? As late as February 19, 1953, Watson leaned toward matching each base with a like base to form the structure (that is, A with A, T with T, and so on), while Crick advocated for complementary pairings (A with T, and G with C), in part because the amount of adenine always equaled the amount of thymine, and the amount of guanine always equaled the amount of cytosine. "When one of us got on the wrong track, the other one got out of it," remembered Crick.

In late February 1953, a visiting scientist suggested that the rules of hydrogen bonding would make the complementary pairings work within a helical structure, allowing A to bond to T, and C to G. Then, on the evening of February 27, Watson fiddled with the model of DNA and crabbed about the difficulty of making the helical structure work when the sugar-phosphate backbone was on the inside. As Watson told me, "Francis, I think, aware how hard it was to build a structure, any structure, just said, 'Build it [the phosphates] on the outside.' And I gave the flippant reply, 'It'd be too easy.'"

"Then why don't you do it?" Crick responded.

An elegant double-helix structure resulted the next morning, with each base arranged so that it naturally attracted its mate. Further, the model could "unzip" and make copies of itself, which provided insight into how DNA might replicate. Though it would take another week to finalize the model, Watson wrote that very day, at lunch, "Francis winged into the Eagle to tell everyone within hearing distance that we had found the secret of life."

It's poignant that although Rosalind Franklin and Maurice Wilkins didn't fight, they didn't talk either. It reminds me of the lyricist Alan Jay Lerner's memories of the decline of his relationship with the composer Frederick Loewe, with whom he made *My Fair Lady* and *Camelot*. "Too much was never said," Lerner wrote in his memoir *The Street Where I Live*. "In the end we were a little like the couple being discussed in one of Noel Coward's early plays. 'Do they fight?' said one. 'Oh, no,' said the other. 'They're much too unhappy to fight.'"

Many couples, by contrast, are quite happy fighting. Orville and Wilbur Wright, for example, went at each other relentlessly. "They would get into terrific arguments," their mechanic, Charles Taylor, remembered. "They'd shout at each other something terrible. I don't think they really got mad, but they sure got awfully hot. One morning following the worst argument I ever heard, Orv came in and said he guessed he'd been wrong and they ought to do it Will's way. A few minutes later Will came in and said he'd been thinking it over and perhaps Orv was right. First thing I knew they were arguing the thing all over again, only this time they had switched ideas."

"I love to scrap with Orv," Wilbur said. "Orv is such a good scrapper."

It may seem strange, but the pleasure of jabbing at each other is not necessarily inferior to that of scratching each other's backs. They may actually be very much the same kind of pleasure. According to the research of psychologist James W. Pennebaker at the University of Texas on the word content of correspondence, high indices of conflict are positively associated with an experience of intimacy. Think about the people you can really argue with. They're often your dearest friends.

Conflict can also be a form of social play, which is, across many species, a source of pleasure and closeness. Some animal species seem to employ a fifty-fifty rule, arranging things so that, no matter how strong or weak the play partners are relative to each other, each tends to win or lose the play just as often.

In creative pairs, the principal form of social play is through banter, evoked by C. S. Lewis in his book *Surprised by Joy:* "When you set out to correct his heresies, you will find that he forsooth has decided to correct yours! And then you go at it, hammer and tongs, far into the night, night after night, or walking through fine country that neither gives a glance to, each learning the weight of the other's punches, and often more like mutually respectful enemies than friends. Actually (though it never seems so at the time) you modify one another's thought; out of this perpetual dogfight a community of mind and a deep affection emerge."

To the untrained eye such dogfights can be scary to watch: Elizabeth Cady Stanton's daughter Margaret remembered seeing her mother and Susan B. Anthony marching off in opposite directions. "And just as I have made up my mind that this beautiful friendship of forty years has at last terminated," she recounted, "I see them walking down the hill, arm in arm . . . When they return they go straight to work where they left off, as if nothing had ever happened . . . They never explain, nor apologize, nor shed tears, nor make up, as other people do."

Even when it's unpleasant in the moment, conflict may be generative in the medium or long term, as it offers, to use the technical phrase, *prosocial functions.* For example, conflict can highlight differences in perspective; it might be the quickest way to discover a problem that needs solving.

The marriage researcher John Gottman said couples likely to remain married exchange five positive remarks for every one that's negative. Research by the consultant Marcial Losada and the management scholar Emily Heaphy quantified positive and negative comments in business teams, finding that top performers had nearly six positive exchanges for every negative one — and medium-performance teams averaged about two positive to one negative. Low-performing teams had about three negative exchanges for every positive one.

Given criticism of other Losada research, there are reasons to be skeptical of the precision of these numbers, but the point for me is that they highlight the general necessity of affirmations existing alongside challenges in the right proportion. The tricky thing in creative work, though, is teasing apart affirmations and challenges. Negative interactions may have positive *outcomes.* A criticism or rejection that at first feels like a bee sting may be regarded later as more like the poke of a doctor's needle. It's the same pain in the moment, but it may eventually seem medicinal when one comes to appreciate what it provoked. John Gottman found in a study that peaceful couples early in their relationships reported more marital happiness than couples who bicker. But in follow-ups three years later, the peaceful couples were far more likely to be divorced or headed for divorce, while the bickering couples tended to have worked out their troubles and stuck together.

Gottman also emphasizes that conflict needs to be distinguished from contempt. The former can be like rain on a house — no threat to the structure and good for the gardens. The latter is like termites eating the foundation. He stresses the importance of "repair"— which may be a traditional makeup moment or simply be a bit of lightness. Consider the couple Gottman describes arguing about what kind of car to buy. Olivia wants a minivan. Nathaniel wants a Jeep. They've had the argument before. "The more they talk about it," Gottman observed, "the higher the decibel level gets." But then something shifts: "Olivia puts her hands on her hips and, in perfect imitation of their four-year-old son, sticks out her tongue. Since Nathaniel knows that she's about to do this, he sticks out his tongue first. Then they both start laughing."

Repair moments may gesture at shared meaning and purpose, but the point is that they are small — not a lifeboat, just a patch kit. The boat is all the good that's carried the relationship thus far.

For pairs, conflict may be the crack in everything that Leonard Cohen sang about — "that's how the light gets in." The pair's potential arises in the first place from foundational differences in temperaments or styles or backgrounds or modes of thinking. It *should* take work to relate. With rigid power, the burden of repair falls entirely on one party, but true creative pairs will always, to some degree, have to reach each other.

Anyway, the last thing a pair wants is total stability. The Wright brothers showed that not just in their process but in their product. As they argued with each other in their father's house in Dayton or in the bicycle shop they ran, many of the best scientific minds in the world were trying to conquer the skies. In 1896, when the Wrights' big accomplishment was to make their own brand of bicycle, Samuel Pierpont Langley, an eminent astronomer and physicist, succeeded in flying his Number 5 model airplane over the Potomac River. It was shot into the air by a catapult and traveled nearly three-quarters of a mile.

Langley's next step was to build a powerful, fifty-horsepower engine. This reflected his basic hypothesis that the key to flight was getting a strong and sturdy craft with enough power to barrel up into the sky. Along with other leading minds, he imagined a plane much like a boat. It needed a rudder to steer it and an engine to push it forward. Langley thought stability was essential. He did his tests over the Potomac because the calm winds there seemed like good experimental conditions. All told, Langley spent about $50,000 on his efforts, about $1.3 million in modern terms.

The Wright brothers spent only about $1,000 over the course of their experiments. Nor did they have Langley's arsenal of technical support. The engine for their flyer was only about a fifth as powerful as his, twelve horsepower. When they were ready to test their first glider, they wrote to the United States Weather Bureau asking for wind conditions in various parts of the country. One of the windiest places, the Outer Banks of North Carolina, also boasted wide, flat beaches and was sparsely inhabited. So they went there, to Kitty Hawk.

Orville and Wilbur Wright became the first in flight because they applied a mechanical principle that followed their collaborative method. The key to keeping a craft in the air, they grasped, was not to make it strong and sturdy. On the contrary, it had to be flexible. The plane itself — and the pilot at its controls — must be able to adjust easily and quickly. In the sky, with winds rushing and ever changing, there was no such thing as inherent stability — only a dynamic stability, which, though it might sound like a contradiction, actually had a lot to do with embracing instability.

21

Varieties of Alphas and Betas

The Hitchcock Paradox

The necessary flexibility in power can manifest in a variety of ways. Consider the extreme situation where one partner seeks to dominate relentlessly and ruthlessly. Alfred Hitchcock is a legendary example. In 1961, he put an obscure thirty-one-year-old model named Tippi Hedren under contract. She thought she'd be a background actor on TV. Then she learned that Hitchcock had cast her as the star in his next feature film, *The Birds*.

"I really found it so new and difficult," Hedren said, noting that she "overcompensated by working too hard, by sometimes being too accommodating." "She was very nervous and unsure of herself," said the actor Martin Balsam, who worked with her during a screen test, "but she had studied every line and every move that was asked of her, and she tried very hard to do everything."

Here was a blank slate, exceedingly eager, entirely submissive — just what Alfred Hitchcock liked. "I controlled every movement on her face," he said. "She wasn't allowed to do anything beyond what I gave her. It was my control entirely." Hitchcock began to dictate to her what clothes to wear, what food to eat, and whom she could see. To keep tabs on her, he had her tailed by members of his crew.

This was his thing. When he hired Kim Novak to star in *Vertigo*, he had her over to his house and talked about everything *but* the film, choosing topics he knew she'd be unfamiliar with. "By the end of the afternoon," the film's producer said, "he had her right where he wanted her, docile and obedient and even a little confused." It's tempting to write Hitchcock off as a monster, but at the upper reaches of many industries we often find leaders with a power style edging into the tyrannical. *Vogue* editor in chief Anna Wintour's leadership style earned her the nickname Nuclear Wintour. Scott Rudin, the superproducer behind everything from *The Truman Show* to *The Book of Mormon,* was reported by the *Wall Street Journal* to have fired 250 assistants over a five-year period. (Rudin said the correct number was 119.) He once fired an assistant for bringing him the wrong kind of muffin. He threw his office phone at assistants so frequently that they measured the cord. "The rookies often stood too close," one told the *Journal.*

According to Mark Lipton, a professor of management at the New School, stark bullying, tantrums, and other behaviors associated with nine-year-olds commonly intersect with high-level vision, leadership, and prestige. Many CEOs behave so badly, he said, that they exhibit classic symptoms of psychopathology. "What saves them," Lipton told me, "and I see this in just about every instance where they remain effective, is a deputy, or a spouse — someone who is by their side."

To succeed in these situations, betas must find a way to both submit and engage — to work in a position of great asymmetry while still making their creative presence felt. In the psychoanalyst Michael Maccoby's studies of narcissistic visionaries, he found they typically depend heavily on sidekicks Maccoby calls "productive obsessives." These sidekicks have to be sensitive to the narcissists' needs — but stand up to them when necessary. In Apple's early days, when Steve Jobs pressured Steve Wozniak to change the hardware to make the computer smaller and more affordable, Wozniak shot back: "If that's what you want, go get yourself another computer." Jobs backed down. All of Jobs's top partners, Walter Isaacson observed, had the quality of being "deferential" but also "pushing back"—"a tricky balance to maintain." "I realized very early that if you didn't voice your opinion," Jobs's COO Tim Cook said, "he would mow you down . . . So if you don't feel comfortable disagreeing, then you'll never survive."

"It's true of alphas in general," the executive coach Eddie Erlandson told me, "that working for them is not for the weak of heart." But as much as alphas want to dominate, they also want to be effective. They may bristle at pushback, but they need it.

That pushback might mean bringing the gloves to the alpha's face. Or it might mean simply summoning the energy—and will and talent—to stay in the ring. Hitchcock's pattern was to choose an actress, isolate and unsettle her, and withhold signs of approval, which would keep her on a gerbil wheel, running round and round, striving to be noticed, striving for praise. "He controlled me totally," Joan Fontaine said. "He kept me off balance, much to his own delight. He would constantly tell me that no one thought I was any good except himself, and that nobody really liked me and nobody would say anything good about me except himself."

Fontaine may have been knocked off balance, but she righted herself artfully. In 1940 and 1941, she starred in two Hitchcock releases—*Rebecca* and *Suspicion*. She was nominated for an Academy Award for both performances and won an Oscar in the second instance.

How is it that something creative can emerge from a situation that might well be described as abusive? It seems to go like this: the alpha behaves in a tyrannical way, inducing some flavor of fear in his subordinate, who then works all the harder to please or satisfy—or to challenge him. As William James suggested, "the fighting impulse" has been appealed to; "pugnacity and pride" have been roused. This leads to good work—so much that even the abused underlings often want to do it again. And if *they* don't, there are others waiting.

Hitchcock surely had no shortage of actors, even though he once left his leading man and lady handcuffed to each other for much of the day, claiming that he had lost the key, when in fact he had deposited it with the studio guard. But for the extremes of domination, nothing beats the story of the climactic scene in *The Birds* where Tippi Hedren's character is trapped in an attic. Hedren was told they'd use mechanical birds, but she came to the set to find a cage built to keep the live birds in the room. They spent a week on the scene—"really the worst week of my life," Hedren said. "Each day I thought—and they told me—just one more hour, just one more shot." But when she collapsed on the ground—as the scene demanded—the birds would fly off too quickly. Hitchcock had wardrobe sew loops to Hedren's clothes and he tied the birds to the loops. Her fright, exhaustion, and ultimate surrender didn't need to be acted.

At one point, Hedren was so beaten down physically and emotionally that her doctor insisted Hitchcock cancel shooting for a week. She spent the week away from the set—but then she came back and finished the film. This is the core characteristic of betas working with extreme alphas. They return. According to Hedren, on the set of the next film they did together, *Marnie,* Hitchcock insisted she make herself available to him sexually. "That was the moment," she said, "after three years of trying to cope, when I finally had enough — that was the limit, that was the end." Hitchcock couldn't force her to work, but, extreme alpha to the last, he refused to let her out of her contract for another three years.

The ultimate irony of extreme alphas is that they often have someone who dominates them. We've touched on this in the discussion of the star and the director. Valentino Garavani is the epitome of an alpha male — a swaggering, indomitable figure — except, from the account Matt Tyrnauer has given of their relationship, it is clear that Giancarlo Giammetti is actually the dominant presence. Gertrude Stein appropriated her partner Alice B. Toklas's identity — she wrote under Toklas's name — to create a self-serving portrait of herself. But as the *New York Times* reported in its obituary of Toklas, "If Miss Stein dominated the couple's salon, Miss Toklas seemed to command Miss Stein." In 1935, Stein was giving a shipboard interview to a group of reporters in New York when, the *New York Herald Tribune* reported, "Miss Toklas's slight, menacing figure appeared in the doorway. 'Come, lovey,' said Miss Toklas, in a steely-sweet voice. 'Say good by to your guests. They are leaving.' Miss Stein leaped to her feet and bounded off into the corridor."

The star may present as swaggering and all-powerful, but this is a symptom of a profound uncertainty. It's natural, then, for the star to associate with someone who is quietly self-assured — who can assure *him.* The frontperson may still need to be seen as in control — that's often part of the shtick. But he is constantly watching his bellwether.

Perhaps the height of this paradox can be seen with Hitchcock, whose wife, Alma, was "the ultimate arbiter" for his movies, wrote Donald Spoto. "To tell the truth," said Elsie Randolph, an actor who was close with the couple, "she bossed him."

Of course, alpha/beta dynamics do not need to be fraught. Not everyone wants to be the boss. "I'm a professional number two man," Kris Lotlikar, the cofounder of Renewable Choice, a green energy company, told me. "This is what I do best, support someone who has the charisma to sell the world on a vision that I share, and that I help create." Quayle

Hodek, the company's CEO, considers Lotlikar his "best friend and partner," but he told me that one key to their relationship is the lack of ambiguity around who gets the final call.

Another common strategy for pairs is to work with authority not as a matter of endemic fact but as a position. Often power is a direct function of roles—each partner will have the final say in his domain. At *South Park,* Trey makes the final calls on the shows themselves but Matt tends to run lead on business deals. My editor and I have an understanding that, if we disagree about a matter in the text and are not able to come to an agreement, I have the final call, but he has the final say on the cover.

Several pairs told me they solve conflicts by deferring to whoever feels most strongly about the topic at hand. One pair I interviewed went to a couples therapist to negotiate power domains. "We fight like any couple," said Cathryn Michon, who makes films with her husband, W. Bruce Cameron. "But you can't do it in front of a film crew." Since Bruce dealt with budgets, they agreed he'd have authority on money questions. Since the film they were working on at the time was adapted from Cathryn's book, she got the last word on character and story. "We just laid out clear areas of responsibility and authority," Cathryn said. "This is how armies function. And film sets are like an army."

Surprisingly, rigid divisions of power can actually lead to the most fluid exchanges. Kris Lotlikar and Quayle Hodek, the cofounders of Renewable Choice, both told me that Kris, the ostensible deputy, ends up making more management decisions day-to-day. Knowing that a disagreement could be brought to an end at any moment, Quayle told me, makes it far less likely that disagreements will escalate, and easier for him to defer to Kris's judgment.

Turn-taking may also be a potent strategy when each member of a pair is a natural alpha. Kate Ludeman and Eddie Erlandson, authors of *The Alpha Male Syndrome,* say they commonly find multiple alphas in organizations. They propose that each alpha should identify his strengths, be it as a "commander," "visionary," "strategist," or "executor."

The case of the subordinate alpha is a curious one—the aggressive, domineering type who nevertheless finds himself in thrall to a partner. I've seen this a number of times. Ralph Abernathy deferred to Martin

Luther King Jr. but acted superior to everyone else. Vincent van Gogh put himself in a position where he depended entirely for his sustenance on his brother Theo, yet Vincent was an extremely dominant character. Suzanne Farrell, at times, put an extraordinary drive for domination aside in relation to her primary partner.

James Watson is another example. He told me he was "always the younger brother" in relation to Francis Crick, which is intriguing on both sides, because Crick presents as rather the less competitive of the two of them. He had, Horace Freeland Judson writes, "a talent for friendship in science," and over his career "coordinated the research of many other biologists, disciplined their thinking, arbitrated their conflicts, communicated and explained their results." Watson, by contrast, developed a reputation for battle. Competition, he said, "is the dominant motive in science. It starts at the beginning: if you publish first, you become a professor first; your future depends on some indication that you can do something by yourself. It's that simple. Competitiveness is very, very dominant. The chief emotion in the field. The second is you have to prove to yourself that you can do it — and that's the same thing."

Watson has said that, six or seven times in his life, "I had to create a situation where if I lost, I'd be out of a job." Unless you do that, he said, "someone will run over you." In one of those situations, at Harvard University, Watson was on the biology faculty with the eminent scientist E. O. Wilson, who pronounced him "the most unpleasant human being" he had ever met at work.

When I asked Watson why he and Crick never worked together after they discovered the mechanism for life in less than a year and a half, he said, "You couldn't be with Francis and be the boss. Whereas I enjoy being the boss."

"Crick was the only person to whom you would take second place?"

"Yes," he said.

22

"What About McCartney-Lennon?"

The Dance of Power

It makes intuitive sense that the subordinate alpha — that paradoxical creature — would recur in high-level creative pairs. Having a clear alpha lays a foundation of clarity. Yet adding a second alpha to the mix — who will defer only to his partner and, even then, with the odd, bottled-up energy of someone acting decidedly out of character — injects the dynamic with the possibility of surprise.

When I came to recognize this, I understood how the great success and great turmoil of John Lennon and Paul McCartney were both parts of the same dance: how leery regard ran alongside genuine alliance; how intimate enmity joined with rivalrous affection.

I use dance as a metaphor but it is not far from the literal truth. There were certain steps that repeated in a reliable sequence over time. Like the approach and withdrawal of an actual dance, the basic moves were challenge and accommodation. But there were also definite reversals, when the leader let the follower carry him.

Though what came before and after it was prodigious, I think it's safe to say that there were two creative peaks in the Lennon-McCartney partnership as songwriters and bandleaders: *Sgt. Pepper's Lonely Hearts Club Band* and *The Beatles* (commonly known as *The White Album*). These records differ from each other sharply. And they were radically different experiences for the musicians, producers, and engineers involved. In popular lore, *Pep-*

per is the apogee of union between John and Paul. *The White Album,* which Paul called "the tension album," looks like the peak of discord.

But as we've seen, unity and conflict are mingled in pairs. Opposition (and all its attendant emotions) is an integral part of creation, even more on the whole than cooperation. The goal throughout Part V has been to conceive of how to unify these qualities, how to consider them together.

Most stories will sharply demarcate enemies and require one or the other to triumph in a finite struggle. These sorts of stories are linear. You can literally draw them out on a line (as screenwriters do in a common exercise) with slashes along the way: a journey begins; challenges are met; defeats or triumphs ensue, leading to great changes.

The shape of the Lennon-McCartney relationship was more like a spiral, the repetition of a certain pattern with ascending complexity. (Imagine the spiral here as three-dimensional, like "the widening gyre" of William Butler Yeats.) To understand their late great moves — to see just how cooperation and competition played out in their great achievements — we need to look at the pattern over time. When we do it, we see the truth is that the *Sgt. Pepper* sessions and the *White Album* sessions were very much part of the same dynamic. They just came at different points in a distinct cycle.

Back in 1957, Paul joined the band with John as its leader. He accepted those terms, perhaps in part out of political dexterity, but also because he found it natural to defer to John. "In those days," Cynthia Lennon wrote, "Paul tried hard to impress John, posing and strutting with his hair slicked back to prove that he was cool . . . [John] was everything Paul wanted to be — laid-back, self-assured and in charge. As the schoolboy he still was, Paul could only aspire to those things."

In the months that followed, Paul taught John guitar chords — he'd been playing banjo chords on his guitar the day they met — helped him develop as a songwriter, and began to make suggestions for the band. John was the band's leader, but Paul and John established themselves as a unit, and Paul often operated as John's proxy. He appointed himself the band's PR man, for example.

The immense opportunity and vulnerability of Paul's position is that it was never exactly clear how far John would let him go. In Hamburg, John developed a signature move: while Paul was crooning at the front of the stage, he would creep around in the back, twist up his face, and make a spectacle of himself. One time, with Paul in the midst of a serious spoken-word piece in the bridge of a song, John stopped the band cold. "They sent me up rotten," Paul said, "especially John. They all but laughed me off the stage." This was John letting Paul know he was boss.

By Hamburg, the complexity of their positions was growing. Casual observers tended to view Paul as the leader, said their friend Astrid Kirchherr, the German photographer and artist. Paul "was by far the most popular with the fans," she said. "He always did the talking and the announcing and the autograph bit." When the band auditioned for Parlophone Records, George Martin considered them in the mold of rock groups with a single leader and thought, at first, that the natural frontman would be Paul.

But in the inner circle, the real locus of power was unmistakable. "John of course was the leader," Astrid Kirchherr said. "He was far and away the strongest."

As much as Paul pushed John — and put himself out front — he also made his deference explicit. In the band's first-ever radio interview, a DJ named Monty Lister asked each member of the band what instrument he played. When George Harrison said "lead guitar," Lister asked him: "Does that mean that you're sort of the leader of the group?"

"No, no," George said. "Just ... well, you see, the other guitar is the rhythm. Ching, ching, ching, you see."

Paul broke in. "He's solo guitar, you see. John is, in fact, the leader of the group."

But Paul often led the leader. Consider the moment Paul's brother, Michael, cited as an illustration of his "innate sense of diplomacy." It was in Paris in 1964. George Martin had arranged for the band to record "She Loves You" and "I Want to Hold Your Hand" in German. When the band missed their studio appointment, Martin came around to their suite at the George V hotel. They played slapstick and dived under the tables to avoid him.

"Are you coming to do it or not?" Martin said.

"No," Lennon said. George and Ringo echoed him. Paul said nothing.

"Then a bit later," Michael said, "Paul suddenly turned to John and said, 'Heh, you know that so-and-so line, what if we did it this way?' John listened to what Paul said, thought a bit, and said, 'Yeah, that's it.'" And they headed to the studio.

How would we chart the lines of authority for this decision? You could say Lennon made the call to refuse the recording session, then reversed himself, the band following him both times. But Paul was the real mover. That he avoided a direct confrontation only underscores his operational strength. "John was the noisiest of the four," said Tony Barrow, who helped handle press for the band. But Paul "was the most persuasive, and the one who wielded the real power with Brian Epstein. John would make a lot of noise," Barrow said, "but not get his own way. Then Paul would go in and persuade Brian that what John had suggested was the right thing to do."

Every pair has its own power dance, a choreography of thrusts and parries, of dips and turns, that shapes its way of moving across life's stage. These steps may play out in an afternoon, but we can also look at their broad outline over time. For Lennon and McCartney, the pattern looked like this:

1. John is dominant but open to connection.
2. Paul is aggressive and impressive but ultimately deferent.
3. John's dominance established, Paul steps up to lead in the areas of his strength. John leads the band; Paul leads John — advising him, teaching him, and acting on his behalf.
4. John moves (usually abruptly) to reestablish his dominance over Paul.

To see John reasserting control, let's return to the matter of their songwriting credits. We've seen that the two quickly agreed to co-own their work. But that left the question: How would the credit line be written? According to the Beatles authority Mark Lewisohn, the contract — drafted in 1962 — reflected an understanding that whoever led the effort on any given song would have his name go first on that song. Accordingly, the first contract with their music publisher, for the songs "Love Me Do" and "P.S. I Love You," both of which Paul had initiated, had McCartney's name first. All of the eight originals on their first LP, *Please Please Me*, released in March 1963, are listed on the album as *McCartney-Lennon*.

Then John changed his mind. He and Brian Epstein met with Paul and told him that the credit would now read *Lennon-McCartney*.

From Paul's many accounts of this conversation, it's clear that he felt blindsided. "I said: 'Whoooooah. What about McCartney-Lennon?'" he recalled. "They said: 'It just sounds better as Lennon-McCartney.' I said: 'McCartney-Lennon sounds pretty good.'"

But he came to acquiesce. "I stepped down," he told Coleman.

Anyone who wants to understand how Lennon-McCartney worked — how they thrived and how they suffered — should look closely at this exchange, because it not only suggests the pattern between the two of them but also points to the complex *internal* dynamic that each individual had with respect to power. As we survey the complications in *relationships,* we also need to remember that each individual is a bundle of complications, even paradoxes. The relationships take shape from those individual characteristics, and the individual characteristics are shaped by the relationship.

John Lennon was an exceptionally dominant personality who nevertheless depended, also to an exceptional degree, on connections with others. From his early childhood, he needed to be the boss of any situation. But he couldn't stand to be alone. "Though I have yet to encounter a personality as strong and individual as John's," said his friend Pete Shotton, "he always had to have a partner." As we've seen, he hardly felt like he existed when he was alone. He would push his friends — be rough with them, even brutal. But he could not stand to see them go.

He lived at the extremes of both dominance and submission.

Paul harbored his own paradox, which was the inverse of John's. On the face of it, he was all deference and affable charm — and he did have a genuine willingness to take direction from prevailing winds. But this masked a determination to come out on top, and perhaps even a deep sense of isolation in his psyche. Unlike John, who went out of his way to show his aggression (it often was his way of covering up vulnerability), Paul went out of his way to keep his aggression hidden. When he was angry at his parents as a boy, he told Hunter Davies, he would sneak up to their room, rip the edge of the lace curtains, and think to himself: "That's got them." While Paul's public persona is affable and diplomatic, people who know him well call him "hard to get to know" and "controlling."

To watch how Paul has returned over the years to the credit issue is telling. In his solo years, he has raised the subject many times in interviews and has acted repeatedly to reverse the credit order. He has admitted a "slight resentment" that his name goes second on songs like "Yesterday" and insisted that "I have learned not to mind." It's obviously not true that he has learned not to mind; if he had, he wouldn't keep bringing it up. He's also told the story of his exchange with Brian and John in a variety of ways, in one instance noting that he had had the idea "since" the meeting that the songs should be credited differently; in another instance asserting that Brian and John assured him in the original meeting, "We'll do this for now and we can change it around to be fair at any point in the future."

An interview Paul gave for the *Beatles Anthology* project, in the mid-1990s, is especially revealing. McCartney gave the backstory that, before the credit issue was decided, in 1963, John and Brian had gone away on holiday to Spain. This trip has often been alluded to as an erotic adventure, and in fact John conceded several times that they had sexual contact. "John was a smart cookie," Paul said. "Brian was gay, and John saw his opportunity to impress upon Mr. Epstein who was the boss of this group. I think that's why he went on holiday with Brian . . . He was that kind of guy; he wanted Brian to know whom he should listen to. That was the relationship. John was very much the leader in that way, although it was never actually said."

With John and Paul — as in so many relationships — so much was never actually said. As the dance metaphor suggests, what matters was not what they explained to each other, or even understood of each other, but how they moved with and around each other.

John's move to claim the lead position in the credits was part of a period, from roughly 1963 to 1965, where he also asserted himself as a songwriter. Though John and Paul both had hits in this era, John had the slight edge, and considering that he had previously been the junior partner to Paul as a songwriter, it reflected a real comeback. Paul's reaction was to elevate his own game, and they went on like this, getting better all the time.

We're ready, now, to return to where we started in this book's prelude — to a moment of chemistry between John Lennon and Paul McCartney so piquant that it set the tone for their whole relationship. On March 29, 1967, they spent five hours in the music room of Paul's house on Cavendish Avenue. By the end, they had mostly finished the lyrics for a new song, one meant for Ringo Starr to sing on their next album. In between bouts of trading ideas and playing alongside each other, they horsed around with songs from their stage days in Hamburg, and Paul played for John, for the first time, the song that became "The Fool on the Hill."

From Paul's place to the EMI Studios on Abbey Road was a few minutes' drive. John, Paul, George, and Ringo met there, started work around 7:00 p.m., and went until 5:45 a.m., by which time they had recorded ten takes of "With a Little Help from My Friends." The next day, they assembled before the photographer Michael Cooper, who shot them in old-style band costumes of yellow (John), pink (Ringo), turquoise (Paul), and red (George) against a background designed by Peter Blake and Jann Haworth with cutouts of figures from Marilyn Monroe to Karl Marx to Stuart Sutcliffe. It was for the cover of *Sgt. Pepper's Lonely Hearts Club Band*.

"It was a peak," Lennon said of the album. "Paul and I were definitely working together, especially on 'A Day in the Life.'" Indeed, that song brought into one track all the singularity and variation of their partnership. Far from the simple joining of two fragments — as lore has it — the song is two distinct pieces, but they were developed and shaped together, all in a spirit best captured by John's remark in 1968: "Now and then we really turn each other on with a bit of song." "The way we wrote a lot of the time," he said later, "you'd write the good bit, the part that was easy, like 'I read the news today' or whatever it was, then when you got stuck or whenever it got hard, instead of carrying on, you just drop it; then we would meet each other, and I would sing half, and he would be inspired to write the next bit and vice versa."

"A Day in the Life" showed how they could enter the same room, but from different doors. The fragment John led on looked with amazement and abstraction on the events of everyday life; Paul's looked directly at everyday life until amazement and abstraction struck like a blow.

The *Pepper* sessions ran from November 1966 to April 1967 and included what the engineer Geoff Emerick estimated to be more than seven hundred studio hours, on top of copious sessions for Paul and John, in which they shaped every song on the album. John initiated "Lucy in the Sky with Diamonds" after he saw a drawing his son Julian made. He showed the picture to Paul — they both saw the chance to play with imagery like that of Lewis Carroll's *Alice in Wonderland* — and they finished the song together. "I offered 'cellophane flowers' and 'newspaper taxis,'" Paul said, "and John replied with 'kaleidoscope eyes' . . . We traded words off each other, as we always did." When Paul sang a song with the chorus "Getting better all the time," as Paul tells it, "John just said in his laconic way, 'It couldn't get no worse,' and I thought, Oh, brilliant! This is exactly why I love writing with John."

It's crucial that, for both men, prodigious aggressive energies had an outlet in the creative work itself. This is a critical distinction between pairs who work well with conflict and those who suffer greatly from it. I think of this quality of exchange as "domesticating the tension," making whatever animosity exists between a pair into the work itself and thus a source of greater intimacy and creativity.

The artists Lisa and Janelle Iglesias offer another glimpse of this principle in action. Though they have individual art practices, they work together as Las Hermanas Iglesias, exploring joint interests in what Lisa called "fusion and hybrids and bi-culturality." Janelle is a year younger, "though most of the time people think we're twins," Lisa told me. At first, when I asked Lisa whether they were competitive, she didn't miss a beat: "No," she said. "We've never been. We've always really looked up to each other and wanted to emulate each other in a lovely way." This was one of my first interviews for the book and at the time I just thought, *Hmmm. I guess some pairs don't have that.* But as I explored the Iglesias sisters' work, I saw that the performances often played out competitive scenarios in exaggerated and silly ways. They filmed a contest to see who could put on an entire suitcase's worth of clothes first. They competed to see who could stuff the most cherries in her mouth. They made piñatas, one for Lisa and one for Janelle, and then beat each other's piñatas into a pulp. But what stayed with me most from the interview wasn't the work itself—it was Lisa's broad smile when she talked about it. This was fun. When I told her about research on how fighting can be a source of bonding, she said, "Yeah, one of the things we do when we're having arguments is play Ping-Pong."

"And the person who wins gets their way?" I asked.

"No," she said. "We don't even keep score. It's just a way to take our aggression out."

Paul McCartney ran the *Sgt. Pepper* sessions, with John by his side. One night, for instance, when they were working on "Getting Better," the engineers played the track "over and over again," wrote Hunter Davies, while

George Harrison went off to chat with a friend. Ringo Starr was off that night; they had a backing track and intended just to do vocals. "Paul and John listened carefully," Davies wrote. "Paul instructed the technician which levers to press, telling him what he wanted, how it should be done, which bits he liked best. George Martin looked on, giving advice where necessary. John stared into space."

After they played the song for what seemed, to Davies, "the hundredth time," Paul said he wasn't happy with it and that they'd better get Ringo in to do it all over again. Then Paul suggested a new mix, and after that he said that he was pleased; they didn't need Ringo after all.

"But we've just ordered Ringo on toast," John joked.

This was typical. John and Paul brought in the songs they'd worked out in private, and, as a leadership unit — but with John as the dreamy king and Paul as the fervent deputy — they brought them to life.

The depth and character of the relationship between them can be seen in the unusual turn of events of that same session. Late that night, after they'd sung "Getting Better" for what seemed to Davies "the thousandth time, " John rifled through his silver pillbox, where he kept a range of stimulants. "'He would open it up," Paul remembered, "and choose very precisely: 'Hmm, hmmm, hmmm. What shall I have now?'"

Soon thereafter, John said he felt "very strange." George Martin suggested some fresh air, and he took him to the roof, where John admired the stars with an enthusiasm Martin found puzzling. John had accidentally taken a large dose of LSD.

With his trip in full swing, John felt nervous — and needed a lot of reassurance. They decided to knock off at two in the morning, which was early for them in those days, and Paul brought John back to his house. John could count on this: If something went bad, Paul would take care of it. If John made an audacious request, Paul would translate it. If John said something ugly to George Martin or someone else in the studio, Paul would smooth it over. If John accidentally took a large tab of LSD, Paul would take him home.

Except, this night, Paul decided to take the next step. "I thought, 'Maybe this is the moment where I should take a trip with him,'" Paul remembered. "It's been coming for a long time."

When Paul took his tab, he recalled, "we looked into each other's eyes, the eye contact thing we used to do, which is fairly mind-boggling . . . It was amazing. You're looking into each other's eyes and you would want to look away, but you wouldn't, and you could see yourself in the other person."

Like dreams or the themes that emerge in stream-of-consciousness writing, the preoccupations that come to people on acid trips can be enormously revealing. Paul spent much of his trip moving between his house and the garden. "Oh no, I've got to go back in," he would tell himself. "I've got to do it, for my well-being." And in the meantime, he said, "John had been sitting around very enigmatically and I had a big vision of him as a king, the absolute Emperor of Eternity. . . ." Finally, after four or five hours, Paul cried uncle and said he wanted to go to bed.

"Go to bed?" John said. "You won't sleep!"

"I know that," Paul said. "I've still got to go to bed." And as he lay there, "I could feel every inch of the house, and John seemed like some sort of emperor in control of it all. It was quite strange. Of course he was just sitting there, very inscrutably."

The resonances here with his remarks made while quite sober are palpable: "I always idolized him," Paul said of John. "We always did, the group. I don't know if the others will tell you that, but he was our idol.

"We were all in love with John," he said.

The other force that animated the creative triumph with *Sgt. Pepper* was external. A common enemy—as much as a common goal—can channel and dissipate tension. Just look at the sci-fi movies where enemy nations suddenly gather together to fight the Martians. For John and Paul, the Martians were a group from Southern California called the Beach Boys, whose album *Pet Sounds* they heard in May 1966. The album "blew me out of the water," McCartney said. "Without *Pet Sounds*," George Martin said, "*Sgt. Pepper* . . . wouldn't have happened. *Revolver* was the beginning of the whole thing. But *Pepper* was an attempt to equal *Pet Sounds*."

As the Beatles worked on *Sgt. Pepper*, the Beach Boys' maestro, Brian Wilson, worked on his next album, *Smile*.

When Wilson heard the first results of the *Pepper* sessions—"Strawberry Fields Forever"—he was in Los Angeles driving to the Dolores Restaurant on Santa Monica Boulevard for a burger and fries. He had to pull the car to the side of the road. "I locked in with it," he said of the song. He shook his head and said to his friend in the car, "They did it already."

"Did what?" his friend asked.

"What I wanted to do with *Smile*. Maybe it's too late."

Brian Wilson ended up falling into a serious depression. *Smile* would take him more than thirty-five years to complete. It's a poignant story, in part because he didn't have anyone in his own circle who could check and balance him, challenge and buoy him, the way John and Paul did for each other. He was in his own world. And in a way, this is the problem that came to the Lennon-McCartney partnership. By beating back all competition, they led themselves into a world of their own. Where do you go from the top of the world?

This was the question that both John and Paul were asking themselves in the fall of 1967, and the answers they came up with, and the paths they went down, led them to the next phase of their relationship. It is often portrayed as the beginning of the end, but that's not the best way to understand it. Rather, it was a continuation of the dynamics they had established essentially the moment they met.

Paul's preoccupations were what could the band do next, what new media could they conquer, what other vistas. For a boy-king like him — twenty-five years old and among the most successful entertainers in history — there was a fine line between confidence and grandiosity, and he certainly rode that line hard in late 1967 and 1968 — dreaming up a new film for the Beatles, *Magical Mystery Tour*, that they would direct themselves, and a business enterprise, called Apple Corps, that would expand the band's vision into record and film production, electronics, and retail.

John signed on without fuss to Paul's plans because he had a very different goal in mind. From the time of *Revolver* forward, he had been preoccupied with the saving power of acid, which subdued his aggressive nature. "Even a couple of years ago," Ivan Vaughan told Hunter Davies in 1967, "the old animosities were still there: refusing to talk to anybody, being rude, slamming the door. Now he's just as likely to say to people, 'Come in. Sit down.'" By the time of the *Sgt. Pepper* sessions, Geoff Emerick wrote, "it was evident that John's personality was changing. Instead of being opinionated about everything, he was becoming complacent; in fact, he seemed quite content to have someone else do his thinking for him, even when he was working on one of his own songs . . .

"No doubt Paul was aware of the situation," Emerick wrote, "and he was seizing the opportunity to step in and expand his role within the band."

Lennon was still in his accepting phase, standing by. As much as he was pleased with *Sgt. Pepper* — he clearly thought it was the best thing the Beatles had ever done — he was often in a state of psychological distress, even spiritual malaise. One night, he locked himself in his bathroom and begged God to reveal himself. "I just fucking got down on me knees," he said, "and I cried, 'God, Jesus or whoever the fuck you are — *wherever* you are — will you please, just once, just *tell* me what the hell I'm supposed to be doing."

It was a sign of his vulnerability that he became entranced with Alexis Mardas, a fast-talking Greek native whom John met through the scene around the Indica Gallery. Mardas was a television repairman, but he had big visions of electronic wonders, including wallpaper loudspeakers, an artificial sun, and a flying saucer he would coat with magic paint to make it invisible. John called him "Magic Alex" and he introduced him to Paul as "my new guru." ("But I didn't treat him that way," Paul said. "I thought he was just some guy with interesting ideas.")

It was George Harrison who brought the next guru into their circle, the Maharishi Mahesh Yogi, a little dervish of a man, an inveterate giggler, an entrepreneurial wizard who developed Transcendental Meditation and began to teach it on world tours. In February 1968 all four Beatles decamped to his ashram in Rishikesh, India. Ringo stayed about two weeks; Paul about five. John and George stayed about two months and left in a rush when Magic Alex whipped up rumors that the Maharishi made advances on his female disciples. John decided it must be true and turned on the Maharishi with wrath. (The song "Sexy Sadie" articulated his anger. "I copped out," John said, "and wouldn't write Maharishi, what have you done, you've made a fool of everyone.")

With his gurus, John played out his familiar power pattern: he made himself a pupil — but then, suddenly and aggressively, he struck out at them.

One fact of the Rishikesh adventure that gets less attention than it should is how John and Paul spent much of their time — which was singing and playing acoustic guitars and writing. At least fifteen Lennon-

McCartney songs that would appear on Beatles albums, including a good portion of *The White Album*, were written in that time.

When the studio sessions began for *The White Album*, John Lennon was in a new frame of mind. The sleepy, spacy quality in evidence during *Pepper* was gone, replaced by a trenchant and overtly hostile quality. Now he called *Pepper* "the biggest load of shit we've ever done" and insisted that these new recordings would need to be honest and raw, without elaborate production. "There was an aggressiveness I had never seen in him before," Geoff Emerick said of the first session. "By the end of the night he was almost psychotic."

From John's point of view, he was just taking charge again. "I was again becoming as creative and dominating as I had been in the early days," Lennon said, "after lying fallow for a couple of years." Though it was obviously causing tension in the studio, John read that as evidence that he was doing what he needed to do. "It upset the applecart," John said. "I was awake again and they weren't used to it."

I always thought we'd die together. Sometimes, I wish that we had.

—*Ralph Abernathy*

PART VI

INTERRUPTION

At 10:47 a.m. on March 30, 1988, Marina Abramović stepped onto the Great Wall of China where it begins in the mountains near the Yellow Sea and began to walk west. At the same moment, her partner, Ulay, stepped onto the Great Wall where it ends in the Gobi Desert and began to walk east.

They had been planning the performance for about eight years, raising money, securing permission from the Chinese. They originally intended to marry at the meeting point. But for several years before the walk, their artistic and romantic partnership had been fraying. A piece that grew out of their collaboration was, for some time, the only thing holding the collaboration together — and so they reconceived its meaning. On June 27, after walking three months for a combined 2,400 miles, they met near a cluster of Buddhist, Taoist, and Confucian temples. They embraced, took photographs, and then parted.

"He went to his jeep and I went to my jeep," Marina told me. "I left the country the next day." Four months later they walked the meeting moment again for a film crew—a reunion to reenact their disunion. They barely spoke for years after that. They have not worked together since.

It's fitting and proper to talk about the end of pairs. As long as we define end as the cessation of active engagement, we can say that it will surely come to all. Either someone dies, or the project ends, or troubles become more than the partnership can bear. These troubles usually grow organically out of the qualities that led the two people to each other in the first place. Outside forces play a role too, usually by exacerbating an inherent tension.

But the other meaning of "end"—the cessation of all ties—is another matter entirely. My experience is that no pair ever ends in this sense of the word. The analogy of a divorced couple with kids suggests some of the practical questions that emerge (like who has what rights) and the passions that are aroused (like how to handle feelings for an estranged intimate from whom one cannot, alas, fully separate).

But for creative partners post-"divorce," life can be even weirder than for ex-spouses. An individual's very self has taken shape through work shared with another person. So what exists of that self now? These questions go far beyond the legal or the emotional. They are existential, and they long endure. Even when one partner dies, what has come to life between partners lives on, in the shadows. We have to reckon at this stage with something far more complex than stories with unhappy endings. We have to reckon with the unhappiness of losing the shape of story itself.

23

"Listen, This Is Too Crazy . . ."

Stumbles

From what I've seen, there are two ways the work of a pair becomes interrupted: by stumble and by wedge.

I use the word *stumble* because the same energies that push a pair forward can also knock them over. Think of a toddler hurtling down a path. He may well fall, and you can't cry "Stop" often or loud enough to stop him without stopping childhood itself. You don't root for the kid to get hurt but you do root for him to take the risk. You wish you could be so brave.

"Why do pairs break up?" I asked Diana McLain Smith, a family therapist turned adviser to leadership teams, and she told me that to answer the question, you have to go back to how pairs begin in the first place.

"Opposites do attract," Smith told me, "and people see in someone different from them the potential to create something they can't do on their own. So they enter the relationship celebrating the differences. At some point, it's inevitable that the differences pose challenges that people don't know how to deal with. They find the exchange more noxious than creative. So now they have to negotiate differences that are not as happy making."

But by responding to the difficulties, the partners may exacerbate them. "Say you have somebody who is extremely spontaneous and action-oriented," Smith said, "and she connects with someone who is more grounded and reflective. The wild one finds the relationship centering, and the even-keeled person appreciates the stimulation. Over time, though, the more even-keeled person may feel overwhelmed by the randomness and the spontaneous person may start to feel more constrained. But the person who is more spontaneous will tend to amplify her needs — turning up the volume; maybe throwing tantrums or sulking — and the person who is more even-keeled mutes her needs. Now they're in a pattern, and it's self-reinforcing. The thing each one of them does brings out *more* of the thing they don't know how to deal with in the other." The worst part of these destructive patterns, Smith told me, is that each person in the pair doesn't see them as patterns — or as anything mutual. He or she just attributes the problems to the other partner. "It's like the fundamental attribution error. In relationships, when times are bad, people say, 'We have a fundamental problem. It's you.'"

One of my favorite end-of-relationship studies is by the sociologist Diane Felmlee. She asked people what had initially attracted them to an ex and what repelled them at the end. For about 30 percent of people, both answers were really the same, just cast in a very different light. One subject found his or her partner — Felmlee didn't identify gender — "sweet and sensitive" at first but later "too nice." One partner was wonderfully "strong-willed" and later obnoxiously "domineering." A partner with a great "sense of humor" later "played too many jokes." The study subjects seem to have lost their tolerance for the qualities that attracted them in the first place.

In the heat of the moment, each person wants to blame the other. The irony is that this is what makes the relationship seem unbearable in the end, because people come to feel helpless, Smith told me. "They come to think that the only way out is to exit."

"You mean to say," I asked, "that people don't really want out of the relationship itself, they just want out of the dynamic?"

"That's right," she said. "They don't want to go away from the person, necessarily. They want away from the feeling."

So this is the first answer to how creative work between people gets interrupted: by forces that arise organically out of the terms on which the work began. The people we're drawn to may unsettle us. They probably *should* unsettle us. But the differences that arouse us can later come to seem impossible. Graham Nash, for instance, found David Crosby's defiance invigorating — Crosby was the unruly yang to Nash's yin. Yet Crosby eventually pushed Nash to the breaking point when Crosby's willful, erratic nature became entwined with drugs and alcohol. The nadir, Nash told me, was a 1979 studio session where Crosby showed up strung-out, slit-eyed, covered in sores. "His voice was rough, husky; our harmonies were strained," Nash wrote in his memoir. "I couldn't vibe him out. I couldn't anticipate him anymore."

The music had always saved them, Nash told me, and he nurtured hopes it would again, even as Crosby nodded out during breaks. One night, the band warmed up for a new Nash song called "Barrel of Pain." "We had a great jam going," Nash recalled, "it was rocking like mad." As the studio amps vibrated with the sound, a crack pipe Crosby had laid on one of them slid off the edge, fell to the ground, and shattered. "I had tried everything with David," Nash told me. "I tried doing drugs with him. I tried doing less than him. I tried doing more than him. I tried staying away from drugs to watch him."

But what happened next was too much even for Nash.

Crosby stopped playing to try to put the pieces of the pipe together.

"That was it for me," Nash told me. "That was my darkest moment. When Crosby stopped the jam, I just went, 'Holy fuck.' That's when I realized that the drugs were more important to Crosby than the music."

"It was as clear as it could be," Crosby added.

"Even at the time?" I asked.

"Oh no, not for me," Crosby answered. "I was in a haze. But a few days later, Graham called me up and he said, 'Listen, this is too crazy . . .'"

Notice that Nash characterized the break not as personal exasperation but as a rupture of their shared faith. "We always promised that the music would be sacred," Nash told me. A mutual deference to whatever is sacred allows a pair to abide. It keeps them upright.

"I'd say that the key word is *humility*," *South Park* staff writer Vernon Chatman told me, reflecting on Matt Stone and Trey Parker, who, as I finished this book, had just wrapped their seventeenth season of the show, launched the fourth production of *The Book of Mormon,* and formed their own studio. "When two people come up against each other," Chatman said, "it's just natural that their egos are going to get battered. Humility is the thing that makes you recognize, 'That's my ego and has nothing to do with the larger issue.' It's just that thing where, 'There is me, there is you, and there is us.' And us is the biggest thing and you have to be reverent to it."

Chatman paused. "It's funny, because I'm saying all this shit like 'humility' and 'ego' and 'reverent,' but if you asked Matt and Trey they'd just say: 'It's like Van Halen. It's like a band. And the band is bigger than anyone in it.'"

Nash called it faith, Chatman humility. This devotion to the partnership may also come down to loyalty. No matter how far Elizabeth Cady Stanton pushed her, Susan B. Anthony remained at her side. "Like husband and wife," Stanton wrote, "each has the feeling that we must have no differences in public."

Irritations and divergences between two people are as inevitable as the chattering of the mind in meditation; for a partnership, the equivalent of returning to the breath is returning to the joint purpose.

But this may grow more challenging over time, because annoyances can increase with exposure, and with success. J.R.R. Tolkien was uneasy with C. S. Lewis's tendency to proselytize even when they were exchanging pages as young men in the 1930s. By 1947, after publishing fifteen books and running a radio broadcast during the war, Lewis had become, *Time* magazine declared in a cover story, "one of the most influential spokesmen for Christianity in the English-speaking world . . . for his listeners, almost as synonymous with religion as the Archbishop of Canterbury." This pop theology aggravated Tolkien, who believed preaching should be left to the clergy, and it contributed to a severe strain between the writers.

Irritants may begin as generative—like the proverbial sand grain in the oyster—but, over time, become merely irritating. Dean Martin and Jerry Lewis's act was built on Jerry looking to get a rise out of Dean, and Martin dressing him down or flicking him away. In one sketch, Martin (playing himself) is literally driven mad when every character he encounters—from the taxi driver to the man on the street to the psychiatrist himself—is Jerry Lewis. For years, there was palpable pleasure in Martin's exasperation. But as time wore on, the exasperation took on a life of its own.

One reason relationships can tip quickly is that both positive and negative stories tend to be reinforcing. The psychologist Sandra Murray has found that, early in relationships, stories often skew to the positive. The presence of illusions—"motivated misunderstandings," Murray calls them—are positively associated with "greater satisfaction, love and trust, and less conflict and ambivalence in both dating and marital relationships." And people not only tell themselves illusory stories, Murray found, but react to threats by deepening their attachment to them. That is, A not only idealizes B but reacts to troubling qualities in B by burnishing that ideal.

What often happens at the end of a relationship, Murray suggests, is that this feedback loop gets broken. Somehow, the troubling qualities of B are just too much for A to bear. And with the idealized narrative in tatters, a new narrative is constructed, casting the once-heroic, do-no-wrong partner as a goat who can do no right. Both stories, Murray argues, are ultimately meant to be protective—the first sort to protect A from worry and doubt, the second to protect A from the discomfort of ambivalence.

This helps explain the rapid fall of a partnership like Martin and Lewis, who went, in what seemed like a blink of an eye, from rambunctious friends to wary enemies. At their nadir, Lewis wrote in his memoir, he steeled himself to approach Dean and told him that he really thought what made their partnership magic was "the love that we had—that we still have—for each other . . .

"He half-closed his eyes, gazing downward for what felt like a long time," Lewis wrote. "Then he looked me square in the face. 'You can talk about love all you want,' Dean said. 'To me, you're nothing but a fucking dollar sign.'"

24

The Paradox of Success

Wedges

As with the human body, any major system failure can take down a pair, and the systems aren't always operating in stable conditions. As the world around the pair changes, the experiences of the two within it are naturally affected too. A wedge is whatever gets between two people or exacerbates an ongoing challenge.

Perhaps the most salient wedge for successful pairs is success itself. After two seasons of *Chappelle's Show*, 2003 and 2004, critics called it the best thing on television; the first season became the best-selling TV series on DVD ever. (It still is.) But with the explosive success of his show mocking racial stereotypes, Dave Chappelle feared he was fueling those same stereotypes. He grew suspicious of his colleagues. "If you don't have the right people around you, and you're moving at a million miles an hour, you can lose yourself," he said.

According to the show's co-creator, Neal Brennan, cracks in the partnership showed when they went to negotiate with Comedy Central to extend the show. Brennan pressed Chappelle to make a deal as a producing team first. Brennan's view was that Chappelle had nothing to lose, because Comedy Central needed him as both a producer and a star. Once the production contract was locked up, Brennan argued, Chappelle could go and "clean up" with his own deal as talent. "You could make the case that I was pleading that to get more money," Brennan told me. "But, in my mind,

I was pleading that to have a partner. I felt like we were going to kill together or we were going to bomb together."

Chappelle made his own deal with Comedy Central, reported to be worth $50 million for two seasons, leaving Brennan to negotiate separately as a producer, but the conflict between Chappelle and Brennan was only one spark in Chappelle's flameout. After taping just a few episodes of the third season, he fled the set, and the country, without telling his colleagues, friends, or family. "Success takes you," Chappelle said on his return, "where character cannot sustain you." The show never resumed. Chappelle has returned to the stage sporadically since then, and he and Brennan talk frequently. Asked if they will ever work together again, Brennan told me: "No fucking way."

Success was a wedge between Steve Jobs and Steve Wozniak too, not because of a crackup but because it led them down different paths. Apple Computer exploded in the late 1970s and early 1980s but Wozniak never took to management, and he lionized the kind of work that could be done alone. He went back to finish his engineering degree. He took up flying. After a plane crash, he left Apple — returning several years later as a bench engineer in the Apple II division. In 1988, after selling a company that created a universal remote control, he decided to teach elementary school. A 1998 *Wired* profile described him as "possibly the world's best Tetris player."

Meanwhile, Jobs — a textbook narcissist whose machinations were relentless — built an iconic career marked by at least one spectacular collaborative failure (with Apple CEO John Sculley) and a series of enormous successes: with Pixar's Ed Catmull and John Lasseter during his exile from Apple and, after his return, with a series of partners, including COO Tim Cook, retail chief Ron Johnson, and designer Jonathan Ive. "If I had a spiritual partner at Apple, it's Jony," Jobs told his biographer Walter Isaacson. "Jony and I think up most of the products together and then pull others in and say, 'Hey, what do you think about this?'" From these conversations, we can trace the gestation, or at least a critical shaping, of the iMac, the iPhone, and the iPad. The irony is that Woz is remembered as the sweet one, and Jobs as the brute, but the latter partner consistently did better work with people.

Success does more than create conditions that challenge a partnership;

it can lead to ideas that are fundamentally at odds with partnering. An impressive body of evidence shows that even *notions* of wealth and power can be fundamentally divisive to relationships. The psychologist Kathleen Vohs and colleagues have found that people with money on their minds are less likely to give time to colleagues who need help and more likely to sit farther away from others at meetings. Asked to choose between collaboration and solo ventures, they choose the latter. "Money brings about a self-sufficient orientation in which people prefer to be free of dependency and dependents," Vohs wrote. The psychologist Paul Piff's research has shown that high socioeconomic status can make people more selfish and insular (as well as less ethical and compassionate).

Success can also bring to the surface quarrels about credit that would otherwise remain underground. When Martin Luther King Jr. won the Nobel Peace Prize, in 1964, Ralph Abernathy was mortally offended that in the procession to the ceremony in Oslo, Sweden, he and his wife were assigned to ride in a car behind King; as Abernathy loudly insisted, he always rode *with* his partner. Abernathy appealed to King, who demurred, and then, Taylor Branch wrote, "stood frozen with embarrassment" as Abernathy tried to push his way past security. Later, Abernathy and his wife argued that they were entitled to half the prize money (about $54,000 — more than $400,000 in modern terms). This led to an "estrangement," one movement insider said, that remained a lasting presence between the civil rights partners.

Yet, however much the relationship was strained, it did not give way. In 1965, King insisted to the board of the Southern Christian Leadership Conference that it formally designate Abernathy his successor.

The most common wedge comes in the form of a third person who gets between a pair. When we consider the significance of this factor, we get a new insight into the strength of pairs that endure. One of the remarkable features of Matt Stone and Trey Parker's story, for instance, is the consistency and quality of the people around them — among many others, their lawyer, Kevin Morris, who represented them well before *South Park,* including the years when, Matt said, "he didn't make a dollar off us"; their executive producer, Anne Garefino, who has been on board since the *South Park* pilot in 1997 and now serves as CEO of an innovative corporation that manages the show's creative property; and their animation director, Eric Stough, who has known Trey Parker since middle school.

I know, this begins to sound like credits on a TV show, and no one watches those, but let yourself be bored for a moment because there's a great deal of infrastructure around an effective pair that should be boring to the general public. As a rule, if interest is drawn to that part of the organization, it's because things aren't going well. I made the point in the introduction that the dichotomies that we see in pairs are fractal; that is, they suggest a pattern that plays out on a variety of scales. We've already seen how the model applies inside the thinking mind.

There's also an extension *around* a pair of the same dynamics we see *within* a pair. So between Matt and Trey, one common dynamic is Matt = doer; Trey = dreamer. But Matt-Trey also form a unit in relation to Kevin Morris, and this relationship has its own dynamic: Matt-Trey = dreamer; Kevin = doer. This relationship between a pair and a third is often a stabilizing force. One common problem occurs when the third shifts course, or does something shifty, or disappears, or in any way ceases to play a healthy role. Even one change of this kind can be a full-force gale; two such changes can be a hurricane. In the late 1960s, John Lennon and Paul McCartney had three.

25

Failure to Repair

Why Did Lennon-McCartney Split?

On August 27, 1967, just months after the release of *Sgt. Pepper*, the Beatles' manager, Brian Epstein, died of a drug overdose. He was thirty-two years old. "We don't know what to say," John Lennon told reporters. "We loved him and he was one of us." It's a poignant remark because the band never again found someone they loved who would run their shop. For some time, they made the tragic mistake of neglecting to look. Instead, John and Paul took on not just the band's management but a vast and scattered expansion, beyond music into retail, film, and electronics, and beyond business into what Paul proudly called "Western communism."

Around this same time, George Harrison, a steady presence since he'd joined the band at fourteen years old, began to buck his role. Fascinated with Indian music, embraced by Bob Dylan as a peer, Harrison lost patience with his subordinate position to John and Paul. "Off to the side in the Beatles," Greil Marcus wrote, "you could always feel George Harrison pressing, sense his exclusion from the hot center where the geniuses held court, wonder if his resentments would ever flame up and burn." In the late 1960s, he reached that temperature.

Finally, women took new places in John's and Paul's lives. "At a certain age," Paul said, "you start to sort of think, 'Wow, you know I've got to get serious . . . I can't just be a playboy all my life.'" In December 1967, Paul proposed to his longtime girlfriend Jane Asher, but this turned out to be the endgame of their relationship, not a new beginning, and it unleashed a season of torrential change in John's and Paul's romantic lives — and brought women into what had been, for a long time, a closed scene between them, and within the band. "Now it would be seen as very chauvinist of us," Paul said. "Then it was like: 'We are four miners who go down the pit. You don't need women down the pit, do you?'"

These changes had a major effect on Lennon-McCartney, but only because of the inherent instability of their dynamic, the same instability that provided so much of the creative force. So far, we've talked about internal dynamics (and the stumbles that arise from them) and external conditions (the wedges that get between people). But of course, stumbles and wedges intersect and amplify each other, and what results can be confounding to participants and observers alike.

But confusion itself isn't fatal to creative work. Nor is a feeling of rejection or betrayal, or a wish to get the hell away. No, the only thing that is fatal to creative work is when the creatives stop working.

The wellspring of trouble for John and Paul, as with any pair, was the complex characters of the principals — and the spring of 1968 found both at the apogee of their peculiarities. John's ferocious charisma, his pathological ambivalence, his needy, dreamy, hungry nature had never abated, nor had his yearning for something bigger than Lennon-McCartney, bigger than the Beatles, bigger than any physical realm. John always had a dream: first it was rock 'n' roll itself, then fame, then to open the doors of perception — he often fell in with a guru, grew disillusioned, and needed someone or something else very quickly.

In early May, shortly after John returned from India — made a fool, he thought, by the Maharishi — he and Paul traveled to New York City to promote Apple Corps. This was the new holding company for the Beatles, and the absolute height of Paul's audacity, the apex of his incessant desire for more — more experiences, more control — combined with his unflagging sense that, at least with John Lennon by his side, he could do absolutely anything. With *Sgt. Pepper* behind them, and his vision for an aesthetic empire coming to life, Paul may have gotten the idea that he would be allowed a very long leash.

It was inevitable that John would yank his collar. The only surprise is the way he did it. They returned to England on May 16, 1968. On May

17, John had a revelation while tripping. "I've something very important to tell you all," he announced to the band at a meeting he convened. "I am . . . Jesus Christ come back again. This is my thing." He was "dead serious," his friend Pete Shotton said. Apparently John had the idea that *he* could be the guru he was waiting for. That lasted about a day. On May 18, 1968, with his wife, Cynthia, away on vacation, John placed a call to an avant-garde artist he knew. Her name was Yoko Ono, and she arrived at his house by taxi late at night.

There are so many legends and counterlegends about Yoko Ono and John Lennon that it is hard to get to the truth, especially because the testimony of the principals — John and Yoko themselves — can't be taken at face value. Yoko has said, for example, that John pursued her — and she eluded him — between when they met in November 1966 and when they became a couple in May 1968. But Yoko had solicited John avidly as a patron.

We should also steer clear of the opposite myth — that Yoko put John under her spell. To the contrary, for the sake of our story, it's vital to recognize his agency. The myth of Yoko swooping in and plucking John in her pincers is the ultimate storytelling cop-out, because it distracts from the more significant thing, which is the nature and direction of John's power. He was a vulnerable man, after all, but not weak; erratic but not passive.

My sense is that John saw in Yoko a singular concatenation of opportunity. She could be his mystical guru, his physical lover. She could revive the spirit of Stu Sutcliffe and show him what true art looked like.

She could also be a stick he could use to bash the back of his partner's head, which had, John certainly noticed, gotten even bigger in the last few years. What better way to strike back than to return to the primal root of power — to say, in words and deed: I care about you less than you care about me. I am ready, even eager, to leave you.

Indeed, on top of whatever other reasons John had for suddenly deciding that Yoko needed to be by his side at all hours — including at Abbey Road, including at writing sessions with Paul — there is the element of the long-standing infinite game. It's hard to believe, for example, that it is merely coincidence that John's Jesus freak-out, immediately followed by his Yoko freak-out, occurred just after he'd witnessed, at extremely close hand, a jolt of electricity between Paul and a woman named Linda

Eastman, who within months would be Paul's girlfriend and within a year would be his wife. Linda connected with Paul on the New York trip, and he invited her to ride in the limousine on the way to the airport. "There was something awfully steamy going on in that car . . . a lot of body heat," another passenger in the car said. "It was palpable; you could feel it." Two days after Paul brought his future wife in front of John, John found himself a new woman — and a new partner. He always had to top Paul.

The thing with John and Paul and women — it had been mixed up for a long while. In the Liverpool days, Paul had bought gold engagement bands for himself and his girlfriend Dot, and when John saw the rings, he turned to his girlfriend Cynthia and said, "Perhaps we should get engaged too." Paul broke up with Dot. John married Cyn soon after because he found out she was pregnant.

Flash-forward to 1968: In May, John let Cyn discover him with Yoko in their own house. In July, Paul pulled the same stunt with Jane Asher, who found him in bed with another girl at *their* house. Flash-forward about another year: On March 12, 1969, Paul and Linda got married. Straightaway, John began to inquire about how he could marry Yoko quickly. The ceremony happened on March 20 in Gibraltar.

The other thing I have to mention — it would be authorial malpractice not to mention it — is the obviously not-typical-heterosexual profile of John Lennon. This was a man who said of his lover Yoko Ono at the apparent height of his obsession with her: "It's just handy to fuck your best friend . . . And once I resolved the fact that it was a woman as well, it's all right." John told Yoko that he liked her because she was like a "bloke in drag . . . like a mate," and Yoko told him repeatedly that she considered him a "closet fag."

I don't see John as closeted in the typical sense, but there was weirdness between him and women, and he had a yearning for a certain kind of closeness with men that one feels in the pit. It's not part of the project here to discern the details of his sexuality. But the idea that John's attention simply wandered from Paul and the band because of his other interests, that he just fell in love with Yoko in the traditional way, doesn't ring true.

Nor did Yoko's presence suddenly mean an end to the music. Though the *White Album* sessions were often tense and unpleasant — the engineer Geoff Emerick disliked the scene at Abbey Road so much that he flat-out quit — the work didn't suffer, and the interconnections between songs, though more fraught and worked through with less generosity than in the past, still had tremendous heat. John led the sessions with "Revolution 1" and Paul helped dress that song to within an inch of its life before answering with "Blackbird," which may be his masterpiece. John made a role raid on Paul's oeuvre with "Julia" and "Good Night," and Paul did the same with "Helter Skelter" and "Why Don't We Do It in the Road." Even John's rage had a creative outlet; maddened by the endless takes of a swooning "Ob-La-Di, Ob-La-Da," he left the studio in a huff, only to return in a stoned swagger, commandeer the piano, and bang out the song at a much faster tempo, which became the recorded version.

No matter how thick the tension got, it still had a place in the room. And Paul was determined to carry on. Though Paul felt wounded by the way John withdrew from him and challenged by the way John began to roll over him, he returned with his own signature move: a blend of assertion and accommodation. Paul saw that John was going too far but he said he understood that was John's way. He held out hope that they could get back to the music. This had worked in the past.

The opposite of love is not hate; it's indifference. This is especially important to consider given how pairs may remain nominally together but only as performers or business partners — they may cease to create without any kind of explicit split. See the Rolling Stones' Mick Jagger and Keith Richards, or the Eagles' Glenn Frey and Don Henley (in their reunion years), or the Who's Pete Townshend and Roger Daltrey when they go on the road. They're like tribute bands to themselves.

Some pairs stop burning down the house and settle into profitable routines. John and Paul had the opposite problem. The yearning and desire to create with each other remained palpable, but the structure around them began to smolder, losing its roof, then its walls, and finally its foundation. John could taunt Paul, and Paul could placate John — but now George Harrison began to bristle, picking fights with both of them, and Yoko's presence only provoked George more. It's one thing for a little brother to get bossed by his big brother. It's another thing for a little brother to get bossed by his big brother's new girlfriend.

Paul's pattern was to make obvious signs of deference to John and then creep back to assert his leadership, with John's tacit approval, under the cover of another authority (Brian Epstein, say). Now there was no Brian

Epstein — no manager at all. For Paul to exercise leadership, he had to do it explicitly. This was never really his strong suit; as he hectored the band into working, he sounded more and more like the sort of schoolmaster they had created the band to avoid. In early 1969, in the sessions for what became *Let It Be*, George said he was done.

Yet this did not bust up the band. They were more like family than colleagues. The centripetal forces pushing them toward a common center were strong enough for them to withstand extreme centrifugal forces whirling them outward. Making music together had gotten down into their marrow. All the problems — the George problem, the Yoko problem, the no-manager problem, all intensifying and complicating the John-and-Paul power-struggle problem — were in full swing in January 1969 when they ascended to the roof of Apple Corps for their iconic final concert. They assumed their old positions.

John was stage left, Paul stage right, both looking out into the crowd — or, in this case, the surrounding rooftops — but able to turn in an instant to see each other. George stood to their left, facing both of them. On "Don't Let Me Down," John forgot the words in the third verse and went into a nonsense refrain, pure gibberish, but literally without a missed beat, he and Paul turned to each other and picked up with the correct lyrics as though nothing had happened. John beamed. Paul bobbed his head up and down in primal affirmation.

It's hard to find a better illustration of what the marriage expert John Gottman calls "repair" — a return to the strength of a partnership that tempers the effects of its weaknesses. There were many other examples. In April 1969, John and Paul recorded the vocals for "You Know My Name (Look Up the Number)," a fantastically weird B-side that Paul said is "probably my favorite Beatles track . . . just because it's so insane." Also in April, just back from his "bed-in" honeymoon with Yoko, John rushed to Paul's doorstep with "The Ballad of John and Yoko." With George and Ringo unavailable, John and Paul cut the song in one long day, John taking the guitars and lead vocal, Paul on bass, drums, piano, maracas, and harmony vocals.

One might even find repair in the heartbreak songs "Two of Us," "Oh! Darling," and "The Long and Winding Road." John had broken Paul's heart, but, for a time, Paul still had John to make music with him about it.

Yet while John and Paul could fall into rhythm in the studio, they could not work out issues of control and authority outside it. Apple was skidding on ice, and someone had to take the wheel. Still on his power trip, John found himself sweet-talked by a canny, dubious manager named Allen Klein and signed with him summarily. (Klein was the ultimate wedge: he won John over in part by demonstrating his knowledge of John's individual contributions to the Lennon-McCartney canon.) George and Ringo followed John and went with Klein—pure primate politics there. But Paul would not. He didn't trust Klein, and for good reason, it turned out. But his protests in this period were worse than futile: they only stirred John up more. "Look, John, I'm right," Paul said in one dispute. "You fucking would be, wouldn't you?" John shot back. "You're always right, aren't you?"

For a time, they had been a band without a manager. Now they had a manager without a band because Paul wouldn't work with Klein and insisted on having the entertainment lawyers Lee and John Eastman—Linda's father and brother—in the mix. So the conflict between John and Paul spun into a proxy war between Klein and the Eastmans.

In the end, the earthquakes and aftershocks made the music impossible, at least for a while. Nursing his wounds, Paul went off and made an album all his own—only to learn that Klein (supported by John and George) wanted the release delayed to make way for the Beatles' *Let It Be*. And some of those songs recorded in early 1969 had now been remixed, in a fashion horrifying to Paul and without his input. Paul's description of the pinch he felt is telling about how the infinite game became interrupted. He began to feel, he said, "like I'm a junior with the record company, like Klein is the boss and I'm nothing. Well, I'm a senior. I figure my opinion is as good as anyone's, especially when it's my thing. I figured I'd have to stand up for myself eventually or get pushed under."

26

The Never Endings

Did Lennon-McCartney Ever Split?

But when did John and Paul end their partnership? It's not when they fought over Allen Klein. That played out for several years (even longer when you consider that John, George, and Ringo ended up firing Klein and suing him). It's not when John told Paul he was leaving the band, in September of 1969, because the following February, John told the BBC that the interruption "could be a rebirth or a death. We'll see what it is. It'll probably be a rebirth."

The usual end given in Beatles narratives is when Paul released a new album in April 1970 with a self-authored Q&A that included the question: "Are you planning a new album or single with the Beatles?" and the answer: "No." This led the *Daily Mirror* to scream on its front page PAUL IS QUITTING THE BEATLES, and, in smaller type, "Lennon-McCartney Song Team Splits Up." The story spun quickly around the world.

When John saw the papers, he fumed that *he* should have announced the split. But he also chided Paul for taking things too far: "He can't have his own way, so he's causing chaos," he told *Rolling Stone*. "I put out four albums last year, and I didn't say a fucking word about quitting."

But Paul didn't quit either. The very next question in his self-interview was: "Is this album a rest away from the Beatles or the start of a solo career?" The answer: "Time will tell. Being a solo album means it's 'the start of a solo career . . .' and not being done with the Beatles means it's just a rest. So it's both."

Even Paul's lawsuit against John, George, and Ringo, filed on December 31, 1970, can't be given as the end, because it was so clearly a struggle over the business ties that the relationships had been enveloped in.

The reason we can't assign a date to when John and Paul definitively split is that it never definitively happened. It's tempting to think about the end of a partnership as being like the end of an opera, where two people come to dramatic conflict, sing in each other's faces, and decide to separate, weeping, like with Marina and Ulay's Great Wall walk. But more often, the end of a partnership is like one of those country songs where the character leaves home and never comes back, and no one — not the one who left, not the one who was left, not the one who's listening to the song — really knows why.

One reason it's so murky is that there's no final way out of the kind of creative partnership that we've been studying. To make work with another person is to open a kind of joint bank account in which two individuals deposit energy, time, creative daring — but where rights of withdrawal are beyond either individual's control.

"Just now again," Paul said in 1971, "I feel I can do what I want. So it's like there was me, then the Beatles phase, and now I'm me again." That, at least, was his aspiration, or perhaps we should say his fantasy, and the history of the partnership itself has been badly obscured by words spoken in its grip — mainly the illusion of distinct, measurable contributions to the Lennon-McCartney oeuvre. In 1970, Jann Wenner asked John Lennon when the songwriting partnership with Paul ended. "I don't know, around 1962, or something." He laughed, and it sounds like a nervous laugh, or maybe he was announcing a joke: 1962 was when Paul and John first began laying their compositions down on studio tape at Abbey Road, and though John's remarks were deeply inconsistent, a view took hold among close observers that the fabled partnership had for a long while been a fiction. Ten years later, after Lennon casually described the exchange between himself and Paul that created "We Can Work It Out," the writer David Sheff challenged him: "Haven't you said that you wrote most of your songs separately, despite putting both of your names on them?"

"Yeah," Lennon said. "I was lying," and he laughed. "It was when I felt resentful, so I felt that we did everything apart."

Today, many people who consider themselves knowledgeable take pride in their ability to distinguish between Lennon's and McCartney's work on Beatles songs, but this is really just a species of the lone-genius myth. It's ironic, since the myth prevents so many people from forming relationships in the first place, because they are in the grip of the idea that they can do it alone. And the same myth comes around and prevents us from seeing what happened between two people who really did take the leap (and who suffered the consequences).

By consequences, I mean that neither man could be rid of the other—not rid of their shared history, certainly, nor even rid of their yearning. "I know that Paul was desperate to work with John again," Linda McCartney told *Playboy* in 1984, referring to the decade between the cessation of their work and John's assassination in 1980.

For his part, John—true to his cycle—eventually spun himself through his period of fury at Paul, a period where he said he felt that he had been locked in a room with some guys and he absolutely had to get out. Even this period, it should be said, bore more in common with what we'd call an adversarial collaboration than with naked enmity—many highlights of John's work in the early 1970s ("Imagine," say) had his native honesty and lyricism along with a soaring, anthem-like quality he had learned from Paul. Paul, too, did *his* best work ("Maybe I'm Amazed," for example) with his innate melodic range and a concision and emotional vulnerability that he would drift farther and farther away from. "I suppose musically I'm competing with the other three, whether I like it or not," Paul said in 1971. The same year, John said that he expected his new album would "probably scare [Paul] into doing something decent and then, then he'll scare me into doing something decent, like that."

Just a few years after their breakup was in the headlines, it seemed quite possible that these most intimate enemies could join again onstage or in the studio. In 1973, John separated from Yoko. The business imbroglio was partly settled. Around 1974, John began to talk with fondness and enthusiasm about his old bandmates, and he began to answer the constant questions about reunion first with playful neutrality ("You never know, you never know") and then with avowed intention. For some time, it seems that the real obstacle to a Beatles reunion was George. "I've lost all that negativity about the past and I'd be happy as Larry to do 'Help!'" John told the journalist Chris Charlesworth in March 1975. "I've just changed completely in two years. I'd do 'Hey Jude' and the whole damn show, and I think George will eventually see that. If he doesn't, that's cool." That fall,

John said, "I personally would like the Beatles to make a record together again, but I don't really know how the other three feel about the idea."

One poignant evocation of John's yearning came when he joined Elton John onstage at Madison Square Garden on Thanksgiving night 1974. Backstage at Madison Square Garden, he was so nervous that he threw up in a toilet bowl. He insisted that Elton's writing partner, Bernie Taupin, go out onstage with him. Taupin walked with him a few paces and then said, "You're on your own."

When John came out, the crowd went so wild that the sprung floors underneath the Garden began to bounce. John wore a dark jacket and a black shirt with a gardenia pinned to it. It was the last time he would perform for the public. He and Elton played three songs, the last of which was "I Saw Her Standing There"—"a number," John said, "of an old, estranged fiancé of mine called Paul."

Like so many of John's phrases, this one doesn't make literal sense — *estranged* is past tense, about something broken; *fiancé* is all about expectation, the promise of eternal union. Yet, like so many of John's phrases, it works as poetry — it told the truth.

John and Paul had a major rapprochement in this period. They talked after Paul's dad died. They saw each other frequently. They once jammed together. Paul invited John to sit in on a session for his album *Venus and Mars,* which he recorded at Allen Toussaint's studio in New Orleans. One night John pulled Art Garfunkel aside to ask him about his recent reunion with Paul Simon. "I'm getting calls from my Paul," Lennon said, "who's doing an Allen Toussaint project. And he wants to know if I'm available for the recording. What should I do?"

Garfunkel said he should absolutely do it — so did May Pang, John's occasional companion at the time.

The saga of their yearning and missed connections lasted throughout the 1970s. The full story of why they never made music together again would take a whole other book to relate, but if it were written, we would see it was stumbles and wedges, stumbles and wedges, all the way through.

Even John's death didn't spell a proper end. When Bruce Springsteen said in his eulogy for Clarence Clemons, "Clarence doesn't leave the E Street Band when *he* dies. He leaves when *we* die," this wasn't just a romantic thought. Clarence and Bruce had the luxury of going out on good terms. Paul McCartney, by contrast, was left with a series of mixed messages and frustrated connections and outright insults from his partner to turn over for the rest of his days.

Survey the nearly thirty-five years of remarks from Paul McCartney, and it's immensely clear how alive this partnership — in all its glory and wounds and confusion — is in his life. In a 1984 interview, Paul was asked if he ever talked to Yoko Ono about John. "Yes. We did," he said. "In fact, after he died, the thing that helped me the most, really, was talking to Yoko about it. She volunteered the information that he had . . . really liked me. She said that once or twice, they had sat down to listen to my records and he had said, 'There you are.' So an awful lot went on in the privacy of their own place." He made the subtext explicit in a 1987 interview that he appreciated being told John "really did love me. Because it looked like he didn't."

Paul's uncertainty about whether John liked him — and whether he respected him — is a constant theme. He's sure, Paul has said, that John *must* have thought him special "because he'd have got rid of me . . . He didn't suffer fools gladly." Paul has also repeated, many times, the story of John's saying about one of his songs, "'That's a good one, there.'" "I just felt great," Paul said. "That was true praise." It's hard to avoid the conclusion that he is trying to reassure himself. He's also come to talk with some frequency about how he has conversations with John in his mind, though it's clear that no one could play with the same roughness and surprise as the real John Lennon. In October 2013, reviewing McCartney's sixteenth studio album as a solo artist — called *New* — the *Guardian* critic Alexis Petridis observed that McCartney had worked with four producers who'd made notable contributions, but it was obvious they were overly deferential.

"It's a shame, but perhaps therein lies the paradox of Paul McCartney's latter-day career," Petridis wrote. "The one thing he really needs is the one thing that he can't have, because it doesn't exist: an equal."

John and Paul are sui generis, but this is still a common story: you leave the guy who makes you miserable — but no one ever again makes you so great. According to the psychologist Diana McLain Smith, it's common for partners who have a stoppage amid conflict to suffer. "If they go away without seeing how they've contributed to the dynamic," she told me, "it's a real tragedy, because they've lost their chance to learn something. When you're up against the wall with another person—this sounds like a bromide but I've seen it over and over—you have a chance to learn something that no one else is going to teach you, because if you learn how to deal with the difference, you can transform yourself and grow, and suddenly the context, which presents as a ceiling on creativity, becomes a much higher floor.

"But if the relationship had an unresolved tension," she went on, "and every relationship that ends does, and both people are always contributing—then it's very much alive for both people, regardless of where they go or what they do. Even if you never see that person again, they will be a presence in your psyche with whom you have an ongoing dialogue. And you can always speculate about it but it's never as satisfying or fruitful without the other person there."

Are there any relationships that end naturally—the equivalent of the old lady dying at ninety-nine years old and everyone saying, "She had a good long life"? "Some relationships do have an expiration date," Smith told me. "It would be the one where the function and the purpose of the relationship doesn't exist anymore. According to both people. And that happens."

Perhaps the Watson-Crick relationship is an example. Certainly, unlocking the key to life through DNA fulfilled their mutual sense of purpose, though the existence of tension between them emerged in 1968 when Watson showed Crick a draft of his memoir *The Double Helix*, which began with the line "I have never seen Francis Crick in a modest mood." Crick wrote his ex-partner that the book was a "violation of friendship" that "grossly invades my privacy," but Watson published it anyway. Crick later said, "The person who comes out worst [in the book] is Jim." The two strong personalities were capable of butting heads still.

Suzanne Farrell and George Balanchine worked together until 1982, when he became too ill to work. The last pieces Balanchine choreographed were solos for her. When he died, in April 1983, she said she felt like an orphan, and when she retired from dance, in 1989, her future as a creative force in Balanchine's company was exceedingly uncertain. Eventually, she fell out with Balanchine's successor and ceased to have any formal association with the New York City Ballet. Then, in 2000, Farrell created her own company, at the Kennedy Center in Washington, DC, and she is now regarded as Balanchine's chief interpreter, essentially taking on for young dancers the role he played in her life.

From what I've seen, many individuals in pairs find themselves unable to adjust when they lose their partners. This is especially poignant with Ralph Abernathy and Martin Luther King Jr., given the way they played their roles with each other to the very end of King's life. On April 3, 1968, Abernathy and King came to Memphis to support a strike of sanitation workers. A meeting at the Mason Temple was called for, and, on a night with rain, thunder, and heavy winds, an exhausted King asked Abernathy to go in his stead. But Abernathy saw too many journalists and photographers for him to take the stage alone. "Martin, all the television networks are lined up waiting for you," Abernathy told his partner on the phone. "The people who are here want you, not me."

Lying on the bed at the Lorraine Motel, King said, "Okay, I'll come."

Abernathy did his usual warm-up talk and then introduced King, who began his speech by thanking him. "Ralph Abernathy is the best friend that I have in the world," he said, though of course these were the least noticed lines in a speech that became known for King's spiritual ruminations on the prospect of an assassination. "Well, I don't know what will happen now," he said. "We've got some difficult days ahead. But it really doesn't matter with me now, because I've been to the mountaintop."

The next night, at the Lorraine — outside room 306, known as the King-Abernathy Suite, because they stayed there together so often — King was shot on the balcony while Abernathy was in the room. "I wheeled," Abernathy wrote in his memoir, "looked out the door, and saw only Martin's feet." He rushed to him and cradled him in his arms. "His eyes grew calm," Abernathy wrote, "and he moved his lips. I was certain he understood and was trying to say something. Then, in the next instant, I saw the understanding drain from his eyes and leave them absolutely empty."

Having spent much of his career in his partner's shadow, after King's assassination Abernathy found this shadow widened and darkened. His was a triple blow: He had to operate without his partner. He had to function in ways that didn't suit him. (As King had arranged, Abernathy stepped up to lead the Southern Christian Leadership Conference, but he was not cut out to be the onstage star.) And he had to do all this in constant comparison to a martyr and civic saint. In his 1989 memoir, Abernathy revealed

King's marital infidelities—and was widely accused of betraying King and his legacy. A telegram came to Abernathy from prominent black leaders, warning him that the book would "rob you of your place in history." Abernathy died the next year. In 2013, amid celebrations for the fiftieth anniversary of the March on Washington, the historian David J. Garrow summed up Abernathy's place in the history of the occasion: "ignored and forgotten."

For Orville Wright, life without his brother Wilbur was like an engine with no fuel. Wilbur died of typhoid in 1912, nine years after their first successful flight. Orville sold their company three years later and spent the rest of his life tinkering and receiving occasional honors. He never married. He died in Dayton in 1948.

After losing their partners to death, many individuals find themselves even worse off—like an engine filled with gas but with no motor oil. The works do not come to rest; they overheat and burn out. Consider poor Theo van Gogh. On July 27, 1890, Vincent shot himself in the stomach. Theo sat with him as he died. Almost immediately, Theo's role as the sane, steady helper evaporated. To his brother, he had been ordered and clear, alternately avuncular and chiding. In their joint work, Theo often entertained risks but returned to a practical path. And despite ill health, he had laid the foundation for a conventionally good life—he had married and had a son he named for his brother.

But after Vincent's suicide, Theo lost the plot. He had a sudden mania for showing his brother's work and moved to a new apartment where he could hang Vincent's paintings as though in a museum. He quit his job, wanting to establish a new business immediately, and sent a telegram to Paul Gauguin that suggested a manic episode: "Departure to tropics assured, money follows." He signed it, "Theo, Director."

Theo's former employers described him as "a madman of sorts, like his brother the painter."

The artist Camille Pissarro reported that Theo had become "violent; he who loved his wife and his son so dearly, he [now] wanted to kill them."

In September, Theo complained that his "nerves . . . have got the upper hand." In October, his brother-in-law Andries Bonger asked the physician who had cared for Vincent to see Theo but to pretend it was an "impromptu visit." "Everything irritates him," Bonger wrote, "and gets him beside himself."

By mid-October, Theo was in an asylum. He was moved to another asylum, where, in late January 1891, he died. The cause of death, read the hospital notes, was "chronic illness, excessive exertion and sorrow." Though Theo may have suffered from other ailments — syphilis perhaps — Chris Stolwijk and Richard Thomson note in their biography that the circumstances of his death "remain mysterious" and he may have killed himself. In March 1891 the critic Octave Mirbeau wrote of Theo and his brother, "Mort aussi de la même mort que lui." He may have meant that they died *for* the same thing, but one possible translation is that they died *of* the same thing.

The larger story here is how relationships shape who we are. The coda to the Wordsworths' narrative is an amazing illustration. On the day of William Wordsworth's wedding, his sister grieved as if it were a funeral. Dorothy lived with William and his bride for the next twenty years. But she had "lived for and through her brother," said Frances Wilson, the author of *The Ballad of Dorothy Wordsworth*. "And when he no longer had need of her, you know, there wasn't any point to her life anymore . . . And so for 20 years, she lived in the top of the house like the mad woman in the attic in *Jane Eyre*."

When William died, she changed once more. "She suddenly becomes her old self again . . . having been unrecognizable for 20 years," Wilson said. "She became an adult again and became beautiful, wild, amazing, fascinating Dorothy again. So it's as if . . . when he'd gone, she could breathe again."

The fact of never endings will always butt up against our desire for a neat conclusion. Closure is a myth, but the idea wouldn't have such an appeal if it didn't resonate with a deeply held need to order experience into stories. Graham Nash told me the crack-pipe story as if it were an utter break with Crosby, but within months, they were playing at an antinuke benefit Nash had helped organize. Nash didn't want CSN at the gig, but the event needed a headliner, so he called Crosby and Stills both. If some partners find they can't get away from their exes soon enough, others find that confluence has set in so deep that they can never really get away.

After doing jail time, Crosby got clean, and these days they play together "every chance we get," Nash told me. When I last saw them, in

2013, they were performing at a benefit at the Pasadena Playhouse. Nash introduced a song called "Lay Me Down" by referring to the time "David and I did our solo record." He caught himself — he meant *duo*. "Solo, yeah," Nash said. "That's how close I think we are."

But even unhappy endings bring home the final lesson of creative exchange, which is that when you get mixed up with another person, you become something else — for better and worse. Once in, there is no way out.

Consider Marina Abramović and Ulay. Their last performance at the Great Wall of China was one of the most affecting — and apparently unambiguous — ending stories in the history of collaboration, and it had an equally effective epilogue in the moving reunion at the Museum of Modern Art, included in the documentary *Marina Abramović: The Artist Is Present*. The film followed the 2010 MoMA Marina retrospective and centered on her three-month performance in which she sat placidly every day, eight hours a day, six days a week, while members of the audience took turns sitting across from her and staring. At one point, Marina opened her eyes to see who the next person in front of her was, and she saw Ulay. Her eyes grew wet. She reached out and took his hands. The audience broke into applause. "The Reunion of These Two Artists Will Make You Cry," read the headline on BuzzFeed. The video zoomed around the web.

When I began to research Marina and Ulay for this book, much of what I knew of their relationship came from this documentary. In addition to the scene at the MoMA, the film shows them driving upstate to Marina's country house and sharing a meal — and includes Ulay reflecting on their work, wistfully, generously (and at times, it seems, with a longing to return to it). In my first interview with Marina, we spent most of the time talking about the work she and Ulay had done together and didn't get to the breakup years for a while, so the idea of their happy reunion stuck in my head.

But when I talked to Ulay in November 2013, I quickly saw that the story was more complicated. Though he said he had "no hard feelings" about Marina, he also pointed out that her MoMA retrospective had included works they created together that were, he said, "our common spiritual property." "There were a lot of our common works," he told me, "and also her work sitting at the table was actually our *Nightsea Crossing* piece cut in half. Rather than me, she invited seven hundred or seven thousand other people. She didn't inform me, she didn't ask me, whatever. She just went ahead. Some people in New York—pretty serious people, I won't mention the names—said actually it should have been called *The Artist Is Not Present*."

Later that day, I talked to Marina, and I mentioned my conversation with Ulay.

"We're actually not talking," she said. "Did he tell you that?

"He send me the letter from his lawyer, that I'm not doing as I'm supposed to do. And I have this huge list of things that he's not doing right, so I got fed up with this, so we're not speaking."

The dispute had to do with the material in their archive, which Marina bought from Ulay, eleven years after their split, for $210,000. They drew up a contract with terms that "aimed to cover every eventuality," Marina's biographer, James Westcott, wrote, noting that they had what amounted to a "divorce settlement" meant to put "disputes to rest."

But, of course, no divorce agreement can put disputes to rest. The very conditions that make them necessary—when rapport and trust have been broken—often make them ineffective. And so a pair like Marina Abramović and Ulay are left standing on either side of a breach, unable to cross it, and unable to walk away. What lies in the breach is a piece of themselves.

"Is this anything new," I asked Marina, "or has this been a constant battle?"

"Constant battle," she said. "Constant. Constant. But you know, the things with the couple is disaster generally." She laughed. "If one of them die maybe it's more lucky because there is good memory. Otherwise it is a mess."

We talked some more about the ownership of the archive, then—out of nowhere, or so it seemed—she brought up the Great Wall walk. I took notice, because Ulay, unsolicited, had also brought up the performance, mentioning that in the documentation for the piece, Marina was crying—he said he thought it was a performance for the cameras.

Marina had a bone to pick too. "You know," she said, "the one thing that I will never forgive him, it's that he literally—walking the Chinese wall, he stopped on the point where it was between Taoist and Confucius monastery because that was a beautiful spot to meet, and he wait there three days, which I have to walk extra to meet him. I want to kill him."

I began to ask her another question, but she cut in.

"I'm always getting to bad mood when we talk about this. It's like, how many years is now since '88?"

"That's twenty-five years."

"Oh my God, twenty-five years. Can you imagine? And it's still not settled? It'll probably never settle till we die."

It is joy to be hidden but disaster not to be found.

— *D. W. Winnicott*

Epilogue: Barton Fink at the Standard Hotel

December 24, 2013

I am disorganized, moody, vain — a writer, in other words, and though I've leaned heavily on my editor, principally, plus a battalion of friends and colleagues while writing this book, there is no saving me from myself when a deadline nears and I have to produce more or less alone.

I thought I would finish this book by Thanksgiving, and I rented my house for the winter holidays to finance a trip to Mexico. With the book decidedly not finished, and the rental too late to cancel, I booked a room instead in downtown Los Angeles. You may have heard the phrase *drop-dead deadline*. Mine is January 2. I've been here since December 21. This morning, as I walked the hallway toward my room — deep red carpet; clean white walls; a long walk because the elevators are on the west side and my room faces east — I thought of another writer on deadline in a Los Angeles hotel.

In the Coen brothers' film, Barton Fink checks in to the Hotel Earle to write a screenplay and, near the end of the movie, finds himself handcuffed to the bed while the hotel burns around him.

I feel like this is where I'm headed, metaphorically speaking.

I'll be straight with you. This is no Hotel Earle. The wallpaper is not peeling. No large sweaty man has asked me to hold a box. My room is clean and modern, and light pours in through tall windows. The view has a cityscape quality, like the set behind David Letterman's desk, that gives you that feeling of being an observer of something grand and intricate but also towering over it.

Room service is twenty-four hours. The menu includes fresh watermelon juice.

Actually, if you wanted to design a pod from which to live with maximum comfort and minimal relational obligation, this would be an outstanding prototype. And this is my concern — that I have come to an absurd manifestation of my isolated condition.

Further absurdity: I now fear that I will fail to properly finish this book on creative relationships and that said failure will proceed directly from my failure to manage my own.

Let me catch you up. The subtext of this book is that from the moment I had the idea, I thought about Eamon Dolan — thought about him as an editor for the project and as an example of the chemistry that I intended to investigate. In the five years since then, I've lived every theme I describe here through our relationship, and I offer the following snapshots — one corresponding to each of the major stages we've explored — by way of gesturing at the depth and breadth of the connection.

1. Eamon runs his own imprint at Houghton Mifflin Harcourt, where his office door is covered by six hundred refrigerator magnets (including a photograph of Gilda Radner, the back end of an elephant, and a map of Texas with a working thermometer). The magnets speak to his eclectic interests, his voracious curiosity, his openness to the odd and authentic. I try to be authentic but I am certainly odd, and the sound of Eamon's voice has always served to flip a switch in me. When I get him on the phone, the electricity is palpable.

Our sympathies run deep, yet we are entirely unalike. He is a linear and rational thinker, whereas my thinking is circular and emotional. He is a steady, sanguine man; I am melancholy and hypomanic. He presents as even-keeled and maintains considerable reserve; I am erratic and known to overshare. He is efficient; I am . . . I don't know. What do you call someone who takes five years to write a book? *Inefficient* seems a little kind.

It's strange how connection is so comforting and unsettling at the same time. As I work with Eamon, I often feel like a stranger to myself. Not a foreigner, exactly. But definitely someone I'm curious about and perplexed by. I frequently feel sharper, smarter, better. Yet I also feel certain that I have left aspects of myself behind. Sometimes with pleasure, sometimes with dismay, I wonder: *Who is this person wearing my clothes? "Joshua Wolf Shenk"? Who is that guy?*

2. Joshua Wolf Shenk in this context is the author of an Eamon Dolan Book. I told Eamon when he bought the proposal at the Penguin Press that we ought to put his name on the cover, *edited by*. He demurred (though I believe he was tickled by the thought). A year later, he left Penguin to create his own imprint at Houghton Mifflin Harcourt, so my wish to have the credit line on the book jacket came true.

In our conversations, I move between *I* and *mine* and *we* and *ours* fluidly (as does he), and though I don't stop to unpack it every time, I'm aware that I'm riding a line between individual identity and joint identity. I find this exhilarating and terrifying. Shortly before Eamon told me he was moving houses, I heard the news through the grapevine, and as I considered the prospect of being stranded — an author's contract is with the publishing house, not an editor — I thought I would have to abandon the book if I could not move with him, because I wouldn't be able to write it without him. It's ironic, because in the years since then, in moments of high frustration, I several times went over in my mind my legal options for withdrawal per that same contract I signed in 2010 with Penguin (and that was taken up in 2011 by Houghton Mifflin Harcourt). These thoughts of leaving are like those of the small child who puts an apple and a stuffed animal in his backpack and walks out the front door. My wanting to leave is tied up in the emotions of being unable to leave.

3. In terms of the primary archetypes laid out in this book, I'm the star, while Eamon directs. I am liquid, and Eamon contains. My job is to push against the conventions of "big idea" books. Eamon's job is to hold the project to the primary necessities of the form.

Yet we are not stereotypes. For example, finding and naming the thematic stages has been my work principally (this is the work of a container). I've also pushed for organization via the traditional mode of narrative; Eamon has pushed for a more audacious organization by idea. About a year ago a friend of mine, an accomplished editor and Pulitzer Prize–winning writer, told me that the plan for the book — to consider scores of stories alongside one another — was nuts. I called Eamon afterward and said, "My friend says this is nuts and I have to say I agree." Eamon said it was not nuts and I trusted him and followed his direction.

4. The distance between writer and editor is both profound and negligible. Eamon and I have gone months without talking. And we have talked for multiple hours on consecutive days. Though I tend to live with highly fluid boundaries, I'm acutely aware of a steady remove from Eamon that I respect. For example, I have his mobile number — he called me on it once and I saved the number — but I've never used it. I've never texted him. On nights or weekends, I send an e-mail or leave a message on his office voice mail.

At these times I regard Eamon as being on another planet, more or less, and I regard myself as a kind of space agent, beaming out messages to the beyond. Sometimes answers come back. Living this way feels immensely connected and, I will say, also lonely, in a Major Tom or "Rocket Man" sort of way.

5. It's natural to ask how conflict can be avoided. But the better question is: How can it be maximized in the context of a productive ongoing relationship?

I rely on Eamon's steady dispassion to balance my emotional extremes. I rely on his being decisive and unrelenting. I call and propose three ideas, and, after appropriate discussion, he renders a verdict, something along the lines of "Try number one. Drop number two. Do more research on number three and get back to me."

But at times Eamon's direct, decisive style has felt hurtfully cold. For example, Eamon believes — he has told me several times — that the main work of discussing early drafts is to focus on what needs improvement, whereas I feel the need for bountiful encouragement and coaxing alongside admonitions to improve. My needs may be excessive. Correct that — I'm sure my needs are excessive, but my point here is that when I went over his responses to my first full draft, I became depressed and the book ground to a halt.

This was in the spring of 2013. According to the original schedule, I was supposed to deliver revisions and rewrites on June 1, but it quickly became clear that this was not going to happen, and the book was rescheduled.

The next deadline for the book was November 1. I missed it.

Describing the destructive patterns that relationships can fall into, the psychologist Diana McLain Smith identified a dynamic that I now think of as the horrifying amplification. This is the situation where two partners, each finding his needs unmet and frustrated by the other's contrasting style, respond by bringing their styles even more fully to bear. From my side of things, I felt like I was slow in part because I needed more encouragement, more support, more structure. Even as I ran late, I presented these needs. As you can imagine, Eamon was disinclined to meet them. To the contrary, he became more stern, more distant, and, in one instance, totally irate, writing me that "all the practical issues aside, you have what I would call a moral deadline — an obligation to deliver what you promise, to not make excuses, and to not implicitly blame me for your perseveration."

At this point in the book business, the agent steps in, and mine did, and she delivered the news to me that my next deadline was January 2 — this one to respond to Eamon's edits and submit a *final* final manuscript, which would go to production. I had two and a half weeks to do it. Then I got the flu. Then my ninety-nine-year-old grandmother died. Then I came home and had to cede my house to a paying stranger. Now it's now and I'm Barton Fink at the Standard Hotel.

To heighten the stakes: Eamon, in his last round of edits, instructed me to end the book with an exhortation to readers "to embrace the possibility of creative pairs in our own lives." But to exhort, I have to step away from my pose as journalist-scholar and introduce myself. I like the idea of the epilogue of a book being similar to the talkback after a play. When the playwright comes out from behind the curtain, he can make a self-deprecating joke or offer a revealing anecdote that charms the audience. But if his eyes are bloodshot and his jacket is ripped, the audience is going to be *worried*.

I certainly don't feel like a man in a position to exhort.

I struggled with this for a while before it occurred to me that I may be just the one to exhort because I am among those who very much need exhorting to. So here we go.

The first thing to do is try.

Start small. Connection will not swoop down on you like a hawk seizing a mouse, and even if it does come toward you like a boat while you're floating in the ocean, you will still need to grab the rungs of the ladder and climb onto it, and the first step may not be the hardest, but it is, often, the wildest. The gap from zero to one, from an abyss where anything is possible to a particular place where the possibilities are distinct, may be hard to conceive.

To try, press the green button — not the red one — when your phone rings.

To try, ask for help — send an e-mail: "This is Major Tom to Ground Control."

To try, find a stranger who gets you or a friend you think is strange. Go to a place where people share your interests, like a writers' conference or a skate park.

To try is to risk humiliation. I heard a lecture some months ago on fear and the lecturer confessed that she *felt* fear speaking to us from the stage. She went on to talk about the evolutionary biology of fear, how we are built to flee from predators, to evacuate our excess solids and liquids and run. Someone asked, in the Q&A, what would account for the fear of public speaking since there were evidently no lions in this lecture hall. The room puzzled over this for a few minutes, then someone said: It's because being chased by lions in evolutionary time was no greater threat than being abandoned by the pack. To be abandoned by the pack was death — to say something wrong was to risk this abandonment.

Fear is the emotion we feel when we need to flee danger. Shame is the emotion when the dangerous thing is what we feel.

To try may be to lip-synch to a Bon Jovi song on the Jumbotron at a Celtics game. It may be to do your thing, or help someone else with her thing, or sit around with someone and say, "We need a thing. What's our thing?"

To try is to risk succeeding. What we fear isn't our weakness but our power. This is probably true. It's also true that we don't get what we want, we don't get what we deserve — we get what we can stand.

December 26

This morning I sent a flurry of text messages and e-mails. Sent parts of what you've just read to Jenny, to Josh. Called Matthew. Texted Jillian: *Can you talk today?* I felt a little foolish. No one answering.

Then Matthew called back and we talked through the whole thing about Eamon. I decided to send him a note, a combination of apology re deadlines and a confession of my problem exhorting. "This is Major Tom to Ground Control."

Jenny wrote me back. Helpful. Ted called and I was writing. My finger hovered over the red button but I pressed the green one instead.

The next thing to do is accept.

Accept that your partner is a pain in the ass. Accept that you are a pain in the ass, so the two of you are made for each other. Accept that what makes you furious about your partner is wrapped up with what excites you. What you most love and what drives you most crazy is the same thing, just on a bad hair day.

Accept that the people you need will please you and disappoint you but that the index of the creative experience is not your pleasure or disappointment. Your thoughts and emotions are not immaterial, but they are not the crux of the matter. The crux of the matter is the work.

Accept that reality is not in your mind. Reality is between you and another person.

Once, I interviewed a scholar of Martin Buber named Claire Sufrin because I wanted to know more about the dialogical idea that underlies his book *I and Thou*. Buber's basic premise is that there are two kinds of meetings: the I/it, in which the subject approaches the object as something to be used toward an end, and the I/Thou, in which two entities have what Buber called an encounter, a true meeting, in which there is a recognition of totality. The subject/object distinction dissolves.

The I/Thou relationship, for Buber, is the essence of the holy.

While this basic idea is fairly clear, *I and Thou* is arcane and philosophical and hard to parse, so that's why I talked to Claire Sufrin. She started off by telling me that *Thou* is a holdover from an early translation and that the book really ought to be called *I and You*. The point is not to encounter the divine but to encounter another individual — even a nonhuman thing, Buber proposes — and through this meeting to touch divinity (for the atheists, read: ultimate goodness).

I asked Claire: Did Buber ever suggest steps toward such an encounter

r aspects of the encounter? (You know by now how much of my job has
een to break down the ineffable into pieces, into steps, into stages.)

"No," she told me, "and that is a large part of his point — that we have
choice between thinking about things as a whole or as a sum of their
arts. Imagine that you meet someone and you leave and say, 'That was
erson X,' and you describe that person: 'Pretty tall, has brown hair, wears
lasses,' and so on. You enumerate that person's characteristics in order to
reate a fairly detailed realistic description. That's an I/It relationship. You
re seeing the person in their parts and details.

"To have an I/Thou relationship with that very same person," Claire
ontinued, "to share something that speaks to what's most meaningful
the world — if you have an encounter like that, you come away and you
an't actually describe who it was. You would struggle to describe it, to
ven talk about it, and yet internally you feel like you've been changed."

Accept that this is possible.

Accept that you can surrender to whatever is larger than you or to
whatever within you leads in that direction.

he next thing to do is play your part. *Part* in the dictionary —"a piece or
egment of something." *Play* —"engage in activity for enjoyment and rec-
eation rather than a serious or practical purpose."

Creative work depends on play. Creators face the shackles of the world
s it is and try to discover the world as it can be. The way out of the shack-
es isn't to find the key or to strain like the Hulk until they burst. The way
ut of the shackles is to stop believing in them.

To play your part, do what you do best.

To play your part, talk to someone. Talk to your partner.

Be as honest as you can be in such a way as to make him hear it. Some
people need a cup of sugar for every drop of criticism. Give them the sugar.
Some people can take the medicine straight. Pour it out in generous doses.

Talk to yourself. Since I researched the part of the book about the dialogical nature of thinking, I've spent a lot of time trying to cultivate a conversation in my own mind. My therapist gave me the same instruction:
"Talk to yourself like you'd talk to your child." It feels weird at first, but it
helps.

You seem frustrated, I say to myself.

I am, I answer. *I have more to do than I have time for.*
What is it you have to do? Can we put it on a list?

Self-talk shouldn't substitute for talking to other people. But self-talk can
be helpful preparation for social talk, and the right kind of social talk can
facilitate creative self-talk. This is a tricky thing to get right, because social talk can also knock us sideways, and self-talk can also lead us down
rabbit holes. Play with it.

December 29

I've been counting down every day since I've been here — day nine, day
eight, day seven, and so on — but just this afternoon I started to become
acutely aware of the *hours.* When I'm far from a deadline, it feels totally
abstract. As I get closer, I know it's real but it's still an idea. At a certain
point, I begin to feel the deadline like a physical thing. I feel it in my gut
that someone is actually going to be on the other end of these words.

I got that feeling this morning, sat in it all afternoon; it was all around
me, viscous. Somehow, a few minutes ago, I lost it. I snapped back into
myself again. I lost the connection.

The next thing to do is watch some Louis CK and go to sleep.

December 30

When I went over how my relationship to Eamon corresponds to the
themes of the book, I didn't know what to say about the last part. Now I
offer this.

6. To make things, we break things. To make ourselves, we break ourselves. Imagine the best you've ever felt and the worst thing you've ever
feared. Seeing a connection through to its potential will bring you both.

It's tempting to think about interruption as an end of relationships and
of repair as a way to stave off the end. On a practical level, it's true: repair
is the difference between relationships that last and those that founder.

But repair ≠ restoration. Repair is not eliminating the cracks that let
the light in. It's about tolerating them. Repair, for me and Eamon, is in
the small talk we make when we get on the phone. Repair is in the fatty
thoughts that we cook until they are lean. I always feel repaired when I

present a problem and he answers with one or another of his maxims, such as: "The art of book writing is not in addition but subtraction"; and "Instinct is the subconscious expression of experience"; and "Let your freak flag fly."

Repair is doing whatever it takes to work.

And so, in the end, I am not handcuffed to the bed as the building burns. I may be physically apart, but I am not alone. It is necessary at times to fall back into the abyss of one's mind, and it is necessary to return, to charge again into the space between yourself and others, whatever that looks like, to take someone's hand, and head out of the room of isolation, and into the bustle of connection, to remember that, for any of us, any ordinary street crossing can become our Abbey Road.

The next thing to do is finish, or, at least, surrender. Give over the thing you've both created and start the process over.

Los Angeles, California
January 2, 2014

Acknowledgments

Eamon Dolan is the co-creator of this book, and I thank him first and last. My agent, Betsy Lerner, guided the project with characteristic devotion, skill, and good humor. Thanks, as well, to Ben Hyman, Larry Cooper, Tracy Roe, Taryn Roeder, and Ayesha Mirza at Houghton Mifflin Harcourt, and Yishai Seidman at Dunow, Carlson and Lerner.

In the early phases when drafts were so ugly they could hardly be graced with that name, and again in the final months when the race was on, Meehan Crist made this book more lucid, better reasoned, and more lyrical. Thanks, too, to Meghan O'Rourke for her editorial advice and fellowship, and to Jenny Mayher, editor, writer, librarian, activist — and my ideal reader for twenty-five years.

As is often the case with offstage collaborators, Eileen Gibson Funke's role can only be described using a string of nouns. Researcher does not suffice, though she researched pairs in great depth and with great finesse. She also helped organize what sometimes felt like limitless material, functioning at times as editor at large, project manager, sounding board, and contributor. She was also, for three years, the one I could always turn to whenever I needed support — or a good laugh.

Sue Parilla's role *can* be described in a phrase — fact checker — but this does not convey the skill and discernment that someone like Sue brings to bear. Yes, she made sure the book correctly described the fourth position in ballet, and properly spelled "Slurpee." But she also waded chest-high into the swamps of knowledge this book touches on — a hundred such swamps in this book—and made herself such an expert that she could alert me not just to black-and-white facts but to many shades of accuracy. As if this were not enough, she topped off her dogged commitment and impeccable judgment with enormous kindness.

Josh Axelrad has been my primary reader for some years and went through most of this book several times. Many times have I quoted to him what Wilbur said of Charlotte: "She was in a class by herself. It is not often that someone comes along who is a true friend and a good writer. Charlotte was both."

Thanks to my other Charlottes, great minds and devoted friends and sharp readers: Jillian Lauren, Todd Hasak-Lowy, Alex Beers, Adam Piore, Elizabeth Scarboro, John Gilmore, Ari Handel, Elisabeth Subrin, Mari Brown, Ted Rose, Pari Chang, Martina Dolejsova, Michael Kadish, Agatha French, Bevan Thomas, Andy Walter, Tessa Blake, Jamie Blaine, Gareth Cook, Julie Perini, Stephen Elliott, John Cloud, Brooke Delaney, Mara Naseli, Dan Kennedy, Anna Schuleit Haber, Julian Rubinstein, Mary Ann Marino, Brian Hecht, Sara Marcus, Nell Casey, Alissa Quart, Bliss Broyard, and Rachel Lehmann-Haupt.

Thanks to the Webbers: Lea Thau, for her steadfast encouragement, and Oliver Wolf Shenk, for his turtle walks and giraffe impressions, and to Lucy, Henry, Abraham, and Anabel.

Thanks to Jon Shenk and Bonni Cohen for their love and example.

Thanks to Nicholas Lemann, Bruce Feiler, and Andrew Proctor for generous counsel.

I would not be a writer if it weren't for my brother David Shenk, who shared with me his wisdom, as he always has, from start to finish.

Special thanks to Sam Linsky and Jennifer Senior, who helped me get this project off the ground.

Some critical ideas in this book were developed at the Arts in Mind Series, exploring the intersections of creativity and psychology. Thanks to my colleagues M. Gerard Fromm, Edward R. Shapiro, Jeremy Safran, Lisa Lewis, Jane Tillman, Lee Watroba, Catherine Boutwell, and Alexandra Shaker.

I will largely restrain myself from acknowledging, again, the many scholars and creative pairs who shared their knowledge with me, opened their homes and studios to me, and in many cases reviewed the work for accuracy; they are named in the sources and I am deeply grateful. But I need to highlight Robbi Behr and Matthew Swanson, co-creators of Idiots' Books and Bobbledy Books, who gave of their experience as a creative pair with generous devotion and relentless honesty. Every major theme I develop in the book was tested and refined with their example in mind — often on the phone with them, or on Skype, or in e-mails. If this book had godparents, it would be Robbi and Matthew.

In the nascent stages of this book, the scholar Elyse Graham was my compatriot and teacher, and Stacey Kalish was my researcher in chief.

Thanks to John Schuster, Gwyneth Shanks, Grace Littlefield, Kelly Diamond, Kevin Dutch, Domenic Priore, Joe Marchia, and Kate Midden; and to Sean Hemeon, Jelena Mrdja, Devin Lytle, Iris Porter, Lenae Day, Patricia Beltran, and Estela Martinez Beltran.

This project began with a series in *Slate* commissioned by David Plotz and edited by Michael Agger, and a portion of it found a home in the *Atlantic,* thanks to Scott Stossel, Toby Lester, and Kasia Cieplak-Mayr von Baldegg.

Portions of this book were written at Yaddo (2012), The MacDowell Colony (2011), the Norman Mailer Center (2010), and the Blue Mountain Center (2009). Thanks to the staff who make these sublime places possible and to the fellows who bring them to life. I'm grateful, too, for the community and resources afforded by Suite 8 in Silver Lake, the Huntington Library, the Writers Junction, the Brooklyn Creative League, the Brooklyn Writers Space, the Wertheim Study at the New York Public Library, the Erikson Institute for Education and Research at the Austen Riggs Center, and the Rose O'Neill Literary House at Washington College.

Thanks to the teachers and staff at the Los Angeles Family School.

It's staggering for me to review this list, especially because it is so paltry (a) in its acknowledgment of those named and (b) in how few of the people who have affected and shaped my life *have* actually been named. It is true, as Shelley said, that we are a sum of all our influences; it is true that any name on any book cover is but a hyperlink, and that readers — to know the full picture of how it was done — ought to click on it and see the complete list of associates, and each of *those* names, too, should be a hyperlink, and so on.

But since this is not possible, you can focus your gaze again on a place no less mysterious, no less amazing — the space between me and Eamon Dolan, whom I thank again, and last, and who has my lasting thanks.

Selected Sources

For complete citations, see the book's endnotes. What follows is an overview of my principal sources, organized alphabetically by pairs, followed by my research highlights for major topics, such as creativity, relationships, and social psychology.

Ralph Abernathy and Martin Luther King Jr.

I began with Abernathy's book *And the Walls Came Tumbling Down: An Autobiography*. His reminiscences are also a strong presence in a book edited by his daughter Donzaleigh Abernathy called *Partners to History: Martin Luther King Jr., Ralph David Abernathy, and the Civil Rights Movement*. King's writings are collected in a book edited by Clayborne Carson, *The Autobiography of Martin Luther King Jr.* For any study of the civil rights era, Taylor Branch's three volumes are seminal: *Parting the Waters: America in the King Years, 1954–63; Pillar of Fire: America in the King Years, 1963–65;* and *At Canaan's Edge: America in the King Years, 1965–68*. Branch shared his thoughts with me in an interview.

Marina Abramović and Ulay

Marina Abramović: The Artist Is Present, a documentary directed by Matthew Akers and Jeff Dupre, gives an outstanding overview of the Abramović-Ulay pairing and includes considerable footage of their performances. The catalog to Marina's 2010 Museum of Modern Art retrospective, edited by the curator Klaus Biesenbach, has the same title as the film. James Westcott's *When Marina Abramović Dies* is the standard biography of the artist and has a thorough treatment of the Marina-Ulay years. I also consulted Thomas McEvilley's *Art, Love, and Friendship: Marina Abramović and Ulay, Together and Apart*. I spoke with Marina and Ulay several times each, and Ulay shared with me an as-yet-undistributed documentary on his own career called *Project Cancer: Ulay's Journal from November to November*, directed by Damjan Kozole. Chrissie Iles, a curator at the Whitney Museum, also offered her insights.

Susan B. Anthony and Elizabeth Cady Stanton

Both Stanton's and Anthony's voices are easily accessible via Stanton's *Eighty Years and More: Reminiscences* and *The Selected Papers of Elizabeth Cady Stanton and Susan B. Anthony*. Geoffrey C. Ward's *Not for Ourselves Alone: The Story of Elizabeth Cady Stanton and Susan B. Anthony*, a companion piece to the Ken Burns documentary of the same name, is an intimate look at these partners. I consulted Jean H. Baker's *Sisters: The Lives of America's Suffragists*; Elizabeth Griffith's *In Her Own Right: The Life of Elizabeth Cady Stanton*; and Vivian Gornick's *The Solitude of Self: Thinking About Elizabeth Cady Stanton*. The scholar Ellen DuBois shared her expertise in an interview.

George Balanchine and Suzanne Farrell

The documentary *Suzanne Farrell: Elusive Muse* turned me on to this story, which I developed aided by Farrell's memoir *Holding On to the Air*, written with the help of Toni Bentley, herself a former dancer at the New York City Ballet and an admired writer on dance and other subjects. Bentley offered context and amplification for the story in an interview. Studies of Balanchine include the fine slim volume *George Balanchine: The Ballet Maker*, by Robert Gottlieb, and Bernard Taper's *Balanchine: A Biography*. *I Was a Dancer*, by Jacques d'Amboise, Farrell's frequent dance partner, offered his perspective. Francine Prose's essay on Farrell in *The Lives of the Muses: Nine Women and the Artists They Inspired* is one of many outstanding portraits in the book, which also includes portraits of Alice Liddell, Elizabeth Siddal, Lou Andreas-Salomé, Gala Dalí, Lee Miller, Charis Weston, and Yoko Ono. "Second Act," Joan Acocella's 2003 *New Yorker* profile of Farrell, was essential, and I benefited from Jennifer Homans's writing on Farrell's recent life as a company leader.

Simone de Beauvoir and Jean-Paul Sartre

I first encountered Hazel Rowley's *Tête-à-Tête: Simone de Beauvoir and Jean-Paul Sartre* through a review by Louis Menand in the *New Yorker,* though I later learned that Rowley considered Menand's conclusions "completely opposed to my own." I also appreciated Daniel Bullen's essay on the pair in *The Love Lives of the Artists: Five Stories of Creative Intimacy* (which also profiles Rilke and Lou Andreas-Salomé, Alfred Stieglitz and Georgia O'Keeffe, Diego Rivera and Frida Kahlo, and Henry Miller and Anaïs Nin). For anyone wanting a deeper dive, Sartre's and Beauvoir's own works await. Beauvoir published five volumes of memoirs alone, and then there is her *Letters to Sartre* and his *Witness to My Life: The Letters of Jean-Paul Sartre to Simone de Beauvoir 1926–39.*

Larry Bird and Magic Johnson

The HBO documentary *Magic and Bird: A Courtship of Rivals,* directed by Ezra Edelman, is a thorough and intimate portrait featuring interviews with the principals as well as with the journalist Jackie MacMullan, who was the force behind *When the Game Was Ours* (a book that drew on MacMullan's more than one hundred interviews, including with Magic and Bird themselves). A joint interview with Magic and Bird on the *Late Show with David Letterman* on April 11, 2012, was also helpful.

Neal Brennan and Dave Chappelle

I interviewed Neal Brennan in April 2012 and February 2013. Dave Chappelle declined my request for an interview. I appreciated "If He Hollers Let Him Go," an essay on Chappelle by Rachel Kaadzi Ghansah that appeared in the *Believer,* as well as Kevin Powell's piece in *Esquire* titled "Heaven Hell Dave Chappelle." Chappelle told his own version of his breakdown in a lengthy interview with Oprah Winfrey in February 2006.

Warren Buffett and Charlie Munger

Outstanding biographies have been written about both men: Warren Buffett was profiled in Alice Schroeder's *The Snowball: Warren Buffett and the Business of Life,* and Charlie Munger was the subject of Janet Lowe's

Damn Right!: Behind the Scenes with Berkshire Hathaway Billionaire Charlie Munger. Michael Eisner's *Working Together: Why Great Partnerships Succeed,* written with Aaron R. Cohen, has a good portrait of the pair (along with profiles on Eisner himself and Frank Wells, Bill and Melinda Gates, Brian Grazer and Ron Howard, and many others).

Francis Crick and James Watson

Crick and Watson both left memoirs of their adventures with DNA: Watson's *The Double Helix: A Personal Account of the Discovery of the Structure of DNA,* and Crick's *What Mad Pursuit: A Personal View of Scientific Discovery.* Horace Freeland Judson's *The Eighth Day of Creation: The Makers of the Revolution in Biology* gives a thorough history of their work and its milieu. I also drew on the *Nova* documentary *Secret of Photo 51,* about Rosalind Franklin, and the PBS film *The Secret of Life,* directed by David Glover, which has an extensive companion website, http://www.pbs.org/wnet/dna/episode1. Victor McElheny's *Watson and DNA* is an erudite guide to the discoveries. The NIH archive has the script of a BBC broadcast called *The Race for the Double Helix — Providence and Personalities,* published by the *Listener* on July 11, 1974, which provides a rare transcription of interviews with key players. Robert Wright's essay on Watson and Crick for *Time* in 1999 is a concise and artful treatment, as is Nicholas Wade's 2003 *New York Times* piece "A Revolution at 50." I interviewed Dr. Watson at the Cold Spring Harbor Laboratory in August 2013.

David Crosby and Graham Nash

Both artists have memoirs — Nash's is *Wild Tales: A Rock & Roll Life,* and Crosby has two, *Long Time Gone* and *Since Then: How I Survived Everything and Lived to Tell About It,* both written with Carl Gottlieb. The writer Steve Silberman's essay on Crosby and Nash for Crosbynash.com gets to the heart of their story, and thanks to Silberman's introduction, I spent several evenings with Crosby and Nash before and after performances in 2012 and 2013. Dave Zimmer's *Crosby, Stills & Nash: The Biography* is an authoritative history of the band.

The Curies

I started with Lauren Redniss's stellar graphic narrative *Radioactive: Marie and Pierre Curie: A Tale of Love and Fallout* and turned next to Marie Curie's

Pierre Curie (with autobiographical notes), followed by their daughter Eve Curie's *Madame Curie: A Biography*, and Susan Quinn's *Marie Curie: A Life*.

Emily Dickinson

Brenda Wineapple's *White Heat: The Friendship of Emily Dickinson and Thomas Wentworth Higginson* not only lays bare this critical connection but serves as a model for the scholarship of relationships. (Wineapple has practice; she also wrote *Sister Brother: Gertrude and Leo Stein*.) A second essential text is Ellen Louise Hart and Martha Nell Smith's collection of Dickinson's writings to her sister-in-law Susan Huntington Dickinson, called *Open Me Carefully*. I interviewed Smith several times and drew on her book *Rowing in Eden: Rereading Emily Dickinson*. I also benefited from conversations with Christopher Benfey, the author of *A Summer of Hummingbirds: Love, Art, and Scandal in the Intersecting Worlds of Emily Dickinson, Mark Twain, Harriet Beecher Stowe, and Martin Johnson Heade*.

Valentino Garavani and Giancarlo Giammetti

Matt Tyrnauer's work on this couple is dynamite: "So Very Valentino," a feature in *Vanity Fair*, August 2004, and the documentary film *Valentino: The Last Emperor*. Tyrnauer also sat with me for an interview.

Steve Jobs and Steve Wozniak

Walter Isaacson's biography *Steve Jobs* is indispensable, as is Wozniak's memoir *iWoz: Computer Geek to Cult Icon*. I also drew on Gary Wolf's 1998 *Wired* profile of Wozniak, "The World According to Woz"; Michael Malone's *Infinite Loop: How Apple, the World's Most Insanely Great Computer Company, Went Insane*; and the documentary *Steve Jobs: One Last Thing*.

John Lennon and Paul McCartney

I started with, and often returned to, *The Beatles* by Hunter Davies, who watched John and Paul write and record. He captures the flavor of the characters and their scene superbly, and this is the first brick in a towering wall of primary material on Lennon and McCartney. Memoirs by other principal witnesses include Geoff Emerick's *Here, There and Everywhere: My Life Recording the Music of the Beatles* (written with Howard Massey); Pete Shotton's *John Lennon: In My Life* (written with Nicholas Schaffner);

and Cynthia Lennon's *John*. I also drew from Alistair Taylor's *With the Beatles;* Derek Taylor's *It Was Twenty Years Ago Today;* Tony Barrow's *John, Paul, George, Ringo & Me;* Tony Bramwell's *Magical Mystery Tours;* George Martin's *All You Need Is Ears* (with Jeremy Hornsby); and May Pang's *Loving John* (with Henry Edwards). The journalist Ray Connolly's *The Ray Connolly Beatles Archive* is also a good primary source.

The interviews of John and Paul themselves are foundational, and the website Beatlesinterviews.org has an impressive number of transcriptions. Paul's primary contributions to the history comes in *Paul McCartney: Many Years from Now,* a combination of biography and oral history done with Barry Miles, and *The Beatles Anthology,* both the documentary and book. *Anthology* also gathers up many of John's remarks, as well as recollections of George Harrison, Ringo Starr, and others. Major Lennon interviews include his 1970 sessions with *Rolling Stone*'s Jann Wenner — which are available online, in a book by Wenner (*Lennon Remembers*), and in the original audio via free podcast — and his 1980 *Playboy* interview with David Sheff, which can be found in Sheff's *All We Are Saying.*

Mark Lewisohn's work is another cornerstone for Beatles research. *The Complete Beatles Recording Sessions: The Official Story of the Abbey Road Years, 1962–1970* emerged from his thorough review of the working tapes at Abbey Road. (I'm told by Beatles geeks that John Winn's two volumes on Beatles recordings — *Way Beyond Compare* and *That Magic Feeling* — supplement Lewisohn nicely.) Lewisohn also created *The Beatles Day by Day,* which, along with Keith Badman's two-volume *The Beatles Diary,* accounts for all their known movements. The first of Lewisohn's three volumes on the band, *The Beatles: All These Years, Volume 1 — Tune In,* which takes the band through 1962, is breathtaking and will be remembered as the turning point between journalism on the band and proper history. Several books go through every Beatles song: I consulted Ian MacDonald's *Revolution in the Head: The Beatles' Records and the Sixties,* and musicologist Walter Everett's astonishingly detailed two-volume *The Beatles as Musicians: The Quarry Men Through* Rubber Soul and *The Beatles as Musicians:* Revolver *Through the* Anthology.

I relied heavily on Beatlesbible.com, which has entries on all the major topics and cites the primary sources. Conversations in the site's Fab Forum were also helpful. The *New York Times* music writer Allan Kozinn, author of the outstanding *The Beatles*, generously offered his thoughts and directed me to good sources, as did the scholar Kenneth Womack, author of *Long and Winding Roads: The Evolving Artistry of the Beatles*, among other works on the band. Michael McCartney, whose *Remember: The Recollections and Photographs of the Beatles* includes a proper print of the seminal photograph he took of John and Paul writing "I Saw Her Standing There," shared with me his memories of the day. Pauline Sutcliffe, author (with Douglas Thompson) of *Stuart Sutcliffe: The Beatles' Shadow and His Lonely Hearts Club*, shared her brother's diaries and letters with me. Four surviving members of the original Quarry Men — John Duff Lowe, Len Garry, Rod Davis, and Colin Hanton — sat with me for an interview, and Davis kindly fielded my questions about the band's early days in Liverpool.

I also drew on Bob Spitz's *The Beatles;* Jonathan Gould's *Can't Buy Me Love: The Beatles, Britain, and America;* Peter Doggett's *You Never Give Me Your Money: The Beatles After the Breakup;* Mark Hertsgaard's *A Day in the Life: The Music and Artistry of the Beatles;* Philip Norman's *John Lennon: The Life* and *Shout!;* Howard Sounes's *Fab: An Intimate Life of Paul McCartney;* Larry Kane's *Ticket to Ride* and *Lennon Revealed;* Tim Riley's *Lennon;* Lewis Lapham's *With the Beatles;* Alan Clayson's *Backbeat: Stuart Sutcliffe: The Lost Beatle;* Rupert Perry's *Northern Songs: The True Story of the Beatles' Song Publishing Empire;* and Doug Sulpy and Ray Schweighardt's *Get Back: The Unauthorized Chronicle of the Beatles' "Let It Be" Disaster.*

C. S. Lewis and J.R.R. Tolkien

I owe a debt to Diana Pavlac Glyer for her intricate examination of Lewis, Tolkien, and their collaborators in *The Company They Keep: C. S. Lewis and J.R.R. Tolkien as Writers in Community,* and for several interviews. Humphrey Carpenter's *J.R.R. Tolkien: A Biography* was helpful, as was Carpenter's *The Letters of J.R.R. Tolkien* and *Letters of C. S. Lewis* as edited by W. H. Lewis. For more on Lewis, I turned to A. N. Wilson's *C. S. Lewis: A Biography,* George Sayer's *Jack: A Life of C. S. Lewis,* and *The Letters of C. S. Lewis to Arthur Greeves (1914–1963),* edited by Walter Hooper. Colin Duriez's *Tolkien and C. S. Lewis: The Gift of Friendship* lent color to otherwise inaccessible moments. Lewis's own reflections on relationships in *Surprised by Joy* and *The Four Loves* were a great aid.

Jerry Lewis and Dean Martin

Jerry Lewis's memoir *Dean and Me (A Love Story)*, written with James Kaplan, was my principal source, along with Nick Tosches's *Dino: Living High in the Dirty Business of Dreams*.

Henri Matisse and Pablo Picasso

The Museum of Modern Art's landmark 2003 show *Matisse Picasso* yielded a thorough catalog and a revealing interview by Charlie Rose of the MoMA curators Kirk Varnedoe and John Elderfield. I also drew on Jack Flam's *Matisse and Picasso: The Story of Their Rivalry and Friendship*; Yve-Alain Bois's *Matisse and Picasso*; John Richardson's 2003 *Vanity Fair* essay "Between Picasso and Matisse"; and Paul Trachtman's *Smithsonian* feature *Matisse & Picasso*. The MoMA curator Anne Umland helped me look for the relationships between the painters' work via study of originals in the museum's gallery.

Trey Parker and Matt Stone

Arthur Bradford's Comedy Central special *6 Days to Air: The Making of South Park* opened up this pair for me. Bradford showed me footage from his upcoming documentary feature on Parker and Stone and shared his observations, as did Kevin Morris, their lawyer; Vernon Chatman, the *South Park* staff writer; and Jason McHugh, an old friend and colleague. Among the many features on Stone and Parker, I found most helpful their 2000 interview with *Playboy*; Vanessa Grigoriadis's piece "Still Sick, Still Wrong," in *Rolling Stone*; and the 2011 *60 Minutes* profile.

Rilke

I relied heavily on the scholar Lewis Hyde's introduction to a recent edition of *Letters to a Young Poet*; Sven Birkerts's fine essay on Rilke included in his collection *Reading Life: Books for the Ages*; and Mark M. Anderson's "The Poet and the Muse" from the *Nation*, on Rilke and Lou Andreas-Salomé.

Theo and Vincent van Gogh

The foundation for any research on Vincent van Gogh is his own correspondence, and his letters are artfully presented at Vangoghletters.org.

An earlier translation, which also includes other family members' letters, is available at Webexhibits.org/vangogh. Many of Theo's letters have gone missing, but his voice can be heard in the correspondence with his fiancée, Jo Bonger, collected in a book called *Brief Happiness*. I dearly appreciated George Howe Colt's treatment of Vincent and Theo in *Brothers: On His Brothers and Brothers in History*, which offered many other affecting portraits, including that of James and Stanislaus Joyce. Colt shared his thoughts with me in an interview. Jan Hulsker's *Vincent and Theo van Gogh: A Dual Biography* is a major study. For more on Theo I drew on Marie-Angelique Ozanne and Frederique De Jode's *Theo: The Other van Gogh;* Chris Stolwijk and Richard Thomson's *Theo van Gogh, 1857 to 1891: Art Dealer, Collector, and Brother of Vincent;* Steven Naifeh and Gregory White Smith's *Van Gogh: The Life;* Deborah Silverman's *Van Gogh and Gauguin: The Search for Sacred Art;* Martin Gayford's *The Yellow House: Van Gogh, Gauguin, and Nine Turbulent Weeks in Provence;* and Adam Gopnik's *New Yorker* essay "Van Gogh's Ear." The writer Gregory Curtis, author of a forthcoming study of van Gogh's final months, was a regular sounding board and guide.

The Myth of the Lone Genius

Mark Rose's history of invention and copyright, *Authors and Owners,* is seminal, and Rose unpacked the history of the emergence of the "lone genius" idea for me in several interviews, as did James Shapiro, the Shakespeare scholar whose works include *Contested Will: Who Wrote Shakespeare?,* and James J. Marino, author of *Owning William Shakespeare: The King's Men and Their Intellectual Property.* Marjorie Garber's essay "Our Genius Problem" in the *Atlantic* in December 2002 lays out the history of the genius idea. I learned about Alfonso Montuori through his article "Deconstructing the Lone Genius Myth: Toward a Contextual View of Creativity," written with Ronald E. Purser, and Montuori was a helpful guide to other work as well. Though it was published near my deadline, too late for me to digest, Darin M. McMahon's *Divine Fury: A History of Genius* is a potent cultural history.

In what follows, I've included only books, though of course I am indebted to many great articles in academic journals, newspapers, and magazines, documentary films, and interviews online. An asterisk indicates that I interviewed the author.

CREATIVITY

Teresa Amabile, *Creativity in Context*

Teresa Amabile and Steven Kramer, *The Progress Principle: Using Small Wins to Ignite Joy, Engagement, and Creativity at Work*

Frank Barron, *No Rootless Flower: An Ecology of Creativity*

*Frank Barron, Alfonso Montuori, and Anthea Barron, *Creators on Creating: Awakening and Cultivating the Imaginative Mind*

Ori and Rom Brafman, *Click: The Forces Behind How We Fully Engage with People, Work, and Everything We Do*

Whitney Chadwick and Isabelle De Courtivron, *Significant Others: Creativity and Intimate Partnership*

Elizabeth G. Creamer, *Working Equal: Academic Couples as Collaborators*

Mihaly Csikszentmihalyi, *Creativity: Flow and the Psychology of Discovery*

*Michael P. Farrell, *Collaborative Circles: Friendship Dynamics and Creative Work*

Richard L. Florida, *The Rise of the Creative Class: And How It's Transforming Work, Leisure, Community, and Everyday Life*

Howard Gardner, *Creating Minds: An Anatomy of Creativity Seen Through the Lives of Freud, Einstein, Picasso, Stravinsky, Eliot, Graham, and Gandhi*

Edward Hirsh, *The Demon and the Angel: Searching for the Source of Artistic Inspiration*

Steven Johnson, *Where Good Ideas Come From*

*Vera John-Steiner, *Creative Collaboration*

Robert Kanigel, *Apprentice to Genius: The Making of a Scientific Dynasty*

Wayne Koestenbaum, *Double Talk: The Erotics of Male Literary Collaboration*

Bruce Nussbaum, *Creative Intelligence: Harnessing the Power to Create, Connect, and Inspire*

*Anne Paris, *Standing at Water's Edge: Moving Past Fear, Blocks, and Pitfalls to Discover the Power of Creative Immersion*

Mary Helena Pycior, Nancy G. Slack, and Pnina G. Abir-Am, eds., *Creative Couples in the Sciences*

*Keith Sawyer, *Group Genius: The Creative Power of Collaboration*

*Clay Shirky, *Cognitive Surplus: Creativity and Generosity in a Connected Age*

Robert B. Silvers and Barbara Epstein, *The Company They Kept: Writers on Unforgettable Friendships*

Twyla Tharp, *The Creative Habit* and *The Collaborative Habit*

Harriet Zuckerman, *Scientific Elite: Nobel Laureates in the United States*

POWER AND COMPETITION

V. Frank Asaro, *Universal Co-Opetition: Nature's Fusion of Competition and Cooperation*

David P. Barash, *Beloved Enemies: Our Need for Opponents*

Adam M. Brandenburger and Barry J. Nalebuff, *Co-Opetition*

Po Bronson and Ashley Merryman, *Top Dog: The Science of Winning and Losing*

Richard Conniff, *The Ape in the Corner Office: Understanding the Workplace Beast in All of Us*

*Frans de Waal, *Our Inner Ape: A Leading Primatologist Explains Why We Are Who We Are*

*Dario Maestripieri, *Games Primates Play: An Undercover Investigation of the Evolution and Economics of Human Relationships*

Dorothy Rowe, *Friends and Enemies: Our Need to Love and Hate*

RELATIONSHIPS AND PSYCHOLOGY

Diane Ackerman, *A Natural History of Love*

Jose Luis Alvarez and Silviya Svejenova, *Sharing Executive Power: Roles and Relationships at the Top*

*Arthur Aron and Debra J. Mashek, *Handbook of Closeness and Intimacy*

*Elaine Aron, *The Highly Sensitive Person*

David Bakhurst and Christine Sypnowich, *The Social Self*

Ellen Berscheid and Pamela C. Regan, *The Psychology of Interpersonal Relationships*

Melinda Blau and Karen L. Fingerman, *Consequential Strangers: The Power of People Who Don't Seem to Matter . . . but Really Do*

*Stuart L. Brown, *Play: How It Shapes the Brain, Opens the Imagination, and Invigorates the Soul*

*John T. Cacioppo and William Patrick, *Loneliness: Human Nature and the Need for Social Connection*

Susan Cain, *Quiet: The Power of Introverts in a World That Can't Stop Talking*

Nicholas A. Christakis and James H. Fowler, *Connected: The Surprising Power of Our Social Networks and How They Shape Our Lives*

*Amy C. Edmondson, *Teaming: How Organizations Learn, Innovate, and Compete in the Knowledge Economy*

*Susan T. Fiske, *Social Beings: Core Motives in Social Psychology*

*Alan Fogel, *Developing Through Relationships*

Barbara L. Fredrickson, *Love 2.0: How Our Supreme Emotion Affects Everything We Feel, Think, Do, and Become*

Sai Gaddam and Ogi Ogas, *A Billion Wicked Thoughts: What the Internet Tells Us About Sexual Relationships*

Jolene Galegher, Robert E. Kraut, and Carmen Egido, *Intellectual Teamwork: Social and Technological Foundations of Cooperative Work*

*Alison Gopnik, *The Philosophical Baby: What Children's Minds Tell Us About Truth, Love, and the Meaning of Life*

Daniel Goleman, *Social Intelligence: The New Science of Human Relationships*

John Gottman, *The Seven Principles for Making Marriage Work*

Adam Grant, *Give and Take: Why Helping Others Drives Our Success*

Richard J. Hackman, *Leading Teams: Setting the Stage for Great Performances*

Julian Jaynes, *The Origin of Consciousness in the Breakdown of the Bicameral Mind*

*J. A. Scott Kelso, *Dynamic Patterns: The Self-Organization of the Brain and Behavior*

J. A. Scott Kelso with David A. Engstrøm, *The Complementary Nature*

*Michael Maccoby, *Narcissistic Leaders: Who Succeeds and Who Fails*

*Annie Murphy Paul, *The Cult of Personality Testing: How Personality Tests Are Leading Us to Miseducate Our Children, Mismanage Our Companies, and Misunderstand Ourselves*

*James W. Pennebaker, *The Secret Life of Pronouns: What Our Words Say About Us*

*Esther Perel, *Mating in Captivity: Reconciling the Erotic and the Domestic*

*Daniel H. Pink, *To Sell Is Human: The Surprising Truth About Moving Others*

Lee Ross and Richard E. Nisbett, *The Person and the Situation: Perspectives of Social Psychology*

Daniel J. Siegel, *The Developing Mind: How Relationships and the Brain Interact to Shape Who We Are*

Diana McLain Smith and Peter Senge, *Elephant in the Room: How Relationships Make or Break the Success of Leaders and Organizations*

*Michael L. Stallard, *Fired Up or Burned Out: How to Reignite Your Team, Passion, Creativity, and Productivity*

*Frank J. Sulloway, *Born to Rebel: Birth Order, Family Dynamics, and Creative Lives*

Nassim Nicholas Taleb, *Antifragile: Things That Gain from Disorder*

*George E. Vaillant, *The Wisdom of the Ego; Triumphs of Experience: The Men of the Harvard Grant Study;* and *Adaptation to Life*

Eudora Welty and Ronald A. Sharp, *The Norton Book of Friendships*

ADDITIONAL INTERVIEWS

Melea Acker, Mark Allen, Benjamin Ball and Gaston Nogues, Robbi Behr and Matthew Swanson, Deborah Bell, Roberto Benabib and Jenji Kohan, Jeremy Bernstein, Christina Biedermann, Tessa Blake and Ian Williams, Laurent de Brunhoff and Phyllis Rose, Bethany Burum, Jessica Chaffin and Jamie Denbo, David Crosby and Graham Nash, Lee Damsky, Richard Danielpour, Ian Desai, Matthew Dickman, Deborah Dowling, Amy Edmondson, Eddie Erlandson, Frank Escher and Ravi GuneWardena, Charles Fernyhough, Susan Fiske, Chris Fowler, Peter Freed, Ronald K. Fried, M. Gerard Fromm, Daniel Gilbert, Sam Gosling, Ari Handel, Glen Hansard and Markéta Irglová, Sheila Heti and Margaux Williamson, Quayle Hodek and Kris Lotlikar, Lisa Iglesias, Molly Ireland, Gavin Kilduff, Mark Lipton, Josh Loeb and Zoe Nathan, Michael R. Maniaci, Dan McAdams, Eric Moskowitz and Amanda Trager, Conan O'Brien, Annalise Ophelian, Ira Robbins, James L. Sacksteder, Sharon Salzberg, George Saunders, Lawrence Schiller, Edward R. Shapiro, Carl Sheingold, Jeff Simpson, Jill Soloway, Abraham Stoll, Claire Sufrin, Yla R. Tausczik, Tenzin Geyche Tethong, Hannah Tinti, Billie Tsien and Tod Williams, Abigail Turin, Timothy Wilson.

James P. Carse's brilliant work *Finite and Infinite Games: A Vision of Life as Play and Possibility* is hard to categorize. Tony Kushner's afterword to *Angels in America,* in which he discusses his relationship with Kimberly Flynn and Oskar Eustis, serves as a kind of manifesto on the fundamental of social connection to creativity. It stayed with me throughout this project. William James and Martin Buber have been the godfathers of this book, James as the psychologist I most appreciate and Buber as the fount of the spiritual vision that guided it. Misha Glouberman and Sheila Heti's *The Chairs Are Where the People Go: How to Live, Work, and Play in the City* also affected me deeply.

Notes

Please send any corrections or amplifications to Po2@shenk.net.

Prelude

xi *"its beings"*: Martin Buber, *To Hallow This Life: An Anthology* (New York: Harper, 1958), 51.

"*And also plays*": Tony Kushner, *Angels in America, Part Two: Perestroika* (New York: Theatre Communications Group, 1993), 155. I've ascribed this thought to Kushner, who articulates it forcefully and develops it with the example of his own life and work, but I need to say that he himself ascribes the idea to Marx. The full quote is "Marx was right: The smallest indivisible human unit is two people, not one; one is a fiction."

xiii *March 29, 1967:* Hunter Davies, *The Beatles* (1968; New York: W. W. Norton, 1996), 263, describes the session happening "mid-March" but the context suggests that it was the evening of the first session for "A Little Help from My Friends," which Mark Lewisohn, *The Complete Beatles Recording Sessions* (New York: Harmony Books, 1988), 106, assigns to March 29. When I asked Davies about the discrepancy, he wrote me: "As a rule, trust Mark L. rather than me" (Hunter Davies, e-mail to the author, January 31, 2014). All the other details in the prelude are drawn from Davies, *The Beatles,* 263–68.

order of the lines: They also changed *do* to *would,* as becomes apparent.

Introduction: 1 + 1 = Infinity

xv *"of great men"*: Thomas Carlyle, *On Heroes, Hero-Worship, and the Heroic in History* (Project Gutenberg, 2012, http://www.gutenberg.org/files/1091/1091 -h/1091-h.htm).

"must make him": Herbert Spencer, *The Study of Sociology* (London: C. Kegan Paul, 1881), 34.

xvi   *sixteenth-century Florence:* Gene A. Brucker, *Renaissance Florence* (Berkeley: University of California Press, 1969).

    Enlightenment London: For a terrific introduction to the significance of culture, see Steven Johnson, *Where Good Ideas Come From: The Natural History of Innovation* (New York: Penguin, 2010). In his TED talk on the book, at TEDGlobal, Oxford, England, July 2010, Johnson explained how the rise of the coffeehouse was integral to the spread of the Enlightenment, because it brought people from all backgrounds and fields of expertise together, creating what Johnson dubbed a "liquid network." The first coffeehouse in England, the Grand Café, opened in 1650 in Oxford, at the dawn of the Enlightenment, and, Johnson explained, "an astonishing number of ideas from this period have a coffeehouse somewhere in their story" (http://www.ted .com/talks/steven_johnson_where_good_ideas_come_from.html).

    the campus of Pixar: Keith Sawyer, "Group Genius at Pixar," *Creativity & Innovation* (blog), September 12, 2008, http://keithsawyer.wordpress.com /2008/09/12/group-genius-at-pixar. Also see Keith Sawyer, *Group Genius: The Creative Power of Collaboration* (New York: Basic Books, 2007).

    a good story: I mean *story* first in the literal sense that lone heroes make for rousing tales. The hero's journey identified by Joseph Campbell—and later adapted into an industry-defining guidebook for screenwriters in Christopher Vogler, *The Writer's Journey: Mythic Structure for Writers* (Studio City, CA: Michael Wiese Productions, 2007)—starts and ends with a sole protagonist. This rule is sacrosanct everywhere from pulp novels to literary memoir, from commercials to video games. The second meaning of *story* is as a unit of significance that helps us organize our understanding of complex phenomena. This is what Joan Didion meant by "we tell ourselves stories in order to live" (Joan Didion, *We Tell Ourselves Stories in Order to Live: Collected Nonfiction* [New York: Random House, 2006]). Reality itself emerges from our selection and interpretation, our imposition of narrative lines on circumstances that might otherwise elude our mental grasp.

xviii *five years:* Connell Barrett, "Tiger's Caddie Steve Williams Tells All," *Golf Magazine,* February 22, 2009, http://www.golf.com/tour-and-news/tigers-caddie -steve-williams-tells-all.

    their collective work: William Grimes, "Jeanne-Claude, Christo's Collaborator on Environmental Canvas, Is Dead at 74," *New York Times,* November 19, 2009, http://www.nytimes.com/2009/11/20/arts/design/20jeanne-claude.html ?_r=0. According to this piece, the initial decision to leave Jeanne-Claude uncredited—and the reversal—was mutual: "To avoid confusing dealers and the public, and to establish an artistic brand, they used only Christo's name. In 1994 they retroactively applied the joint name 'Christo and Jeanne-Claude' to all outdoor works and large-scale temporary indoor installations. Other works were credited to Christo alone."

"secret weapon": Dale Pollock, *Skywalking: The Life and Films of George Lucas* (New York: Harmony Books, 1983), 228.

"those films": Denise Worrell, *Icons: Intimate Portraits* (New York: Atlantic Monthly Press, 1989), 192. For a thorough treatment of Marcia Lucas, see Michael Kaminski, "In Tribute to Marcia Lucas," http://secrethistoryofstar wars.com/marcialucas.html.

Matthew effect: Robert K. Merton, "The Matthew Effect in Science," *Science* 159, no. 3869 (1968): 56–63, and "The Matthew Effect in Science II: Cumulative Advantage and the Symbolism of Intellectual Property," *Isis* 79, no. 4 (1988): 606–23.

xix *trained doctors:* Vivien T. Thomas, *Partners of the Heart: Vivien Thomas and His Work with Alfred Blalock: An Autobiography* (Philadelphia: University of Pennsylvania Press, 1995); Katie McCabe, "Like Something the Lord Made," *Washingtonian* (August 1989).

"but in Maxwell Perkins": The original article is Bernard De Voto, "Genius Is Not Enough," *Saturday Review of Literature,* April 21, 1936. A. Scott Berg quotes the De Voto review at length in his biography *Max Perkins* (New York: Dutton, 1978), xv–xvii.

"for myself": A draft of Wolfe's note to Perkins, in which he explains his decision to break with Scribner, is heartbreaking. See Ted Mitchell, ed., *Thomas Wolfe: An Illustrated Biography* (New York: Pegasus Books, 2006), 217–18.

without cracking up: F. Scott Fitzgerald, "The Crack-Up," *Esquire,* February 1936, http://www.esquire.com/features/the-crack-up.

"taken for granted": Lawrence Lessig, *The Future of Ideas* (New York: Random House, 2001), 13.

xx *colleagues and acolytes:* Richard Posner, "The Courthouse Mice," *New Republic,* June 5, 2006, http://www.newrepublic.com/article/the-courthouse-mice.

Justin Bieber: Lizzie Widdicombe, "Teen Titan," *New Yorker,* September 3, 2012, http://www.newyorker.com/reporting/2012/09/03/120903fa_fact_wid dicombe?currentPage=all.

Mario Batali: The restaurateur's partner is Joe Bastianich; see Foster Kamer, "Joe Bastianich and the Gospel of *Restaurant Man*," *New York Observer,* May 30, 2012, http://observer.com/2012/05/joe-bastianich-profile-restaurant -man-interview-05302012/.

Doris Kearns Goodwin: Goodwin, like many major authors, employs a substantial number of research assistants. In the midst of a scandal some years ago, she described a process that included four research assistants, three of them full-time and one part-time. David D. Kirkpatrick, "Historian Says Borrowing Was Wider Than Known," *New York Times,* February 23, 2002, http://www.nytimes.com/2002/02/23/books/23BOOK.html.

brands: This may seem pejorative, but I don't intend it to be. First, the work of a social enterprise is prodigious, and people who lead great teams or who are themselves enmeshed in teams someone else leads deserve as much, if not more, appreciation than the putative lone genius. Second, *brand* is not a diss but a cold-eyed description of the phenomenon in play. The relationship between the author and the body of work, explains Mark Rose in *Authors and Owners* (Cambridge, MA: Harvard University Press, 1993), 1, is pervasive in the culture, including in "our system of marketing cultural products. Joyce Carol Oates, Saul Bellow, Zane Grey, Pablo Picasso, Leonard Bernstein, Stephen Spielberg, Clint Eastwood: the name of the author—or artist, conductor, or, sometimes, star, for in mass culture the authorial function is often filled by the star—becomes a kind of brand name, a recognizable sign that the cultural commodity will be of a certain kind and quality."

love/belonging needs: About.com reproduces a common graphic illustrating Maslow's hierarchy: http://psychology.about.com/od/theoriesofperson ality/a/hierarchyneeds.htm. His original paper on the topic, A. H. Maslow, "A Theory of Human Motivation," *Psychological Review* 50 (1943): 370–96, is online at the website Classics in the History of Psychology, http://psychclas sics.yorku.ca/Maslow/motivation.htm.

xxi *"resources: information":* Johnson, *Where Good Ideas Come From,* 245.

"upon his consciousness": Percy Bysshe Shelley, *Prometheus Unbound: A Lyrical Drama in Four Acts* (London: J. M. Denton, 1898), xviii.

xxii *"part of the problem":* Diana McLain Smith, interview with the author, June 18, 2013.

Sigmund Freud and Wilhelm Fliess: Michael P. Farrell, *Collaborative Circles: Friendship Dynamics and Creative Work* (Chicago: University of Chicago Press, 2001), 38.

power positions harden: José Luis Alvarez and Silviya Svejenova, *Sharing Executive Power: Roles and Relationships at the Top* (Cambridge: Cambridge University Press, 2005).

"special consecration": Georg Simmel, "The Number of Members as Determining the Sociological Form of the Group: I," *American Journal of Sociology* 8 (1902): 1–46, 158–96.

xxiii *"keep turning up":* Johnson, *Where Good Ideas Come From,* 18.

xxiv *"to the culture":* Mihaly Csikszentmihalyi, *Creativity: Flow and the Psychology of Discovery and Invention* (New York: HarperCollins, 2009), 25.

xxv *struggle for faith:* Louis Menand, "William James & the Case of the Epileptic Patient," *New York Review of Books,* December 17, 1998, http://www.ny books.com/issues/1998/dec/17/.

1. *"You Remind Me of Charlie Munger"*

3 *"You remind me of Charlie Munger":* Janet Lowe, *Damn Right!: Behind the Scenes with Berkshire Hathaway Billionaire Charlie Munger* (Hoboken, NJ: John Wiley and Sons, 2000), 2.

to meet: Ibid., 73.

4   *"to meet each other":* Steve Jobs: One Last Thing, directed by Sarah Hunt and Mimi O'Conner (2011), http://program.lunchbox.pbs.org/program/steve-jobs-one-last-thing/.

Pierre Curie: Denis Brian, *The Curies: A Biography of the Most Controversial Family in Science* (Hoboken, NJ: John Wiley and Sons, 2005), 15.

one intermediary: Gueorgi Kossinets and Duncan J. Watts, "Empirical Analysis of an Evolving Social Network," *Science* 311 (January 2006). The numbers cited are not in the paper but are from Duncan J. Watts in an e-mail to the author.

even in ordinary encounters: John T. Cacioppo and William Patrick, *Loneliness: Human Nature and the Need for Social Connection* (New York: W. W. Norton, 2008), 33–34, 178.

take the first step: Ibid., 231.

5   *play of that name:* John Markoff and Somini Sengupta, "Separating You and Me? 4.74 Degrees," *New York Times,* November 21, 2011, http://www.nytimes.com/2011/11/22/technology/between-you-and-me-4-74-degrees.html.

"consequential strangers": Melinda Blau and Karen L. Fingerman, *Consequential Strangers: The Power of People Who Don't Seem to Matter . . . but Really Do* (New York: W. W. Norton, 2010).

occasional or rare contact: Mark Granovetter, "The Strength of Weak Ties," *American Journal of Sociology* 78, no. 6 (May 1973), 1371, http://www.stanford.edu/dept/soc/people/mgranovetter/documents/granstrengthweakties.pdf. "Of those finding a job through contacts," Granovetter wrote, "16.7% reported that they saw their contact often at the time, 55.6% said occasionally, and 27.8% rarely."

"magnet place": Michael P. Farrell, *Collaborative Circles: Friendship Dynamics and Creative Work* (Chicago: University of Chicago Press, 2003), 19.

6   *in Jerusalem:* Daniel Kahneman, *Thinking, Fast and Slow* (New York: Farrar, Straus and Giroux, 2011), 4–5.

Stanford's grad school: Stephanie Sammartino McPherson, *Sergey Brin and Larry Page: Founders of Google* (Minneapolis: Twenty-First Century Books, 2011), 23.

the structure of DNA: Watson and Crick details from Horace Freeland Judson, *The Eighth Day of Creation: Makers of the Revolution in Biology* (Cold Spring Harbor, NY: Cold Spring Harbor Laboratory Press, 2004), 68, 108, 110; "DNA and the Cavendish Laboratory" (Cambridge: University of Cambridge, Cavendish Laboratory, 2003), http://www-outreach.phy.cam.ac.uk/resources/dna/fullstory.pdf.

Smith's creative alter ego: Patti Smith, *Just Kids* (New York: HarperCollins, 2010), 23–25.

civil rights movement: Ralph David Abernathy, *And the Walls Came Tumbling Down: An Autobiography* (New York: HarperCollins, 1991), 89.

as Zuckerberg's COO: Miguel Helft, "Mark Zuckerberg's Most Valuable Friend," *New York Times,* October 2, 2010, http://www.nytimes.com/2010/10/03/business/03face.html. The host of the party was Dan Rosensweig; see Ken Auletta, "A Woman's Place," *New Yorker,* July 11, 2011, http://www.newyorker.com/reporting/2011/07/11/110711fa_fact_auletta.

7   *become her chief aide:* Elisabeth Griffith, *In Her Own Right: The Life of Elizabeth Cady Stanton* (Oxford: Oxford University Press, 1984), 72–74; Geoffrey C. Ward, *Not for Ourselves Alone: The Story of Elizabeth Cady Stanton and Susan B. Anthony: An Illustrated History* (New York: Knopf, 2001), 40, 58.

leading men: Suzanne Farrell, *Holding On to the Air: An Autobiography* (Gainesville: University Press of Florida, 2002), 32.

a scholarship: Ibid., 37.

left the room: This is the version of the scene Farrell (Ficker) gave in *Suzanne Farrell: Elusive Muse,* directed by Anne Belle and Deborah Dickson (PBS, 1996), though in *Holding On to the Air,* she described Balanchine's inspecting her feet before leaving.

had been accepted: Farrell, *Holding On to the Air,* 43.

"historical moment": Matt Tyrnauer, interview with the author, February 12, 2014. For details on the meeting of Valentino and Giancarlo, see Tyrnauer, "So Very Valentino," *Vanity Fair,* August 2008, http://www.vanityfair.com/culture/features/2004/08/valentino200408, and *Valentino: The Last Emperor* (Acolyte Films, 2009).

8   *the coffeehouse:* Steven Johnson, *Coffee Fueled the Age of Enlightenment* (FORA.tv, 2012), http://www.dailymotion.com/video/xgjlhj_steven-johnson-coffee-fueled-the-age-of-enlightenment_news#.Ue7NglPo-2w.

"the creative class": Richard L. Florida, *The Rise of the Creative Class: And How It's Transforming Work, Leisure, Community, and Everyday Life* (New York: Basic Books, 2002).

on separate floors: Robert Kraut, Carmen Egido, and Jolene Galegher, "Patterns of Contact and Communication in Scientific Research Collaboration," in *CSCW '88: Proceedings of the 1988 ACM Conference on Computer-Supported Cooperative Work* (presented at the ACM Conference on Computer-Supported Cooperative Work, New York: Association for Computing Machinery, n.d.), 1–12.

from one another: Kyungjoon Lee et al., "Does Collocation Inform the Impact of Collaboration?," *PLoS ONE* 5, no. 12 (December 15, 2010). "The results of this first-of-a-kind study suggest that although emerging communication technologies have radically transformed the style and scope of collaboration around the world, physical proximity continues to play a critical role in predicting the impact of scientific research. Although causal relationships cannot be inferred from observational data, a few important associations can be identified. First physical proximity of collaborators was found to be positively associated with publication impact."

9   *rather than telecommute*: Claire Cain Miller and Catherine Rampell, "Yahoo Orders Home Workers Back to the Office," *New York Times*, February 25, 2013, http://www.nytimes.com/2013/02/26/technology/yahoo-orders-home-workers-back-to-the-office.html. Also see "Bodies Matter: The Inconvenient Truth in Marissa Mayer Banning Telecommuting at Yahoo," *Forbes*, http://www.forbes.com/sites/toddessig/2013/02/28/bodies-matter-the-inconvenient-truth-in-marissa-mayer-banning-telecommuting-at-yahoo.

"As few as possible": Claire Suddath, "Why Won't Yahoo! Let Employees Work from Home?" *Businessweek*, February 25, 2013, http://www.businessweek.com/articles/2013-02-25/why-wont-yahoo-let-employees-work-from-home.

four times as important as words: Michael Argyle et al., "The Communication of Inferior and Superior Attitudes by Verbal and Non-verbal Signals," *British Journal of Social and Clinical Psychology* 9, no. 3 (1970): 222–31; Christopher K. Hsee, Elaine Hatfield, and Claude Chemtob, "Assessments of the Emotional States of Others: Conscious Judgments versus Emotional Contagion," *Journal of Social and Clinical Psychology* 11, no. 2 (1992): 119–28, http://www2.hawaii.edu/~elaineh/84.pdf.

"neural WiFi": Daniel Goleman, *Social Intelligence: The New Science of Human Relationships* (New York: Random House Digital, 2006), 67.

improvisation in jazz: Frank J. Bernieri and Robert Rosenthal, "Interpersonal Coordination: Behavior Matching and Interactional Synchrony," in *Fundamentals of Nonverbal Behavior*, eds. Robert Stephen Feldman and Bernard Rimé (Cambridge: Cambridge University Press, 1991), 403.

"complexity of the dance": Goleman, *Social Intelligence*, 35.

"from another planet": Mick Wall, *Enter Night: A Biography of Metallica* (New York: St. Martin's Press, 2011), 21.

10   *"to jam with"*: Ibid., 26.

Ulrich remembered: Lars Ulrich, interview with Howard Stern, September 20, 2011, http://www.youtube.com/watch?v=Qtt0uKGrfl4&feature=youtube_gdata_player.

one hundred million albums: "Q Prime: Metallica," n.d., http://www.qprime.com/band/8.

"more than just a normal human being": Steven Naifeh and Gregory White Smith, *Van Gogh: The Life* (New York: Random House, 2011), Kindle edition.

for nine years: Mary Moorman, *William Wordsworth: A Biography: The Early Years, 1770–1803* (Oxford: Oxford University Press, 1957), 15–18.

to write screenplays: "Coen Brothers," Wikipedia, http://en.wikipedia.org/wiki/Coen_brothers.

2. Identical Twins from the Ends of the Earth

11   *he looked like Elvis:* Hunter Davies, *The Beatles* (1968; New York: W. W. Norton, 1996), 33.

      hit the UK charts: "The History of Heartbreak Hotel," *Independent,* http://www.independent.co.uk/arts-entertainment/music/features/the-history-of-heartbreak-hotel-471131.html.

      "until Elvis": Davies, *The Beatles,* 19.

12   *"Tutti Frutti":* Mark Lewisohn, *The Beatles: All These Years, Volume 1—Tune In* (New York: Crown, 2013), 136.

      standing ten deep: Howard Sounes, *Fab: An Intimate Life of Paul McCartney* (Cambridge, MA: Da Capo, 2010), 19.

      "connector of connoisseurs": Lewisohn, *Tune In,* 129.

      immigrants to Liverpool: Bob Spitz, *The Beatles: The Biography* (Boston: Little, Brown, 2006), 45–49.

      "let's go": Lewisohn, *Tune In,* 55.

      "love of the same": For a brief overview and references to scholarly sources, see Aaron Retica, "Homophily," *New York Times,* December 10, 2006, http://www.nytimes.com/2006/12/10/magazine/10Section2a.t-4.html.

      ethnicity, and race: Miller McPherson, Lynn Smith-Lovin, and James M. Cook, "Birds of a Feather: Homophily in Social Networks," *Annual Review of Sociology* 27 (2001): 415–44.

      torn out too: James Westcott, *When Marina Abramović Dies: A Biography* (Cambridge, MA: MIT Press, 2010), 85.

      "something like this": *Marina Abramović: The Artist Is Present,* directed by Matthew Akers and Jeff Dupre (Show of Force, 2012).

13   *independent thinking:* Paul Gompers, Vladimir Mukharlyamov, and Yuhai Xuan, "The Cost of Friendship" (working paper, National Bureau of Economic Research, June 2012), http://www.nber.org/papers/w18141.

      "no progression": William Blake, *The Marriage of Heaven and Hell* (Mineola, NY: Courier Dover, 1994), 29. Blake is referring not to contrary *people* but to contrary energies. He writes, "Attraction and Repulsion, Reason and Energy, Love and Hate, are necessary to Human existence."

      "into a third": Philip Furia, *Ira Gershwin: The Art of the Lyricist* (Oxford: Oxford University Press, 1997), 244.

      "matrices, of thought": Arthur Koestler, *The Act of Creation* (New York: Dell, 1964), 121.

      the personal computer: Geoff Colvin, *Talent Is Overrated: What Really Separates World-Class Performers from Everybody Else* (New York: Portfolio, 2010).

      paradigm shifts: Thomas S. Kuhn, *The Structure of Scientific Revolutions* (Chicago: University of Chicago Press, 1962).

14   *uncomfortable questions:* J. Richard Hackman, interview with Diane Coutu, *Harvard Business Review* (May 2009), http://hbr.org/2009/05/why-teams-dont-work.

new to one another: Brian Uzzi and Jarrett Spiro, "Collaboration and Creativity: The Small World Problem," *American Journal of Sociology* 111 (September 2005): 447–504. This study has often been cited with the mistaken assumption that it refers to the makeup of teams behind specific musicals. Jordan Ellenberg clarifies in his *Slate* piece "Six Degrees of Innovation," March 23, 2012, http://is.gd/u9V9FQ.

"each other out": Diana McLain Smith, interview with the author, June 14, 2013.

15 *"The penitentiary"*: Philip Norman, *John Lennon: The Life* (New York: Doubleday, 2008), 108.

"ingenious": Paul McCartney, interview with Terry Gross, *Fresh Air*, http://www.npr.org/templates/story/story.php?storyId=127411144.

in the UK: Barry Miles, *Paul McCartney: Many Years from Now* (New York: Henry Holt, 1998).

"hearing that": McCartney, interview with Terry Gross.

Pete Shotton, John's best friend, recalled: Spitz, *The Beatles*, 96.

with his dad: Miles, *Many Years from Now*, 24.

for Sinatra: "The Making of 'Sgt. Pepper,'" *The South Bank Show*, season 15, episode 25, June 14, 1992.

16 *"was unreal"*: Jann Wenner, *Lennon Remembers* (London: Verso, 2001).

could hardly play: Pete Shotton and Nicholas Schaffner, *John Lennon: In My Life* (New York: Thunder's Mouth Press, 1994), 51–52.

petty crime: Davies, *The Beatles*, lxxxi. John said, "Had it not been for the Beatles, I would probably have ended up like Freddie."

Pete Shotton remembered: Shotton and Schaffner, *John Lennon*, 61.

path he considered: Davies, *The Beatles*, 59. Paul also discussed this in a 1987 interview with Terry Wogan, http://www.youtube.com/watch?v=IU1H9myxGdg, at about 10:50.

17 *"like cats"*: Spitz, *The Beatles*, 97.

"going to live and be": Steve Wozniak, *iWoz: Computer Geek to Cult Icon* (New York: W. W. Norton, 2006), 92.

18 *same body*: L. Jon Wertheim, "Togetherness," *Sports Illustrated*, April 26, 2010; Eric Konigsberg, "Unseparated Since Birth," *New York Times*, August 30, 2009, http://www.nytimes.com/2009/08/30/magazine/30brothers-t.html; Burkhard Bilger, "Perfect Match," *New Yorker*, August 31, 2009, http://www.newyorker.com/reporting/2009/08/31/090831fa_fact_bilger.

3. *"Like Two Young Bear Clubs"*

19 *common image*: For instance, Francis Crick described himself as being "electrified" on meeting Watson in 1951; see Horace Freeland Judson, *The Eighth Day of Creation: Makers of the Revolution in Biology* (Cold Spring Harbor, NY: Cold Spring Harbor Laboratory Press, 2004), 112.

"ten days": Judith Thurman, "Marina Abramović's Performance Art," *New Yorker*, March 8, 2010, http://www.newyorker.com/reporting/2010/03/08/100308fa_fact_thurman.

"to spit fire": Janet Flanner, "Master," *New Yorker*, October 6, 1956, 77.

"learning and confidence": Ralph David Abernathy, *And the Walls Came Tumbling Down: An Autobiography* (New York: HarperCollins, 1991), 89.

"sharpening each other": John Battelle, *The Search: How Google and Its Rivals Rewrote the Rules of Business and Transformed Our Culture* (New York: Penguin, 2005).

"smack or so": C. S. Lewis, *All My Road Before Me: The Diary of C. S. Lewis, 1922–1927* (Boston: Houghton Mifflin, 1992), 393.

20 *"modern" works*: Diana Pavlac Glyer, *The Company They Keep: C. S. Lewis and J.R.R. Tolkien as Writers in Community* (Kent, OH: Kent State University Press, 2007), 156.

"Tolkien was both": C. S. Lewis, *Surprised by Joy: The Shape of My Early Life* (New York: Harcourt Brace Jovanovich, 1966), 216.

"biting the coals": C. S. Lewis, *They Stand Together: The Letters of C. S. Lewis to Arthur Greeves (1914–1963)*, ed. Walter Hooper (New York: Collier Books, 1986), 298.

"northernness": Glyer, *The Company They Keep*, 4.

"quipping with one another": Ibid.

the film The Kids Are All Right: Lisa Cholodenko, interview with the author, July 15, 2012. Blumberg confirmed the exchange in an e-mail to the author, January 21, 2014.

"sharing stories": Walter Isaacson, *Steve Jobs* (New York: Simon and Schuster, 2011), 25.

21 *in private*: Ken Auletta, "A Woman's Place," *New Yorker*, July 11, 2011, http://www.newyorker.com/reporting/2011/07/11/110711fa_fact_auletta.

"thirteen hours": William McGuire, ed., *The Freud-Jung Letters: The Correspondence Between Sigmund Freud and C. G. Jung* (Princeton, NJ: Princeton University Press, 1994), ix.

"other way around": J. Richard Hackman, interview with Diane Coutu, *Harvard Business Review* (May 2009), http://hbr.org/2009/05/why-teams-dont-work.

"the obnoxious one": Larry Page and Sergey Brin, interview with Charlie Rose, July 26, 2001. This exchange begins around 43:00.

22 *security and novelty*: Esther Perel, *Mating in Captivity: Reconciling the Erotic and the Domestic* (New York: HarperCollins, 2006).

Part II: Confluence

25 *in 1962*: Mark Lewisohn, *The Beatles: All These Years, Volume 1—Tune In* (New York: Crown, 2013), 785. Lewisohn says the session was "probably" in late

November. Barry Miles, *Paul McCartney: Many Years from Now* (New York: Henry Holt, 1998), 93, dates it in September.

at work: Miles, *Many Years from Now,* 35.

"Like mirrors," Paul said: Ibid.

lying on top of it: I'm drawing many of the details of this scene from Michael McCartney's photograph, the best print of which is in Michael McCartney, *Remember: The Recollections and Photographs of the Beatles* (New York: Henry Holt, 1992), 106–7. That they pulled the chair in from the dining room and the description of Paul's guitar came from a tour I took of the McCartney boyhood home. Andy Babiuk, author of *Beatles Gear: All the Fab Four's Instruments, from Stage to Studio* (San Francisco: Backbeat Books, 2009), identified the guitars for me, though Paul's guitar can't be precisely determined. Gibson has details on the John Lennon guitar at http://is.gd/QSNErx. In the Babiuk book, see pages 72–73.

26   *"beauty queen":* This second line, later deleted, has been reported a few ways. Miles, *Many Years from Now,* 97, has "She'd never been a beauty queen." Bill Harry, *The Paul McCartney Encyclopedia* (London: Virgin Books, 2002), 439, has just "Never been a beauty queen."

Clean? Lean?: Miles, *Many Years from Now,* 93.

offered this: Harry, *The Paul McCartney Encyclopedia,* 439.

"pop at work": This is a quote from Michael McCartney's book *Remember,* though it's not clear if he's quoting Paul or giving a summation.

"eyeball to eyeball": David Sheff, *All We Are Saying: The Last Major Interview with John Lennon and Yoko Ono* (New York: St. Martin's, 2010), 137.

their publishing: Rupert Perry, *Northern Songs: The True Story of the Beatles' Song Publishing Empire* (London: Omnibus Press, 2009).

27   *"shared and matched":* Lewisohn, *Tune In,* 704.

"couple identity": Michael R. Maniaci, "Couple Identity," in *The Encyclopedia of Human Relationships,* eds. Harry T. Reis and Susan Sprecher (Thousand Oaks, CA: SAGE Publications, 2009), 336–38.

shared mind: Jordan Zlatev et al., *The Shared Mind: Perspectives on Intersubjectivity* (Amsterdam: John Benjamins Publishing, 2008).

4. Presence → Confidence → Trust

29   *Berkshire Hathaway:* Progression of the Buffett and Munger relationship from Janet Lowe, *Damn Right!: Behind the Scenes with Berkshire Hathaway Billionaire Charlie Munger* (Hoboken, NJ: John Wiley and Sons, 2000), 4, 63, 74–75, 78–79, 93, 100, 254, and Alice Schroeder, *The Snowball: Warren Buffett and the Business of Life* (New York: Random House, 2009), 208, 222, 228, 250, 479. Per Lowe's timeline on page 254 of *Damn Right,* Munger and Buffet began buying shares in Blue Chip Stamps in 1965.

shared their work: Diana Pavlac Glyer, *The Company They Keep: C. S. Lewis and J.R.R. Tolkien as Writers in Community* (Kent, OH: Kent State University Press, 2007), 3–4.

30 *the partnership developed:* All the quotes from Neal Brennan in Part III come from his interviews with the author on February 22, 2013, and November 26, 2013.

resumé or Wikipedia: Harry Collins, *Tacit and Explicit Knowledge* (Chicago: University of Chicago Press, 2010).

31 *"to stand close":* Diane Ackerman, *A Natural History of Love* (New York: Vintage, 1995), xx.

"between two brains": Daniel Goleman, *Social Intelligence: The New Science of Human Relationships* (New York: Random House, 2006).

guts and necks: Joshua Wolf Shenk, "What Makes Us Happy?," *Atlantic*, June 2009, http://www.theatlantic.com/magazine/archive/2009/06/what-makes -us-happy/307439/.

"yes to it": Gertrude Stein, *The Making of Americans, Being a History of a Family's Progress* (Champaign, IL: Dalkey Archive Press, 1995), xxix.

32 *"an evening of such delight":* For an understanding of this progress between Lewis and Tolkien, turn to Glyer, *The Company They Keep,* 5, 7, 8, 48, 113–16, and J.R.R. Tolkien, *The Letters of J.R.R. Tolkien*, ed. Humphrey Carpenter, with Christopher Tolkien (Boston: Houghton Mifflin, 2000), 362.

"minds alive today": "Penn & Teller: Interview," *Time Out,* http://www.time out.com/london/comedy/penn-teller-interview.

"each other's lives": David Remnick, "Bloodbrother: Clarence Clemons, 1942–2011," June 19, 2011, http://www.newyorker.com/online/blogs/newsdesk /2011/06/bloodbrother-clarence-clemons-1942-2011.html.

33 *road for a tour:* Ben Sisario, "Clarence Clemons, E Street Band Saxophonist, Dies at 69," *New York Times,* June 18, 2011, http://www.nytimes.com /2011/06/19/arts/music/clarence-clemons-e-street-band-saxophonist -dies-at-69.html; Jon Pareles, "'Born to Run' Reborn 30 Years Later," *New York Times,* November 15, 2005, http://www.nytimes.com/2005/11/15/arts /music/15bruc.html.

"ladder won't collapse": I'm drawing this example from an excellent blog post by Sandy Ikeda, http://thinkmarkets.wordpress.com/2009/02/08/on -confidence-andor-trust/, citing Adam B. Seligman, *The Problem of Trust* (Princeton, NJ: Princeton University Press, 2000).

"that gave us": Walter Isaacson, *Steve Jobs* (New York: Simon and Schuster, 2011).

"about others": Robert J. Shiller, "Animal Spirits Depend on Trust," *Wall Street Journal,* January 27, 2009, http://online.wsj.com/news/articles/SB12330 2080925418107.

elicits vulnerability: The table at http://bit.ly/OsfYRP gives a good overview, drawn from C. Ashley Fulmer and Michele J. Gelfand, "At What Level (and in

Whom) We Trust Across Multiple Organizational Levels," *Journal of Management* 38 (July 2012): 1167–1230.

"be caught": George Saunders, interview with the author, April 1, 2013.

to benefit another: Sandra L. Shallcross and Jeffry A. Simpson, "Trust and Responsiveness in Strain-Test Situations: A Dyadic Perspective," *Journal of Personality and Social Psychology* 102, no. 5 (2012): 1031–44.

solid profit: Schroeder, *The Snowball*, 345.

"a meal a day": David Wild, "*South Park*'s Evil Geniuses," *Rolling Stone*, February 19, 1998, http://www.rollingstone.com/culture/news/south-parks-evil -geniuses-19980219.

dirty clothes: 6 Days to Air: The Making of "South Park," directed by Arthur Bradford (Comedy Central, 2011).

"our own thing going": Ibid.

34　*"forget your buddies"*: Jason McHugh, interview with the author, December 13, 2013.

5. The Turn of Faith

35　*meat-delivery truck*: Suzanne Farrell, *Holding On to the Air: An Autobiography* (Gainesville: University Press of Florida, 2002), 200.

most of their meals: Ibid., 44.

Igor Stravinsky: Jennifer Dunning, "Balanchine and Stravinsky, Reunited," *New York Times*, January 18, 2007, http://www.nytimes.com/2007/01/18/ arts/dance/18stra.html.

New York City Ballet: For Balanchine details: Associated Press, "Russian Tea Room to Become Rubble," *Boca Raton News*, December 31, 1995, http://news .google.com/newspapers?nid=1290&dat=19951231&id=LjNUAAAAIBAJ&sj id=R44DAAAAIBAJ&pg=6660,5105000. On Tanaquil Le Clercq: Anna Kisselgoff, "Tanaquil Le Clercq, 71, Ballerina Who Dazzled Dance World," *New York Times*, January 1, 2001, http://www.nytimes.com/2001/01/01/nyregion /tanaquil-le-clercq-71-ballerina-who-dazzled-dance-world.html. On the New York City Ballet: "Our History," accessed February 3, 2014, http://www.nyc ballet.com/explore/our-history.aspx.

eighty-some members: Joan Acocella, "Profiles: Second Act," *New Yorker*, January 6, 2003, http://www.newyorker.com/archive/2003/01/06/030106fa _fact_acocella.

"inner clock," he said: Farrell, *Holding On to the Air*, 68.

36　*"maybe less"*: Ibid., 49.

member of the company: Ibid., 54.

mellifluous Farrell: Ibid., 43.

her doctor's orders: Robert Gottlieb, *George Balanchine: The Ballet Maker* (New York: HarperCollins, 2010), 130.

refusing to answer his phone: Suzanne Farrell: Elusive Muse, directed by Anne Belle and Deborah Dickson (PBS, 1996).

with her hands: Jacques d'Amboise, *I Was a Dancer* (New York: Knopf, 2011), 281.

"strange musical cues": Farrell, *Holding On to the Air,* 78.

"not ready for it": Ibid., 79.

37 *"Just been born":* Ibid., 80.

fourteen months: Acocella, "Profiles."

no more jumps: Ibid.

38 *"turn of faith":* Farrell, *Holding On to the Air,* 94–95.

"would have been frightening": Ibid., 95.

"out of a hat": Ibid.

"kept going": Adams, interview with David Daniel.

39 *"every American company":* Acocella, "Profiles."

"work on it": Elusive Muse.

"we were accomplices": Farrell, *Holding On to the Air,* 95.

Don Quixote: Jennifer Dunning, "Love Retrieved, Imperfect and Unbalanced," *New York Times,* September 16, 2007, http://www.nytimes.com/2007/09/16/arts/dance/16dunn.html.

"for each other": Elusive Muse.

two of them: Farrell, *Holding On to the Air,* 123.

6. "Everybody Just Get the Fuck Out"

40 *Bach fugue:* Christopher Hogwood, "Bach-Stravinsky, *Four Preludes and Fugues from Das Wohltemperirte Clavier,*" March 15, 2012, http://www.hogwood.org/archive/composers/others/bach-stravinsky-four-preludes-and-fugues.html.

middle of a scene: "How Writers Write: Graham Greene," William Landay, http://www.williamlanday.com/2009/07/08/how-writers-write-graham-greene/.

"the ritual": Twyla Tharp, *The Creative Habit: Learn It and Use It for Life* (New York: Simon and Schuster, 2003), 14.

private meetings: Miguel Helft, "Mark Zuckerberg's Most Valuable Friend," *New York Times,* October 2, 2010, http://www.nytimes.com/2010/10/03/business/03face.html.

41 *at a pub:* Diana Pavlac Glyer, *The Company They Keep: C. S. Lewis and J.R.R. Tolkien as Writers in Community* (Kent, OH: Kent State University Press, 2007), 5.

Lewis's apartment: C. S. Lewis, *The Collected Letters of C. S. Lewis* (New York: HarperCollins, 2009), 181, 297, 336.

with a call: Alice Schroeder, *The Snowball: Warren Buffett and the Business of Life* (New York: Random House, 2009), 322.

incessant chatter: Horace Freeland Judson, *The Eighth Day of Creation: Makers of the Revolution in Biology* (Cold Spring Harbor, NY: Cold Spring Harbor Laboratory Press, 2004), 112.

C. S. Lewis writes in The Four Loves: C. S. Lewis, *The Four Loves* (New York: Mariner Books, 1971), 80.

"interrelated and interdependent": Marina Abramović, interview with the author, November 11, 2013.

42   *"Dave Chappelle's typist":* Scott King, "Just for Laughs Exclusive — Neal Brennan Interview," *Chicago Now,* June 14, 2011, http://www.chicagonow.com/class-act-comedy/2011/06/just-for-laughs-exclusive-neal-brennan-interview/.

"gave us such joy": Alex Danchev, *Georges Braque: A Life* (New York: Skyhorse Publishing, 2012).

modern art: For a good account of Braque and Picasso, see Janet Flanner's profiles of Braque, "Master," *New Yorker,* October 6, 1956, and "Master II," *New Yorker,* October 13, 1956. For a briefer account, see Michael Brenson, "Picasso and Braque, Brothers in Cubism," *New York Times,* September 22, 1989, http://is.gd/aBreQU.

"gestalt Vulcan": Michael D. Eisner with Aaron R. Cohen, *Working Together: Why Great Partnerships Succeed* (New York: HarperCollins, 2010), 108.

"reason was forbidden": John Nathan, *Sony* (Boston: Houghton Mifflin, 2001), 2.

to pass one's lips: Mark Snyder, "Self-Monitoring of Expressive Behavior," *Journal of Personality and Social Psychology* 30, no. 4 (1974): 526–37.

43   *"going to work out":* Graham Nash, interview with the author, April 18, 2012.

"completely absent": Daniel Kahneman, biographical essay, http://www.nobelprize.org/nobel_prizes/economic-sciences/laureates/2002/kahneman-bio.html.

"this thing here": Eisner and Cohen, *Working Together,* 67.

"for an hour": Helft, "Mark Zuckerberg's Most Valuable Friend."

"even comes close": Lea Thau and Catherine Burns, e-mails to the author, February 22, 2012.

"heightening its meaning": E. B. White, *Here Is New York* (New York: Harper and Brothers, 1949), 29.

44   *quickness to respond:* Elaine Hatfield, *Emotional Contagion* (Cambridge: Cambridge University Press, 1994), 29–37.

largely nonconscious: For a great summary of this research, see Molly E. Ireland and James W. Pennebaker, "Language Style Matching in Writing: Synchrony in Essays, Correspondence, and Poetry," *Journal of Personality and Social Psychology* 99, no. 3 (2010). For an overview of mimicry, see Tanya L. Chartrand and Rick van Baaren, "Human Mimicry," *Advances in Experimental Social Psychology,* vol. 41, ed. Mark P. Zanna (San Diego: Elsevier Academic

Press, 2009), 219–74, http://www.sciencedirect.com/science/article/pii/S00 6526010800405X.

look alike: R. B. Zajonc et al., "Convergence in the Physical Appearance of Spouses," *Motivation and Emotion* 11, no. 4 (1987): 335–46.

45 *in their eyes:* Schroeder, *The Snowball,* 24.

"coordinative structure": Kevin Shockley, Daniel C. Richardson, and Rick Dale, "Conversation and Coordinative Structures," *Topics in Cognitive Science* 1 (2009), 305–19.

"and knowledge": Ireland and Pennebaker, "Language Style Matching in Writing," 550.

or *and* but: James W. Pennebaker, *The Secret Life of Pronouns: What Our Words Say About Us* (New York: Bloomsbury Press, 2013), 6.

"read, say, and hear": James W. Pennebaker and Cindy K. Chung, "The First Romney-Obama Debate: Off to the Races," *Wordwatchers* (blog), October 3, 2012, http://is.gd/uH73rq.

type, frequency, and grammatical structure: Pennebaker, *The Secret Life of Pronouns,* 5.

46 *already diverged:* Ireland and Pennebaker, "Language Style Matching in Writing."

Lennon and McCartney: "After a while, they'd finish each other's sentences," said one of the original guitarists, Eric Griffiths. Bob Spitz, *The Beatles: The Biography* (Boston: Little, Brown, 2006), 112.

Matt Stone and Trey Parker: "Subversive, Satirical and Sold Out," *60 Minutes* (CBS, 2012), http://www.cbsnews.com/video/watch/?id=7411226n.

Daniel Kahneman and Amos Tversky: "We were not only working, of course — we talked of everything under the sun, and got to know each other's mind almost as well as our own. We could (and often did) finish each other's sentences and complete the joke that the other had wanted to tell, but somehow we also kept surprising each other." Daniel Kahneman, "Autobiographical Statement: Daniel Kahneman," n.d., http://www.haverford.edu/kinsc/Biog raphy/Psych/Armstrong/autobio_final_1.htm.

"a powerhouse": Graham Nash and David Crosby, interview with the author, April 18, 2012.

"going to tell him": The Coen Brothers, directed by Sarah Aspinall (BBC, 2000).

47 *"do the thing":* David Zax, "Funny Business," *Yale Alumni Magazine* (September/October 2012).

"so fast": "Subversive, Satirical and Sold Out," *60 Minutes.*

"And I would just go, 'Okay'": "Comedians in Cars Getting Coffee: Larry Eats a Pancake," accessed February 3, 2014, http://comediansincarsgettingcoffee .com/larry-david-larry-eats-a-pancake, at around the 10:30 mark.

48 *"didn't give a damn for the critics":* Vera John-Steiner, *Creative Collaboration* (Oxford: Oxford University Press, 2000), 15.

begin to think: James W. Pennebaker, interview with the author, June 23, 2010.

"transactive memory": Daniel M. Wegner, "Transactive Memory: A Contemporary Analysis of the Group Mind," in *Theories of Group Behavior* (New York: Springer, 1987), 185–208.

"what we don't": Daniel M. Wegner, "Don't Fear the Cybermind," *New York Times,* August 4, 2012, http://www.nytimes.com/2012/08/05/opinion/sun day/memory-and-the-cybermind.html?_r=0. Also see Daniel M. Wegner, Toni Giuliano, and Paula T. Hertel, "Cognitive Interdependence in Close Relationships," in *Compatible and Incompatible Relationships,* ed. William Ickes (New York: Springer, 1985), 253–76; http://link.springer.com/chapter/10 .1007/978-1-4612-5044-9_12.

49 *"Googling* each other": Clive Thompson, "Is Google Wrecking Our Memory?," *Slate,* September 20, 2013, http://is.gd/FXt0yB.

action or watching it: Lea Winerman, "The Mind's Mirror," *Monitor on Psychology* 36, no. 9 (October 2005): 48, http://www.apa.org/monitor/oct05/ mirror.aspx.

psychology and neuroscience: "Social Cognition," *ScienceDaily,* http://www .sciencedaily.com/articles/s/social_cognition.htm.

50 *"become ourselves":* Patti Smith, *Just Kids* (New York: HarperCollins, 2010), Kindle edition.

become more: Described variously as "exploration," "curiosity," "competence," or "self-improvement," this drive can be seen in kids who dive headlong into games. This motivation out of innate interest—not for any discrete rewards—has been shown, empirically, to be the distinguishing characteristic of high performance, as Harvard Business School professor Teresa Amabile wrote in *The Progress Principle.* See Teresa Amabile and Steven Kramer, *The Progress Principle: Using Small Wins to Ignite Joy, Engagement, and Creativity at Work* (Boston: Harvard Business School Publishing, 2013). Also see Barbara Chai, "How to Stay Motivated—and Get That Bonus," *Wall Street Journal,* December 31, 2009, http://online.wsj.com/article/SB10001424052748704 1528045746282304288690074.html.

"as one's own": Martin Reimann and Arthur Aron, "Self-Expansion Motivation and Inclusion of Brands in Self," in *Handbook of Brand Relationships,* eds. Deborah J. MacInnis, C. Whan Park, and Joseph R. Priester (Armonk, NY: M. E. Sharpe, 2009), 68.

descriptions of themselves: Arthur Aron and Elaine N. Aron, "Self and Self-Expansion in Relationships," in *Knowledge Structures in Close Relationships: A Social Psychological Approach,* eds. Garth J. O. Fletcher and Julie Fitness (New York: Psychology Press, 1996), 333.

"others in the self": Ibid., 329.

"we're the same person": This same body of experiments helps explain the emotion of splitting from a partner. Losing someone you're intimately con-

nected with often leads to a rapid de-expansion of self—that is, if you experienced expansion in the relationship—and that hurts. By contrast, a breakup may actually put a person in a better mood if the bond was causing more restriction than expansion (Arthur Aron, interview with the author, June 8, 2012).

"relationship with your partner": Arthur Aron et al., "Inclusion of Other in the Self Scale and the Structure of Interpersonal Closeness," *Journal of Personality and Social Psychology* 63 (1992): 596–612.

7. *"No Power in Heaven, Hell or Earth"*

53   *fifty-fifty:* Michael D. Eisner, with Aaron R. Cohen, *Working Together: Why Great Partnerships Succeed* (New York: HarperCollins, 2010), 102.

"extremely easy": Kevin Morris, interview with the author, October 17, 2013.

freedom of living alone: Marie Curie, *Pierre Curie* (with autobiographical notes), trans. Charlotte and Vernon Kellogg (New York: Macmillan, 1923), 170–71. Online at http://www.aip.org/history/curie/credits.htm#refs.

54   *"fiercely to her independence"*: Eve Curie, *Madame Curie: A Biography* (Cambridge, MA: Da Capo, 2001), 120.

"an hour of love": Ibid.

science over marriage: Ibid.

he still lived with his parents: Susan Quinn, *Marie Curie: A Life* (Cambridge, MA: Da Capo, 1995), 115.

and to science: Eve Curie, *Madame Curie,* 129.

55   *"further and further"*: Herman Melville, "Hawthorne and His Mosses," *Literary World,* August 17 and 24, 1850. Scholars believe that *Moby-Dick* was critically affected by Melville's relationship with Hawthorne. In July 1850, Melville said his book on a whaling voyage was "in sight of port." In August he met Hawthorne and moved near him in the Berkshires. He apparently began revising *Moby-Dick* in November. Melville wrote to Hawthorne's wife that her husband "first revealed to" him "the speciality of many of the particular subordinate allegories," and "intimated the part-&-parcel allegoricalness of the whole." The scholar David B. Kesterson writes: "The major occurrence in Melville's life, then, during the writing of *Moby-Dick* was the growing friendship with Nathaniel Hawthorne," and Kesterson quotes the scholar Howard Vincent saying that Hawthorne was "the one writer in America who had expressed the tragic point of view, which was deeply felt, but not hitherto declared, by Melville himself. Hawthorne was the catalyst speeding Melville's accumulated reflections into expression" (David B. Kesterson, "Hawthorne and Melville," lecture delivered in Salem, MA, September 23, 2000, Phillips Library, Peabody Essex Museum).

"our scientific dream": Eve Curie, *Madame Curie,* 129.

she slowly moved in his direction: Her trepidation about joining Pierre had to do with whether she could put anything above her commitment to her country. She'd objected when a friend became engaged to a German, telling her that she had "sign[ed] on with a foreign crew." "Your heart," she wrote her friend, "cannot be free / But must be Polish everywhere" (Quinn, *Marie Curie,* 117).

live with her there: Eve Curie, *Madame Curie,* 129–35.

done without hesitation: Quinn, *Marie Curie,* 116.

56 *"eternally wedded together":* Penny Colman, *Elizabeth Cady Stanton and Susan B. Anthony: A Friendship That Changed the World* (New York: Henry Holt, 2011), 130.

"as did he": J. A. Kaplan, "Deeper and Deeper: Interview with Marina Abramović," *Art Journal* 58, no. 2 (1999): 9.

magnetism of tempered steel: Eve Curie, *Madame Curie,* 152.

57 *discovered radioactivity:* Marie's words from ibid., 96: Marie's experiments proved that "the radiation of uranium compounds can be measured with precision under determined conditions, and that this radiation is an atomic property of the element of uranium. Its intensity is proportional to the quantity of uranium contained in the compound, and depends neither on conditions of chemical combination nor on external circumstances such as light or temperature." See Marie Curie, *Pierre Curie,* 45.

polonium: Marie Curie, *Pierre Curie,* 46, 90.

which they named radium: Ibid., 54.

"the work of the Curies": Eve Curie, *Madame Curie,* 159.

"we observed": Ibid., 160.

"country of one of us": Ibid., 161.

"that of a dream": Quinn, *Marie Curie,* 156.

fashion or physics or popular music: "Creativity results from the interaction of a system composed of three elements: a culture that contains symbolic rules, a person who brings novelty into the symbolic domain, and a field of experts who recognize and validate the innovation" (Mihaly Csikszentmihalyi, *Creativity: Flow and the Psychology of Discovery and Invention* [New York: Harper-Collins, 2009], 6).

58 *"baby face":* Hunter Davies, *The Beatles* (1968; New York: W. W. Norton, 1996), 45. One of John's recollections in *The Beatles Anthology* (San Francisco: Chronicle Books, 2000), 12, seems to bely this history; there he said, "I had to make the decision whether to let George in. I listened to him play and said, 'Play "Raunchy."' I let him in and that was the three of us then." But I think this is a case of John collapsing a more protracted discussion. According to Barry Miles, in *Paul McCartney: Many Years from Now* (New York: Henry Holt, 1998), Paul had to lead a "campaign" to get George into the group. Miles writes that John was "astonished" by the "Raunchy" solo

but "there was one big problem: George was only fourteen at the time and no way was John Lennon going to have a fourteen-year-old in his group." Miles finishes the story the same way Pete Shotton does. It's not so much that Paul persuaded John as that John relented after George's great persistence.

"tagging after John": Pete Shotton and Nicholas Schaffner, *John Lennon: In My Life* (New York: Thunder's Mouth Press, 1994), 57.

"so did Paul": The Beatles, *The Beatles Anthology*, 30.

"anyone else": Davies, *The Beatles*, 48.

"wrong with me": The Beatles, *The Beatles Anthology*, 14.

59   *Beat ideal*: According to Ellis Amburn, *Subterranean Kerouac: The Hidden Life of Jack Kerouac* (New York: St. Martin's, 1999), 342, Lennon told Jack Kerouac directly that the name Beatles was inspired by the Beats, though the origin of the name has a variety of other explanations. See Howard Sounes, *Fab: An Intimate Life of Paul McCartney* (Boston: Da Capo, 2010), 31–32.

"I'd believe him": The Beatles, *The Beatles Anthology*, 69.

guiding force in his life: Larry Kane, *Lennon Revealed* (Philadelphia: Running Press, 2007), 52.

"John's attention": Miles, *Many Years from Now*, 65.

60   *"survival for me"*: The Beatles, *The Beatles Anthology*, 56.

"'lot of trouble'": Ibid., 14.

"always give in": Ibid., 56.

"Massey and Coggins": Ibid.

"he chose me": Ibid.

61   *"you'll get work someday"*: Barry Miles, *The Beatles Diary, Volume 1* (London: Omnibus Press, 2009), e-book.

"cheered for the first time": Ibid.

adding Ringo Starr: The Beatles, *The Beatles Anthology*, 70, 72.

Japage 3: Mark Lewisohn, *The Beatles: All These Years, Volume 1—Tune In* (New York: Crown, 2013), 201.

contracts with Epstein: Ibid., 705.

"rest of the world": Alistair Taylor, *With the Beatles* (London: John Blake Publishing, 2003), 123.

Part III: Dialectics

62   *"great area of speculation"*: Andrew Dickson White Museum of Art, *Earth Art* (Ithaca, NY: Office of University Publications, Cornell University, 1970), 69–70.

63   *bacteriophages*: "Discovery of the Function of DNA Resulted from the Work of Multiple Scientists," n.d., http://www.nature.com/scitable/topicpage/dis covery-of-the-function-of-dna-resulted-6494318.

64   *coordination dynamics*: See J. A. Scott Kelso and David A. Engstrøm, *The Com-

plementary Nature (Cambridge, MA: MIT Press, 2005), and J. A. Scott Kelso, *Dynamic Patterns: The Self-Organization of Brain and Behavior* (Cambridge, MA: MIT Press, 1995).

spotter and a sniper: Milo S. Afong, *HOGs in the Shadows: Combat Stories from Marine Snipers in Iraq* (New York: Penguin, 2007), 4.

8. In the Spotlight (in the Shadows)

65   *"Woodstock of capitalism":* Dan McCrum, "Fans Flock to 'Woodstock of Capitalism,'" *Financial Times,* May 6, 2012.

  "nothing to add": Janet Lowe, *Damn Right!: Behind the Scenes with Berkshire Hathaway Billionaire Charlie Munger* (Hoboken, NJ: John Wiley and Sons, 2000), 5.

66   *her mother famous:* Judith Thurman, "Wilder Women," *New Yorker,* August 10, 2009, http://www.newyorker.com/arts/critics/atlarge/2009/08/10/090810 crat_atlarge_thurman.

  "move my lips": Lowe, *Damn Right,* 5.

  "the pleasure of it": Ernest De Selincourt, ed., *The Letters of William and Dorothy Wordsworth,* vol. 2 (Oxford: Clarendon Press, 1967), 454.

  account of it: Wordsworth's "Daffodils," https://wordsworth.org.uk/daffodils .html.

  patron, researcher, gopher, and babysitter: For an artful account of the Joyce brothers, see George Howe Colt, *Brothers: On His Brothers and Brothers in History* (New York: Simon and Schuster, 2012), 242–46.

67   *"self-reliant crusader":* Ian Desai, "Gandhi's Invisible Hands," *Wilson Quarterly* (Autumn 2010), http://www.wilsonquarterly.com/essays/gandhis-invisible -hands.

  "rural churches": Taylor Branch, interview with the author, December 30, 2013.

  "Mr. Rough and Mr. Smooth": Taylor Branch, *Parting the Waters: America in the King Years, 1954–1963* (New York: Simon and Schuster, 1998), Kindle edition.

  "dearest friend and cellmate": "America's Gandhi: Rev. Martin Luther King Jr.," *Time,* January 3, 1964, http://content.time.com/time/magazine/article/0,91 71,940759,00.html#ixzz2rGRGiQ4n.

68   *"ever does it":* Ann Romines, *Constructing the Little House: Gender, Culture, and Laura Ingalls Wilder* (Amherst: University of Massachusetts Press, 1997), 48.

  researcher, and secretary: The best source here is Stacy Schiff, *Vera (Mrs. Vladimir Nabokov): Portrait of a Marriage* (New York: Random House, 1999). I'm drawing on the *New York Times* review of the book, April 27, 1999, in which Michiko Kakutani summed up Vera's roles as "editor, typist, agent, secretary, chauffeur, nursemaid, go-between, buffer, researcher and butterfly-catching companion"; http://www.nytimes.com/1999/04/27/books/books-of-the-times-behind-a-sorcerer-s-magic-a-formidable-assistant.html.

69 *going broke: Valentino: The Last Emperor,* directed by Matt Tyrnauer (Acolyte Films, 2009). This information is given at about 16:15.

toilet-seat covers: Giancarlo Giammetti and Armand Limnander, *Private: Giancarlo Giammetti* (New York: Assouline, 2013), 144–45.

"'*Let's do bathrooms*'": Cathy Horyn, "Q & A: Giancarlo Giammetti," *On the Runway* (blog), November 21, 2007, http://runway.blogs.nytimes.com/2007/11/21/q-a-giancarla-giammetti/.

footnote: *outside of their minds:* Jeff Tweedy: *Sunken Treasure — Live in the Pacific Northwest* (Nonesuch, 2006), directed by Christoph Green and Brendan Canty.

70 "*in the back*'": Derek Blasberg, "The Private Eye of Giancarlo Giammetti," *Wall Street Journal,* October 10, 2013, http://online.wsj.com/news/articles/SB10001424052702304213904579095250925722872.

"*in front of me*": Colt, *Brothers.*

"*a lot of patience*": *Valentino: The Last Emperor.*

"*making them together*": Colt, *Brothers,* 233.

71 *uncle Vincent's firm:* Uncle Vincent was a partner in the firm of Goupil et Cie, and, though he retired in 1872, he left money in the firm until 1878. Chris Stolwijk, Richard Thomson, and Sjraar Van Heugten, *Theo van Gogh, 1857 to 1891: Art Dealer, Collector, and Brother of Vincent* (Amsterdam: Van Gogh Museum, 2002).

to the middlebrow: Simon Schama, *The Power of Art* (London: BBC Books, 2006), 300.

"*such was the case here*": Vincent van Gogh to Theo van Gogh, January 10, 1876, http://www.webexhibits.org/vangogh/letter/3/050.htm.

their exalted expectations: Anna van Gogh to Theo van Gogh, May 31, 1873, http://vangoghletters.org/vg/context_1.html. As the essay notes, Vincent was briefly considered a wearer of the crown, but the image was used repeatedly by his parents in connection with Theo: "Always remain our joy and crown"; "Look after yourself always, and be aware that you are our crown and joy"; "Continue to be our joy and crown, that is the greatest treasure we desire." "A remark of Mrs. van Gogh's shows that this crown metaphor embraced more than just the person who wore it; it covered the honor and merits of the whole family." She wrote to Theo when it looked as if Vincent was going off the rails in the Borinage: "Now that the eldest has shaken the coronet it is our redoubled hope that the second one will straighten the coronet again."

insane asylum: Vincent van Gogh to Theo van Gogh, November 18, 1881, http://vangoghletters.org/vg/letters/let185/letter.html. See note 3 there for a list of the letters that mention Vincent's father's wish to commit him.

73   *"and so false"*: Theo van Gogh to Elisabeth van Gogh, October 13, 1885, http://www.webexhibits.org/vangogh/letter/17/etc-fam-1886.htm.

     "his new calling": Debora Silverman, *Van Gogh and Gauguin: The Search for Sacred Art* (New York: Farrar, Straus and Giroux, 2000), 18.

     "whatever happens": Vincent van Gogh to Theo van Gogh, May 28, 1888, http://webexhibits.org/vangogh/letter/18/492.htm.

     "as a revolutionary or rebel": Vincent van Gogh to Theo van Gogh, about September 22 and 28, 1884, in http://vangoghletters.org/vg/letters/let461/letter.html.

74   *"in one another"*: Theo van Gogh to Jo Bonger, August 1, 1887, in H. van Crimpen, ed., *Brief Happiness: The Correspondence of Theo van Gogh and Jo Bonger* (Amsterdam: B. V. Waanders Uitgeverji, 2000), 66.

     "Flemish cattle drovers": Colt, *Brothers*, 223.

     "not a grey harmony": Vincent van Gogh to Horace M. Livens, August–October 1887, http://www.webexhibits.org/vangogh/letter/17/459a.htm.

75   *images of Theo:* In June 2011, the Van Gogh Museum in Amsterdam announced that it would rename an 1887 painting by Vincent van Gogh long known as *Self-Portrait in Straw Hat.* In preparation for a show on the painter's years in Antwerp and Paris, a senior researcher, Louis van Tilborgh, determined that the painting was, in fact, a portrait of Theo van Gogh. The image shows a man wearing a blue coat over a white shirt, a blue bow tie, and a yellow straw hat (http://www.vangoghmuseum.nl/vgm/index.jsp?page=1937&lang=en). Several days after the revelation, *ArtInfo* published a story about scholars' responses in which the curator Belinda Thomson, author of *Van Gogh Paintings: The Masterpieces,* told the magazine that she believed there was a second portrait of Theo; see "Is an 1887 van Gogh 'Self-Portrait' Really of Theo?" *Blouin ArtInfo* (blog), June 21, 2011, http://blogs.artinfo.com/artintheair/2011/06/21/is-an-1887-van-gogh-self-portrait-really-of-theo.

9. Jokestein and Structureberg

76   *"it would squeal"*: Geoff Emerick and Howard Massey, *Here, There and Everywhere: My Life Recording the Music of the Beatles* (New York: Penguin, 2006), Kindle edition. Several other quotes from Emerick that follow are from the same source.

     "in that way": David Sheff, *All We Are Saying: The Last Major Interview with John Lennon and Yoko Ono* (New York: St. Martin's, 2010), 173.

77   *play dissonant chords:* Tim Riley, *Lennon: The Man, the Myth, the Music — the Definitive Life* (London: Virgin Books Limited, 2011), 118.

     out of tune: Jack Douglas, who produced *Double Fantasy,* said in the PBS documentary *LennoNYC,* directed by Michael Epstein: "And the funny thing was he used to deliberately put his D string out of tune. He'd tune up and tune the D flat and I said to him, 'Why do you do that?' . . . And he said, 'Well, because when we used to make those Beatles records they were just mono mixes and they would go on the radio and my Aunt Mimi would say, "John, is one of these guitars you?"' And [John] would say 'Yup. That one. See the one that's slightly out of tune, that's me,' and he never stopped doing that." Yet people with better ears than me tell me that Lennon's guitar is surely in tune for many Beatles recordings; this is why I qualify this statement with "at times."

"raw, raunchy sound": Richard Danielpour, interview with the author, July 24, 2012.

"rebel a bit": Philip Norman, *John Lennon: The Life* (New York: Doubleday, 2008), e-book.

"fuckin' jewelry": Philip Norman, *Shout!: The Beatles in Their Generation* (New York: Fireside, 2005), e-book. For a thorough treatment of this episode, see Andrew Grant Jackson, "The Beatles Play for the Queen," *Slate*, November 4, 2013, http://is.gd/dpTVD7, part of the Blogging the Beatles project.

"rattle your jewelry": "The Beatles — 'Twist and Shout,' Royal Command Performance, London Palladium, 1963," YouTube video, posted by alanivory1, March 18, 2011, http://www.youtube.com/watch?v=6O9Ef1PkVj4.

"Very nice!" (Laughs): Kevin Howlett, *The Beatles: The BBC Archives: 1962–1970* (New York: Harper Design, 2013), 67–69.

78 *"wanted to play"*: Barry Miles, *Paul McCartney: Many Years from Now* (New York: Henry Holt, 1998), 34.

"that John did": Paul McCartney, interview with Paul Gambaccini, *Rolling Stone*, January 31, 1974, http://www.rollingstone.com/music/news/paul-mccart ney-is-not-dead-and-neither-is-the-past-19740131?print=true. This online version of the article gives *slagging* as *slugging*, but this must be a typo or a mistake by the author. *Slagging* is the apt word for what Paul is describing, and one Paul used many times to convey just this meaning.

"amenable to change": Emerick and Massey, *Here, There and Everywhere*, 100.

"lateral thinking": Cynthia Lennon, *John* (New York: Three Rivers Press, 2005), Kindle edition.

79 *restoration of same*: Frank Barron, *No Rootless Flower: An Ecology of Creativity* (Cresskill, NJ: Hampton Press, 1995), 88.

The Birth of Tragedy: Friedrich Wilhelm Nietzsche, *The Birth of Tragedy* (Oxford: Oxford University Press, 2000).

"energy and attention": Barron, *No Rootless Flower*, 91.

"the ones who do": A version of this ad is online: "Here's to the Crazy Ones (1997)," YouTube video, posted by vintagemacmuseum, May 23, 2010, http://www.youtube.com/watch?v=tjgtLSHhTPg.

80 *"all over again"*: Françoise Gilot and Carlton Lake, *Life with Picasso* (New York: Anchor Books, 1989), 152–59.

81 *head guy*: Mel Brooks and Carl Reiner, interview with Steve Heisler, *A.V. Club*, December 1, 2009, http://is.gd/8vHmHM.

82   *piano tune:* This demo is widely available on the web, including here: "John Lennon's Original Tempo 'Help!' [Home Demo] — 1965," YouTube video, posted by xXOneHotLennonXx, November 4, 2011, http://www.youtube.com/watch?v=MR6r9-sRfoo.

    "the window, you know": Sheff, *All We Are Saying,* 177.

    complained about it: Jann Wenner, *Lennon Remembers* (London: Verso, 2001), 98.

    marriage between the two: I'm summarizing from a lecture I heard Donald Hall give at the Bennington Writing Seminars in June 2009.

83   *"the conversation":* Miles, *Many Years from Now,* 67.

    "cloud your mind up": Ibid., 272.

    "a thousand trips": Wenner, *Lennon Remembers,* 52.

    around the mike: Emerick and Massey, *Here, There and Everywhere.*

84   *reel-to-reel tape recorders:* Mark Lewisohn, *The Complete Beatles Recording Sessions* (New York: Harmony Books, 1988), 72.

    material world: See *The Beatles Bible* on "Tomorrow Never Knows," http://www.beatlesbible.com/songs/tomorrow-never-knows.

10. Inspiration and Perspiration

85   *"far from the truth":* Randall Stross, *The Wizard of Menlo Park: How Thomas Alva Edison Invented the Modern World* (New York: Random House, 2008), 166.

86   *99 percent perspiration:* Wolfgang Mieder, Stewart A. Kingsbury, and Kelsie B. Harder, eds., *A Dictionary of American Proverbs: Oxford Paperback Reference* (Oxford: Oxford University Press, 1992), 397.

    "details to others": Kathleen McAuliffe, "The Undiscovered World of Thomas Edison," *Atlantic,* December 1995, http://www.theatlantic.com/magazine/archive/1995/12/the-undiscovered-world-of-thomas-edison/305880/.

    results-oriented: Vera John-Steiner, *Creative Collaboration* (Oxford: Oxford University Press, 2000), 39.

    at times, brooding: Description of their personalities and Wilbur's glimpse into flight can be found in Tom D. Crouch, *The Bishop's Boys: A Life of Wilbur and Orville Wright* (New York: W. W. Norton, 1989), 14–15, 159.

    "make it work": Ibid., 516. For another sketch of the brothers' differences, see ibid., 13–16. For Wilbur's lead role in the quest to fly, see ibid., 162–63.

    $58.4 million: "In the Saleroom: Jeff Koons' Balloon Dog (Orange)," last modified November 13, 2013, http://www.christies.com/features/in-the-saleroom-jeff-koons-balloon-dog-orange-4222-3.aspx. The hammer price was $52 million but the final price includes the buyer's premium.

    Coosje van Bruggen: Guy Raz, "An Art Factory Goes Out of Business," NPR.org, http://www.npr.org/templates/story/story.php?storyId=127239760. Carlson is hardly the sole actor in such a production. As we'll see, the man called out in this example as the doer is himself the dreamer in relation to partners or employees who execute what he suggests.

started another operation: "Carlson Arts LLC Re-Launches Company Providing Custom Fabrication Services for Artists, Architects and Other Design Professionals," last updated November 10, 2010, http://www.prnewswire.com/news-releases/carlson-arts-llc-re-launches-company-providing-custom-fabrication-services-for-artists-architects-and-other-design-professionals-108444334.html.

87   *"comic sensibility":* "Seinfeld: How It Began," on *Seinfeld,* seasons 1 and 2 (Sony Pictures Home Entertainment, 2004).

models out of Legos: 6 Days to Air: The Making of "South Park," directed by Arthur Bradford (Comedy Central, 2011).

Kyle, Kenny, and Butters: South Park, http://www.imdb.com/title/tt0121955/.

for $270,000: Vanessa Grigoriadis, "Still Sick, Still Wrong," *Rolling Stone,* March 8, 2007.

went to McDonald's: Arthur Bradford, interview with the author, August 9, 2013.

88   *"once a week":* Jason McHugh, interview with the author, September 27, 2013.

"gaining ground": Kevin Morris, interview with the author, October 17, 2013.

debt crisis or WikiLeaks: Arthur Bradford, interview with the author, August 9, 2013.

"through it before": Kevin Morris, interview with the author, December 5, 2013.

"encourage him": Jaime J. Weinman, "South Park Has a Silent Partner," *Maclean's,* April 23, 2007.

11. Turn-Taking

90   *"follow that forever":* Jason McHugh, interview with the author, December 13, 2013.

91   *absolutely depend on:* Diana Pavlac Glyer, *The Company They Keep: C. S. Lewis and J.R.R. Tolkien as Writers in Community* (Kent, OH: Kent State University Press, 2007), 4–5, 40, 46–50. Glyer borrowed the term *resonators* from Karen Burke LeFevre, who got the term from Harold Lasswell. See Elizabeth G. Peck and JoAnna Stephens Mink, eds., *Common Ground: Feminist Collaboration in the Academy* (Albany: SUNY Press, 1998), 221. Some historians cite Lewis as the first person to see Tolkien's *Lay,* but Carpenter references the tepid response Tolkien got in 1926 from his old teacher in Humphrey Carpenter, *J.R.R. Tolkien: A Biography* (New York: HarperCollins, 2011), 166.

great importance: Carpenter, *J.R.R. Tolkien,* 145.

encouraging him: If Lewis didn't like a passage, he would say, "Better, Tolkien, please!"; Glyer, *The Company They Keep,* 118.

"legions of his marshalled hate": Revisions described in ibid., 113.

"incorporated into the text": Ibid., 116.

92   *Lewis's first edits:* Ibid.

335 million copies: Ed Grabianowski, "The 21 Best-Selling Books of All Time," HowStuffWorks.com, December 19, 2011, http://entertainment.howstuff -works.com/arts/literature/21-best-sellers.htm; "List of Best-Selling Books," Wikipedia, January 26, 2014, http://en.wikipedia.org/w/index.php?title= List_of_best-selling_books&oldid=592551463.

"often brutally frank": Glyer, *The Company They Keep*, 17–18. The original source is Lewis's brother Warnie's preface to C. S. Lewis, *The Collected Letters of C. S. Lewis* (New York: HarperCollins, 2009), 34.

"Grand Pooh-Bah": George Meyer, interview with Eric Spitznagel, *Believer*, September 2004, http://is.gd/0BIgRj.

"your baby's sick": Adam Grant, *Give and Take* (New York: Viking, 2013), 86.

93   *"not a risk"*: Matthew Swanson, e-mail to the author, November 3, 2012.

12. *"Everything's the Opposite"*

94   *situational cues:* Walter Mischel, *Personality and Assessment* (New York: Psychology Press, 2013).

excrement in the cells: Quiet Rage: The Stanford Prison Experiment, directed by Kim Duke (BBC, 2002).

95   *"people are doing"*: Frank J. Sulloway, interview with the author, November 14, 2012.

the status quo: Frank J. Sulloway, *Born to Rebel: Birth Order, Family Dynamics, and Creative Lives* (New York: Vintage Books 1997), 330.

96   *"tennis, and track"*: Frank J. Sulloway, "Why Siblings Are Like Darwin's Finches: Birth Order, Sibling Competition, and Adaptive Divergence Within the Family," in *The Evolution of Personality and Individual Differences*, eds. David M. Buss and Patricia H. Hawley (Oxford: Oxford University Press, 2010), 86–119, http://www.sulloway.org/Sulloway. This quote is from page 107.

struck out more: Frank J. Sulloway, interview with the author, November 14, 2012.

"What the hell is water?": David Foster Wallace, *This Is Water* (Boston: Little, Brown, 2009).

fundamental attribution error: Lee Ross, "The Intuitive Psychologist and His Shortcomings: Distortions in the Attribution Process," in *Advances in Experimental Social Psychology*, vol. 10, ed. L. Berkowitz (New York: Academic Press, 1977), 173–220.

97   *90 percent do:* David Belton, *American Experience: The Amish* (PBS, 2012).

a perpetual adolescence: As David Shenk wrote in *The Genius in All of Us* (New

York: HarperCollins, 2010), talent itself and genius are not innate, genetic aptitudes but skills a person develops as he's driven constantly by social and cultural interactions.

98 *"stagnant and stingless"*: William James to Alice James, about December 26, 1878, in William James, *The Letters of William James: Volume 1*, ed. Henry James (Boston: Atlantic Monthly Press, 1920), available via Project Gutenberg 2011, www.gutenberg.org/ebooks/40307.

100 *"other extreme is 'bad'"*: Mihaly Csikszentmihalyi, *Creativity: Flow and the Psychology of Discovery and Invention* (New York: HarperCollins, 2009), 36. A summary of Csikszentmihalyi's dichotomies of the creative personality can be found on the web page "What Is Creativity?" from California State University, Northridge, citing Csikszentmihalyi, *Creativity*, 58–73.

"an ongoing process": Alfonso Montuori, "Frank Barron: A Creator on Creating," *Journal of Humanistic Psychology* 43 (2003): 7, http://www.ciis.edu/Documents/Academic%20Departments/TID/Frank%20Barron-JHP.pdf.

positive disintegration: For an overview of this theory, see http://positivedisintegration.com.

101 *"don't get paid"*: 6 Days to Air: The Making of "South Park," directed by Arthur Bradford (Comedy Central, 2011).

"stuff like that": Vernon Chatman, interview with the author, November 12, 2013.

102 *"Jesus Christ!"*: Bradford, *6 Days to Air*.

"Everything's the opposite": David Sheff, *All We Are Saying: The Last Major Interview with John Lennon and Yoko Ono* (New York: St. Martin's, 2010).

103 *"subtracted from ourselves"*: William Todd Schultz, e-mail to the author, September 23, 2012.

"side of King": Taylor Branch, interview with the author.

104 *"She's fired"*: "Subversive, Satirical and Sold Out," *60 Minutes* (CBS, 2012), http://www.cbsnews.com/video/watch/?id=7411226n.

Jobs the visionary: Walter Isaacson, *Steve Jobs* (New York: Simon and Schuster, 2011), 30.

or other people: Steve Wozniak, *iWoz: Computer Geek to Cult Icon* (New York: W. W. Norton, 2006), Kindle edition.

"a single person": Gary Wolf, "The World According to Woz," *Wired*, September 1998, http://www.wired.com/wired/archive/6.09/woz_pr.html.

entire fictional universe: Diana Pavlac Glyer, *The Company They Keep: C. S. Lewis and J.R.R. Tolkien as Writers in Community* (Kent, OH: Kent State University Press, 2007), 7, 59.

good and evil: Humphrey Carpenter, *J.R.R. Tolkien: A Biography* (New York: HarperCollins, 2011), 201; Glyer, *The Company They Keep*, 85.

such facility and ease: Glyer, *The Company They Keep*, 5–8, 48–49, 58.

105 *"between the poles"*: Vernon Chatman, interview with the author, November 12, 2013.

13. The "Other" of the Psyche

107 *"betrothed himself"*: Rainer Maria Rilke, *Letters to a Young Poet,* trans. Joan M. Burnham (San Francisco: New World Library, 2000), Kindle edition.

"the Duino Elegies*"*: Mark M. Anderson, "The Poet and the Muse," *Nation,* June 14, 2006.

work on publishers: Sven Birkerts, *Readings* (Minneapolis: Graywolf Press, 1999), 189. Birkerts wrote: "Although he may have looked like a 'silhouette among solids,' he was of this world enough to be a canny self-promoter. He had been sending his youthful poems, stories, and plays to editors and publishers all over Germany and Central Europe. (The popular image of Rilke as a creature of pure spirit, aloof from the hustle of the marketplace, derives more from his later years. Then, thanks to the devotion of his publisher, Anton Kippenbeg, and the generosity of a number of wealthy friends, he was free to cultivate his Muse as he saw fit.)"

108 *relationships with others:* For a good introduction to object relations theory, see Victor Daniels's website at the Psychology Department of Sonoma State University: http://www.sonoma.edu/users/d/daniels/objectrelations.html.

"indeed the self": Donald W. Winnicott et al., *Psycho-Analytic Explorations* (Cambridge, MA: Harvard University Press, 1989), 418.

the actual words: Charles Fernyhough, "Alien Voices and Inner Dialogue: Towards a Developmental Account of Auditory Verbal Hallucinations," *New Ideas in Psychology* 22 (2004): 49–68.

109 *relate to others:* Daniel Goleman, *Social Intelligence: The New Science of Human Relationships* (New York: Random House, 2006).

mental health and empathy: Daniel J. Siegel, *Mindsight: The New Science of Personal Transformation* (New York: Bantam Books, 2010).

"don't actually exist": Paul Bloom, "First Person Plural," *Atlantic,* November 2008, http://www.theatlantic.com/magazine/archive/2008/11/first-person-plural/307055/.

110 *"this flushes up"*: Lewis Hyde, introduction to Rainer Maria Rilke, *Letters to a Young Poet and the Letter from the Young Worker,* ed. Charlie Louth (New York: Penguin Books, 2013), 9.

111 *"already been the audience"*: Paul Zollo, *Songwriters on Songwriting* (Cambridge, MA: Da Capo, 2003), 119–20.

"than it is you": Henry David Thoreau, *Walden.* This is from chapter 5, "Solitude," online at http://thoreau.eserver.org/walden05.html.

112 *"'Go bother Leonard Cohen'"*: Elizabeth Gilbert, "Your Elusive Creative Genius," February 2009, http://www.ted.com/talks/elizabeth_gilbert_on_genius.html.

"show to begin": Zollo, *Songwriters on Songwriting,* 120.

113 *"originality is through imitation"*: "Poetry Student Workshop at the White House," May 11, 2011, http://www.whitehouse.gov/photos-and-video/video/

2011/05/11/poetry-student-workshop-white-house. Billy Collins's remarks begin around 31:15.

an exchange within: One of the challenges of grappling with this is that we can't be fully aware of it as it is happening. We *can* be aware of what Collins describes as the period of "slavish imitation," like when Hunter S. Thompson retyped pages from *The Great Gatsby.* In my own writing, there are moments when I hear flashes of, say, David Foster Wallace (preening, neurotic, attempting to be lyrical and piercing) or of, say, Michael Pollan (earnest, informed, attempting to be clear and instructive). All of the writers I read intently — and all of the many other rhythms and meanings I ingest in conversation, from the car radio, on billboards I encounter walking down the street — echo around in me and get mixed up somehow with my style. But an authentic voice is something like a soup, which is best when it's blended. You may recognize a chunk of this ingredient here or there. But you should mostly be tasting the soup itself, not its separate ingredients.

Critics will sometimes dismiss work as derivative, but this is not precisely what they mean, because of course everything is derivative. What they mean is that the derivative quality of the work is *evident,* that it has not been blended well enough to feel original. T. S. Eliot put it this way: "Immature poets imitate; mature poets steal; bad poets deface what they take, and good poets make it into something better, or at least something different." The work is to ingest what we get from around us, bringing it inside and then out again in something effectively new ("unique, utterly different from that from which it was torn," Eliot said). Think about Jeff Buckley doing Leonard Cohen's "Hallelujah," or Gus Van Sant reworking the story of Shakespeare's *Henry IV, Part I.* The influences may be felt, the old text may be palpable, but the product is something entirely new.

114 SAME QUESTION: Susan Cain, *Quiet: The Power of Introverts in a World That Can't Stop Talking* (New York: Random House, 2012), 77.

"scrap of paper": Pete Shotton and Nicholas Schaffner, *John Lennon: In My Life* (New York: Thunder's Mouth Press, 1994), 121.

"come down": Hunter Davies, *The Beatles* (1968; New York: W. W. Norton, 1996), 295.

115 *absorbed in company:* Tenzin Geyche Tethong, interview with the author, November 15, 2010. For my first reference to the gentleman as "Tenzin Geyche Tethong" and my subsequent use of "Tenzin Geyche," I am following the form found in a book by His Holiness the Dalai Lama and Victor Chan, *The Wisdom of Forgiveness* (New York: Riverhead Books, 2004); excerpt online at http://www.wisdomofforgiveness.com/ex_intro.htm.

owned by Emerson: Richard Smith, "Thoreau's First Year at Walden in Fact & Fiction," talk delivered at the Thoreau Society annual gathering, July 14, 2007, http://thoreau.eserver.org/smith.html.

116 *"which my songs live"*: Lewis Hyde, introduction to Rilke, *Letters*, 7.
   "Letters *from* a Young Poet": Ibid.

14. Creative Monks and Siamese Twins

121 *on separate projects*: Horace Freeland Judson, *The Eighth Day of Creation: Makers of the Revolution in Biology* (Cold Spring Harbor, NY: Cold Spring Harbor Laboratory Press, 2004), 193.
   "alone for a bit": Francis Crick, *What Mad Pursuit: A Personal View of Scientific Discovery* (New York: Basic Books, 1990), 70.
   "as we liked": David Crosby and Graham Nash, interview with the author, April 18, 2012.
   almost never be in physical proximity: David Littlejohn, in *The Ultimate Art: Essays Around and About Opera* (Berkeley: University of California Press, 1992, 246), identifies a rare instance of contact. He writes, "[Strauss and Hofmannsthal's] motor trip together through northern Italy in March 1913 comes to the reader of the correspondence as something of a shock. It was one of their rare face-to-face encounters. Strauss, typically, was the one to offer the invitation. Hofmannsthal, typically, raised objections. 'Your kind, attractive proposal that I might accompany you on a car journey from Ala was altogether unexpected, and not easy to fit in with everything I had planned. But . . . this personal contact (which we have never before had over anything we have done before) might greatly benefit our chief joint work'— by which he meant *Die Frau ohne Schatten*, the opera they were working on at the time."
   "curiously evasive": Edward Sackville-West, ed., *A Working Friendship: The Correspondence Between Richard Strauss and Hugo von Hofmannsthal* (London: Collins, 1961), xx. Sackville-West is the biographer I refer to.

122 *"take me kindly"*: Hofmannsthal's plea makes for interesting reading alongside Winnicott's finding that "at the center of each person is an incommunicado element, and this is sacred and most worthy of preservation." Lesley Caldwell and Angela Joyce, *Reading Winnicott* (New York: Routledge, 2011), 192. "I am," Hofmannsthal wrote Strauss, "a much more bizarre kind of person than you can suspect; what you know is only a small part of me, the surface; the factors which govern me you cannot see. And so I am grateful to you for not prodding me . . . Please do not do it, even indirectly." Hofmannsthal seemed to suggest that elements of his imagination could, like sterile instruments in a hospital, be infected once brought to a certain kind of relational air: "Do not remind me of things," he pleaded, "for then I shall remind myself and as a result admonish myself. So bizarre is my constitution in such matters that, having once spoken to you of a certain possibility (a subject taken from late classical antiquity), your repeated allusions to this idea, your taking it up, your acquaintance with it, made the whole period distasteful to me and

have driven it out of my thoughts and dreams, perhaps for good." Sackville-West, *A Working Friendship*, xvii–xviii.

"House or town": Alfred Habegger, *My Wars Are Laid Away in Books: The Life of Emily Dickinson* (New York: Random House, 2002), 521.

with the door ajar: Ibid., 517.

virginal white: Ibid., 516.

a tenth of what she wrote: Emily Dickinson Museum, "Emily Dickinson's Letters," http://www.emilydickinsonmuseum.org/letters.

"energy and commitment": Christopher Benfey, interview with the author, June 29, 2010.

special sympathy: Richard Benson Sewall, *The Life of Emily Dickinson*, vols. 1–2 (Cambridge, MA: Harvard University Press, 1994), 463.

123 *for a sabbatical in Europe:* Brenda Wineapple, *White Heat: The Friendship of Emily Dickinson and Thomas Wentworth Higginson* (New York: Random House, 2009), 80.

"Preceptor": Ibid., 11.

"many of her best": Ibid., 4.

saved her life: Ibid., 13.

"Imagination" itself: Ellen Louise Hart and Martha Nell Smith, eds., *Open Me Carefully: Emily Dickinson's Intimate Letters to Susan Huntington Dickinson* (Ashfield, MA: Paris Press, 1998), 242. The line was: "To be Susan is Imagination. To have been Susan, a Dream."

only to Shakespeare: Dickinson wrote: "With the exception of Shakespeare, you have told me of more knowledge than anyone living" (ibid., 238).

two hundred and fifty poems: Christopher Benfey, interview with the author, June 29, 2010.

"idolatry, not indifference": Hart and Smith, *Open Me Carefully*, 221.

"nearer her they get": Ibid., 215–16.

124 *"electric passion":* Hart and Smith, *Open Me Carefully*, xvii.

Elizabeth Barrett Browning: Páraic Finnerty, *Emily Dickinson's Shakespeare* (Amherst: University of Massachusetts Press, 2008), 95.

Harper's Magazine: Roger Lundin, *Emily Dickinson and the Art of Belief* (Grand Rapids, MI: Wm. B. Eerdmans, 2004), 128.

work to the Atlantic Monthly: Thomas Wentworth Higginson, "Letter to a Young Contributor," *Atlantic Monthly*, April 1, 1862, http://www.theatlantic.com/magazine/archive/1862/04/letter-to-a-young-contributor/305164/.

"I have none to ask": Thomas Wentworth Higginson, "Emily Dickinson's Letters," *Atlantic Monthly*, October 1891, http://www.theatlantic.com/past/unbound/poetry/emilyd/edletter.htm.

"shuts the Door—": This famous poem can be seen at Poets.org, http://www.poets.org/viewmedia.php/prmMID/20283.

intriguing and startling: Wineapple, *White Heat*, 5.

"not to live near her": Habegger, *My Wars Are Laid Away in Books,* 524.

125 *"highly sensitive person":* Elaine Aron, *The Highly Sensitive Person: How to Thrive When the World Overwhelms You* (New York: Broadway Books, 1996), Kindle edition.

"overwhelming situations": Elaine Aron, "The Highly Sensitive Person," http://www.hsperson.com/pages/test.htm.

maximize it: H. J. Eysenck and M. W. Eysenck, *Personality and Individual Differences: A Natural Science Approach* (New York: Plenum, 1985).

has a negative effect: R. M. Yerkes and J. D. Dodson, "The Relation of Strength of Stimulus to Rapidity of Habit-Formation," *Journal of Comparative Neurology and Psychology* 18 (1908): 459–82. This paper is online at *Classics in the History of Psychology,* http://psychclassics.yorku.ca/Yerkes/Law/.

matching suits: The best way to see the matching suits is to *see* them, in a Google Image search for *Gilbert and George matching suits.* As the pictures make clear, matching ≠ identical.

"we are an artist": Interview with Gilbert and George, *Journal of Contemporary Art,* n.d., http://www.jca-online.com/gilbertandgeorge.html.

126 *comes in duplicate:* The material on this pair is drawn from my interview with AndrewAndrew, September 9, 2011, and Michael Schulman, "Mirror Images in the DJ Booth," *New York Times,* January 5, 2011.

15. *"Somehow We Also Kept Surprising Each Other"*

129 *"each other's presence":* Donald Hall, "Ghost in the House," *Unholy Ghost: Writers on Depression,* ed. Nell Casey (New York: HarperCollins, 2001), 165.

times a day: Lisa Kogan, "The *O* Interview: Gayle and Oprah, Uncensored," *O,* August 2006, http://is.gd/79iy. For not living in the same city, see Frank Bruni, "The Sidekick No More," *New York Times,* March 18, 2011.

the first time: James C. McKinley Jr., "Still Making Music Together, Far Apart," *New York Times,* September 27, 2013, http://is.gd/3Y0vyw.

"I was there": "Subversive, Satirical and Sold Out," *60 Minutes* (CBS, 2012), http://www.cbsnews.com/video/watch/?id=7411226n.

the old days: Arthur Bradford, interview with the author, August 9, 2013.

130 *"You deal with it":* "Penn and Teller: Reddit's Top Ten Questions," 2011, http://bit.ly/1fJ9Xbi. The clip begins around 20:40.

131 *written and illustrated story:* Paul Lewis, "Cécile de Brunhoff, Creator of Babar, Dies at 99," *New York Times,* April 8, 2003, http://www.nytimes.com/2003/04/08/obituaries/08BRUN.html.

"all the time": Phyllis Rose and Laurent de Brunhoff, interview with the author, November 9, 2009.

132 *"meet only periodically":* All the quotes from Daniel Kahneman here come from a biographical sketch on the Nobel Prize website, http://www.nobelprize.org/nobel_prizes/economic-sciences/laureates/2002/kahneman-bio.html.

For a good summation of the work of Kahneman and Tversky, see Michael Lewis, "The King of Human Error," *Vanity Fair*, December 7, 2011, http://www.vanityfair.com/culture/features/2011/12/michael-lewis-201112.

"a side each," Ringo said: The Beatles, *The Beatles Anthology* (San Francisco: Chronicle Books, 2000), 258.

an hour's drive away: Ibid., 214.

"Dead cool, really": Peter A. Carlin, *Paul McCartney: A Life* (New York: Touchstone, 2009), 124–26.

watching TV: Ibid., 136.

"son of a bitch": Adam Goodheart, interview with the author, June 2, 2009.

133 *it's too close:* Abigail Turin, interview with the author, March 29, 2012.

"our own agency": Esther Perel, *Mating in Captivity: Reconciling the Erotic and the Domestic* (New York: HarperCollins, 2009), 16.

footnote: *to keep in equilibrium:* Marilynn Brewer, *Handbok of Self and Identity,* Mark R. Leary and June Price Tangney, eds. (New York: Guilford Press, 2003), 480–91.

134 Sweet Thursday: John Steinbeck, *Sweet Thursday* (New York: Penguin, 1996), 122.

"conscious intentionality": Mihaly Csikszentmihalyi, *Creativity: Flow and the Psychology of Discovery and Invention* (New York: HarperCollins, 2009), Kindle edition.

footnote: *"dreamt a solution":* Sam McNerney, "Relaxation & Creativity: The Science of Sleeping on It," *Big Think,* May 8, 2012.

"accepted and applied": Ibid.

135 *"relatively uninhibited":* Greg Feist, interview with the author, June 8, 2013.

"go it alone": This quote was in a story that went out on the Associated Press in January 1967, published, among other places, in the *Independent,* January 23.

"normal again": Jonathan Gould, *Can't Buy Me Love: The Beatles, Britain, and America* (New York: Random House, 2008), 371.

16. "Desire for That Which Is Missing"

136 *constantly moving:* NASA, "What Is Microgravity?," http://www.nasa.gov/centers/glenn/shuttlestation/station/microgex_prt.htm.

"for her," wrote Robert Gottlieb: Robert Gottlieb, *George Balanchine: The Ballet Maker* (New York: HarperCollins 2004), 131.

"spiritual consummation": Suzanne Farrell, *Holding On to the Air: An Autobiography* (Gainesville: University Press of Florida, 2002), 125.

137 *"choreographing my life": Suzanne Farrell: Elusive Muse,* directed by Anne Belle and Deborah Dickson (PBS, 1996).

"love the man": Farrell, *Holding On to the Air,* 126.

with her suitor: Ibid., 145.

"in the studio working": Ibid., 147.

138 *"synapse to cross"*: Esther Perel, *Mating in Captivity: Reconciling the Erotic and the Domestic* (New York: HarperCollins, 2006), Kindle edition.

"he does not exist any longer": Simone Weil, *Gravity and Grace* (New York: Routledge, 2012), 146.

poet and scholar Anne Carson notes: Anne Carson, *Eros the Bittersweet* (Champaign, IL: Dalkey Archive Press, 1986), 3.

"nor in one's being": Ibid., 10.

"of the poets": Ibid., 20.

"not possess it": Elusive Muse.

139 *retain their power:* Francine Prose, *The Lives of the Muses* (New York: HarperCollins, 2009), 3.

"works of art": Ibid., 271.

sublimation: The modern authority on adaptations is the psychiatrist George Vaillant; he explores them in his books *Adaptation to Life* (Cambridge, MA: Harvard University Press, 1977) and *The Wisdom of the Ego* (Cambridge, MA: Harvard University Press, 1993).

"visions and confessions": Joan Acocella, "Profiles: Second Act," *New Yorker,* January 6, 2003, http://www.newyorker.com/archive/2003/01/06/030106fa_fact _acocella.

did not have sex: Farrell, *Holding On to the Air,* 166.

140 *"initiating and receiving"*: Ibid., 163.

"not to be": Carson, *Eros the Bittersweet,* 30.

"anyone's list": Farrell, *Holding On to the Air,* 140.

wed "shortly": Ibid., 170.

141 *"such a big deal"*: Ibid., 171.

"thought he wanted": Ibid., 183.

"support or hang me": Ibid., 148.

"nice, quiet boy": Ibid., 179.

142 *"Paul should leave"*: Ibid., 188.

"not dancing tonight": Ibid., 189.

seventeen years: According to the Bruce Springsteen database, Bruce's first show with the core lineup of the E Street Band — including Clarence — was October 25, 1972, at the Shipbottom Lounge in Point Pleasant, New Jersey. By the Main Point show in Bryn Mawr, Pennsylvania, on September 19, 1974, the band had its name; http://www.brucespringsteen.it/e_streetx.htm.

"or whatever": Peter A. Carlin, *Bruce* (New York: Simon and Schuster, 2013), 355.

143 *"fucking phone call"*: Ibid., 356–57.

twenty-three years old: Anna Kisselgoff, "Suzanne Farrell Resigns from City Ballet," *New York Times,* May 13, 1969.

"*run off with a biker*": Joan Acocella, "Second Act."

"*what artistically*": Farrell, *Holding On to the Air*, 202.

"*spiritual daughter*": Elusive Muse.

double bed: Ibid.

144   "*Love, Suzi*": Farrell, *Holding On to the Air*, 213.

"*get to work*": Elusive Muse.

six years before: Farrell, *Holding On to the Air*, 219–20.

"*not a child anymore*": Toni Bentley, interview with the author, October 29, 2012.

red, gold, and black ribbons: Farrell, *Holding On to the Air*, 227.

145   "*dynamic, colorful, tender*": Arlene Croce, *Writing in the Dark, Dancing in the "New Yorker": An Arlene Croce Reader* (New York: Farrar, Straus and Giroux, 2000), 100.

"*had your marriage*": Elusive Muse.

compagnons de voyage: Vincent van Gogh to Theo van Gogh, mid-August 1879, http://www.webexhibits.org/vangogh/letter/8/132.htm.

"*cut off my head*": George Howe Colt, *Brothers: On His Brothers and Brothers in History* (New York: Simon and Schulster, 2012), 253.

146   "*still here*": Emile Bernard, *Lettres de Vincent van Gogh à Emile Bernard*, 1911, http://www.vggallery.com/misc/archives/bernard.htm.

"*later on*": Vincent van Gogh to Theo van Gogh, February 21, 1888, http://vangoghletters.org/vg/letters/let577/letter.html.

"*with people*": Colt, *Brothers*, 195.

"*father superior*": Vincent van Gogh to Theo van Gogh, October 3, 1888, http://is.gd/Sb02fe.

may have received word: It's an open question whether Vincent knew about his brother's engagement at the time he cut his ear. The general consensus in recent decades has been that he had not, though Martin Bailey, writing in *The Art Newspaper*, December 30, 2009, http://www.theartnewspaper.com/articles/Why-Van-Gogh-cut-his-ear-new-clue/19968, makes an intriguing case in the other direction. To me, the most potent evidence comes in Theo's letter to his fiancée, January 1, 1889, in *Brief Happiness*, 76–77, describing his encounter with Vincent at the hospital. "When I mentioned you to him," Theo wrote, "he evidently knew who & what I meant & when I asked whether he approved of our plans, he said yes, but that marriage ought not to be regarded as the main object in life."

December 23, 1888: Vincent van Gogh to Theo van Gogh, December 23, 1888, http://www.webexhibits.org/vangogh/letter/18/565.htm.

at a brothel: Ibid.

"*as much as possible*": Vincent van Gogh to Theo van Gogh, April 21, 1889, http://vangoghletters.org/vg/letters/let760/letter.html.

147   "'*on the Rhône*'": Jo van Gogh, *Memoir of Vincent van Gogh*, http://is.gd/jEw6HN.

17. My Most Intimate Enemy

151 *"anybody like that existed"*: Larry Bird, Earvin Johnson, and Jackie MacMullan, *When the Game Was Ours* (Boston: Houghton Mifflin Harcourt, 2009), ix. *"I had to beat"*: Ibid., v.

"blown away by his stats": *Magic and Bird: A Courtship of Rivals*, directed by Ezra Edelman (HBO Studios, 2010), http://www.hbo.com/sports/magic-and -bird-a-courtship-of-rivals#.

13.3 rebounds: Kent Hannon, "17 Indiana State," *Sports Illustrated*, November 28, 1977, http://si.com/vault/article/magazine/MAG1093086/index.htm. *"Larry Bird is for real"*: *Magic and Bird*.

152 *"It's Magic Johnson"*: Bird, Johnson, and MacMullan, *When the Game Was Ours*, 3.

cover boy too: Douglas S. Looney, "And for My Next Trick, I'll . . . ," *Sports Illustrated*, April 30, 1979, http://sportsillustrated.cnn.com/vault/article/ magazine/MAG1094877/3/index.htm.

undefeated season: Bird, Johnson, and MacMullan, *When the Game Was Ours*, 298.

fourteen of twenty-one shots: Larry Schwartz, "Plain and Simple, Bird Is One of the Best," ESPN.com, http://espn.go.com/sportscentury/features/ 00014096.html.

in the towel: The entire championship game is online, http://www.youtube .com/watch?v=OB_tnVltEOw.

to the least successful: James P. Carse, *Finite and Infinite Games: A Vision of Life as Play and Possibility* (New York: Ballantine Books, 1987), Kindle edition.

race toy cars: Christian Jarrett, "Faster, Higher, Stronger," *Psychologist* 25 (2012): 504–7.

Steve Jobs versus Bill Gates: "Steve Jobs, Bill Gates and Microsoft. It's Complicated," video compilation, posted by Boomer, April 8, 2013, http://everysteve jobsvideo.com/steve-jobs-bill-gates-and-microsoft-its-complicated/.

153 *Abraham Lincoln versus Stephen Douglas*: Roy Morris Jr., *The Long Pursuit: Abraham Lincoln's Thirty-Year Struggle with Stephen Douglas for the Heart and Soul of America* (Washington, DC: Smithsonian, 2008).

Jack Nicklaus versus Arnold Palmer in golf: Ian O'Connor, *Arnie & Jack: Palmer, Nicklaus, and Golf's Greatest Rivalry* (Boston: Houghton Mifflin Harcourt, 2008).

Muhammed Ali versus Joe Frazier in boxing: *Thrilla in Manilla* (HBO, 2009.)

Chris Evert versus Martina Navratilova in tennis: *Unmatched*, directed by Lisa Lax and Nancy Stern Winters (ESPN Films, 2010).

"can't win": Mark Stephens, who writes as Robert X. Cringely, states that Gates told him this while he was reporting a piece for *Vanity Fair* that never ran (Robert X. Cringely, "Masters Tournament," Cringely.com, April 9, 2010, www.cringely.com/2010/04/09/masters-tournament/).

in the world: Kristin Schweizer, "Apple Overtakes Coca-Cola as Most Valuable Brand," *Bloomberg Technology*, September 30, 2013, http://www.bloomberg .com/news/2013-09-0/apple-overtakes-coca-cola-as-most-valuable-brand -study-finds.html.

"splendid success": Roy Basler, ed., *The Collected Works of Abraham Lincoln*, vol. 2 (New Brunswick, NJ: Rutgers University Press, 1953), 383–84.

held Lincoln's hat: Russell McClintock, "Lincoln and the Little Giant," *New York Times*, March 29, 2011, http://opinionator.blogs.nytimes.com/2011/03/29 /lincoln-and-the-little-giant/.

154   *down by two*: *Magic and Bird*.

"actually, it was": Bird, Johnson, and MacMullan, *When the Game Was Ours*, 82–83.

"the other eighty": *Magic and Bird*.

"I finally got Magic": Bird, Johnson, and MacMullan, *When the Game Was Ours*, 115.

"over it yet": Ibid., x.

"and you know he was": *Magic and Bird*.

"working after that": Ibid.

155   *"a beer"*: Bird, Johnson, and MacMullan, *When the Game Was Ours*, 190.

"the way it is": *Magic and Bird*.

"I'd be less": Andre Agassi, *Open* (New York: Random House, 2009), 354. Of course, I need to mention that Agassi's book was ghostwritten by the journalist and memoirist J. R. Moehringer, who created the text from interviews with Agassi but insisted that his name not appear on the cover or title page. "The midwife doesn't go home with the baby," he said. "It's Andre's memoir, not our memoir" (Charles McGrath, "A Team, but Watch How You Put It," *New York Times*, November 11, 2009, http://www.nytimes.com/2009/11/12/ books/12agassi.html).

"characteristics of the situation": Gavin J. Kilduff, Hillary Anger Elfenbein, and Barry M. Staw, "The Psychology of Rivalry: A Relationally Dependent Analysis of Competition," *Academy of Management Journal* 53 (2010): 943–69.

seconds in a 5K: Frieda Klotz, "The Upsides and Dark Sides of Rivalry: A Q&A with Gavin Kilduff," *Strategy + Business*, September 9, 2013, http:// www.strategy-business.com/blog/The-Upsides-and-Dark-Sides-of-Rivalry -A-Q-A-with-Gavin-Kilduff?gko=dddb8.

156   *"women in the world"*: Paul O'Neil, "Twin Lovelorn Advisers Torn Asunder by Success," *Life*, April 7, 1958, 102–12.

157   *"hick from French Lick"*: Ira Berkow, "Larry Bird a Joy, Even When Ailing," *New York Times*, May 26, 1985, http://www.nytimes.com/1985/05/26/sports /sports-of-the-times-larry-bird-a-joy-even-when-ailing.html.

as good as he got: Sam Linksy, e-mail to the author, January 30, 2014.

mowed his front lawn: Magic and Bird.

"big, big fun": The Announcement — the Magic Johnson Story, directed by Nelson George (ESPN, 2012.)

"the same brain": Magic and Bird.

"mirrors of each other": Ibid.

spurred by similarity: Klotz, "The Upsides and Dark Sides of Rivalry."

"does to you": Magic Johnson and Larry Bird, interview with David Letterman, April 11, 2012.

158 *"wish us ill":* David P. Barash, "Why We Need Enemies," *Chronicle of Higher Education,* May 6, 2013.

stories we tell ourselves: T. R. Sarbin, ed., *Narrative Psychology: The Storied Nature of Human Conduct* (Santa Barbara: Praeger, 1986).

psychologist Dan McAdams said: Benedict Carey, "This Is Your Life (and How You Tell It)," *New York Times,* May 22, 2007, http://www.nytimes.com/2007/05/22/health/psychology/22narr.html?pagewanted=print&_r=0.

life stories of redemption: Dan P. McAdams, "The Redemptive Self: Generativity and the Stories Americans Live By," *Research in Human Development* 3 (2006): 81–100.

"the black dog": Anthony Storr, *Churchill's Black Dog, Kafka's Mice, and Other Phenomena of the Human Mind* (New York: Ballantine Books, 1990).

"victorious battle": Carey, "This Is Your Life."

159 *improved performance:* Kilduff, Elfenbein, and Staw, "The Psychology of Rivalry."

"intimate enemy": William James to Dickinson S. Miller, August 30, 1896, *Atlantic Monthly,* http://www.theatlantic.com/past/issues/96may/nitrous/jamii.htm.

"divorce each other": Larry Bird and Bob Ryan, *Drive: The Story of My Life* (New York: Doubleday, 1989), xii.

"together in the finals": Magic and Bird.

retire from basketball, effective immediately: Rick Weinberg, "Magic Johnson Announces He's HIV-Positive," ESPN.com, http://sports.espn.go.com/espn/espn25/story?page=moments/7.

"depressed": Scott Jordan Harris, "The Magic of Magic and Bird," RogerEbert.com, May 19, 2012, http://www.rogerebert.com/far-flung-correspondents/the-magic-of-magic-and-bird.

160 *"it really wasn't": Magic and Bird.*

"wouldn't feel right": Ibid.

18. Luke Skywalker and Han Solo

161 *for modern art in the twentieth century:* Paul Trachtman, "Matisse & Picasso," *Smithsonian,* February 2003, http://www.smithsonianmag.com/arts-culture/matisse-amp-picasso-75440861/#ixzz2rozHIm7N.

"chess game": Ibid.

"duel": Sarah Boxer, "Artists Dueling, Curators Dealing," *New York Times,* February 9, 2003, http://www.nytimes.com/2003/02/09/arts/art-architecture
-artists-dueling-curators-dealing.html?pagewanted=all&src=pm.

by Joseph Conrad: John Richardson, "Between Picasso and Matisse," *Vanity Fair,* February 2003, http://www.vanityfair.com/style/features/2003/02/
picasso-matisse200302.

162   *"continuing the play":* James P. Carse, *Finite and Infinite Games: A Vision of Life as Play and Possibility* (New York: Ballantine Books, 1987).

amazed dismay: John Abell, "This Day in Tech," *Wired,* August 6, 2009, http://
www.wired.com/thisdayintech/2009/08/dayintech_0806/.

Evil Empire: Leander Kahney, "Mac Loyalists: Don't Tread on Us," *Wired,* December 2, 2002, http://www.wired.com/gadgets/mac/news/2002/12/56575
?currentPage=all.

Applesoft BASIC: The Wikipedia entry here is thorough: http://en.wikipedia
.org/wiki/Applesoft_BASIC. I also found the WikiAnswers capsule of the
Apple-Microsoft history helpful: http://is.gd/ZHbfiw.

163   *Macintosh applications:* Caroline Moss, "In 1983, Steve Jobs Hosted Apple's
Version of 'The Dating Game' and Bill Gates Was a Contestant," *Business Insider,* November 24, 2013, http://is.gd/8QozGw.

critical at the time: Daniel Eran, "Mac Office, $150 Million, and the Story
Nobody Covered Sunday," *Roughly Drafted,* March 11, 2007, http://is.gd/M
320F8.

different names: This is the Toyota Aygo, which is also sold as the Peugeot 107
and the Citroën C1. "Peugeot Follows Toyota Car Recall," *BBC,* January 30,
2010, http://news.bbc.co.uk/2/hi/business/8489079.stm.

compact disc: "How the CD Was Developed," *BBC,* August 17, 2007, http://
news.bbc.co.uk/2/hi/technology/6950933.stm.

hierarchical positions: Elaine N. Aron, "Ranking and Linking, for Better and
for Worse," January 9, 2010, *Attending to the Undervalued Self* (blog), http://
www.psychologytoday.com/blog/attending-the-undervalued-self/201001/
ranking-and-linking-better-and-worse.

"become individualistic": V. Frank Asaro, *Universal Co-Opetition: Nature's Fusion of Competition and Cooperation* (New York: Bettie Youngs Book Publishers, 2011), Kindle edition.

164   *"to fall behind":* Sheila Heti, e-mail to the author, September 1, 2013.

165   *"forms of usefulness":* William James, *Talks to Teachers on Psychology; and
to Students on Some of Life's Ideals* (New York: Henry Holt, 1899), https://
archive.org/details/talkstoteacherso1899jame.

"Strawberry Fields Forever": An exceptional account of the development of the
song is at *The Beatles Bible,* http://www.beatlesbible.com/songs/strawberry
-fields-forever.

"Penny Lane": Barry Miles, *Paul McCartney: Many Years from Now* (New York: Henry Holt, 1998), 306.

"each other's songs": Ibid., 307.

"better all the time": "The Making of 'Sgt. Pepper,'" *The South Bank Show*, season 15, episode 25, June 14, 1992. The visual language on Paul's point is essential, so I recommend watching the video, which is available online. In the YouTube version I saw, the documentary was split into three parts, and his comments begin in the third part, around 3:00, http://www.youtube.com/watch?v=CPH4pRgZSv.

166   *kids in his gang*: Mark Lewisohn, *The Beatles: All These Years, Volume 1—Tune In* (New York: Crown, 2013), 51. Lewisohn explains that Strawberry Field — that was the proper name, but it was popularly known in the neighborhood as Fields — was a Salvation Army residence "for children of broken homes." Jackie Spencer, an authority on Liverpool history, told me that "orphanage" is also correct. Jackie Spencer, e-mail to the author, January 29, 2014.

"meet at Penny Lane": Miles, *Many Years from Now*, 307.

"am I a genius": David Sheff, *All We Are Saying: The Last Major Interview with John Lennon and Yoko Ono* (New York: St. Martin's, 2010), 157.

"tune and harmony": Ian MacDonald, *Revolution in the Head: The Beatles' Records and the Sixties* (Chicago: Chicago Review Press, 2007), 223.

167   *trump the other:* Sheff, *All We Are Saying*, 175.

"double A side": The Beatles, *The Beatles Anthology* (San Francisco: Chronicle Books, 2000), 239. There had been two double A sides before this: "We Can Work It Out" / "Day Tripper" in December 1965, and "Eleanor Rigby" / "Yellow Submarine" in August 1966. The fourth single to bear this designation was "Come Together" / "Something" in October 1969.

"for the bond": Bill Harry, *The Paul McCartney Encyclopedia* (London: Virgin Books, 2002), 500.

inspire and direct: For the distinction between power and authority, I'm drawing on conversations with the psychiatrist Edward R. Shapiro, the former medical director/CEO of the Austen Riggs Center.

lost everything: The Armstrong Lie, directed by Alex Gibney (Sony Pictures Classics, 2013).

168   *excessive selfishness:* Alexia Elejalde-Ruiz, "Are You a Niceaholic?," *Chicago Tribune*, January 27, 2013, http://is.gd/zC0F3V.

"lack of change": Asaro, *Universal Co-Opetition.*

"even possible": Alfonso Montuori, "Frank Barron: A Creator on Creating," *Journal of Humanistic Psychology* 43 (2003), http://www.ciis.edu/Documents/Academic%20Departments/TID/Frank%20Barron-JHP.pdf.

"the professor": Jack Flam, *Matisse and Picasso: The Story of Their Rivalry and Friendship* (New York: Basic Books, 2008), 12.

"any man": Michael Kimmelman, "A Matisse Encore with Picasso for Just a Week," *New York Times*, January 22, 1993, http://is.gd/Tq0Zjs.

rather than mannered: See, for example, Peter Conrad, "The Many Faces of Pablo Picasso," *Observer*, February 7, 2009, http://www.theguardian.com/artanddesign/2009/feb/08/pablo-picasso-art.

struggled in high society: John Elderfield and Kirk Varnedoe, interview with Charlie Rose, August 22, 2003.

169   *in effigy*: Laurette E. McCarthy, *Walter Pach (1883–1958): The Armory Show and the Untold Story of Modern Art* (Uniontown: Penn State Press, 2011), 48.

"male gaze": Tyler Green, "The Response to Matisse's 'Blue Nude,'" November 3, 2010, Artinfo.com, http://blogs.artinfo.com/modernartnotes/2010/11/the-response-to-matisses-blue-nude/.

like African masks: http://www.moma.org/collection/object.php?object_id=79766.

"work of a madman": Trachtman, "Matisse & Picasso."

twentieth-century art: See, for example, Peter Plagens, "Which Is the Most Influential Work of Art of the Last 100 Years?," *Newsweek*, June 23, 2007, http://is.gd/Gv2Uqn.

"challenge with the other": Elderfield and Varnedoe, interview with Charlie Rose, August 22, 2003.

170   *"roped together"*: *Picasso and Braque: The Cubist Experiment, 1910–1912*, Kimbell Art Museum, May 29, 2011, to August 21, 2011, http://is.gd/bPYPxm. See also William Rubin et al., *Picasso and Braque: Pioneering Cubism* (New York: Museum of Modern Art, 1989).

Saturday-evening salons: Richardson, "Between Picasso and Matisse."

"there is only Matisse": Flam, *Matisse and Picasso*, xi.

"that is Picasso": Ibid.

19. *"We All Want the Hand"*

171   *"from the opening"*: "The Pez Dispenser," *Seinfeld*, season 3, episode 14, January 15, 1992.

"superiority over the other": James Boswell, *Life of Johnson*, ed. Charles Grosvenor Osgood (1917), http://www.gutenberg.org/files/1564/1564-h/1564-h.htm.

172   *stable over time*: Richard Conniff, *The Ape in the Corner Office: Understanding the Office Beast in All of Us* (New York: Crown Business, 2005), 71.

popular vote: Ibid., 125–26.

"emotional convergence": Daniel Goleman, *Social Intelligence: The New Science of Human Relationships* (New York: Random House, 2006), 24.

173   *has facilitated*: In place of a reference, a confession — I have a research file on this point but I neglected to note the source or author and have been unable to identify either. Here is the original language, expressed better than I have it in the text: "Lateral relationships may be less intimate than asymmetrical

ones. Witness two friends who look to connect with each other when each is available, to talk when each prefers to talk. Friend one will call when he most prefers to talk, but this is not likely to be when friend two most prefers to talk, and friend two will decline the call. Friend two will return the call when he most prefers to talk, but friend one is now absorbed in matters of greater preference, and *he* will decline the call. Each is free and independent and floating in his own universe.

"In conditions of asymmetry, this changes. The powerful one in the exchange sets the terms by which he engages — say, the hour for a call — and the supplicant agrees to these terms, makes himself available. Thus the exchange happens, it is on the volume and depth and potency of exchanges — not on any sense of equality — that intimacy is made." If a reader can help me identify the source, please write me at Po2@shenk.net.

"knew my place": James Watson, interview with the author, August 21, 2013.

"moved Jim": Horace Freeland Judson, *The Eighth Day of Creation: Makers of the Revolution in Biology* (Cold Spring Harbor, NY: Cold Spring Harbor Laboratory Press, 2004), 194.

"position by force": Frans de Waal, *Our Inner Ape: A Leading Primatologist Explains Why We Are Who We Are* (New York: Penguin, 2006), Kindle edition.

174 *someone facing them:* For a nice survey of this research, see "Losing Touch: Power Diminishes Perception and Perspective," http://insight.kellogg.north western.edu/article/losing_touch/.

"in the air": Amy Cuddy, interview with Leigh Buchanan, *Inc.,* May 1, 2012, http://www.inc.com/magazine/201205/leigh-buchanan/strike-a-pose .html.

less powerful people: Dacher Keltner, Deborah H. Gruenfeld, and Cameron Anderson, "Power, Approach, and Inhibition," *Psychological Review* 110, no. 2 (April 2003): 265–84.

company money: Andrew Ross Sorkin, "Tyco Details Lavish Lives of Executives," *New York Times,* September 18, 2002, http://www.nytimes.com/2002 /09/18/business/tyco-details-lavish-lives-of-executives.html.

"once we have power": Dacher Keltner, "The Power Paradox," *Greater Good,* December 1, 2007, http://greatergood.berkeley.edu/article/item/power _paradox.

175 *"greater the risks"*: Kate Ludeman and Eddie Erlandson, "*The Alpha Male Syndrome* — Synopsis," http://www.worthethic.com/the-alpha-male-syndrome .html.

made about them: Dacher Keltner, Jason Marsh, and Jeremy Adam Smith, *The Compassionate Instinct: The Science of Human Goodness* (New York: W. W. Norton, 2010), 220.

176 *"really different thing"*: Jillian Lauren, interview with the author, February 11, 2013.

for the follower: Jamie Rose, *Shut Up and Dance!: The Joy of Letting Go of the*

Lead — on the Dance Floor and Off (New York: Penguin, 2011), Kindle edition.

above them: Keltner, Marsh, and Smith, *The Compassionate Instinct*, 220.

intend and believe: Ibid.

from the minority: I encountered Gruenfeld's research in a profile on her work on the Stanford Graduate School of Business website: "Better Decisions Through Teamwork," April 1, 2004, http://www.gsb.stanford.edu/news/research/ob_teamdecisionmaking.shtml. Professor Gruenfeld confirmed the finding mentioned in the text (e-mail to the author, January 30, 2014) and pointed me to two papers: Deborah H. Gruenfeld, "Status, Ideology, and Integrative Complexity on the U.S. Supreme Court: Rethinking the Politics of Political Decision Making," *Journal of Personality and Social Psychology* 68 (January 1995): 5–20, and Deborah H. Gruenfeld and Jared Preston, "Upending the Status Quo: Cognitive Complexity in U.S. Supreme Court Justices Who Overturn Legal Precedent," *Personality and Social Psychology Bulletin* 26 (October 2000): 1013–22.

177   *"wants to handle":* Conniff, *The Ape in the Corner Office*, 113.

"stage, not yours": Neal Brennan, interview with the author, November 26, 2013.

both pleased: Ibid.

"dance them": Jacques d'Amboise, *I Was a Dancer* (New York: Knopf, 2011), 282.

Corcoran's attention: Tim Rice, "A Day in The Life of Barbara Corcoran and Her Executive Assistant," *Inc.*, January 18, 2014, http://is.gd/qADla5.

record deal: David Howard, *Sonic Alchemy: Visionary Music Producers and Their Maverick Recordings* (Milwaukee, WI: Hal Leonard Corporation, 2006), 106–7.

"That was it": *Amazing Journey: The Story of the Who,* directed by Murray Lerner and Paul Crowder (Universal Studios, 2007). Unless otherwise specified, the Who story comes from this source.

178   *"on and off the stage":* Ibid. The speaker of these lines is not on camera, but it's given over an image of Townshend and Daltrey and it sounds to me very much like Daltrey. Listen for yourself at about 43:30.

Townshend unconscious: This is an oft-told story, included in *Amazing Journey.* Here is Roger Daltrey telling it to Howard Stern: http://www.youtube.com/watch?v=ZVjDbTb0420.

20. "I Love to Scrap with Orv"

179   *"systems, or interests":* Amy C. Edmondson and Diana McLain Smith, "Too Hot to Handle? How to Manage Relationship Conflict," *California Management Review* 49 (Fall 2006): 7; available online at http://dianamclainsmith.com/wp-content/themes/dms/pdf/thth.pdf.

180   *"our guts out at each other":* Mary McNamara, "TV Show–Running Couples: The Ultimate Working Marriage," *Los Angeles Times,* March 6, 2011, http://

articles.latimes.com/2011/mar/06/entertainment/la-ca-showrunners -20110306.

"through and through": Klaus Kinski, *All I Need Is Love: A Memoir* (New York: Random House, 1988), 203.

he said, is "politeness": Francis Crick, interview with the BBC, December 11, 1962, in Paul Strathern, *Crick, Watson and DNA* (New York: Anchor, 1999), e-book.

"bewildered me": This description of Franklin and Wilkins's meeting is from the transcript of the *Nova* documentary by Gary Glassman, *Secret of Photo 51* (PBS, April 2003), http://www.pbs.org/wgbh/nova/transcripts/3009_photo 51.html transcripts/3009_photo51.html.

181   *"be quite crucial"*: Francis Crick, *What Mad Pursuit: A Personal View of Scientific Discovery* (New York: Basic Books, 1990), 70.

photograph of Franklin's: Victor K. McElheny, *Watson and DNA: Making a Scientific Revolution* (New York: Basic Books, 2004), 52. McElheny writes that Watson later concluded it had been taken by Franklin's postdoc, Raymond Gosling. But it is generally written about as her photograph.

"mouth fell open": James D. Watson, *The Double Helix* (New York: Simon and Schuster, 1998), 167.

"mouth fell open": "The Race for the Double Helix — Providence and Personalities," *Horizons* (BBC, 1974). A transcript appeared in the *Listener* on July 11, 1974; see http://profiles.nlm.nih.gov/ps/access/SCBBKH.ocr.

each helical twists: Glassman, *Secret of Photo 51*.

amount of cytosine: Judson, *The Eighth Day of Creation*, 171.

"got out of it": "The Race for the Double Helix."

C to G: Judson, *The Eighth Day of Creation*, 172; Susan Aldridge, "The DNA Story," *Chemistry World, Royal Society of Chemistry*, April 2003, http://www .rsc.org/chemistryworld/Issues/2003/April/story.asp.

"'It'd be too easy'": James Watson, interview with the author, August 21, 2013. Crick remembered the eureka moment slightly differently than Watson — that they collectively recognized the structure on the evening of February 27 (per Judson, *The Eighth Day of Creation*, 172). Watson has recounted — to me and in *The Double Helix*, 196 — that he deduced the structure alone on the morning of February 28 on the heels of Crick's comment.

"why don't you do it": McElheny, *Watson and DNA*, 53.

182   *"secret of life"*: Watson, *The Double Helix*, 197.

"'unhappy to fight'": Alan Jay Lerner, *The Street Where I Live* (Cambridge, MA: Da Capo, 1978), 224.

"switched ideas": Charles E. Taylor as told to Robert S. Ball, "My Story," *Collier's*, December 25, 1948, http://bit.ly/1d0w6Wj.

"good scrapper": Tom D. Crouch, *The Bishop's Boys: A Life of Wilbur and Orville Wright* (New York: W. W. Norton, 2003), 103.

experience of intimacy: James W. Pennebaker, *The Secret Life of Pronouns: What*

Our Words Say About Us (New York: Bloomsbury Press, 2013). See also Kate G. Niederhoffer and James W. Pennebaker, "Linguistic Style Matching in Social Interaction," *Journal of Language and Social Psychology* (December 2002). Niederhoffer and Pennebaker propose a coordination-engagement hypothesis as an alternative to the nonverbal coordination-rapport hypothesis. They explain: "The more that two people in a conversation are actively engaged with one another — in a positive or even negative way — the more verbal and nonverbal coordination we expect. Two people who are angry with one another are highly likely to talk in the same way and mimic each other's nonverbal behaviors. However, if either or both are simply not engaged in the conversation, including not listening, thinking about something else, and/or under the influence of psychoactive agents, we would expect a significant drop in both verbal and nonverbal coordination."

pleasure and closeness: Simon DeDeo, David C. Krakauer, and Jessica C. Flack, "Inductive Game Theory and the Dynamics of Animal Conflict," *PLoS Computational Biology* 6, no. 5 (2010).

183 *just as often:* Erika B. Bauer and Barbara B. Smuts, "Cooperation and Competition During Dyadic Play in Domestic Dogs, *Canis familiaris*," *Animal Behaviour* 73 (2007): 489–99. Bauer and Smuts cite three other studies that support the idea of a fifty-fifty rule. The first showed that younger wallabies displayed offensive maneuvers when they played with old animals while old partners adopted defensive roles. A second study found that, in a male-female pair of captive juvenile hamadryas baboons, the strong partner (the male) was disproportionately gentle and restricted rough behaviors. A third study, of captive wolves, dogs, and coyotes, found that the animals "used a common canine play signal, the play bow, to communicate playful intent in association with particularly aggressive maneuvers that might otherwise be misinterpreted as real aggression." But Bauer emphasizes that tactics used to maintain the fifty-fifty rule "remain largely unstudied." For a review, see Sergio M. Pellis, "Keeping in Touch: Play Fighting and Social Knowledge," http://colinallen.dnsalias.org/Secure/TCA/pellis-final.pdf.

"deep affection emerge": C. S. Lewis, *Surprised by Joy: The Shape of My Early Life* (New York: Harcourt Brace Jovanovich, 1966), 199–200.

that's negative: "The Positive Perspective: Dr. Gottman's Magic Ratio!," *Gottman Institute Relationship Blog*, December 3, 2012, http://www.gottmanblog.com/2012/12/the-positive-perspective-dr-gottmans.html. This appears to be drawn from research explored in John M. Gottman, *What Predicts Divorce?: The Relationship Between Marital Processes and Marital Outcomes* (Hillsdale, NJ: Lawrence Erlbaum Associates, 1994).

every positive one: M. Losada and E. Heaphy, "The Role of Positivity and Connectivity in the Performance of Business Teams: A Nonlinear Dynamics Model," *American Behavioral Scientist* 47 (2004): 740–65. For a summary, see Jack Zenger and Joseph Folkman, "The Ideal Praise-to-Criticism Ratio," *Har-*

vard Business Review (March 15, 2013), http://blogs.hbr.org/2013/03/the -ideal-praise-to-criticism/.

other Losada research: Tom Bartlett, "The Magic Ratio That Wasn't," *Chronicle of Higher Education,* August 5, 2013, http://chronicle.com/blogs/percolator/ the-magic-ratio-that-wasnt/33279.

184 *stuck together:* John Gottman, *The Seven Principles for Making Marriage Work* (New York: Random House, 2002), 145.

"*start laughing*": Ibid., 22.

185 *their experiments:* Tom Crouch, interview with *Nova,* posted November 11, 2003, http://www.pbs.org/wgbh/nova/space/unlikely-inventors.html. For inflation adjustment, I'm comparing 1900 dollars to 2012 dollars using the calculator at Westegg.com.

Kitty Hawk: Crouch, *The Bishop's Boys,* 182.

embracing instability: Ibid., 166–70.

21. Varieties of Alphas and Betas

186 The Birds: Donald Spoto, *The Dark Side of Genius: The Life of Alfred Hitchcock* (Cambridge, MA: Da Capo, 1999), 450; Tim Oglethorpe, "Hitchcock? He Was a Psycho," *Mail Online,* December 20, 2012, http://www.dailymail.co.uk/ tvshowbiz/article-2251425/Tippi-Hedren-tells-Alfred-Hitchcock-turned- sexual-predator-tried-destroy-her.html.

187 "*a little confused*": Quotes about Hitchcock in the three paragraphs preceding this note are from Spoto, *The Dark Side of Genius,* 452, 456–57, 472, 390.

Nuclear Wintour: "Anna Wintour," *60 Minutes* (CBS, 2009), http://www.cbs news.com/videos/anna-wintour/.

"*stood too close*": Kate Kelly and Merissa Marr, "Boss-Zilla!," *Wall Street Journal,* September 24, 2005, http://online.wsj.com/news/articles/SB1127497 46571150033.

"*by their side*": Mark Lipton, interview with the author, August 12, 2011.

"*productive obsessives*": Michael Maccoby, "Narcissistic Leaders: The Incredible Pros, the Inevitable Cons," *Harvard Business Review* (January/February 2000), http://www.maccoby.com/Articles/NarLeaders.shtml.

when necessary: Maccoby, "Narcissistic Leaders."

Jobs backed down: Steve Wozniak, *iWoz: Computer Geek to Cult Icon* (New York: W. W. Norton, 2006), 193.

"*never survive*": Walter Isaacson, *Steve Jobs* (New York: Simon and Schuster, 2011), 460.

"*weak of heart*": Eddie Erlandson, interview with the author, September 2, 2013.

188 *striving for praise:* Michael Thornton, "Hitchcock the Psycho," *Mail Online,* March 21, 2012, http://www.dailymail.co.uk/femail/article-2118385/Hitch cock-Psycho-As-Birds-star-Tippi-Hedren-reveals-tried-destroy-spurned-ad vances-blondes-lived-fear-sadistic-director.html.

"except himself": Spoto, *The Dark Side of Genius,* 219.

with the studio guard: Ibid., 148.

in the room: Tippi Hedren, interview with John Hiscock, *Telegraph,* December 24, 2012, http://www.telegraph.co.uk/culture/film/starsandstories/975 3977/Tippi-Hedren-interview-Hitchcock-put-me-in-a-mental-prison.html.

189 *"that was the end"*: John Triggs, "The Psycho and His Blondes," *Express,* May 27, 2008, http://www.express.co.uk/expressyourself/45830/The-psycho-and -his-blondes.

three years: Hedren, interview with John Hiscock.

the dominant presence: Matt Tyrnauer, "So Very Valentino," *Vanity Fair,* August 2004, http://www.vanityfair.com/culture/features/2004/08/valentino 200408.

"command Miss Stein": "Alice Toklas, 89, Is Dead in Paris," *New York Times,* March 8, 1967, http://www.nytimes.com/books/98/05/03/specials/stein -toklasobit.html.

"into the corridor": Ibid.

190 *"like an army"*: Cathryn Michon, interview with the author, August 24, 2013.

decisions day-to-day: Kris Lotlikar and Quayle Hodek, multiple interviews with the author.

"executor": Kate Ludeman and Eddie Erlandson, *The Alpha Male Syndrome* (Cambridge, MA: Harvard Business School Press, 2006), 39.

191 *to everyone else:* Mike Capuzzo, "Ralph Abernathy's Judgment Day," Philly .com, December 5, 1989, http://articles.philly.com/1989-12-05/news/2615 7645_1_abernathy-white-marble-crypt-judas.

primary partner: For the complexities of the power dynamic between Farrell and Balanchine, see Jacques d'Amboise, *I Was a Dancer* (New York: Knopf, 2011), 282. "In personal relations with Balanchine," d'Amboise wrote, "Suzanne was the perfect hot and cold faucet—warm, caring, and attentive; then cold, distant, and rejecting, juggling him masterfully between the two." Describing Farrell's ultimatum that led to her ousting from the New York City Ballet, d'Amboise wrote that, after her marriage, "Suzanne expected to wield the same power as before, selecting the programs and casting. She felt so assured of Balanchine's worship that she pushed further and further, testing to see how far he would bend."

"their results": Horace Freeland Judson, *The Eighth Day of Creation: Makers of the Revolution in Biology* (Cold Spring Harbor, NY: Cold Spring Harbor Laboratory Press, 2004), 227.

"the same thing": Ibid., 194.

"ever met at work": Quotes in this paragraph from Victor K. McElheny, *Watson and DNA: Making a Scientific Revolution* (New York: Basic Books, 2004), 97–98.

"Yes," he said: James Watson, interview with the author, August 21, 2013.

Watson also described their big-brother/little-brother dynamic in Nicholas Wade's interview in the *New York Times*: "Francis treated me like a younger brother. Very nice — you look after your younger brother. But younger brothers sometimes want to be equal to their older brothers." Nicholas Wade, "A Revolution at 50: Watson and Crick, Both Aligned and Apart, Reinvented Biology," *New York Times*, February 25, 2003, http://is.gd/Nb0NXF.

22. "What About McCartney-Lennon?"

193   *"the tension album"*: Paul McCartney, interview with *Musician* magazine, February 1985. I've not seen the original of this interview and am relying for the citation on William J. Dowlding, *Beatlesongs* (New York: Simon and Schuster, 2009), 219.

Yeats: William Butler Yeats, "The Second Coming," http://www.poetryfoun dation.org/poem/172062.

"aspire to those things": Cynthia Lennon, *John* (New York: Three Rivers Press, 2005), Kindle edition.

band's PR man: Hunter Davies, *The Beatles* (1968; New York: W. W. Norton, 1996), 61.

194   *"off the stage"*: Lewisohn, *Tune In*, 400.

"the autograph bit": Davies, *The Beatles*, 85.

the natural frontman would be Paul: George Martin and Jeremy Hornsby, *All You Need Is Ears: The Inside Personal Story of the Genius Who Created the Beatles* (New York: St. Martin's, 1994), 124.

"the strongest": Davies, *The Beatles*, 85.

"leader of the group": *The Beatles Bible,* http://www.beatlesbible.com/1962 /10/27/the-beatles-first-radio-interview.

"headed to the studio": Davies, *The Beatles*, xxviii.

195   *"right thing to do"*: Peter Doggett, *You Never Give Me Your Money: The Beatles After the Breakup* (New York: HarperCollins, 2011), 32.

McCartney's name first: Lewisohn, *Tune In*.

McCartney-Lennon: TheBeatles-Collection.com has images of the original album: http://is.gd/vBR8wn.

"McCartney-Lennon?": Ray Coleman, *McCartney: Yesterday — and Today* (Detroit: Dove Books, 1996), 96.

196   *"a partner"*: Pete Shotton and Nicholas Schaffner, *John Lennon: In My Life* (New York: Thunder's Mouth Press, 1994).

"That's got them": Davies, *The Beatles*, 24.

197   *"not to mind"*: Coleman, *Yesterday — and Today*, 96.

"in the future": "Sir Paul Defends Credits Switch," BBC News, December 19, 2002, http://news.bbc.co.uk/2/hi/entertainment/2588347.stm.

sexual contact: John to his friend Pete Shotton: "What happened is that Eppy just kept on and on at me. Until one night I just finally pulled me trousers down and said to him; 'Oh for Christ's sake, Brian, just stick it up me fucking arse then.' And he said to me, 'Actually, John, I don't do that kind of thing. That's not what I like to do.' 'Well,' I said, 'what is it you like to do then?' And he said, 'I'd just really like to touch you, John.' And so I let him toss me off" (Shotton and Schaffner, *John Lennon*, 73). In a revised edition of *The Beatles*, Hunter Davies writes: "John told me . . . he had had a one-night stand with Brian on a holiday with him in Spain, when Brian had invited him out a few days after the birth of Julian in 1963, leaving Cyn alone. I mentioned this brief holiday in the book but not what John had alleged had taken place. Partly, I didn't really believe it, though John was daft enough to try almost anything once. John was certainly not homosexual, and this boast, or lie, would have given the wrong impression."

"actually said": The Beatles, *The Beatles Anthology*, 98.

all the time: According to Ian MacDonald, "In the first phase of the Beatles' career (up to and including 'I Want to Hold Your Hand') Lennon and McCartney had been equal in their output of solo and collaborative songs, Lennon stealing fractionally ahead of McCartney on *With the Beatles*. During 'A Hard Day's Night,' Lennon began to work very hard on his songwriting, contributing over half of the group's originals. Rivalry was always hot between them and McCartney's gesture of A-side independence with 'Can't Buy Me Love' must have jolted Lennon who, till then, had regarded himself as undisputed leader . . . Lennon's sudden burst of work allowed him to dominate the band's composing for almost a year. In this light, the imperious 'You Can't Do That,' title and all, sounds very much like the first blow in a deliberate campaign of reconquest." Ian MacDonald, *Revolution in the Head: The Beatles Records and the Sixties* (New York: Henry Holt, 1994), 84.

198   *"Fool on the Hill"*: Davies, *The Beatles*, 268.

5:45 a.m.: Mark Lewisohn, *The Complete Beatles Recording Sessions* (New York: Harmony Books, 1988), 106.

the cover of Sgt. Pepper's Lonely Hearts Club Band: Barry Miles, *Paul McCartney: Many Years from Now* (New York: Henry Holt, 1998), 344.

"'A Day in the Life'": Jann Wenner, *Lennon Remembers* (London: Verso, 2001), 115.

"a bit of song": John Lennon, interview with Jonathan Colt, *Rolling Stone*, November 23, 1968.

"vice versa": Wenner, *Lennon Remembers*, 138.

studio hours: Geoff Emerick and Howard Massey, *Here, There and Everywhere: My Life Recording the Music of the Beatles* (New York: Penguin, 2006), Kindle edition.

on the album: Neville Stannard, *The Long and Winding Road* (New York: Avon Books, 1982), 51, puts the total recording time at more than 700 hours. According to the 2009 *Sgt. Pepper* booklet, it took 129 days and nearly 400 hours to complete the LP.

199 *"we always did"*: Miles, *Many Years from Now*, 312.

"writing with John": Ibid., 314.

cherries in her mouth: The video is online: http://lashermanasiglesias.com/collaborations/lh-competitions.

"aggression out": Lisa Iglesias, interview with the author, October 12, 2009.

200 *"thousandth time"*: All the details of this scene to this point are from Davies, *The Beatles*, 270–71.

"'I have now'": Miles, *Many Years from Now*, 382.

found puzzling: Martin and Hornsby, *All You Need Is Ears*, 206–7.

201 *"very inscrutably"*: Paul's memories of his acid trip with John from Miles, *Many Years from Now*, 383.

"he was our idol": Anthony DeCurtis, *In Other Words: Artists Talk About Life and Work* (Milwaukee, WI: Hal Leonard Corporation, 2006), 61.

"blew me out of the water": *Brian Wilson on Tour*, directed by John Anderson (Sanctuary, 2003).

Pet Sounds: Keith Badman and Tony Bacon, *The Beach Boys: The Definitive Diary of America's Greatest Band on Stage* (San Francisco: Backbeat Books, 2004), 135.

202 *"Maybe it's too late"*: *Beautiful Dreamer: Brian Wilson and the Story of "Smile,"* directed by David Leaf (2004).

power of acid: "John threw himself into it with abandon, convinced that this was the way to greater enlightenment, creativity and happiness" (Cynthia Lennon, *John* [New York: Three Rivers Press, 2005], Kindle edition).

"'Sit down'": Davies, *The Beatles*, 291. Neither Vaughan nor Davies attributed the decline in his aggression to acid, though others have.

203 *"within the band"*: Emerick and Massey, *Here, There and Everywhere*.

"to be doing": Shotton and Schaffner, *John Lennon*, 117.

make it invisible: Emerick and Massey, *Here, There and Everywhere*.

"interesting ideas": Miles, *Many Years from Now*.

"fool of everyone": The Beatles, *The Beatles Anthology*, 286.

204 *in that time*: Songs confirmed to have been written in India: "Cry Baby Cry" (MacDonald, *Revolution in the Head*, 238); "Yer Blues," "Mother Nature's Son," "Julia," "I'm So Tired," and "Dear Prudence" (David Sheff, *All We Are Saying: The Last Major Interview with John Lennon and Yoko Ono* [New York: St. Martin's, 2010]); "The Continuing Story of Bungalow Bill," "Wild Honey Pie," "Rocky Raccoon," "Back in the USSR," "Ob-La-Di, Ob-La-Da," and "I Will" (Miles, *Many Years from Now*); "Revolution" (Stannard, *The Long and Winding Road*, 63); "Polythene Pam" and "Mean Mr. Mustard" (*The Beatles in Their Own Words*, compiled by Barry Miles [New York: Putnam, 1978], 75). "Sexy Sadie" seems to have been written shortly after India; "Why Don't We Do It in the Road" was inspired by India, but it's not clear where it was written. "Blackbird" and "Everybody's Got Something to Hide Except Me and My Monkey" have also been mentioned as India songs.

"we've ever done": Emerick and Massey, *Here, There and Everywhere*.

"almost psychotic": Ibid.

"used to it": Sheff, *All We Are Saying*.

23. *"Listen, This Is Too Crazy . . ."*

210 *"'It's you'"*: Diana McLain Smith, interview with the author, December 9, 2013.

"too many jokes": Diane H. Felmlee, "Fatal Attraction," in *The Dark Side of Close Relationships*, eds., Brian H. Spitzberg and William R. Cupach (New York: Routledge, 1998), 3–32.

211 *"anticipate him anymore"*: Graham Nash, *Wild Tales: A Rock & Roll Life* (New York: Crown, 2013), 262.

"rocking like mad": Ibid., 263.

"drugs to watch him": David Crosby and Graham Nash, interview with the author, April 18, 2012.

"'this is too crazy'": Ibid.

"would be sacred": Ibid.

212 *"anyone in it"*: Vernon Chatman, interview with the author, November 7, 2013.

"differences in public": Elizabeth Cady Stanton, *Eighty Years and More: Reminiscences, 1815–1897* (Amherst, NY: Humanity Books, 2002), 104. This text is also available online at the University of Pennsylvania digital library: http://digital.library.upenn.edu/women/stanton/years/years.html.

in the 1930s: Diana Pavlac Glyer, *The Company They Keep: C. S. Lewis and J.R.R. Tolkien as Writers in Community* (Kent, OH: Kent State University Press, 2007), 9.

"Archbishop of Canterbury": "Religion: Don v. Devil," *Time*, September 8, 1947, http://ti.me/1eLkxwx.

left to the clergy: Glyer, *The Company They Keep*, 83.

is Jerry Lewis: Jerry Lewis and James Kaplan, *Dean and Me (A Love Story)* (New York: Three Rivers Press, 2006), 39–40.

a life of its own: Ibid., 266–70.

213 *discomfort of ambivalence*: Sandra L. Murray and John G. Holmes, "A Leap of Faith? Positive Illusions in Romantic Relationships," *Personality and Social Psychology Bulletin* 23, no. 6 (June 1, 1997): 586–604, doi:10.1177/0146167297236003. This research is profoundly disquieting for the way that it challenges conventional ideas about happiness — which is, alas, so demonstrably a series of illusions that the psychologist R. P. Bentall once wrote, with the zinging truth of satire, a journal article proposing that happiness be classified as a psychiatric disorder ("major affective disorder, pleasant type"). See R. P. Bentall, "A Proposal to Classify Happiness as a Psychiatric Disorder," *Journal of Medical Ethics* 18, no. 2 (June 1992): 94–95.

"fucking dollar sign": Lewis and Kaplan, *Dean and Me*, 277.

24. The Paradox of Success

214 *on DVD ever:* Christopher John Farley, "Dave Speaks," *Time,* May 14, 2005, http://content.time.com/time/magazine/article/0,9171,1061512,00.html.

It still is: Rachel Kaadzi Ghansah, "If He Hollers Let Him Go," *Believer,* http://www.believermag.com/issues/201310/?read=article_ghansah.

"lose yourself": Farley, "Dave Speaks."

215 *"bomb together":* Neal Brennan, interview with the author, February 22, 2013.

two seasons: Andrew Wallenstein, "'Chappelle's Show' Back for a Few Episodes," NPR.org, http://www.npr.org/templates/story/story.php?storyId=5055007.

"cannot sustain you": "Chappelle's Story," Oprah.com, http://www.oprah.com/oprahshow/Chappelles-Story.

"No fucking way": Neal Brennan, interview with the author, February 22, 2013.

1970s and early 1980s: "Apple Turns 30," CNET.com, http://news.cnet.com/2009-1041-6054524.html.

the Apple II division: Steve Wozniak, *iWoz: Computer Geek to Cult Icon* (New York: W. W. Norton, 2006), Kindle edition.

"world's best Tetris player": Gary Wolf, "The World According to Woz," *Wired,* September 1998, http://www.wired.com/wired/archive/6.09/woz.html.

"think about this": Walter Isaacson, *Steve Jobs* (New York: Simon and Schuster, 2011), 342.

216 *"dependency and dependents":* Kathleen D. Vohs, Nicole L. Mead, and Miranda R. Goode, "The Psychological Consequences of Money," *Science* 314, no. 5802 (2006): 1154–56, doi:10.1126/science.1132491.

less ethical and compassionate: Lisa Miller, "The Money-Empathy Gap," *New York,* July 1, 2012, http://nymag.com/news/features/money-brain-2012-7/.

"frozen with embarrassment": Taylor Branch, *The King Years: Historic Moments in the Civil Rights Movement* (New York: Simon and Schuster, 2013), 109.

the prize money: Taylor Branch, *Pillar of Fire: America in the King Years, 1963–1965* (New York: Simon and Schuster, 1997), Kindle edition.

in modern terms: For the sum of the prize money in 1964, see the Nobel Prize website: http://www.nobelprize.org/nobel_prizes/peace/laureates/1964/king-bio.html. For inflation adjustment, see http://www.westegg.com/inflation/infl.cgi.

"estrangement": Branch, *Pillar of Fire.* The "movement insider" is Andrew Young. That the estrangement lasted to the end is from Taylor Branch, interview with the author, December 30, 2013.

"a dollar off us": David M. Halbfinger, "Rewriting Hollywood's Rules," *New York Times,* September 10, 2007, http://www.nytimes.com/2007/09/10/business/media/10morris.html.

show's creative property: Kevin Morris, interview with the author, December 5, 2013.

since middle school: Christie Sounart, "*South Park*'s Unsung Genius," *Coloradan Magazine*, September 1, 2013, http://www.coloradanmagazine.org/2013/09/01/south-parks-unsung-genius.

25. Failure to Repair

218 *"one of us":* The text of this interview is online at *The Beatles Bible,* http://www.beatlesbible.com/1967/08/27/interview-in-bangor-wales/.

neglecting to look: According to Peter Doggett in *You Never Give Me Your Money: The Beatles After the Breakup* (New York: Harper, 2009), 54, Paul began to seek advice on potential managers in the summer of 1968. "After consulting EMI boss Sir Joseph Lockwood and former Conservative Party chairman Lord Poole, he met Lord Beeching, infamous in Britain as the man charged with slashing the rail network into economic shape."

"Western communism": Ibid., 36.

subordinate position to John and Paul: Gary Tillery, *Working Class Mystic: A Spiritual Biography of George Harrison* (Wheaton, IL: Quest Books, 2011), 59–60.

"flame up and burn": Greil Marcus, "A Virtuoso Would Have Destroyed the Beatles," *Guardian,* December 2, 2001, http://www.theguardian.com/culture/2001/dec/03/artsfeatures.thebeatles1.

"'all my life'": *Paul McCartney: Wingspan — an Intimate Portrait,* directed by Alistair Donald (MPL Communications, 2001).

219 *"'do you'":* The Beatles, *The Beatles Anthology* (San Francisco: Chronicle Books, 2000), 110.

220 *"my thing":* Pete Shotton and Nicholas Schaffner, *John Lennon: In My Life* (New York: Thunder's Mouth Press, 1994), 167–68.

"dead serious": Ibid., 167.

late at night: Ibid., 168.

as a patron: Ibid.

221 *"you could feel it":* Bob Spitz, *The Beatles: The Biography* (Boston: Little, Brown, 2006), 761.

"engaged too": Cynthia Lennon, *John* (New York: Three Rivers Press, 2005), Kindle edition.

at their house: Peter A. Carlin, *Paul McCartney: A Life* (New York: Simon and Schuster), 162.

"it's all right": Jonathan Colt, "Yoko Ono and Her Sixteen-Track Voice," *Rolling Stone,* March 18, 1971.

flat-out quit: Geoff Emerick and Howard Massey, *Here, There and Everywhere: My Life Recording the Music of the Beatles* (New York: Penguin, 2006), Kindle edition.

222 *"Blackbird":* The first appearance of "Blackbird" at Abbey Road was June

11, 1968. This was seven days after they made a rough mono remix of take twenty of "Revolution 1." It's uncanny, because this is the exact same interval — seven days — between the completion of "Strawberry Fields Forever," on December 22, 1967, and when Paul brought in the song that would become "Penny Lane." See Mark Lewisohn, *The Complete Beatles Recording Sessions* (New York: Harmony Books, 1988), 90–91, 136.

"Helter Skelter": This song "the end-of-the-world rocker Paul wrote specifically to be the loudest, raunchiest song in the history of recorded music. What he imagined, he said, was the sound of destruction: the collapse of the Roman empire; the musical equivalent of screaming chaos. 'This was the fall, the demise, the going down'" (Carlin, *Paul McCartney,* 161).

the recorded version: Lewisohn, *The Complete Beatles Recording Sessions,* 141.

had worked in the past: A direct line into Paul's thinking at the time can be seen in conversations recorded as part of the sessions for what eventually became the album *Let It Be.* These tapes have never been released, but Doug Sulpy and Ray Schweighardt offer paraphrased accounts of conversations that presumably can't be quoted directly for legal reasons. Here's how Sulpy and Schweighardt describe Paul's thoughts offered on January 13, 1969: "He realizes that the problem is not so much with Yoko as John's reliance on her, although he admits that he doesn't like her presence if only because she's a distraction to *him.* He then goes a step further and sticks up for *John,* claiming that when the two get *really* serious about something John won't allow Yoko to interfere and will actually participate in conversations . . . He admits that John and Yoko go too far in their relationship, but tolerates it because it's always been characteristic of John to go overboard on things" (Doug Sulpy and Ray Schweighardt, *Get Back: The Unauthorized Chronicle of the Beatles' "Let It Be" Disaster* [New York: St. Martin's, 1999], 183). I like the way Peter Carlin characterizes John's moods — "like London's weather in the spring. If you didn't like what you were seeing, just wait ten minutes, and it would change" (Carlin, *Paul McCartney,* 191).

indifference: A version of this thought is associated with Elie Wiesel; see Elie Wiesel, *Against Silence: The Voice and Vision of Elie Wiesel,* vol. 2 (New York: Schocken, 1985), 253.

223　*whirling them outward:* For a concise and potent account of these tensions, see Mikal Gilmore, "Why the Beatles Broke Up," *Rolling Stone,* http://www .rollingstone.com/music/news/why-the-beatles-broke-up-20090903.

primal affirmation: The rooftop concert portion of the *Let It Be* film is widely available online, though it has never been officially released.

"it's so insane": Lewisohn, *The Complete Beatles Recording Sessions,* 15.

harmony vocals: Ibid. Paul described John coming to his house in Barry Miles, *Paul McCartney: Many Years from Now* (New York: Henry Holt, 1998), explaining that John brought the song "around to Cavendish Avenue for me to help finish the last verse he was having a bit of trouble with. He knew he could always leave a couple of sentences out, come and see me and we knew we would always finish them."

224 *Lennon-McCartney canon:* Jann Wenner, *Lennon Remembers* (London: Verso, 2001), 119–20. John: "He not only knew my work and the lyrics that I'd written [but] understood them, and from way back ... That was pretty damn good for me, because it's hard to see me, John Lennon, in amongst all that."

primate politics there: Ringo and George's reasons for going with Klein are given in The Beatles, *The Beatles Anthology*, 324. Ringo's explanation was that he liked him because he "knew music" and "knew records." George liked that Klein was "street people," as opposed to "a class conscious type of person" like Lee Eastman. But George gave as his main reason that "John's with him." There was a pattern of George and Ringo following John on key decisions, which makes implicit sense, considering the hierarchy of the band.

it turned out: For a good short treatment on Klein and the Beatles, see John McMillian, "You Never Give Me Your Money: How Allen Klein Played the Beatles and the Stones," *Newsweek*, December 17, 2013, http://is.gd/svDFZT, an excerpt from McMillian's book *Beatles vs. Stones*.

"aren't you": Miles, *Many Years from Now.* This was not a dispute related to Klein, but it does characterize the tenor of John and Paul's exchanges over the issue of who would run their shop. It happened that the managers Paul wanted—Lee and John Eastman, who became his father- and brother-in-law, respectively, when he married Linda Eastman in 1969—would have been quite a good fit, but that idea was preposterous to John and George.

in the mix: Richard DiLello, *The Longest Cocktail Party* (New York: Playboy Press, 1972), 196.

proxy war between Klein and the Eastmans: The casualties were real enough: John and Paul lost the chance to buy Brian Epstein's company—and thus take back a significant stake in their own enterprise—in part because of bungling by their representatives. When it rains, it pours, goes the cliché, but in this case, there is a causative progression: rain leading to sleet leading to hail. Nervous about the trouble with his marquee talent, Dick James decided to sell his shares of Northern Songs, the company that controlled the Lennon-McCartney catalog. In the scuffle that followed, Allen Klein alerted John that Paul had bought shares of Northern Songs for himself. This made John even less likely to join a coordinated strategy to control a company—and, in fact, it was his shooting his mouth off at a critical moment that caused them to lose the deal.

"get pushed under": Paul McCartney, interview with Richard Meryman, *Life*, April 16, 1971, http://is.gd/Q7ubwW.

26. The Never Endings

225 *suing him*: Pierre Perrone, "Allen Klein," *Independent*, July 6, 2009, http://www.independent.co.uk/news/obituaries/allen-klein-notorious-business-manager-for-the-beatles-and-the-rolling-stones-1732780.html. As a technical matter, Klein's contract wasn't renewed, but given the obvious displeasure with him, *fired* seems a reasonable way to describe it.

"be a rebirth": John Lennon, interview with David Wigg, February 1970. This interview is available on a release called *The Beatles Tapes* and can be heard online at http://www.dailymotion.com/video/xrv35w_the-beatles-tapes-side-1-john_music.

the answer: "No": *The Beatles Bible* has the full self-interview: http://www.beatlesbible.com/1970/04/10/paul-mccartney-announces-the-beatles-split.

around the world: See, for instance, Alvin Shuster, "McCartney Breaks Off with Beatles," *New York Times*, April 11, 1970, http://bit.ly/1j4qQlX.

"word about quitting": Jann S. Wenner, "One Guy Standing There Shouting 'I'm Leaving,'" *Rolling Stone*, May 14, 1970.

227 *"you never know"*: Chris Ingham, *The Rough Guide to the Beatles* (New York: Penguin, 2009), e-book.

228 *"feel about the idea"*: Keith Newham, "John Lennon Is Low Key After Deportation Fight," *Pittsburgh Press*, November 12, 1975.

toilet bowl: Elton John, interview with PBS for "LennoNYC: Beyond Broadcast," *American Masters*, September 30, 2010, http://www.pbs.org/wnet/americanmasters/episodes/lennonyc-beyond-broadcast/episode-4-elton-john/1654.

"You're on your own": Philip Norman, *John Lennon: The Life* (New York: Doubleday, 2008), 199.

began to bounce: Elton John, interview with PBS.

perform for the public: Lennon's absolute last live performance was April 18, 1975, at a salute to Lew Grade, which was later broadcast on television.

"called Paul": Audio of this concert is widely available on the web; *The Beatles Bible* has a transcript of John's remarks at http://is.gd/7u7so8.

"should I do": "It Was 20 Years Ago Today," *Observer*, December 2, 2000, http://www.theguardian.com/theobserver/2000/dec/03/features.review7. Paul's recording for *Venus and Mars* was happening at Allen Toussaint's Sea-Saint studio.

so did May Pang: May Pang, interview with Casey Piotrowski, *The Beatles Show*, May 3, 2008, WPMD-FM, http://is.gd/sK5Bvk.

"when we die": Bruce Springsteen, eulogy for Clarence Clemons, June 21, 2011, http://is.gd/iUprXW.

229 *"suffer fools gladly"*: Barry Miles, *Paul McCartney: Many Years from Now* (New York: Henry Holt, 1998), 151.

"was true praise": The song was "Here, There and Everywhere," and Paul told substantially the same story in his *Playboy* magazine interview in December 1984; in *The Beatles Anthology,* which was published in 1995; in a 1998 BBC interview broadcast as *McCartney on McCartney,* April 8, 1989, http://is.gd/1mbplc; and in a *New Yorker* profile in 2007 written by John Colapinto, "When I'm Sixty-Four," *New Yorker,* June 4, 2007, http://www.newyorker.com/reporting/2007/06/04/070604fa_fact_colapinto. The quote in the text is from Colapinto's piece.

in his mind: Shaun Kitchener, "Paul McCartney Admits Having 'Conversations' with John Lennon's Spirit," *Entertainment Wise,* October 24, 2013, http://www.entertainmentwise.com/news/130314/Paul-McCartney-Admits-Having-Conversations-With-John-Lennons-Spirit.

"an equal": Alexis Petridis, "Paul McCartney: 'New'— Review," *Guardian,* October 10, 2013, http://www.theguardian.com/music/2013/oct/10/paul-mccartney-new-review.

230 *"other person there":* Diana McLain Smith, interview with the author, December 9, 2013.

mutual sense of purpose: "James Watson, Francis Crick, Maurice Wilkins, and Rosalind Franklin," http://www.chemheritage.org/discover/online-resources/chemistry-in-history/themes/biomolecules/dna/watson-crick-wilkins-franklin.aspx.

"is Jim": Nicholas Wade, "A Revolution at 50: Watson and Crick, Both Aligned and Apart, Reinvented Biology," *New York Times,* February 25, 2003, http://is.gd/Nb0NXF.

felt like an orphan: Suzanne Farrell, *Holding On to the Air: An Autobiography* (Gainesville: University Press of Florida, 2002), 286.

231 *played in her life:* Joan Acocella, "Profiles: Second Act," *New Yorker,* January 6, 2003, http://www.newyorker.com/archive/2003/01/06/030106fa_fact_acocella. Also see Jennifer Homans, "The Balanchine Couple," *New Republic,* March 8, 2004, http://www.newrepublic.com/article/79587/the-balanchine-couple.

"Okay, I'll come": For a strong account of Martin Luther King Jr.'s last day, see "Six: 01 — Martin Luther King's Last 32 Hours," http://commercialappeal.com/mlk/.http://media.commercialappeal.com/mlk, and Taylor Branch, *At Canaan's Edge: America in the King Years, 1965–1968* (New York: Simon and Schuster, 1996).

"I've been to the mountaintop": The text and audio of this speech is available at http://americanrhetoric.com/speeches/mlkivebeentothemountaintop.htm.

"absolutely empty": Ralph David Abernathy, *And the Walls Came Tumbling Down: An Autobiography* (New York: HarperCollins, 1991), 440–41.

onstage star: For a brief, poignant treatment of Ralph Abernathy's career after his partner's death, see Mike Capuzzo, "Ralph Abernathy's Judgment Day,"

Philadelphia Inquirer, December 5, 1989, http://articles.philly.com/1989–12 –05/news/26157645_1_abernathy-white-marble-crypt-judas.

232 *King and his legacy:* Art Harris, "A Feud Within the Cause: King Allies Feel Hurt by Abernathy Memoir," *Orlando Sentinel,* http://bit.ly/1aUGzl9.

"your place in history": Michael A. Fletcher, "Ralph Abernathy's Widow Says March Anniversary Overlooks Her Husband's Role," *Washington Post,* http:// wapo.st/LpZvf2.

died the next year: "Ralph D. Abernathy," http://www.biography.com/people/ ralph-d-abernathy-9174397.

"ignored and forgotten": Fletcher, "Ralph Abernathy's Widow."

first successful flight: "Biography of Wilbur Wright," http://wright.nasa.gov/ wilbur.htm.

as he died: Adeline Ravoux, "Memoirs of Vincent van Gogh's stay in Auvers-sur-Oise," trans. Robert Harrison, http://webexhibits.org/vangogh/letter/21/ etc-Adeline-Ravoux.htm.

for his brother: Jan Hulsker, *Vincent and Theo van Gogh: A Dual Biography* (Ann Arbor, MI: Fuller Publications, 1990), 5, 431.

in a museum: Ibid., 450.

"Theo, Director": Ibid., 453.

"his brother the painter": Ibid., 451.

"have got the upper hand": Ibid., 452.

"beside himself": Ibid., 453.

233 *in late January 1891:* January 25, 1891, is the date usually given, but Steven Naifeh and Gregory W. Smith, *Van Gogh: The Life* (New York: Random House, 2011), 867, cite hospital records showing that the body was removed on January 24.

"exertion and sorrow": George Howe Colt, *Brothers: On His Brothers and Brothers in History* (New York: Simon and Schuster, 2012), 256.

he may have killed himself: Chris Stolwijk and Richard Thomson, *Theo van Gogh, 1857–1891: Art Dealer, Collector, and Brother of Vincent* (Zwolle: Waanders, 1999), 56.

"que lui": Ibid., 57.

"could breathe again": "Sister Act: A New Take on Dorothy Wordsworth," NPR .org, http://www.npr.org/templates/story/story.php?storyId=101452310.

Closure is a myth: As the sociologist Nancy Berns observes in her book *Closure: The Rush to End Grief and What It Costs Us* (Philadelphia: Temple University Press, 2011), the idea has no grounding in social science and appears to be a construction of businesses who profit from it — funeral-home directors selling elaborate packages, psychics offering to contact dead loved ones, attorneys suggesting lawsuits, and so on.

Crosby and Stills both: Graham Nash, *Wild Tales: A Rock & Roll Life* (New York: Crown, 2013), Kindle edition.

234　*"how close I think we are"*: Graham Nash and David Crosby, interview with the author, April 18, 2012.

return to it: Admiring all that Marina has achieved for herself in the way of material and reputational success and noting that he would be unable to do it on his own, Ulay says in the film, "But I don't have to. I'm just going to marry her." This is clearly not a fully serious remark, but it doesn't seem as though he's entirely joking either. *Marina Abramović: The Artist Is Present*, directed by Matthew Akers and Jeff Dupre (Show of Force, 2012).

235　"Artist Is Not Present": Ulay, interview with the author, November 10, 2013.
"we're not speaking": Marina Abramović, interview with the author, November 10, 2013.

"disputes to rest": James Westcott, *When Marina Abramović Dies: A Biography* (Cambridge, MA: MIT Press, 2010), 262.

Epilogue: Barton Fink at the Standard Hotel

238　*"not to be found"*: This oft-quoted line originally appeared in Winnicott's paper "Communicating and Not Communicating Leading to a Study of Certain Opposites." The paper can be found in Lesley Caldwell and Angela Joyce, *Reading Winnicott* (New York: Routledge, 2011), and at http://readingsinpsych .files.wordpress.com/2009/09/winnicott-communicating.pdf. In the text, the quotation is in italics. It is often given in error as "*a* joy to be hidden, but *a* disaster not to be found."

239　*hotel burns around him*: For a lush description of the hotel in *Barton Fink,* see Mike D'Angelo, "Barton Fink," *A.V. Club,* September 28, 2009, http://www .avclub.com/article/ibarton-finki-33399.

244　*risk this abandonment*: The lecture was "Fear and Fear Itself," by Tess Girard, at Trampoline Hall, October 7, 2013.
a Celtics game: "The Story of This Viral Video Will Blow Your Mind! (Please Tell Your Friends!)," *AllThingsD,* November 21, 2013, http://allthingsd .com/20131121/the-story-of-this-viral-video-will-blow-your-mind-please-tell-your-friends/.

245　*to touch divinity*: Martin Buber, *I and Thou,* trans. Walter Kaufmann (New York: Scribner, 1970). Buber's book was originally published in 1923, but this is a widely admired translation.

246　*"you've been changed"*: Claire Sufrin, interview with the author, January 20, 2012.
but it helps: Dan Pink writes about self-talk extensively; see Daniel H. Pink, *To Sell Is Human: The Surprising Truth About Moving Others* (New York: Penguin, 2012). For an excerpt of this material, see Daniel H. Pink, "'Can We Fix It' Is the Right Question to Ask," *Telegraph,* June 19, 2010, http://www.tele graph.co.uk/finance/7839988/Can-we-fix-it-is-the-right-question-to-ask .html.

Index

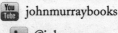